Crime Mapping and Crime Prevention

David Weisburd and Tom McEwen

Editors

CRIME PREVENTION STUDIES
Volume 8

Criminal Justice Press

Monsey, New York, U.S.A.

1998

CRIME PREVENTION STUDIES

Ronald V. Clarke, Series Editor

Printed in the United States of America. No part of this book may be reproduced in any manner whatsoever without written permission, except for brief quotations embodied in critical articles and reviews. For information, contact Willow Tree Press, Inc., P.O. Box 249, Monsey, NY 10952 U.S.A.

ISSN (series): 1065-7029

ISBN: 1-881798-08-9 (cloth)
ISBN: 1-881798-15-1 (paper)

Contents

continued

◆

FOREWORD

This book emerged from the Drug Market Analysis Program (DMAP) sponsored by the National Institute of Justice (NIJ) in five cities across the country. The DMAP aimed for an improved understanding of the dynamics of local drug markets through computer mapping coupled with analytical techniques. In Jersey City, NJ, for example, the project team established a computer mapping capability for the police department, analyzed data on the city's drug markets from a variety of sources, and conducted a successful field test aimed at disrupting local markets. Having established a computer mapping system, they quickly discovered other uses for computer mapping that included crime maps, maps of citizen calls, and maps to assist investigations. In short, any data with addresses could be mapped.

The versatility of computer mapping brings both positive and negative features. On the positive side, it adds a tool for better understanding of crime and its prevention. Analysts can look more closely at crime clusters and crime displacement. Careful mapping can show whether enforcement efforts have been effective and whether areas with crime concentrations are receiving proper attention. Interestingly, computer mapping may also show that crime is not a problem in an area. On the negative side, computer mapping requires us to pay more attention to the analysis that goes into a map's creation, which, in turn, requires more attention to crime prevention theory. It is my belief that theory has been frequently overlooked in computer mapping — a deficiency that is addressed in several of the chapters of this book.

It is clear from NIJ's research efforts that interest is growing in computer mapping among several diverse groups. Crime analysts are interested because of their support role in strategic and tactical operations in law enforcement agencies. Police managers want timely and accurate information for more rapid deployment of personnel, and they want follow-up and assessments of their crime prevention efforts. Computer mapping aids in these aims. Geographers have interests in the distributions, patterns, and relationships of crime, and they strive for new tools to connect crime characteristics and physical surroundings. Finally, criminologists have interest in crime mapping as a means of developing and verifying crime prevention theories.

What I also find of value in the contributions to this book is the range of analytical power that can be achieved with spatial analysis and mapping. On its most basic level, computer maps provide simple descriptions of crime events on a geographic basis, usually emphasized by shading the high- and low-density areas. These maps are simple, straightforward applications that are essential to the everyday work of crime analysis and crime prevention. At the other extreme are maps produced from sophisticated analytical schemes steeped in appropriate theory, in which the geographic area is a part of the spatial analysis and the aim is to show how crime moves or is displaced.

In response to the interest in computer mapping, we have established the Crime Mapping Research Center within NIJ for the purpose of contributing to both applied and basic research in the area of the analytical mapping of crime. The contributors to this book played a part in the foundation of this center. As currently envisioned, the center will fill a void by developing stronger analytical tools for computer mapping.

In summary, I recommend this book to anyone with an interest in computer mapping and its application to crime prevention. The contributions are from leading researchers and practitioners in the field who offer a number of insights on this important subject.

Jeremy Travis
Director,
U.S. National Institute of Justice

ACKNOWLEDGMENTS

We owe a debt of gratitude to many people who have helped us to conceptualize, develop and produce this edited volume. While we cannot name here all of those we have spoken to, or asked advice from, or who kindly offered their time to improve this effort, we want at the outset to identify a few of those who have helped us in particular to produce this work. Perhaps our greatest debt is to Craig Uchida (now at the Office of Community Oriented Policing), who, as Director of Research of the National Institute of Justice, developed the Drug Market Analysis Program with its emphasis on crime mapping. He not only encouraged our efforts but played a pioneering role in bringing computer mapping technologies to criminal justice.

We also want to thank others at the Institute who have supported our efforts, including Richard Titus, who monitored our grant for development of the manuscript, and Nancy La Vigne, the Director of the Center for Computer Mapping. A particular debt is owed to the Director of the National Institute of Justice, Jeremy Travis, who has placed computer mapping on the criminal justice agenda and has taken the time not only to review our publication but to provide a Foreword to it.

Along with contributing author Phil Canter, we want to acknowledge the memory of Kai Martensen, who was an inspiration and mentor to many professionals in the criminal justice field. His professional career of over four decades was devoted to advancing the police profession, including the use of analysis and computer technologies.

Among many who supported our efforts, we especially want to thank Michael Maltz for providing advice and consultation on a diverse set of issues, both historical and technical; Daniel Salem for providing thoughtful assistance; and Joan Peterschmidt for support in organizing the manuscript and preparing the index. Finally we want to thank Ronald Clarke, the editor of the Crime Prevention Studies Series, and Richard Allinson of Criminal Justice Press for their interest in developing a volume devoted to computer mapping issues.

Financial support for development of the volume was generously provided by a grant (92-DD-CX-K031) from the National Institute of Justice. Opinions and positions expressed in the volume are those of the authors or editors and do not necessarily represent the positions or policies of the National Institute of Justice or the Department of Justice.

INTRODUCTION: CRIME MAPPING AND CRIME PREVENTION

by

David Weisburd
Hebrew University and Police Foundation

and

Tom McEwen
Institute for Law and Justice, Inc.

Abstract: *Crime maps have only recently begun to emerge as a significant tool in crime and justice. Until a decade ago, few criminal justice agencies had any capability for creating crime maps, and few investigators had the resources or patience to examine the spatial distribution of crime. Today, however, crime mapping is experiencing what might be termed an explosion of interest among both scholars and practitioners. This introduction begins by examining some early examples of mapping of crime, focusing in particular on factors that inhibited the widespread integration of mapping into crime prevention research and practice in the past. It then turns to innovations in mapping technologies and crime prevention theory that have recently brought crime mapping to the center of trends in crime prevention. The final section introduces the contributions that follow and discusses how they illustrate the many uses of mapping in crime prevention. It examines the pitfalls and problems that researchers and practitioners are likely to encounter in developing and analyzing maps, and the potential advances in crime mapping we might expect in coming decades.*

Address correspondence to: David Weisburd, Institute of Criminology, Faculty of Law, The Hebrew University, Mt. Scopus, Jerusalem, Israel, or Tom McEwen, Institute for Law and Justice, Inc., 1018 Duke St., Alexandria, VA 22314.

Figure 1: Map of Cholera Deaths and Locations of Water Pumps

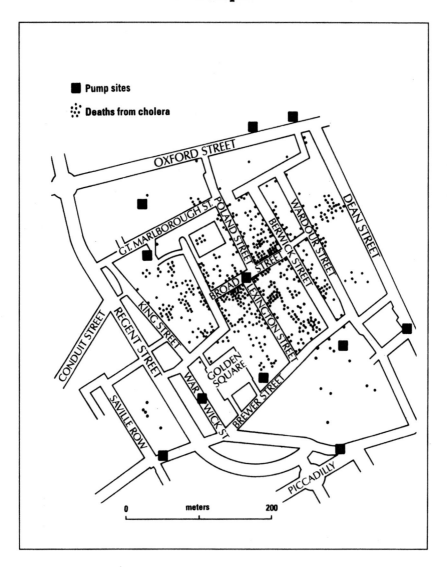

In London in the nineteenth century, cholera was a fearful disease that raged in epidemic proportions and left death and suffering in its wake. The disease seemed to be concentrated in specific neighborhoods. In one epidemic, a physician decided to identify with precision where in the city the deadly disease left its mark, with the hope of finding some pattern to its destruction. Dr. Snow plotted the location of deaths from cholera on a map of central London in September 1854 (see Figure 1). Drawing from a theory that contaminated water causes cholera, he also marked the locations of the area's 11 water pumps. He analyzed the scatter of dots on the map and noticed that they concentrated near the pump on Broad Street. While Dr. Snow suspected the water pump was the problem, he was not entirely certain because one rectangular area near the pump showed no deaths and an area near another pump indicated a second, smaller concentration of deaths. After further inspection, he found that the rectangular space was a brewery where employees did not drink water because they were provided with free beer. Investigation of the other area determined that residents had friends and relatives near the Broad Street pump, and when visiting they often took jugs with them to fill up because the water there seemed to taste better than that from their local pump. Dr. Snow had the handle of the Broad Street pump removed, and the cholera epidemic came to an abrupt halt after having taken more than 500 lives.

Dr. Snow's efforts provide a dramatic example of the use of mapping for informing public policy. But maps themselves have a long history as a basic form of human communication. They have been used to navigate streets and oceans, to portray trends in weather or population, to illustrate political divisions or military strategies, to define boundaries or to reinforce them. For example, a Tahitian native communicated his knowledge of South Pacific geography to Captain Cook by drawing a map, thereby illustrating that the islanders were quite familiar with the idea of mapping. Real estate maps dating to 2000 B.C. found in Mesopotamia and Egypt illustrate the fact that maps are as old as human civilization.

In fiction, detectives often look to maps to untangle complex clues or to bring together seemingly disparate events. A serial murderer may be caught in part because of the clustering of kidnappings in particular types of places. The mystery of the whereabouts of booty from a bank robbery, hidden for half a century, may be unraveled by plotting the locations of cemeteries that lie close enough for a stash to be made before the criminals were caught (Grafton, 1995). Based on what we see in movies and on television, we might expect to see the operations room of a police department laced with colored pins maps. But in practice, crime maps have only recently begun to emerge as a significant tool in crime and justice. Until a decade ago, few criminal justice agencies had any capability for creating crime maps, and few investigators had the resources or patience to examine the spatial distribution of crime. Today, however, crime mapping is experiencing what might be termed an explosion of interest among both scholars and practitioners (see, e.g., Block and Dabdoub, 1993; Eck and Weisburd, 1995; Harries, 1990). Crime mapping has suddenly emerged as a major tool in crime prevention.

In developing this volume, we sought to bring together scholars, crime analysts, and practitioners on the cutting edge of both research and practice in mapping crime. At a time when new mapping technologies are just beginning to be integrated into crime prevention, we wanted to provide examples of how maps could be used in developing policy and theory, and to illustrate the prospects and problems that crime mapping presents. Our volume includes contributions that examine mapping in real life criminal justice contexts, as well as examples of new technologies and future trends that have yet to be implemented in practice. We are concerned with crime prevention theory and crime mapping technologies. Our choice of such a wide range of topics is not accidental: successful mapping of crime demands an integration of theory and data, as well as a practical understanding of the real life context of crime and justice.

In introducing our volume, we think it important to provide historical perspective to the development of crime mapping in crime prevention. We begin by examining some early examples of mapping of crime, focusing in particular on factors that have inhibited the widespread integration of mapping into crime prevention research and practice. We then turn to innovations in mapping technologies and crime prevention theory that have recently brought crime mapping to the center of trends in crime prevention. Finally, we discuss how the contributions that follow illustrate the many uses of mapping in crime prevention, the pitfalls and problems that researchers and practitioners are likely to encounter in developing and analyzing maps, and the potential advances in crime mapping that might be expected in the coming decades.

CRIME MAPPING: EARLY APPLICATIONS

The idea of mapping crime is not new and, in fact, dates back to the early 1800s in France. A review of the historical literature from that period to the present time shows several epochs during which interest in crime mapping was great, but then faded dramatically. In this section, we examine three such periods and discuss the reasons why what seemed like promising beginnings did not lead to sustained interest in crime mapping.

In 1829, Adriano Balbi and Andre-Michel Guerry created the first maps of crime (Kenwitz, 1987; Beirne, 1993). The collaboration itself is of interest because it combined Balbi's training in ethnography and general mapping techniques with Guerry's training as a lawyer interested in patterns of criminality. Using criminal statistics for the years 1825 to 1827 and demographic data from France's latest census, they developed maps of crimes against property, crimes against persons, and levels of education. Comparing these maps, they found that the northeastern portion of France (from Orleans to the Franche-Comte) was better educated, that areas with high levels of crimes against property had low incidences of attacks on people, and that the areas with more property crime were populated by people with higher levels of education (see Figure 2). While the results regarding geographic differences in educational levels came as no great surprise, the others ran counter to popular views at the time. Guerry, however, paid little attention to these reactions because he was not interested in developing or testing theories (Oberschall, 1989).

The Belgian astronomer and statistician Lambert-Adolphe Quetelet attempted to fill the theoretical void. In 1831 and 1832, he independently published three maps dealing with the same themes but spreading across larger areas. Quetelet saw a correlation between crime and several variables including transportation routes, education levels, and ethnic and cultural variations. Quetelet continued theoretical development through his concept of the "average man" and his quest to discover, through statistics and "social physics," the explanation of societal behavior (Quetelet, 1835). His contributions to statistics, which were very controversial at the time, suggested the application from astronomy of the normal distribution and error measurement to social phenomena (Maltz, 1991). Quetelet's use of statistical tools combined with the average man concept was founded on the belief that aggregations of data provide statistical stability, assuming there is no change in any underlying causal relationships. As he stated, "The greater the number of individuals observed, the more do individual peculiarities, whether physical or moral, become

Figure 2: Balbia and Guerry (1829) Maps Comparing Crime and Instruction

effaced, and allow the general facts to predominate, by which society exists and is preserved" (Quetelet, 1835:12, as reported in Stigler, 1986). Indeed, Quetelet found stability over time in crime, birth, and suicide rates and other social phenomena, to the extent that critics said he was questioning the very existence of free will.

Despite groundbreaking work in providing explanations for the distribution of crime, these ecological perspectives were hastily discarded with the advent of a "positivist" criminology eager to locate the causes of crime within the biological and physiological framework of individuals (Morris, 1958; Beirne, 1993). Robinson (1982) draws the following conclusion about the development of thematic maps and Quetelet's (1835) statistical approach:

> Although thematic maps of moral statistics continued to be made [into the 1860s], especially of instruction, their developmental period had run its course. Subsequent attention seems to have been oriented more toward sociological interpretation and away from geographical variation. In a sense this reflects a greater concern with Quetelet's provocative ideas of "social physics" and a lessening of interest in the investigations of regional differences, such as by Dupin, Guerry, and Fletcher [Robinson, 1982:170].

There was also a very practical reason for moving away from the use of maps and regional variations in social and moral statistics. It required a considerable amount of time and effort to collect data, summarize by appropriate areas, and manually create the maps. Whatever the reasons for the demise of interest in mapping of crime, the lesson in our context is that the efforts during this period were based on reasonably good data (as collected by France's censuses), but were weak in other areas. Maps of interest could not be developed on any regular basis; crime theories were not adequately developed; and techniques for analysis were slow, time-consuming, and cumbersome.

The history of mapping in the U.S. stands in sharp contrast to what has just been discussed. We sometimes forget that America is a comparatively young nation. In the early 1800s, many parts of the U.S. were years away from collecting crime and demographic data on a routine basis. A search of the police literature uncovered no references even in the first part of this century to the 19th century mapping efforts in England and France. Instead, what begins to emerge are occasional references to "spot maps" in which pins are physically placed on large street maps. These spot maps were used first with traffic accident data, which predated systematic collection of crime data.[1]

More sophisticated maps were developed by a group of scholars associated with the University of Chicago in the 1920s and 1930s. These urban sociologists, led by Robert Park, looked to characteristics of the urban environment to explain the crime problem in American cities. They mapped crime and other social characteristics in neighborhoods in the city of Chicago. Using these maps, they illustrated the theoretical position that crime was strongly linked to social disorganization and poverty in urban settings. For example, Frederic Thrasher (1927) superimposed the "location and distribution" of gangs in Chicago on a map of urban areas in the city (see Figure 3). He found that gangs were concentrated in areas of the city where social control was weak and social disorganization pervasive. Similar conclusions were reached by Shaw and Myers (1929) in a study of juvenile delinquency conducted for the Illinois Crime Survey. In a map that looks as if it had been generated through modern computer applications (Figure 4) rather than produced by hand, they show that the home addresses of over 9,000 delinquents are clustered in areas marked by "physical deterioration, poverty and social disorganization" (1929:652).

Interest in the ecological correlates of crime faded among American sociologists in the 1930s. The confident assertion by Shaw (1929) that the "study of such a problem as juvenile delinquency necessarily begins with a study of its geographical location" (p.5) was not heeded by those who followed him. Once the relationship between social organization and crime in urban neighborhoods had been illustrated, a new generation of researchers shifted concern to elements of social disorganization and their impacts upon individual predisposition to criminality. The tedious and difficult process of mapping crime in the pre-computer age did not appear to offer potential for new and important insights. A new generation of sociologists concerned with crime sought to understand why certain individuals, both within these socially disorganized areas or outside them, chose to commit crimes while others did not (Merton, 1938; Sutherland, 1939). This question did not demand examination of the location of crime events, but rather led scholars to focus on the motivations of offenders.

The idea of automated crime mapping emerged in the late 1960s. Early applications (Pauly et al., 1967; Carnaghi and McEwen, 1970) showed the potential for visual representations of crime patterns through computer-generated maps. For example, Figure 5 uses such a map to show the distribution of larcenies from automobiles in 1967 in the ninth district in St. Louis, MO. Maps were seen as offering the potential for focusing police resources in more efficient and more effective ways. Similarly, publications on crime analysis strongly advocated automated analysis of crime (Chang et al., 1979; Buck et al., 1973) and illustrated the use of geographic analysis (Brantingham and Brantingham, 1981; Harries, 1974; Pyle, 1974).

Figure 3: The Place of Chicago's Gangland in the Urban Ecology

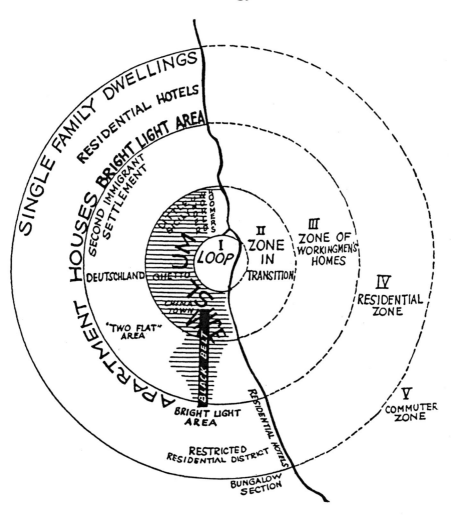

Note: The shaded portion indicates the approximate location of the central empire of gangland.

Figure 4: Home Addresses of Alleged Male Juvenile Delinquents

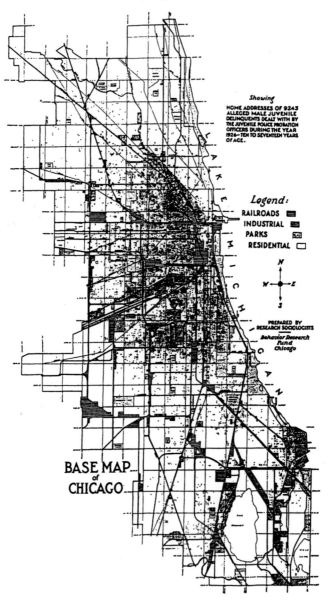

Figure 5: Larcenies from Automobiles in District 9, St. Louis

Data Mapped in 10 Levels Between Extreme Values of 0.00 and 40.00
Data Values Scaled According to Linear Scale.

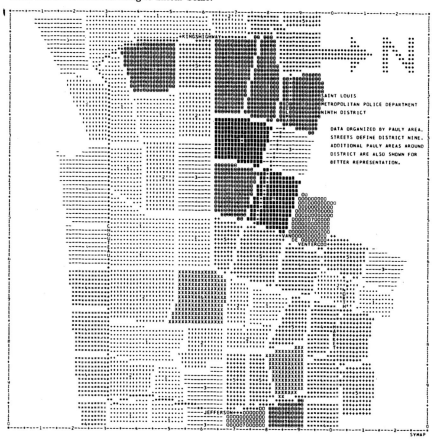

District 9 **** Selected Part One Offenses
From 0001 of 03/06/67 to 2400 of 03/26/67
Crimes Within District: 486 — Total Crimes for This Map: 866

Frequency Distribution of Data Point Values in Each Level

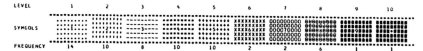

While the potential for computer mapping generated much enthusiasm, few police departments actually integrated crime mapping into police operations. One reason for this failure is that the maps were developed with little sense of organizing theories or perspectives. Moreover, practitioners could count on little help from the academic community, which had long abandoned crime mapping and saw these efforts as representing technological policing applications that were not of their concern. The maps displayed only crime data, and were often not much more sophisticated than simple hand-generated pin maps. They remained an in-house product for police departments because the era of professional policing saw no real need for sharing crime results with either the community, scholars, or even other units of government.

Technical considerations also prevented the rapid spread of automated mapping. The maps required large mainframe computers for development and production, and these were not available to many police departments. Small and medium-sized departments were not automated and most large departments depended for support on the city's data processing section, which did not usually give priority to the needs of the police department. In addition, the computer maps required accurate and up-to-date geographic base files for converting addresses into coordinates. Even large police departments, which had the technical capabilities for creating such files, generally did not want to devote the necessary personnel to this labor-intensive and time-consuming endeavor. Even when the desire for developing maps of crime was present, it was extremely difficult given existing technologies to access crime data quickly in the form necessary for crime analysis. And as difficult as it was to prepare crime data that were under the control of police or other criminal justice agencies, it was that much more difficult to gain information from other agencies. Indeed, in this period there was little use of data across public agencies. Problems existed in both the compatibility of systems that were used and the identification of people or places tracked by specific agencies.

PRACTICAL AND THEORETICAL INNOVATIONS: PAVING THE WAY FOR WIDESPREAD MAPPING APPLICATIONS

Crime mapping has thus informed theory and policy about crime for almost two centuries. Nonetheless, its use has been sporadic. Each time that mapping has emerged as a crime analysis method or crime prevention tool, technological or theoretical barriers have prevented its full-scale development and application. The difficulty of matching data to maps made crime mapping an extremely time-consuming and tedious activity for scholars and practitioners. The lack of good data that could be accessed in a timely fashion often relegated mapping to an interesting but not very practical tool for crime prevention. Similarly, in periods during which the major theoretical questions that informed crime prevention research and policy had little to do with the ecology of crime, a full-scale focus on crime mapping was unlikely.

A comparison of the historical situation with the present suggests that recent interest in crime mapping is likely to have a more substantial and lasting impact on crime prevention theory and applications. In large part this is because of the computer and information revolutions of the last two decades. The expensive mainframe computer, which only large municipalities or agencies could afford in the 1960s and 1970s, has been replaced by cheaper and more efficient microcomputers. Starting with the Apple computer in 1979, the capabilities of microcomputers have increased every year and the costs have decreased. Desktop computers now deliver the power of mainframe computers of the 1980s. What this means is that the hardware necessary to develop computer maps has become available to lone scholars and even the smallest criminal justice agencies. The software has also become cheaper and more efficient. There are still mapping applications that demand access to relatively more expensive mini-computers. But most programs are available for microcomputers, and the power of such applications for integrating and presenting information is continually being updated.

Information systems that accurately record crime events and the processing of offenders have become the rule rather than the exception in American criminal justice agencies. Especially for police, the linkage of such information to places, generally street addresses, has become a central concern. In general, it is the management responsibilities faced by such agencies that have led to this geographic focus. In order to respond quickly and efficiently to emergency calls to the police, accurate coding of street addresses in information systems has become a necessity for modern police departments. Other agencies that want to track the whereabouts of offenders are also concerned that there be accurate identification of where offenders live and work. Advances in information systems now allow even small-scale criminal justice agencies to accurately define street addresses and attach them to coordinates that can be linked to computer maps.

The more general concern for compatibility among systems and data sources has now made it possible for practitioners and scholars to link data about the ecology of crime to a host of other information sources (e.g., census data, hospital records, tax records, and land use information).

At the same time that advances in computer and information systems have largely overturned the technological barriers to mapping of crime, innovations in crime prevention theory have pushed the concept of place to the center of research and practice in controlling crime. For most of this century the focus of crime prevention has been on people and their involvement in criminality (Weisburd, 1997; Brantingham and Brantingham, 1990). The ecology of crime, which is at the core of crime mapping, did not fit easily into this theoretical perspective. In the 1980s, however, the focus of crime prevention began to shift. Following a series of research studies that challenged the effectiveness of offender-based approaches (see, e.g., Martinson, 1974; Visher and Weisburd, 1997), a number of scholars called for a reorientation of crime prevention practice and theory to what may be termed the *context* of crime (Weisburd, 1997). In its broadest terms, this new perspective sought to develop a greater understanding of crime and more effective crime prevention strategies through concern with the physical, organizational, and social environments that make crime possible (see Brantingham and Brantingham, 1990; Clarke, 1980, 1983, 1992, 1995; Cornish and Clarke, 1986) . From the outset, the concept of place became a central concern of scholars in this area (see Eck and Weisburd, 1995).

This shift provided an important theoretical impetus to crime mapping, and encouraged its use not only in the development of practical prevention programs but also in research about the etiology of crime (see, e.g., Brantingham and Brantingham, 1981). If place was to be seen as a focus of crime prevention efforts, then methods that emphasize the ecology of crime had to be developed. If scholars were to understand the relationship between crime and place, then data had to be collected and explored in such a way that spatial relationships became central, rather than peripheral, to their analyses. Crime prevention programs that sought to identify places where crime was common — so called "hot spots" of crime (Sherman and Weisburd, 1995) — necessitated knowledge about the clustering of crime events across addresses in the city. With concurrent advances in computer and information technologies, crime mapping emerged as an indispensable tool of research and practice in crime prevention.

CRIME MAPPING: PROSPECTS AND PROBLEMS

We begin our collection of essays with five papers that illustrate the potential of crime mapping for developing and implementing recent innovations in crime prevention. In the first, Carolyn Rebecca Block shows how computer mapping of crime can facilitate community policing and problem solving. These approaches use an action research model similar to that of situational crime prevention (Goldstein, 1990; Clarke, 1992), and rely upon detailed information about where crime events occur and the factors that facilitate them. Block introduces the concept of a GeoArchive, a geographic database that is developed with the express purpose of providing police and the community with data that can facilitate "problem-solving community policing."

Block also addresses what has become a major problem in the development of computer mapping applications, "data overload." With the development of new information technologies, vast amounts of data can be overlaid onto computer maps. Official crime information itself can include hundreds of thousands and even millions of events. If data from the census, hospitals, and other city agencies are merged, one can see that the analyst can become quickly overwhelmed with maps becoming a mass of uninterpretable points (Maltz et al., 1990). Even if the maps are focused on specific kinds of problems and include only one or two types of information, computer maps quickly begin to be difficult to interpret (see, e.g., Weisburd and Green, 1994). Block suggests methods for managing and analyzing the vast array of information that has become available for crime prevention efforts.

Following Block's contribution are two chapters that illustrate the potential role that mapping can play in building police and community partnerships. In recent years scholars have emphasized the importance of community involvement in crime prevention efforts (see Greene and Mastrofski, 1988; Rosenbaum, 1994). The community is now seen as an important resource for both identifying and solving crime problems. Faye S. Taxman and Tom McEwen suggest that criminal justice and other public agencies working together with the community in "work groups," are likely to develop more effective and long-lasting solutions to crime problems. Maps and geographic data provide work groups with information critical to identifying, understanding and responding to crime problems. Sharing such information among members of work groups provides a basis for developing consensus and cooperation among police, other public agencies, and the community.

Marc Buslik and Michael D. Maltz also illustrate the importance of bringing maps into the community. They argue that sharing information with the public will not only increase cooperation and develop trust, but will aid in analyzing and interpreting the vast amounts of data that are likely to be included in maps. People who live in a community may be able to explain clustering of points on a map through their own experiences in the neighborhood, or the special knowledge of the people who live there. Information sharing that Buslik and Maltz describe as "power to the people" may empower the community and may lead to more effective crime prevention efforts. In this same vein, Buslik and Maltz emphasize the importance of bringing computer applications to those who are closest to problem-solving efforts: just as the community may have special insight and knowledge, patrol officers also gain insight from their direct experiences in the community.

Lorraine Green Mazerolle, Charles Bellucci and Frank Gajewski also raise the issue of who will use computer maps. They focus, however, on a different concern. Too often, computer mapping is viewed as an undifferentiated technology that can be applied in similar form for a myriad of purposes. Mazerolle and her colleagues suggest that mapping systems must be built in response to the specific users and purposes for which they are developed. A mapping system appropriate for a crime analysis unit defining departmental policy is not likely to be relevant for street level officers. In turn, specialized units may need types of information that are not relevant at the departmental level. If a criminal justice agency chooses to develop systems that will be used by specialists, the system configuration will be different than one that was meant for a wider group of officers with less expertise.

Mazerolle, Bellucci and Gajewski also describe the very real problems that face criminal justice agencies in developing mapping systems given current technologies. Many scholars and practitioners have been frustrated by the disjuncture between the promises of computer mapping and the realities of developing such maps with criminal justice information. Data transfer, geocoding, data integration, system customization, and confidentiality all present problems for those who want to develop crime mapping systems. Mazerolle and her colleagues use the example of the Jersey City Drug Market Analysis Program (see Weisburd and Green, 1995) to illustrate these problems and potential solutions to them.

In the final chapter in this section, Philip R. Canter provides a series of examples of how computer maps have aided crime prevention efforts in Baltimore County, MD. This chapter provides concrete examples of how mapping crime has influenced the activities of criminal justice agencies. Mapping has fostered a broader approach to crime problems and gained significant institutional support because of its usefulness as a crime prevention tool.

In the second section of our volume, we turn from crime prevention *practice* to crime prevention *research*. In the first two essays, the importance of cognitive or perceptual maps are explored. Computer mapping has developed for the most part in the context of large, computerized data-bases supplied by criminal justice or other public agencies. The importance of qualitative assessments of crime and crime prevention has most often been ignored. George F. Rengert and William V. Pelfrey, Jr., illustrate the disjuncture between crime maps based on official data about crime and those based on perceptions of crime. Whatever the familiarity of people with a neighborhood, they are unlikely to be able to predict the relative safety of areas with any accuracy. One important, though troubling, finding in this chapter is that both minority and non-minority students and community service recruits in Philadelphia defined dangerousness in relationship to the proportion of minorities that are found in an area. Rengert and Pelfrey's essay suggests that practitioners and scholars should expand the scope of mapping beyond the quantitative data sources that have so far dominated mapping applications.

David M. Kennedy, Anthony A. Braga and Anne M. Piehl show how this approach can be applied in the context of a problem-solving program aimed at juvenile gun violence and gun markets in Boston, MA. Kennedy and his colleagues suggest that qualitative information can be integrated with quantitative data in the context of computer mapping. They argue that the "experiential assets" of practitioners provide an important resource for crime prevention efforts. They use perceptions of gang officers, probation officers, and city employed "street workers" to develop a portrait of where juvenile gangs are found, their number and size, and antagonisms and alliances. Linking these perceptual maps to criminal justice data provides the authors with a fuller picture of the relationship between gangs and gun violence, which has facilitated an innovative problem-solving approach aimed at controlling serious gang violence in Boston.

Patricia L. Brantingham and Paul J. Brantingham suggest that the future will include innovations not only in technology but also in the ways in which we analyze and integrate mapping into crime prevention research. While major advances have been made in mapping applications, similar strides are just beginning to be made in the ways in which we systematize and present information drawn from computer maps. Traditionally, scholars have looked at simple counts of crime or rates of crime in specific areas or places. Brantingham and Brantingham suggest that additional measures are needed to develop a fuller understanding of the ecological distribution of crime problems. They present one such measure, the Location Quotient (LQC), which estimates the mix of crimes rather than the prevalence of crime events. The Location Quotient allows the researcher to define what types of crimes dominate a given area, rather than focusing upon the amount of crime that is present. The LQC emphasizes the contextual view of crime, and illustrates the importance of developing new analytical tools for describing geographic crime patterns.

The final contribution in this section shifts our focus to the use of mapping in developing a broader understanding of the distribution of crime problems. For the most part, computer mapping of crime has reinforced assumptions about the concentration of crime in specific places (see, e.g., Sherman, et al., 1989; Weisburd, et al., 1993; Weisburd and Green, 1993). James L. LeBeau and Karen L. Vincent suggest that computer mapping may also challenge current assumptions about the ecology of crime. Taking the case of repeat-address burglar alarm calls and burglaries, they caution researchers and practitioners regarding the application of hot-spot approaches to some crime problems. In their analyses, LeBeau and Vincent found that burglaries are not likely to occur at the same address multiple times. Alarm calls, in contrast, do repeat at similar addresses, though there are so many false alarms that a concentration on repeat-call locations is not likely to provide much crime prevention value.

In the final section of the volume, we include four essays that examine future prospects for integrating crime mapping into crime prevention research and practice. Our goal here is to identify technologies and issues that are just beginning to be examined, and are likely to concern scholars and practitioners over the next decade. The first two papers examine new technologies for predicting and tracking crime that are in the first stages of their development. Andreas M. Olligschlaeger describes the development of an early warning system that anticipates the emergence of criminal activity in Pittsburgh, PA. This system uses artificial neural networks to identify flare-ups of drug hot-spot areas. Olligschlaeger illustrates how neural networks can be integrated into computer mapping efforts, providing a sophisticated method for identifying where new crime events are likely to develop. While Olligschlaeger points out the barriers that confront full integration of these new technologies today, we believe neural networks are likely to form an important part of crime prevention research and practice in the future.

Severin L. Sorensen also provides a glimpse into future trends in crime mapping technologies. Using the acronym *SMART* (Spatial Management, Analysis and Resource Tracking), he suggests that we are close to achieving real time and place mapping through linkages with Geographic Positioning Systems and Automated Vehicle Location systems. One of the major problems facing crime mapping applications today is the gap between crime events and crime analysis (see Green et al., 1997). Sorensen shows how advances in satellite tracking technologies are making it possible to develop systems in which there is almost immediate access to crime information. Following Sorensen's model for future applications of crime mapping in crime prevention, we might suspect as well that the potential for data overload we described earlier is likely to grow in the coming decade.

The final essay, by John E. Eck, emphasizes the importance of crime prevention theory in crime mapping. We think this an especially appropriate paper to conclude a section on future trends, because crime mapping in crime prevention has often been atheoretical, relying upon maps to lead the way in defining theory and practice. As Eck illustrates, crime mapping without a theoretical context is likely to lead to confusion in both research and policy. The same distribution of points on a map may lead to a number of different potential explanations. More often than not, it is difficult to make sense of the mass of data that computer maps provide without informing analyses with theories about the distribution of crime events.

CONCLUSIONS

The contributors to this book demonstrate the important role that crime maps have begun to play in crime prevention theory and applications. In their professional roles as criminologists, geographers, and crime analysts, they write about the relationships between geographic areas and crime, physical disorder, gangs, and drugs. They show how crime mapping is used in crime prevention programs, and point to future uses of crime mapping in research, theory and practice.

Technological advances in computer mapping and information systems and theoretical innovation in crime prevention have combined to bring crime mapping to the center of crime prevention practice and policy. The time when such maps were an interesting oddity has passed. Crime maps have become an essential tool in crime prevention. The essays in this volume both illustrate this fact and suggest innovative directions for mapping applications.

NOTES

1. This is illustrated in a bulletin issued by the U.S. Federal Bureau of Investigation (1944):

> Spot maps have been used for a number of years by traffic bureaus in police departments throughout the country for the purpose of furnishing a clear, quick, and comprehensive picture of the accident situation and to indicate at a glance the points in the city which present the greatest hazard. Spots maps have also been used in a similar fashion to show the crime hazards of the city. For example, some departments show on a spot map one type of pin indicating the location of the theft of each automobile and a pin of a different shape or color to indicate the location of its recovery. The advantage of a spot map lies in its maintenance and interpretation [p.34].

REFERENCES

Beirne, P. (1993). *Inventing Criminology*. Albany, NY: State University of New York Press.

Block, C.R. and M. Dabdoub (1993). *Workshop on Crime Analysis Through Computer Mapping Proceedings*. Chicago, IL: Illinois Criminal Justice Information Authority.

Brantingham, P.L. and P.J. Brantingham (1981). *Environmental Criminology*. Beverly Hills, CA: Sage.

—— (1990). "Situational Crime Prevention in Practice." *Canadian Journal of Criminology* (Jan):17-40.

Buck, G.A., R. Austin, G. Cooper, D. Gagnon, J. Hodges, K. Martensen and M. O'Neal (1973). *Police Crime Analysis Unit Handbook*. Washington, DC: Law Enforcement Assistance Administration, U.S. Department of Justice.

Carnaghi J. and T. McEwen (1970). "Automatic Pinning." In: S.I. Cohn and W.E. McMahon (eds.), *Law Enforcement, Science and Technology*, vol. III. Chicago, IL: Illinois Institute of Technology Research.

Chang, S.K., W.H. Simms, C.M. Makres, and A. Bodnar (1979). *Crime Analysis System Support: Descriptive Report of Manual and Automated Crime Analysis Functions*. Gaithersburg, MD: International Association of Chiefs of Police.

Clarke, R.V. (1980). "Situational Crime Prevention: Theory and Practice." *British Journal of Criminology* 20:136-147.

—— (1983). "Situational Crime Prevention: Its Theoretical Basis and Practical Scope." In: M. Tonry and M. Morris (eds.), *Crime and Justice: An Annual Review of Research*, vol. 4. Chicago, IL: University of Chicago Press.

—— (ed.) (1992). *Situational Crime Prevention: Successful Case Studies*. Albany, NY: Harrow and Heston.

—— (1995). "Situational Crime Prevention: Achievements and Challenges." In: M. Tonry and D. Farrington (eds.), *Building a Safer Society: Strategic Approaches to Crime Prevention*. Crime and Justice: An Annual Review of Research, vol. 19. Chicago, IL: University of Chicago Press.

Cornish, D.B. and R.V. Clarke (eds.) (1986). *The Reasoning Criminal*. New York, NY: Springer-Verlag.

Eck, J.E. and D. Weisburd (eds.) (1995). "Crime Places in Crime Theory." In: J. Eck and D. Weisburd (eds.), *Crime and Place*. Crime Prevention Studies, vol. 4. Monsey, NY: Criminal Justice Press, pp. 1-34.

Goldstein, H. (1990). *Problem-Oriented Policing*. New York, NY: McGraw-Hill.

Grafton, S. (1995). *'L' is for Lawless*. New York, NY: Henry Holt and Company.

Greene, J.R. and S. D. Mastrofski (eds.) (1988). *Community Policing: Rhetoric or Reality*. New York, NY: Praeger.

Harries, K.D. (1974). *The Geography of Crime and Justice*. New York, NY: McGraw-Hill.

—— (1990). *Geographic Factors in Policing*. Washington, DC: Police Executive Research Forum.

Kenwitz, J.W. (1987). *Cartography In France: 1660-1848*. Chicago, IL: University of Chicago Press.

Maltz, M.D. (1991). "Crime Statistics: A Historical Perspective." In: E.H. Monkkonen (ed.), *Theory and Methods in Criminal Justice History, Part 2*. Ann Arbor, MI: Edwards Brothers.

—— A.C. Gordon, and W. Friedman (1990). *Mapping Crime in Its Community Setting: Event Geography Analysis.* New York, NY: Springer-Verlag.

Martinson, R. (1974). "What Works? Questions and Answers about Prison Reform." *Public Interest* 35:22-54.

Merton, R. (1938). "Social Structure and Anomie." *American Sociological Review* 3:672-682.

Morris, T.M. (1958). *The Criminal Area.* London, UK: Routledge and Kegan Paul.

Oberschall, A. (1989). "The Two Empirical Roots of Social Theory and the Probability Revolution." In: L. Kruger, G. Gigerenzer, and M.S. Morgan (eds.), *The Probabilistic Revolution: Ideas in the Sciences,* vol. 2. Cambridge, MA: Massachusetts Institute of Technology Press.

Pauly, G.A., T. McEwen, and S. Finch (1967). "Computer Mapping-A New Technique in Crime Analysis." In: S.A. Yefsky (ed.), *Law Enforcement Science and Technology,* vol. 1. New York, NY: Thompson Book Company.

Pyle, G.F. (1974). *The Spatial Dynamics of Crime.* Chicago, IL: Department of Geography, University of Chicago.

Quetelet, A. (1835). *Sur l'Homme et le Developpement de ses Facultes, ou Essai de Physique Sociale.* Paris, FR: Bachelier.

Robinson, A.H. (1982). *Early Thematic Mapping in the History of Cartography.* Chicago, IL: University of Chicago Press.

Rosenbaum, D. P. (ed.) (1994). *The Challenge of Community Policing: Testing the Promises.* Thousand Oaks, CA: Sage.

Shaw, C.R. (1929). *Delinquency Areas.* Chicago, IL: University of Chicago Press.

Shaw, C.R. and E.D. Myers (1929). "The Juvenile Delinquent." In: *Illinois Crime Survey.* Chicago, IL: Illinois Association for Criminal Justice.

Sherman, L.W., P.R. Gartin, and M.E. Buerger (1989). "Hot Spots of Predatory Crime: Routine Activities and the Criminology of Place." *Criminology* 27:27-56.

Sherman, L.W. and D. Weisburd (1995). "General Deterrent Effects of Police Patrol in Crime 'Hot-Spots': A Randomized, Controlled Trial." *Justice Quarterly* 12:625-648.

Stigler, S.M. (1986). *The History of Statistics: The Measurement of Uncertainty before 1900.* Cambridge, MA: Belknap Press of Harvard University Press.

Sutherland, E.H. (1939). *Principles of Criminology.* Philadelphia, PA: Lippincott.

Thrasher, F.M. (1927). *The Gang*. Chicago, IL: University of Chicago Press.

U.S. Federal Bureau of Investigation (1944). "Spot Maps in Crime Prevention." *FBI Law Enforcement Bulletin*. Washington, DC: U.S. Department of Justice.

Visher, C. and D. Weisburd (in press). "Identifying What Works: Recent Trends in Crime Prevention Strategies." *Crime, Law and Social Change*.

Weisburd, D. (1997). "Reorienting Crime Prevention Research and Policy: From the Causes of Criminality to the Context of Crime." Washington, DC: U.S. National Institute of Justice.

—— (1994). "Defining the Street Level Drug Market." In: D.L MacKenzie and C.D Uchida (eds.), *Drugs and Crime: Evaluating Public Policy Initiatives*. Thousand Oaks, CA: Sage.

—— (1995). "Policing Drug Hot Spots: The Jersey City Drug Market Analysis Experiment." *Justice Quarterly* 12:711-735.

Weisburd, D., L. Maher and L. Sherman (1993). "Contrasting Crime General and Crime Specific Theory: The Case of Hot Spots of Crime." In: Freda Adler and William S. Laufer (eds.), *New Directions in Criminological Theory*. Advances in Criminological Theory vol. 4, New Brunswick, NJ: Transaction.

Mapping as
a Crime
Prevention Tool

THE GEOARCHIVE: AN INFORMATION FOUNDATION FOR COMMUNITY POLICING[1]

by

Carolyn Rebecca Block

Statistical Analysis Center, Illinois Criminal Justice Information Authority

Abstract: *This chapter presents the main concepts of the GeoArchive as an "information foundation for community policing." Based on the Illinois Criminal Justice Information Authority's experience in developing this innovative idea, many agencies are using a GeoArchive to identify problems and develop strategies for crime prevention and intervention at the neighborhood level. The theory of the GeoArchive and practical suggestions and rules of thumb for developing a GeoArchive are illustrated with examples of how the GeoArchive is being used in current crime prevention strategies.*

INTRODUCTION

A GeoArchive is a database of community and law enforcement data, organized for use in crime analysis, investigation and community problem solving.[2] A type of geographic information system (GIS), a GeoArchive contains address-level data from both law enforcement and community sources, linked to computer mapping capability and

Address correspondence to: Carolyn Rebecca Block, Statistical Analysis Center, Illinois Criminal Justice Information Authority, 120 South Riverside Plaza, Chicago, IL 60606.

organized so that the data can be updated, maintained, mapped, analyzed and used by those who are developing and implementing strategies of crime reduction in the community. When combined with a problem-oriented community policing program, a GeoArchive can become an *information foundation for community policing.*

Crime maps are nothing new. Pin maps have graced walls behind police chiefs' desks since pins were invented. Neither is the "high-tech" version of these pin maps — computer-aided crime mapping — particularly new. What is new is that police districts and community-level organizations now have direct access to and control over computer mapping. This means that those people who have the greatest stake in solving neighborhood problems now have direct access to the information and analysis tools they need to identify and develop effective solutions for specific problems facing their community. The potential effects of this innovation are so fundamental to the nature of local decision making and problem solving that it deserves to be called a "technological revolution."

By itself, however, computer mapping technology will not supply the information needed for problem-oriented community policing.[3] For effective problem identification and problem solving, communities need more than the ability to map data. They must be able to turn spatial data into information. This means that they must compile and organize the vast amount of mapped data generated by day-to-day activity in a neighborhood, relate the data to other information, and then summarize those data quickly and objectively as a basis for making decisions. Increasingly, people eager to meet this challenge have been springing up in a variety of sworn, civilian, technical, practical, academic and community settings across the continent and around the world.[4] These innovative "mapping entrepreneurs" are searching for ways to go beyond making pretty maps towards using spatial data as a foundation for community problem solving. In Chicago, for example, the Illinois Criminal Justice Information Authority is working with the Chicago Police Department and Loyola University Chicago to develop an "Information Foundation for Community Policing," which couples a "GeoArchive" database with spatial analysis and statistical tools (such as the Spatial and Temporal Analysis of Crime [STAC] software package).[5]

Technology by itself is not enough to support problem-oriented community policing, crime analysis, tactical decisions, or the development of investigation strategies and intervention programs. Mapping technology is useful only to the degree that it is coupled with useful data and analysis tools to make sense of those data (Figure 1).

Both community problem solving and law enforcement tactical decisions require a well-organized body of local-level community and law enforcement information (a GeoArchive). In order to develop a strategy for preventing homicide, for example, we must know more than just the patterns and trends of homicide. We also need to know about all the events (lethal and non-lethal, criminal and noncriminal) that may escalate to or presage a homicide. Therefore, a database intended to support such problem solving should link law enforcement and community data at the address level. This we have called a GeoArchive.

In addition to a GeoArchive database, we need tools to help us make sense of all of this information. When it is initially acquired, computer mapping technology is a tremendous boon to crime analysts and local problem solvers; no longer is it necessary to draw maps by hand. All too soon, however, the amount of mapped information becomes too much to handle, many alternative summaries of it are possible, and quick decisions become more and more out of reach. In such situations, an efficient and objective summary of reality provided by statistics and spatial analysis can offer a useful guide to interpretation.[6] Statistics are tools designed to summarize enormous amounts of information and to organize that information to answer specific, practical questions.

But these requirements are difficult to meet. Tools for organizing and analyzing spatial data are still in their infancy, particularly tools that are applicable in practical situations. The GeoArchive and STAC, basic components of the "Early Warning System" project in Chicago Police Area Four and prototypes for the Chicago Alternative Policing Strategy (CAPS) program and the ICAM (Information Collection for Automated Mapping) program, are attempts to develop solutions to these problems.[7] Though we still have much to learn, these pilot projects have taught us a lot about developing and maintaining a GeoArchive, linking it to statistical and spatial analysis tools, and using the two resources together to identify and solve community problems. Using the Chicago experience as an example, this chapter outlines the major things we have learned so far, in the hope that other communities will benefit from our experience.

Figure 1: An Information Foundation for Community Problem-Solving

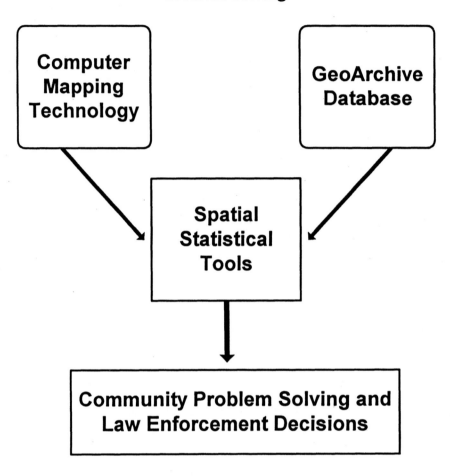

COMPUTER MAPPING AS A TECHNOLOGICAL REVOLUTION

Only a few years ago, the only mapped information available to most police departments was in the form of cardboard pin maps with colored plastic pins. Computer maps required such expensive equipment and such a high level of expertise that they could be produced only by a central city planning agency outside of the police department or perhaps by a central administrative unit within the police department. Mapping software and hardware was complex and expensive, and required experts to use. In addition, it was — and still is — tremendously expensive to create the computerized (digitized) street maps that are necessary for mapping.[8] Access to mapping equipment and automated maps was, therefore, beyond the reach of most departments.

Because cities that did have mapping capability usually housed it centrally, often in an agency outside the police department, police access to mapping was indirect, often cumbersome, and usually time consuming. Local or field-level decision makers had to petition a central "data division" to obtain a map meeting their needs, and the response, even if successful, was seldom timely. Furthermore, the digitized maps, mapped data and area boundaries available from a central source are not always the most useful for identifying and solving community safety problems. Maps that are appropriate for central planning might not be appropriate for local law enforcement decisions.

Times have changed. A combination of three recent innovations in computer mapping technology — accessible mapping software, personal computers and work stations that can handle that software and the U.S. Census's TIGER (Topologically Integrated Geographic Encoding and Referencing) [see Guptill, 1988]) files — have brought computer mapping capability within the reach of local communities (Stallo, 1995). Though some mapping software is still very expensive, requiring years of training and high-powered hardware, software companies have begun to produce mapping packages that are much cheaper and friendlier, and that need no more than an ordinary personal computer (PC) to run them (Sanford, 1995). Also, the Census Bureau's creation of digitized street maps for every U.S. county was a huge breakthrough for local-level mapping. These "TIGER" street map files, available at low cost from the Census or computer software vendors, eliminate the necessity of digitizing the local street map, an extremely expensive task that had been a formidable obstacle to local mapping.

The advent of accessible, PC-based mapping software and inexpensive automated street maps means that computer mapping capability is now available at the local, district and neighborhood levels. As a result of this technological revolution, the ability to identify and solve problems using spatial information is no longer the exclusive purview of analysts and technical experts in large organizations or in city, state or federal governments. It is also available to people trying to identify and solve problems in their own neighborhood.

Accessible computer mapping generates a need for methods and techniques geared to take advantage of spatial information (Guptill, 1988; Block and Green, 1994). When law enforcement and community agencies begin to shop for computer mapping software, they may encounter a vendor who tries to sell them data. They should realize that they already have a multitude of data, and easy access to even more. A police department does not need to buy back its own offense and arrest data from a vendor. For other kinds of data, agencies generally will obtain much better information from each other if they establish their own data-sharing relationships instead of going through a vendor. Instead of more data, what agencies really need are tools to map, organize and summarize the data they already have. With these tools, maps can go beyond description to become a foundation for community problem solving.

Data Overload

The last 10 or 20 years have seen a quiet revolution in criminal justice. Even though conventional wisdom points to a dearth of high-quality criminal justice data, both the quality and quantity of data have improved tremendously in recent decades, as has their availability to decision makers (Block, 1989). Sufficient information is now available to allow for the measurement of basic indicators with a degree of precision that was not only unknown but even unanticipated a few years ago. Even though there is still a lot of room for improvement in the degree of detail and specificity of data available, the criminal justice system generates a tremendous amount of information. Much of it, however, is unused. There may be so many pieces of information that it is impossible for the human mind to assimilate them, sort them out, and summarize them before the window of opportunity for an effective decision has passed. Thus, rather than the major problem being a dearth of data, often the problem is just the opposite — data overload.

Just when information technology has begun to be widely used in law enforcement to bring data overload under control (Manning, 1992), computer mapping is generating yet another surge of data. This is occurring for two reasons. First, computer mapping adds quantities of new information — mapped data sets, automated street maps and boundary maps — to the data repertoire. Second, accessible computer mapping has *changed the nature* of that information with an added dimension — space (see Anselin, 1989). Therefore, mapping generates both a quantitative increase in the amount of data and qualitative changes in the character of data.

Having ready access to spatial information for the first time can be compared to suddenly being granted another sense. Someone without the sense of sight, for example, might be quite capable of perceiving the environment with the other four senses, and if granted the ability to see, would need time to learn how to use this fifth sense and integrate it with the other four. Similarly, now that spatial information is generally available, our first inclination might be to maintain, organize and analyze it in the same way as we have always done. The old ways, however, do not utilize the unique character of the information offered by spatial data. For example, an address-based data set of homicides might support many kinds of spatial analysis; we could ask whether the homicide locations are clustered, whether the homicides tend to be located close to other mapped locations such as taverns or gang territories, or whether they tend to occur on the periphery of a city or in the center. Similarly, with a data set of areas defined within boundaries (such as Census tracts, police districts, gang territories, or crime Hot Spot Areas), we might examine the location of high-crime areas relative to transit stops, or the effect of a Hot Spot Area on crime levels in the area surrounding it. But it is difficult to study issues such as these without a database organized to use spatial information, plus statistical tools to summarize that information.

In addition to the data overload precipitated by the advent of accessible computer mapping, problem-oriented community policing can precipitate its own inundation of data. Though many people have some of the information necessary to identify and solve a community problem, no single individual is likely to have all of it. A tactical officer, a patrol officer, a narcotics officer, a long-time resident and a community worker are all likely to have differing sets of information about patterns of street gang violence, and officers working the night shift may be aware of very different aspects of the neighborhood's problems than officers working the day shift (Block and Green, 1994). Some of this knowledge is spatial; individuals have "cognitive maps" that may differ, even for the same area (Rengert, 1995b; Rengert and Greene, 1994; Mattson and Rengert, 1995). In addition, community information might be forever lost when an especially knowledgeable person moves, retires or is promoted out of the area. In principle, then, a complete problem analysis could require the compilation and evaluation of the body of knowledge representing the experience of all aspects of a community, past and present — an overwhelming task.

Like computer mapping, community policing can produce an enormous increase in the quantity of data as well as a qualitative change in the nature of data. Information necessary for problem-oriented community policing is often different from information usually collected in law enforcement (Sparrow, 1994:124-126). To identify the problems facing a neighborhood and to describe those problems with enough detail to support effective intervention programs, we must have some way to organize and sift through the vast amount of information available about an area from a multitude of sources, each event anchored by location and time, and to make this information easily and readily available to local problem solvers.

No matter how sophisticated it may be, computer mapping technology is not enough by itself to control and manage data overload. In addition to technology, we need tools that can manage data that is organized in different spatial units and that changes over time, and that can link spatial and other kinds of information, such as individual, incident, location and situation characteristics. We also need spatial analysis and statistical tools that can summarize a vast amount of spatial information for quick and objective decision making. Database tools such as the GeoArchive and statistical tools such as STAC can control and manage data overload, so that law enforcement and community information can become a foundation for the tactical, crime analysis and policy decisions of problem-oriented community policing (see Figure 1, above).

In his analysis of evolving interaction between two Chicago street gangs (the Black Gangster Disciple Nation and the Vicelords) from 1987 to 1992, David Curry (1995) used a GeoArchive and STAC to deal with data overload. In the original map (Figure 2), showing all street gang-related offenses attributed to the two gangs in an area on Chicago's West Side, with locations of four schools, Humboldt Park, and the grid of local streets, there is so much data that it is difficult to perceive any pattern. However, when Curry organized the data to examine specific hypotheses, he began to see a pattern that tells a story. First, he separated violent gang offenses attributed to the two gangs, and separated crimes occurring in the earlier years from those occurring in the later years. Second, using consistently defined boundaries and search parameters, Curry used STAC to identify the densest concentrations (Hot Spot Areas) of gang-related crimes attributed to each gang in the two periods.

Figures 3a and 3b indicate that two changes took place between 1987-1988 and 1991-1992: first, a sharp decline in violent gang activity, and, second, a shift in gang territory. The earlier years saw four dense concentrations of violent Black Gangster Disciple Nation (BGDN) activity, centered in two locations to the northeast and southeast of Humboldt Park, and around and between four area schools. Violent Vicelord activity was much less densely compressed, and the most concentrated areas centered on the schools (where they overlapped with BGDN Hot Spot Areas), not the park. By 1991-1992, the level of violent gang-related offenses in the area had fallen sharply, and the BGDN offenses were so widely scattered that STAC did not find a Hot Spot Area. In contrast, Vicelord offenses continued to be concentrated around the schools.

Figure 2: Gang Crimes in Study Area around Four Schools and Park

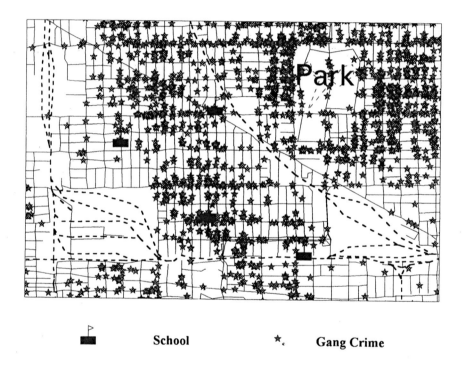

■ School   ⋆꜀   Gang Crime

To move from a data overload situation to a problem analysis, Curry (1995) used a GeoArchive of community data (school and park locations) and law enforcement data (gang offenses), as well as STAC Hot Spot Area analysis. Equally vital to his analysis, however, was the hypothesis that spatial patterns and concentrations of gang-related offenses attributed to the two gangs had changed over time. Such a theoretical perspective, like mapped data, is necessary for effective spatial analysis. However, finding the best theory for a given application can be as problematic as managing and summarizing the data.

Figure 3a: Density Ellipses for Violent Gang Crimes in Study Area for Two Gangs in 1987-88

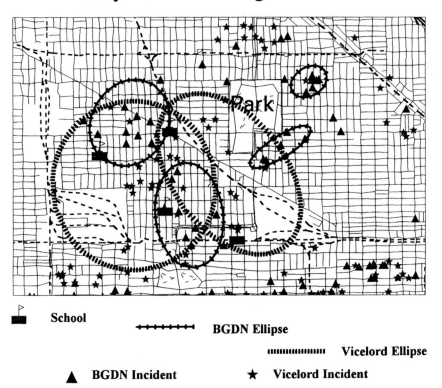

■ School   ┝━━━━━┥ BGDN Ellipse

                        ⅲⅲⅲⅲⅲⅲⅲⅲⅲⅲ Vicelord Ellipse

▲ BGDN Incident   ★ Vicelord Incident

Theory Overload

For law enforcement and community information to make sense as a basis for local-level decisions, we need more than "just a pretty map." As John Eck argues elsewhere in this volume and others have argued previously (Roncek and Maier, 1991; Maltz et al., 1991), the successful analysis of spatial patterns of crime requires that mapping technology be guided by theory that can link place to crime, can unravel the spatial characteristics of different types of crime, and can provide explanations and suggest prevention strategies for the high vulnerability of some neighborhoods or demographic groups. Nevertheless, it is much easier to *assert* that computer mapping technology must be linked to an information-organizing framework built on theory than to actually *do* it. Which theory do we choose? What general theoretical framework(s) or guiding construct(s) apply best to the specific, local problem at hand?

Figure 3b: Density Ellipses for Violent Gang Crimes in Study Area for Two Gangs in 1991-92

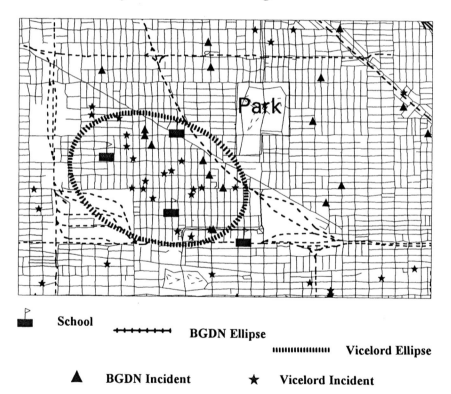

School

BGDN Ellipse

Vicelord Ellipse

▲ BGDN Incident ★ Vicelord Incident

For almost every community safety problem, there are numerous alternative theories that might be used to guide problem identification and intervention strategy development, theories that may suggest different and even completely contradictory interventions. This is equally true, perhaps even more true, when the people involved in problem solving are not aware that they have a theoretical framework. Each individual experiences somewhat different aspects of the same community, and has different ways of understanding community events. Such a perceptual framework is an implicit theory. These diverse but sometimes competing ways of thinking about a community and its problems can be a rich source for innovative problem analysis and solution development (Fisher, 1994). On the other hand, a plethora of theories, whether or not they are formally stated as such, can lead to stagnation or produce only sound and fury. This "theory overload," if not harnessed to the process of community problem solving (Goldstein, 1990), can be a formidable obstacle.

Problem-oriented community policing (Sparrow, 1994; Moore; Goldstein, 1977, 1990) provides a potential solution to theory overload. In community policing, the police department and the community collaborate to set and achieve community safety priorities (Sparrow, 1994). In problem-oriented (or problem solving) policing, the emphasis has evolved from the traditional focus on handling individual incidents as they arise to identifying, analyzing and solving the general problem leading to similar incidents (Goldstein, 1990). Though the concepts of community and problem-oriented policing overlap (Moore and Trojanowicz, 1988), the existence of one does not necessarily imply the existence of the other. Community policing programs vary widely in the degree to which the police department and citizens collaborate to identify and analyze problems and develop solutions for them. If not combined with problem solving, community policing alone is likely to yield only limited and ephemeral benefits (Sparrow, 1994). By the same token, police problem solving may not always involve the community (Ward et al., 1995; Goldstein, 1993; Sparrow, 1994), thus losing access to information and resources available only from people intimately familiar with a specific neighborhood. However, when they do occur together as problem-oriented community policing, the resulting police and community collaboration draws on the knowledge and resources of those who know a community best — people working together to solve its problems. This can be a powerful mechanism for solving theory overload.

Implementation of this solution is not simple, however. Community-centered problem-solving is an art, not a science. It involves many steps, summarized by Spelman and Eck's (1987) acronym SARA (Scanning, Analysis, Response, Assessment).[9] Each of these elements presents a different organizational and logistical challenge. Of the steps in problem solving, perhaps the biggest challenge is analysis, which requires not only compiling and organizing information (grouping incidents as problems), but also relating this information to alternative theories (analyzing relevant interests in the problem, critiquing the current response, and searching for innovative responses). One of the basic tasks of analysis is to collate and compile disparate theories about a problem and its solutions into a common working definition that can be a basis for a collaborative solution — a strategy for intervention or prevention.

As Sparrow (1994:46) puts it, "...to find broadly acceptable solutions to problems (police) need, first, to find broadly acceptable definitions of the problems." But Sadd and Grinc (1996:14) point out that, "One of the principles guiding community policing is recognition that the police must be guided by the values of the community. Identifying these values may not be easy." Pulling the community's theoretical perspectives together to identify and define the problem is a foundation for developing solutions. But theory overload makes this difficult, because there may be as many theories about a problem as there are community members, sometimes more.

Thus, we come full circle: as a potential solution to theory overload, the analysis step in problem-oriented community policing requires that the problem solvers identify and address the various theoretical frameworks in the community. They must, in other words, resolve theory overload in order to resolve theory overload. Herman Goldstein and his colleagues have compiled and tested numerous techniques and social mechanisms aimed at overcoming this dilemma (for an overview, see Goldstein, 1993.) As with many tasks, the effort is aided by the proper tools — database management and statistical tools for compiling, storing, summarizing, analyzing and communicating information.

As a tool for overcoming theory overload, a GeoArchive works in several ways. First, it can serve as a community memory bank (Maltz et al., 1991) — a device for storing, linking and sharing enormous amounts of community information from diverse sources. Further, because maps can be so compelling, particularly maps of someone's own neighborhood, an accessible GeoArchive can increase the amount of interaction among neighborhood players, the clarity of their communication with one other, and the resulting degree of consensus on problem-solving strategies. In addition, a GeoArchive can actually motivate community problem solvers to share information with each other. Thus, a GeoArchive can provide a springboard for problem solvers to identify and evaluate those alternative theoretical frameworks that should be an integral part of problem analysis and the search for solutions.

Building an Information Foundation for Community Problem Solving

No matter how innovative or revolutionary, no technology or theory by itself is a panacea for solving community problems. The most effective problem analysis and problem solving will not emerge from technology or theory alone, but only when they support each other. We need conceptual resources to utilize technological resources effectively, and we need technological resources to make it easier to compile, evaluate, communicate and utilize conceptual resources. Together, computer mapping technology linked to an information-organizing framework that encompasses both law enforcement and community information can become an information foundation for community problem solving.

Data overload and theory overload present obstacles to linking theory and technology. However, two kinds of tools designed to accommodate the unique aspects of spatial data can integrate and make sense of the enormous amounts of information generated by daily interaction in a neighborhood (see Figure 1). Database management and statistical tools, used in combination, can compile, summarize and communicate spatial and other information. With these tools, one of which is the GeoArchive, we can link technology to theory and form a foundation upon which practical applications can be built.

WHAT IS A GEOARCHIVE?

Spatial data overload calls for tools that can do more than just manage large databases. To turn "spatial data into spatial information," we must be able to assimilate, sort, link and summarize data over several dimensions: individual characteristics, spatial relationships, and trends over time.[10] However, the development of data management and statistical tools for geographic analysis has not kept pace with the technological revolution in computer mapping. Database and statistical tools, particularly spatial analysis tools applicable to practical law enforcement situations, are still in their infancy.[11] In response to this situation, the Illinois Criminal Justice Information Authority, working with the Chicago Police Department, Loyola University Chicago and mapping entrepreneurs around the world, has been compiling a portfolio of database and statistical tools to manage, organize and summarize spatial data as a basis for practical community safety decisions. The GeoArchive is one of these tools.

A GeoArchive is a particular kind of GIS.[12] Like all GISs, a GeoArchive is especially organized for spatial data, and contains a digitized map and data geocoded to be located on that map.[13] It can be seen as a large set of map transparencies that can be overlaid on each other. But a GeoArchive has several characteristics that distinguish it from other GIS databases (see Figure 4). A GeoArchive links address-based local-level data from a variety of law enforcement and community sources, and is organized so that it can be updated, maintained, mapped, analyzed and used by those who are developing and implementing strategies of crime reduction in the local community.

Address-Based, Neighborhood-Level Information

Geographic point (address-based) data and area data are key components of GIS databases. In point data, the spatial unit is a dot on the map, representing a single location such as an offense, an offender's residence or a tavern or abandoned building. In area data, the spatial unit is a two-dimensional area surrounded by an enclosed boundary, such as a zip code, a police district or beat, a Census tract or a gang territory.[14] In contrast to other GISs, a GeoArchive must contain *both* area and point data sets, with a database of information behind each. In fact, the most important geographic information in a GeoArchive is point (address or pin) data.

In some GIS databases, the area is the smallest spatial unit of analysis. Any point in such a GIS is either only a map data location with no information behind it, or actually represents an area (i.e., a centroid).[15] Both point data and area data have information behind them in a GeoArchive; they are much more than locations on a map. In the Early Warning System for Street Gang Violence project, for example, each crime incident has about 50 variables associated with it (such as offense type, weapon, number of offenders); each Census tract has numerous demographic variables associated with it (such as total population, percent under age 15); each street gang territory

Figure 4: The GeoArchive and Community Problem-Solving

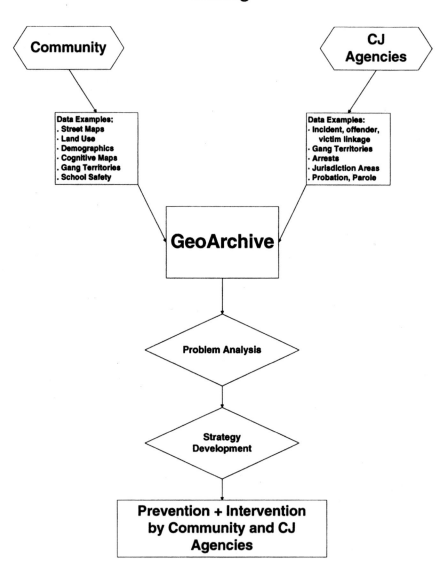

boundary is linked to information about the gang; and so on (Jacob and Block, 1995; Green and Whitaker, 1994; Block and Green, 1994; Bobrowski, 1988).

In a GIS in which area is the smallest spatial unit of analysis, the unit scale is often too large and the boundaries of the units too arbitrarily drawn for the data to be useful for analyzing community problems. Local problems require local address-level information, not address information summarized across areas defined by artificial boundaries. We do not send a squad car to a Census tract to answer a call, but to an address. A GIS that depends too completely on Census or district-level data may be useful for some purposes, such as writing annual reports or long-term forecasting of resource utilization at the district or city level. It will not, however, be a useful tool for daily decisions and community problem solving.

Moreover, address-level information is lost with an area-level GIS. Points can be aggregated to areas, but areas cannot be disaggregated to points. With an address-level database of criminal incidents linked to an area-level database of police districts, it would be easy to count, for example, the number of criminal incidents in every police district. In contrast, with a strictly area-level database of total incidents for each police district, there is no way to determine the exact location of each incident. If forced to aggregate address-level to area-level data, we will lose valuable information.

For example, the Community Areas in Chicago vary widely in their population-based rates of street gang-motivated homicide (Figure 5).[16] The number of homicides occurring between 1987 and 1994 ranged from zero to 63, and the rate per 100,000 population ranged from zero to 21. However, aggregating the data by Community Area obscures the actual pattern of homicides, and may even be misleading (Brantingham and Brantingham, 1981). An address-level map of the same street gang homicides (Figure 6) shows that the overall homicide rate for a Community Area may be a misleading representation of concentrations of homicides (shown as triangles on the map).[17] This happens when arbitrary area boundaries divide a homicide cluster (for example, where Areas 22, 23, and 24 meet), or when a cluster is confined to a small part of a larger area (for example, Areas 8 or 46). Vice Lord activity, for example, is not determined by Community Area boundaries.

Do the densest concentrations of street gang non-lethal violence and drug activity produce a higher risk of street gang homicide? Actually, the risk of street gang-motivated homicide is higher in Hot Spot Areas of street gang-motivated non-lethal violence (narrow-line ellipses in Figure 6), calculated independently of the homicide locations, than in the densest concentrations of street gang drug offenses (heavy-line Hot Spot Areas). For example, the small Hot Spot Area of non-lethal violence in Community Area 8 had 45.7 homicides per square mile, while the large drug offense Hot Spot Area covering most of Areas 23, 25, 26 and 27 contained only 9.1 per square mile. The greatest risk of street gang homicide, however, occurs when non-lethal violent and drug offense Hot Spot Areas intersect. For example, along the border between Areas 23 and 24, where the large drug Hot Spot Area intersects with a violent Hot Spot Area, there were 18.8 homicides per square mile. The portion of Community Area 61 where a violent and drug Hot Spot Area overlap experienced 37.5 homicides per square mile. Thus, neighborhoods unfortunate enough to have both Hot Spot Areas of gang turf violence and of street gang-related drug offenses tend to have a very high risk of lethal gang violence. This kind of analysis would be impossible without address-level data.

But this is not to say that area-level data should be excluded from a GeoArchive. For many reasons, both are necessary. The most obvious reason is that some information that may be vital to informed decisions is defined or available only at the area level. Population data and street gang territory data, for example, are defined only within the boundaries of areas. By linking Census data to the non-lethal street gang data summarized by the Hot Spot Areas in Figure 6, for example, we can measure the per capita rate of non-lethal violent or drug offenses within each Hot Spot Area. In addition, many agency or community decisions are focused on a specifically defined area, such as a beat or a ward. If the GeoArchive is to support analysis in response to specific local-level questions, it must be organized so that information can be aggregated and presented according to the area units that are appropriate to the particular problem.

In addition, the point and area data sets of a GeoArchive should be related to each other, so that analysis can benefit from both. It is often necessary to relate data from one agency to another, such as police data to court data, taking into account that the two agencies "think" according to different district systems. With geocoded addresses of incidents plus the boundaries of police, court, or other areas, this is easy to do. Police incidents, for example, may be aggregated to court areas, or court events (addresses of probationers, for example) aggregated to police areas. The homicides shown in Figure 6

Figure 5: Gang-Motivated Homicides, Mean Annual Rate Chicago Community Areas, 1987-1994

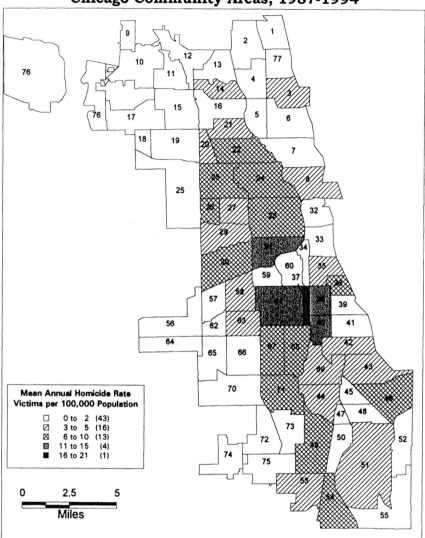

Mean Annual Homicide Rate
Victims per 100,000 Population

☐	0 to 2	(43)
▨	3 to 5	(16)
⊠	6 to 10	(13)
▦	11 to 15	(4)
■	16 to 21	(1)

0   2.5   5
Miles

Source: Chicago Homicide Dataset, Illinois Criminal Justice Information Authority

Figure 6: Gang-Motivated Homicides and Hot Spot Areas of Serious Non-Lethal Violence* and Drugs, Chicago, 1987-1994

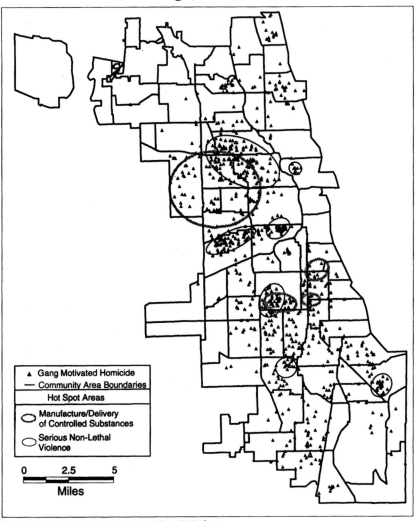

*Based on incidents of aggravated battery and aggravated assault with a firearm.
Source: CPD Offense Data, Illinois Criminal Justice Information Authority

could be aggregated across Community Areas, police districts, or any set of areas having available mapped boundaries. Therefore, a Geo-Archive should be organized so that it is easy to aggregate points across a variety of areas (police districts, probation districts, school districts, Census block groups, Boys and Girls Club neighborhoods, health center catchment areas, and so on). In this way, spatial analysis can focus specifically on the question at hand and on the intended audience for the results, and the results can be easily used and readily interpreted by those making the decisions.

In general, a GeoArchive should be able to handle community safety problems requiring different kinds of information and different levels of aggregation. Analysis of an immediate threat to neighborhood safety often requires information that is timely and specific to a particular situation, while analysis of long-term trends and patterns requires data covering a long time span across a variety of areas. Similarly, solving crime (investigation) and preventing crime may involve different kinds of analysis and require different information. For example, detailed information about individual offenses, offenders and victims is very important to the investigation of a pattern of serial offenses, while crime pattern and crime analysis decisions may call for more information about areas such as drug markets or gang territories.

Community and Law Enforcement Data

The events and environmental situations that surround violence or property crime are not limited to those recorded in official law enforcement statistics. By the same token, community data alone do not provide enough information for community problem solving. To identify community problems, neither criminal justice nor community data are enough by themselves; both are needed (see Figure 4). In addition, the most effective solutions will draw on the resources of both (Sadd and Grinc, 1996:11-12). Though in principle most community policing projects recognize the necessity of community collaboration, there are many difficulties in actually achieving it (for a discussion of some of these, see Sadd and Grinc, 1996). The process of obtaining information from citizens and community agencies and utilizing community resources to solve problems is often *ad hoc* and poorly documented.[18] The *mechanism* of sharing information is seldom addressed. A GeoArchive provides such a mechanism. This section is a quick outline of some of the major law enforcement and community data sets most valuable for a GeoArchive.

Law enforcement information includes a vast amount of point data (location of offenses and arrests, addresses of victims and offenders, citizen calls for service, police response information) and area data (districts, beats, wards). Point data sets, such as crimes known to the police, accumulate at a great rate.[19] By developing and instituting an efficient system for geocoding, however, mapped data can be available to local decision makers within no more than 24 hours after the event.[20] To law enforcement data can be added point and area data from other criminal justice agencies, such as corrections or probation, and from organizations affiliated with the criminal justice system, such as drug abuse intervention agencies or organizations working with ex-offenders.

Data sets of streets, bodies of water and major landmarks (called map data sets) are fundamental to mapping. The accuracy of digitized street map data affects not only the display of streets on a map but the geocoding of address data. Erroneous maps are, therefore, a serious threat to accurate decisions. In the U.S., the availability of Census TIGER street maps is one of the main reasons that computer mapping is now accessible at the community level. Like all data sets, however, the TIGER files do contain some errors. Streets may be missing, either because new streets have been added to the area or because the original map was erroneous; street names may be missing, misspelled or inaccurate; and locations important to police work (e.g., under a viaduct, along a park road, at the lakefront) may not be recognized by the map.[21] This can be rectified, however, by editing the street map file. Therefore, for accurate geocoding and accurate maps, it is vital that the users or managers of a GeoArchive have access to and are capable of modifying the base street map file.

Community point and area data sets that are particularly useful in building a GeoArchive (see Block and Green, 1994, for detail) include: (1) land use data sets containing information on each parcel of land in the city (for example, vacant or not, abandoned or not, residential or commercial, state of repair, specific function such as tavern or convenience store, and so on); (2) public transit data sets (train or bus stops and routes); (3) schools (grammar, high schools, private); (4) community organizations (block clubs, churches, social service agencies); (5) parks and other open areas (with park roads, field houses, lagoons); (6) emergency locations (hospitals, fire houses, police stations); (7) public housing (by type, showing roads and play lots); (8) places holding liquor licenses (by type of establishment and license); (9) public health data (area-level mortality and morbidity rates by specific cause, point data on health problems such as infant mortality or fatal firearm accidents); and, of course, (10) Census data.

In sum, the first and second criteria for a GeoArchive maintain that it should contain a wide variety of data sets, organized to be mapped at various scales and levels of detail and as point, area or line data, depending on the application. As John Eck points out elsewhere in this volume, theory should govern the choice of details to place on a map. For example, transit routes may be mapped as point files (the stops) or as line map files (the routes). Land use data sets may be point files, area files, or both; for example, a point file of convenience stores extracted from a land use file of parcels. Schools, public housing, or city parks may be mapped as point or area files, depending on the scale of the map, and routes to and from school can be shown with a line map file. Area boundaries showing each building and the major entrances and exits of a school campus or public housing complex are more informative for community decisions, but it is easier to create a point file than to create boundaries; updating is also easier with a point file. Census data should be available for a wide choice of scales (block, block group, tract, Community Area). Though tracts cover such a large area that it may be cumbersome to relate them to neighborhood problems, detailed information may be available only at the tract level, not at the smaller block level (Green and Whitaker, 1994).

Easy Accessibility to Local Decision Makers on a Timely Basis

The third criterion for a GeoArchive is that it is a *local* resource for crime analysis and decision making. In contrast to many GIS databases, a GeoArchive should be developed and controlled at the local level (from the bottom up rather than from the top down). Control means that local decision makers can change, update and manipulate GeoArchive data. It is this local, neighborhood control of information that makes the GeoArchive an information foundation for community problem solving. This does not mean that every local Geo-Archive should be built and maintained independently of all others, solely by local efforts and resources; that would be nonsensical. There is no reason for each local decision maker to be required to learn the techniques of geocoding or the intricacies of editing street map files. Similarly, there is no reason why citywide mapped data sets, such as abandoned buildings or liquor licenses, should not be shared across all city neighborhoods. On the contrary, local GeoArchives should be supported by data sets and skills provided by centrally located experts. However, these technocrats should serve the needs of the local-level decision makers, not vice versa.[22]

Local-level data accessibility raises two issues. First, it could be argued that central maintenance is necessary to check for and control errors, and to eliminate the discrepancies that would inevitably occur if every locality were to make independent changes in a data set. If data were corrected and updated at the local level without central coordination, maps in neighboring areas would become increasingly incompatible with one another. On the other hand, those most likely to discover data errors are those people who use the data, in this case, the individuals who work the streets and know them well and the decision makers who analyze the data and map the patterns, not the central data coordinators. One solution to this dilemma is a data clearinghouse, in which local-level users regularly send data corrections and enhancements to a central "holding file," where a holding file manager checks for accuracy and consistency and then makes the enhanced data generally available. With such a clearinghouse system, local decision makers have free rein to create and define data sets that best fit their purposes, but only data approved by the clearinghouse is shared citywide.

A second consideration raised by locally accessible data is data security. This can be a problem not only for law enforcement data, but for community data as well. For example, in the Early Warning System for Street Gang Violence project, an agency's volunteer staff was willing to provide street gang territory information to the GeoArchive, but was concerned that gang members would learn they had done so. It is also important to recognize that officially verified data may not require the same level of security as unverified data. Officially verified data have gone through a review process, are usually standardized in format, have standard codes and an identification number of some kind, and are often considered public information. Whereas unverified investigation data such as lists of suspects, contacts or citizen tips might require high security, officially verified data usually does not.

In the GeoArchive created by the Loyola Community Safety Project for the Rogers Park/ Edgewater community (Block et al., 1993), consideration for security was balanced with a high degree of access to the data. The Rogers Park/Edgewater GeoArchive was queried regularly by community groups, beat committees, aldermen and state representatives. Because of problems of confidentiality and concerns about the value of this information for real estate speculators, all requests for information were approved by the project director or technical coordinator. However, this did not inhibit the community from using the GeoArchive or requesting specific additions and expansions. For example, when Rogers Park community groups and the police district became concerned about the effect that taverns and liquor stores were having on crime in the neighborhood, the Community Safety Project added information on crime in liquor outlets to the GeoArchive and analyzed the relationship between concentrations of liquor stores or taverns and concentrations of crime in these places (Block and Block, 1995). Acting in part on the results of this analysis, the community organizations and the police district launched coordinated projects aimed at reducing levels of violence in the specific places and areas identified as generating the most serious problems.

Though some skeptics might argue that neighborhood-level decision makers such as patrol officers or social agency workers are not capable of using mapped information to identify and solve problems, the ICAM system in Chicago provides empirical evidence to the contrary (Rich, 1996).[23] Developed to support the ambitious CAPS approach to problem-oriented community policing, under which beat officers city-wide focus on problem solving (Rodriguez, 1993; Rich, 1996), the primary goal of ICAM is to bring mapped data to all beat officers in the city quickly — within 24 hours at most. Early, though anecdotal, results indicate that ICAM's accessibility encourages beat officers to analyze and solve problems, and that officers regularly take ICAM maps to community beat meetings (Rich, 1996).

A concomitant goal of CAPS, still in the beginning stages of realization, is to increase the problem solving collaboration between community members and the police, in part by increasing community access to ICAM and other information (Rodriguez, 1993; Baladad, 1996). In some districts, citizens access ICAM information at kiosks and officers regularly sit down with community members around ICAM maps to study a problem. A recent review in the newsletter of a coalition of Chicago neighborhood organizations (Baladad, 1996:11) found that "significant gains have been made in community access to information" under ICAM and CAPS, but noted that access "is still marred by inconsistency" from district to district" and called for more citizen use and requests for ICAM information.

A typical example of a community concern is depicted in Figure 7, which was created at the request of a coalition of community organizations concerned about organizing a task force to confront safety problems in some high-risk areas on the Near North Side.[24] Working with the two local police districts, these organizations used the Hot Spot Areas analysis of gang-related offenses to identify and focus on specific problem areas in their neighborhood.

There may be some disagreement whether the increased availability of information through ICAM is driving increased citizen interest in problem solving, whether — as Baladad argues — the increasing

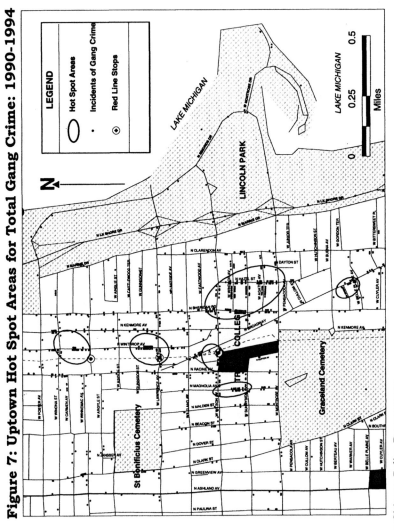

Figure 7: Uptown Hot Spot Areas for Total Gang Crime: 1990-1994

LEGEND

Hot Spot Areas

Incidents of Gang Crime

Red Line Stops

LAKE MICHIGAN

LINCOLN PARK

LAKE MICHIGAN

0   0.25   0.5

Miles

St Bonifacius Cemetery

Graceland Cemetery

Data Source: Chicago Police Department
Illinois Criminal Justice Information Authority

52

awareness of the value of mapped information on the part of community groups and citizens is driving greater access to ICAM, or whether the two processes drive each other. Whatever the reason, it seems clear that ICAM is becoming a catalyst for the decentralized use of information to solve problems. According to Manning (1992), centralized control of information has been an obstacle preventing law enforcement from benefiting from innovative technology. He argues that one reason why information technology has not had much effect on policing so far is that its basic assumption "is a belief in the centrality of information" (p.390).

However, overcoming information centrality is not easy (Hasson and Ley, 1994). On the one hand, to avoid data incompatibility across local-level GeoArchives and to make large and widely used data sets (such as street files, geocoded incidents, land use or other community data) easily available at the district or neighborhood level, it is better to maintain many large, important data sets centrally. On the other hand, the best source for data validity-checking and correction is at the user level, which is often the local level. Building a system to meet these conflicting needs requires creative and innovative management. It may be best to develop this system incrementally, with the collaboration of a Working Group of local GeoArchive users across the city who experiment to find the best system to insure that local GeoArchives would really support local decision making. Instead of being predetermined, the needs of GeoArchive users would become apparent as the project progresses. The evaluators of CAPS have found that such flexibility and willingness to experiment and learn from experience has played an important role in its development (Chicago Community Policing Evaluation Consortium, 1994).

THE GEOARCHIVE AND COMMUNITY POLICING:
PRACTICAL SUGGESTIONS

In creating and working with the GeoArchive in Chicago, we have discovered a number of helpful hints, suggestions and rules of thumb about combining law enforcement and community data. This paper is too short to treat all of these in detail, but several that may be useful to others are discussed below.

Spatial Linking Can Generate Information that Previously Did Not Exist

A common dilemma in data set management is that two data sets cannot be matched, because they do not contain the same identifier. This obstacle may be overcome by matching the coordinates of geocoded addresses. For example, the Authority needed data on convenience store robbery for a cross-state comparative analysis (Amandus et al., 1996), but the location variable in Chicago Police Department incident data does not include a "convenience store" code. The solution was provided by Richard Block, who matched six months of Chicago Police Department address-based incident data compiled for the Chicago CAPS evaluation (approximately 300,000 incidents) to the addresses of convenience stores, creating a data set of offenses occurring at convenience stores. This data set was then used to identify the robberies and their characteristics. A similar technique was also used to identify offenses occurring at taverns or liquor stores, in independent studies by Block and Block (1995) and by Florence (1995).

In addition, a GeoArchive can be used to add new fields, such as incidents occurring at or near an establishment, to the data set behind a point or area file. For example, the Early Warning System project (Jacob and Block, 1995) added a "number of offenders" variable to the incident file, by counting the number of records in the offender-based file with the same incident identification number, and writing the total as a new field in incident file.

Coordinate matching is thus a very powerful technique. With a GeoArchive, you can create new data in two ways: by linking spatial data sets to create a third data set, and by using one data set to create new fields behind another data set. However, as we discovered when applying coordinate matching to criminal incidents and liquor license addresses (Block and Block, 1995), this valuable tool should not be used blindly. In the first matching attempt, only 60% of the addresses of incidents that the police had recorded as occurring at a tavern or liquor store matched the liquor license addresses in a file from the state Department of Revenue. After investigation, we discovered that very few of these mismatches were due to inaccurate information in either data set. Instead, most of the mismatches were caused by a combination of definition differences and map accuracy problems. When these problems and incompatibilities were corrected, the coordinate matching "hit rate" approached 95%.[25]

A GeoArchive Can Stimulate Cooperation among Agencies and between Agencies and the Community

Information sharing is a necessary foundation for community-based crime reduction programs, and, therefore, necessary for a Geo-Archive. By definition, a GeoArchive consists of a compilation of spatial databases originally collected by many different agencies and organizations for many different purposes. This is one of its most valuable attributes. In the mid-1980s, for example, a pilot mapping project in selected Chicago police districts (Maltz et al., 1987) found that information from neighborhood and community groups added to the richness of the spatial database, and allowed officers to identify high-activity areas more accurately.

Though conventional wisdom has it that agencies, and even departments of the same agency, resist sharing data with one other, we have found that maps provide a great incentive for data sharing and communication. For example, Sparrow (1994:121) notes that GISs "constitute an appealing technology around which to form cross-functional teams." This does not happen automatically, however. In our experience, two things will help open and maintain lines of communication. First, the agency requesting data should do everything possible to reduce the provider's cost of data transfer. For example, accept data in the format that is easiest for the provider, avoid requests for any special "selects" or other analysis, and do your own geocoding (but avoid hard-copy data if at all possible). Second, the requesting agency should treat the project as a team effort. This means giving the agency who provided the data copies of the enhanced, geocoded data set and the printed analysis, offering to conduct analysis for them on request, and citing their generosity in publications.

Under these circumstances, most community, city and state agencies or organizations will be more than happy to contribute data to a GeoArchive, especially when they know that it is being developed as an "information foundation" for community problem solving and to reduce levels of violence. In turn, a GeoArchive can increase collaboration and cooperation among community agencies, by providing a storehouse of community information (a community memory bank) that combines and relates information across agencies, and by making it possible to produce maps that can present this information in a visual, readily understandable form. As law enforcement and community groups begin to use GeoArchive maps for decision making, their stake in the quality and availability of that data will increase. As a result, they will share data more readily and become more interested in maintaining data quality. Thus, though cooperative relationships between the police and local communities are not easy, they are possible (Kennedy, 1993; Kennedy et al., 1996) and a GeoArchive can facilitate their development.

Chicago's Early Warning System for Street Gang Violence project is based on the assumption that information compiled by community and neighborhood organizations, as well as by law enforcement, can be used to develop an "early warning system" of neighborhoods in crisis (see Jacob and Block, 1995; Spergel and Curry, 1990). Since much street gang violence is spatially anchored and occurs as the culmination of escalating incidents of revenge and retaliation, continuing escalation would then be prevented by crisis intervention and dispute mediation, using both internal community influences and external police support. Such a program, which requires the strong support of neighborhood agencies, churches, community groups and the police department, showed success in pilot projects in Chicago's Humboldt Park and in Philadelphia (Spergel, 1984; Spergel et al., 1984; Spergel, 1986). As the Violence Reduction Project, the concept is currently being tested in a Chicago neighborhood plagued by extremely high rates of street gang-related violence (Jacob and Block, 1995), and is being replicated in five cities around the country.

One result of Early Warning System analysis useful for the Violence Reduction Project was to relate the home addresses of the most active street gang offenders to the location of the most serious street gang offenses (Jacob and Block, 1995). In the Little Village area on Chicago's West Side (Figures 8 and 9), the predominant street gang-related activity is turf battles between the Latin Kings and the Two-Six street gangs.[26] The densest concentrations of residential addresses of those Latin Kings and Two-Sixers who were identified by police investigation as offenders in serious gang-related violence (homicide, firearm-aggravated battery or firearm-aggravated assault) are defined by the Hot Spot Areas in Figure 8, with the clusters of Latin King residences (narrow-line ellipses) lying generally to the east and the densest clusters of Two-Sixer residences (wide-line ellipses) generally lying to the west. When this map was shown to Violence Reduction Project street workers, they identified most clusters as locations of a hub of a specific faction of the Two-Six or Latin King street gang. Thus, for turf gangs, the core of gang territory can be identified by finding the densest clusters of addresses where the most active gang members live.

However, for turf street gangs, the hub of gang territory does not necessarily define the center of street gang-related violent offenses. The densest concentrations of serious violence committed by the Latin Kings on Two-Six victims or by Two-Sixers on Latin King victims do not coincide with the residence clusters of the offenders, but rather with the residence clusters of the victims (Figure 9). Latin King violent attacks on Two-Sixers (dashed-line ellipses) tend to coincide with Two-Six hub turf, and Two-Six violent attacks on Latin Kings (wide-line ellipses) tend to coincide with Latin King hub turf. (The Hot Spot Area of Latin King attacks on Two-Sixers around Harrison High School are an exception to this pattern.) This suggests a "marauder" pattern, in which members of rival gangs travel to the hub of their enemy's territory in search of potential victims. The location of the Two-Sixer and Latin King hub turf is known not only to project street workers, but to other Little Village residents, and certainly to the rival gang members. The two rival gangs search out their enemies where they believe they are most likely to be found, often in or near the center of their turf.

This pattern is not seen for the entrepreneurial gangs with territories to the north of Little Village. For these gangs, the densest concentrations of street gang-related activity (serious drug offenses such as manufacture and delivery) tend to coincide with the residential clusters of gang member residences. In contrast to gangs in which violent turf battles are the predominant activity, entrepreneurial gangs tend to commit gang-related offenses close to where they live.

Diverse Data Sets Present Not Only Benefits but Also Great Technical Difficulties

The somewhat Panglosian scenario described above, in which agencies cooperate to compile data sets from many sources into a single, related GeoArchive, carries with it some technical obstacles. Some of the greatest difficulties in GeoArchive management and interpretation stem from linking, combining and merging data across agencies and between local and central sources.

First, even the most basic data elements of a GeoArchive may be defined differently from agency to agency. Street address information, for example, which is fundamental to a geocoded address-based data set, may be used differently in two agencies (Block and Block, 1995). In a data set maintained for tax revenue purposes a tavern address might be the mailing address for accounting, while in a data set maintained for police purposes a tavern address could be the actual

Figure 8: Latin King and Two-Six Offender Residency Hot Spot Areas, 1987-1994

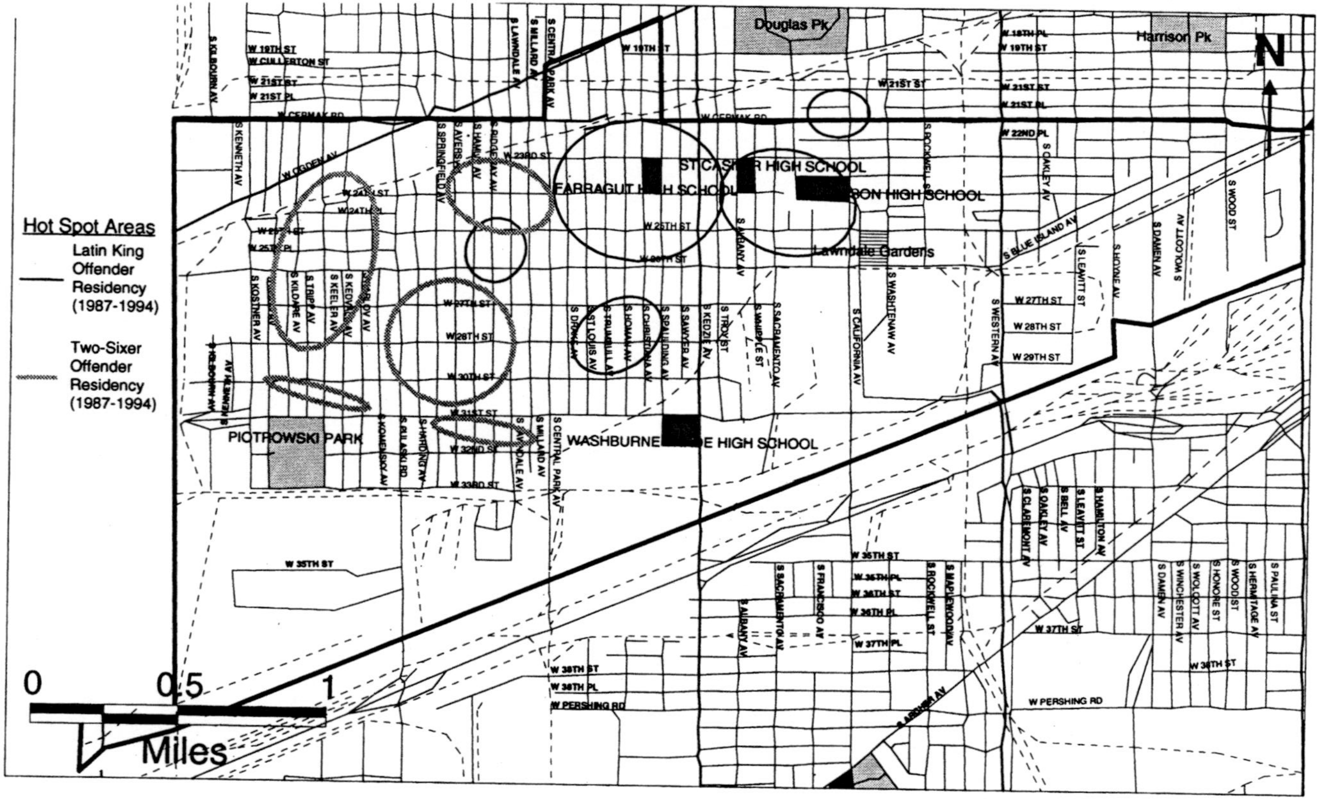

Hot Spot Areas

Latin King
Offender
Residency
(1987-1994)

Two-Sixer
Offender
Residency
(1987-1994)

58

Figure 9: Latin King and Two-Six Violent Hot Spot Areas, 1987-1994

Hot Spot Areas

Two-Six
Violent Hot
Spot Areas
(1987-1994)

Latin King
Violent Hot
Spot Areas
(1987-1994)

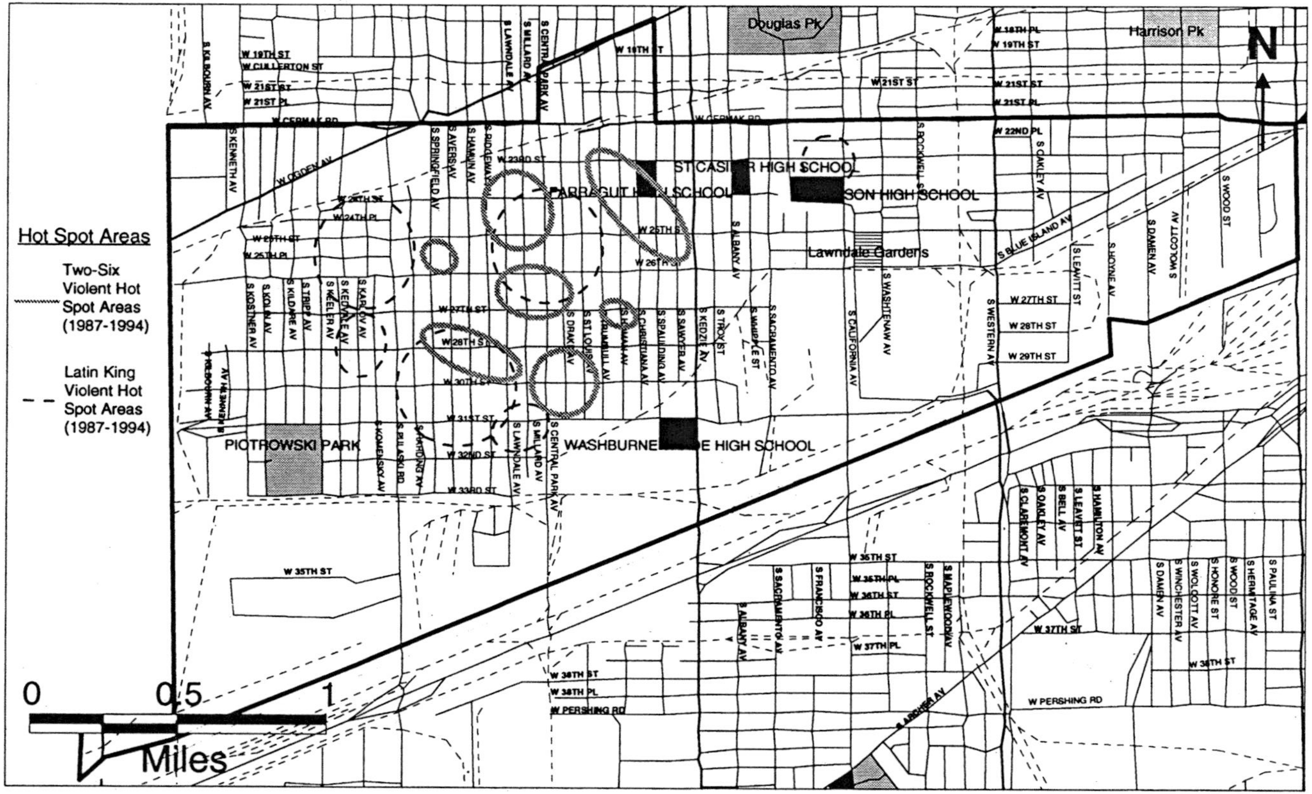

location of the bar; these two street addresses might be several doors apart or around the corner from each other. Though both addresses are accurate, they are not the same. As a result, the accuracy, precision and even definition of address may differ from one agency to another.

Second, for most data sources, information is not static, but is continually being corrected and updated at the source. This raises two issues: the degree to which the GeoArchive data should be synchronized with the source data, and the degree to which the database system should emphasize current versus past data. One trade-off is having GeoArchive data that is consistent with "official" data from the source, versus the dangers of data overload. Every time new source data are received by an archived data set, the new data must be integrated with earlier data so that archived information will not be written over and destroyed (Miller, 1995). Another trade-off is the availability of current versus past information. Timeliness can be vital, not only for investigation but also for targeting areas at high risk of an escalating crisis. On the other hand, past information is often vital to the identification and analysis of a problem.

Chicago's ICAM system approaches this problem by emphasizing current information. Incident data are available to ICAM users no more than 24 hours after the incident occurs (usually much sooner). This emphasis on speedy access is a large factor in the success of ICAM, and a major reason for its widespread use by district-level officers. To achieve this speed, ICAM captures incident information as it travels from the district to the central data division of the police department, before the central office has added any additional information, enhancements or corrections (Rich, 1995).[27] While this creates some differences between the central and local data sets, complete synchronization in this case is less important than current availability of data. For similar reasons, ICAM data sets currently contain only three months of data.[28] This not only helps to avoid data overload, but also the lack of a long time series of archived data in ICAM makes it less necessary to worry about synchronizing ICAM data with centrally archived data sets.

Triangulation: Combining Data from Diverse Sources to Improve the Accuracy of Measurement

Outside of textbook examples, the perfect measure seldom exists. In practical applications, a combination of two or three indicators may each capture a different aspect of the variable to be measured.

This is one of the main benefits of linking law enforcement and community data in a GeoArchive. For example, there is no address-level data on firearm availability in Chicago, though this variable has always been a high priority for the Early Warning System. In a current project, we are hoping to use data sets from three sources — firearm confiscations (Chicago Police Department), multiple buys (Bureau of Alcohol, Tobacco and Firearms) and firearm injuries (Cook County Trauma Registry) — to create a neighborhood-level indicator.

Multiple Data Sets, Users and Uses Create Opportunities But Pose Data Management Problems

Multiple, related databases offer great potential benefit for Geo-Archive users, but only if they are organized and managed so that the data sets are efficiently related to each other but still timely and accessible to users. Multiple GeoArchive databases present several challenges: linking diverse databases to each other and linking the same database to updated versions, assimilating information that accumulates at a great rate, synchronizing multiple and changing data sources within the GeoArchive, and balancing some users' needs for quickly accessible information with other users' needs for exhaustive detail (see Block and Green, 1994, for more detail).

The GeoArchive must be able to generate spatial analysis and maps or sets of maps targeted to meet the varied needs of many users: community agency workers and public officials, detectives and tactical officers, neighborhood patrol officers, crime analysts and others. Various problems may require information at a different level of aggregation, at a different degree of timeliness, or in more or less detail. The information needs of tactical and investigatory support officers are not the same as those of crime analysis; the needs of short-term, crisis decisions and long-term planning vary; and the information necessary to develop a crime prevention strategy may not be the same as that necessary to apprehend an offender.

A GeoArchive with multiple data sets from numerous sources, each with different fields and definitions covering different time spans and requiring periodic updating according to different cycles, creates considerable opportunity for confusion and error. Many of the data sets in a GeoArchive file are huge and detailed. Chicago, for example, accumulates 50,000 to 65,000 incident records a month with many fields of information in each record. To attempt to provide instant and immediate access to such a large, complex database might increase data overload to the point where the GeoArchive becomes too difficult and too slow to be used in practical situations. On the other hand, for many decisions — such as solving an investigation puzzle — minute detail is vital. Similarly, when law enforcement data are being generated every minute, it may be vital for beat officers to have the most current information possible. Yet, solving some neighborhood problems may require comparative information for past months or years. Thus, different users and different decisions require different levels of detail and emphasize either current or long-term data.

The development of street gang territory maps (Block and Block, 1993; Block and Green, 1994; Jacob and Block, 1995) provides an example of multiple data and multiple users, and of combining law enforcement and community data. In the Early Warning System project, the Gang Investigation Section of the police department provided initial information about street gang territory locations (Block and Block, 1993). However, local detectives saw greater detail, with more specific factions, and community leaders saw somewhat different boundaries. In general, the profusion of cognitive maps in a neighborhood produces a variety of perceptions of where street gang territory boundaries lie.

Some of these differences are due to perspective or experience, some due to a focus on the general versus the specific, and others due to actual changes in the territories over time. (One purpose of turf battles is, after all, to change turf boundaries.) However, none of these perspectives is wrong; the problem is how to combine all of these truths into a territory map that is "best" for most decisions. For some decisions it is important to know the specific, current detail of each faction's boundaries, while for others this degree of detail would present a data-overload obstacle to quick decisions. Perhaps the best, but not the easiest, solution is to respond to both needs — to create multiple, related gang territory map files containing multiple levels of detail, update them on a regular basis while maintaining earlier files in an archive, and devise and maintain a simple, current, summary map for rapid tactical decisions.[29]

Methods of Combining Both Point and Area Data in the Same Analysis

The first tenet of a GeoArchive is that it contains both point- and area-level information. To exploit all the information in these point and area data sets, we need to do more than simply describe them on overlapping maps. We need to be able to relate point to area data, and vice versa, in a multivariate analysis. One way to do this is to turn area data into points (for example, population potential; see Choldin and Roncek, 1976; Felson, 1986). Another approach is to turn points into areas.

STAC Hot Spot Areas turn point data into areas that reflect the actual scatter of points over the map (the point pattern). These areas are not arbitrarily determined by boundaries of political units, Census tracts or street patterns, but represent those areas where the points being analyzed (events, places, activities, etc.) are most densely clustered. For mapping, each of these dense clusters is bounded by the best-fitting standard deviational ellipse.[30]

Unlike procedures that are ultimately based on area-level data, such as isolines connecting area centroids (for example, Curtis, 1974) or population potential measures, STAC Hot Spot Areas do not lose the detailed information of point pattern scatter. Unlike topographical isoline maps (see LeBeau, 1995), STAC Hot Spot Area ellipses have defined boundaries that are easy to visualize in relation to other point, area or boundary information on the map. Unlike cognitive maps or expert opinion, STAC Hot Spot Area analysis is an objective, quick, database-driven method for finding dense areas that the expert in question may not know about.[31]

By itself, a point data set cannot define a particularly dense *area*. Though a particular address may be a high-crime place, it is not a Hot Spot Area. If applied to an address, the term "area" takes on a qualitatively different meaning. In addition, a high-crime address could reflect some unique characteristic of the particular location, and irrelevant variables (such as the presence of a pay phone from which calls for service are made) could easily obscure the measurement.[32] As Block and Block (1995) found in the analysis of liquor-license crime, a single address with more crimes than any other address may or may not be located within a high-density crime area. Some high-crime liquor outlets are located in dense areas of liquor-outlet crime, and others are not. By the same token, some low-crime places are located in high-crime areas and others are not. Both the characteristics of the place and the area are important in determining the most effective strategy for intervention in a particular case.

Hot Spot Area ellipses are area summaries of point patterns.[33] To complete the cycle, Hot Spot Areas can be related, in turn, to another set of point data. We can explore, for example, the location of street gang-related homicides relative to Hot Spot Areas of street gang non-lethal violent offenses versus drug offenses (see Figure 6). In addition, two sets of Hot Spot Areas can be related to each other, as in the comparison of clusters of serious street gang offenders (see Figure 8) to clusters of street gang-related offenses (see Figure 9).

Hot Spot Areas can be related to areas defined within arbitrary boundaries, such as Census blocks, Community Areas (see Figure 5 and 6), and more complex aggregates of area-level data (for example, see Hirschfield et al., 1995). In addition, it is simple to calculate a variety of density rates for any Hot Spot Area, not only density per square mile (as in Figure 6), but also rates based on the occurrence of any other appropriate information that can be summed within the Hot Spot Area boundary. In the Early Warning System project, for example, we have found it useful to calculate the density of drug-related offenses in a Hot Spot Area, using the number of abandoned buildings in the area as the denominator of the rate. Finally, as the next section will show, population-based densities can be calculated using Census block data. In general, the opportunities for combining area and point data in the same analysis are numerous and the potential benefits are great.

A Good Descriptive Map May Be Enough for Communicating Information, but for Effective Decision Making Spatial Analysis Tools Are Also Needed

In Manning's (1992:380) review of technology and the police, he complains that "very few uses of information technology are analytic, strategic, or tactical." "Tertiary" information that goes beyond administrative records to support complex analysis and problem solving "is rarely found in policing and, when available, is rarely used" (1992: 380). This situation is not confined to law enforcement, but is also seen in other government agencies (see Sparrow, 1994, for a review of several) and among users of spatial information in general (Bailey, 1994). Though not intended to be a complete introduction to spatial analysis, this section outlines a few of the things we have learned.

The analysis of spatial patterns, like the analysis of other kinds of patterns, can be roughly categorized into descriptive and exploratory techniques versus analytical or hypothesis-testing techniques. For example, cartography — the art of creating maps that present spatial information clearly and concisely — tends to be more descriptive, while spatial statistics describing and evaluating point patterns (Boots and Getis, 1988) tend to be more analytical. However, the line of demarcation is vague. As with other kinds of analysis, a good description can, and indeed must, be the foundation of a causal analysis. In *Mapping It Out*, one of the best practical reviews of techniques for "expository cartography," Monmonier (1993) presents ways to map such analytical concepts as change over time, variation in intensity, flows and processes, and causal models. A "pretty map," therefore, may be the basis for a causal analysis as well as a means of communicating the results of the analysis.

An information foundation for community policing (see Figure 1, above) requires both a GeoArchive and spatial statistical tools, and the statistical toolbox should include not only STAC Hot Spot Area analysis but others as well. The focus of the 1993 Workshop on Crime Analysis through Computer Mapping was "going beyond pretty maps," and the presentations and discussions were organized around techniques to answer three types of spatial analysis questions: analysis of differences across areas, point pattern analysis, and analysis of sequential travel or attack patterns. In addition to tools that approach spatial analysis questions from each of these three perspectives, as Monmonier points out, we also need tools that can present and analyze spatial data over time (see Langran, 1993).

Analysis of differences across areas, often depicted as "thematic" maps with each area shaded according to the intensity of some indicator (for example, see Figure 5), is often the most accessible kind of spatial analysis. Area maps have long been available in automated mapping systems, and they are relatively easy to do by hand. However, statistical methods for the analysis of relative crime density across arbitrary areal units suffer from strong aggregation biases and serious problems in interpretation (Brantingham and Brantingham, 1984). Also, they cannot deal with a reality in which dense areas cross boundary lines or occur along a boundary line. STAC offers a resolution to this problem by turning points into areas. Because it does not rely on predetermined boundaries, STAC fulfills Openshaw's (1994:87) call for spatial analysis techniques that "impose as few as possible additional, artificial, and arbitrary selections on the data."

A common problem in GeoArchive analysis is the calculation of population-based rates for areas where the boundary does not coincide with a standard Census area. Richard Block has developed a method that will produce useful rate estimates (Block, 1995b) when the area in question is sufficiently large relative to the size of a Census block. Given a GeoArchive containing boundaries for the larger area(s) plus Census block data, he calculates the sum of the populations of all Census blocks in which the centroid (the geographical center) is located within the area boundary. This is possible even without mapping the boundary of each Census block, because the centroid coordinates of each block are included in the Census data set. Estimates of the population within a police district, a street gang territory, a Hot Spot Area, or any enclosed boundary can be calculated with this method, thus making it possible to compare the relative density per resident of events or incidents across many variously defined areas.

The identification and description of dense clusters on the map is just one of many practical spatial analysis questions, each requiring a different statistical tool. There are two types of point pattern analysis (Boots and Getis, 1988): those that describe arrangements of points in space (such as the STAC Hot Spot Area ellipse), and those that indicate degree of dispersion versus clustering (such as Nearest Neighbor Analysis). For overviews of spatial statistical tools for point pattern analysis, see Boots and Getis (1988), Block (1995), Canter (1995), Cressie (1991) or Ebdon (1985). For an overview of spatial statistical tools for tracing travel patterns from one point to the next, see Rossmo (1995), and, for early applications, see Pyle et al. (1974) or Brantingham and Brantingham (1981). In general, however, spatial analysis techniques are still underdeveloped, especially techniques that are accessible to practical decision makers. As Openshaw (1994:84) argues, we need techniques "that are able to hunt out what might be considered to be localised pattern or 'database anomalies' in geographically referenced data but without being told either 'where' to look or 'what' to look for, or 'when' to look."

It is also important to remember that the spatial analysis toolbox needs more than one tool; a single kind of analysis may not be enough. Monmonier (1993) strongly urges map makers to create and present more than one kind of map, and argues that it would be unethical not to do so.

> Because the statistical map is a rhetorical device as well as an analytic tool, ethics require that a single map not impose a deceptively erroneous or carelessly incomplete cartographic view of the data (Monmonier, 1993:185).

Richard Block's current study of patterns of street robbery relative to the locations of rapid transit stops utilizes not only several kinds of maps but also several kinds of spatial analysis. Patterns of street robberies in two Chicago police districts from 1993 to 1994 are shown in Figure 10, which includes locations of parks, large cemeteries and major institutions as well as transit stations.[34] Two kinds of spatial analysis are depicted here. First, the number of robberies occurring at a single address is shown by a circle scaled to represent the number. (The legend shows the relative size of the circles from only one incident to a maximum of seven incidents.) Second, Figure 10 shows the Hot Spot Area ellipses resulting from a STAC search for the densest clusters of robberies throughout the entire map.

Figure 10: Northeast Side (Districts 20 and 24) Street Robberies 1993-1994: Number at a Location and Hot Spot Areas

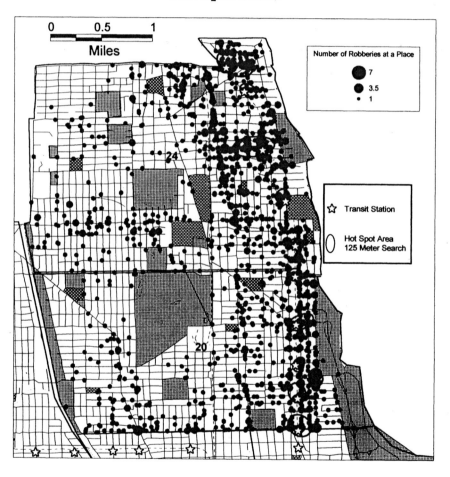

The graduated circles in Figure 10 are a cartographic device developed to handle a problem that is very common in maps of law enforcement data.[35] Criminal incidents do not tend to be randomly scattered across the map. Certain places, like certain groups of people, are relatively vulnerable to crime. In a small-scale map where the maximum number of occurrences at each address are also small, it is possible to use symbols or even actual numbers to depict the number of occurrences at an address. In maps such as Figure 10, however, with counts from zero to seven, symbols or numbers would be difficult to see and interpret. In such cases, we have found that symbols of graduated size are clear and unambiguous (circles or triangles work best).

The graduated circles convey two pieces of information: both the risk of ever having a robbery at an address and the risk of multiple robberies increase toward the eastern border of the map. The heaviest concentration runs along the lakefront, with intermittent dense areas around transit stations. A secondary line of high-risk addresses runs parallel to the first, along a major north/south street (Clark Street). The analysis of STAC Hot Spot Areas takes this a step further. There are ten transit stations on the map, and every one is located within a Hot Spot Area of street robbery offenses. Even though the STAC search encompassed the entire area of both districts, it found a series of small Hot Spot Area ellipses, all but one of which contains a transit station, all located along the rapid transit line.

What mechanisms would drive these patterns? To answer this question, the Community Safety Project measured the Manhattan distance between the location of each street robbery in 1993 and 1994 and the nearest transit station.[36] Because Chicago streets are laid out on a grid with an eighth of a mile (about 600 feet) between each block, the distance in feet between a transit stop (usually located at a corner) and a street robbery is a rough indicator of the number of city blocks a victim would walk away from the station before being robbed. The resulting graph (Figure 11) is an example of analysis based on spatial information, but not presented as a map. [37]

Taken together, these three kinds of spatial analysis indicate that the most dangerous addresses (based on the analysis-level count analysis) and the most dangerous areas (Hot Spot Area analysis) for street robbery in this neighborhood are located close to a rapid transit station. However, the stations themselves are relatively safe (distance analysis). People are less at risk of street robbery when they are at or still very close to a station, but their risk increases rapidly as they move a block (about 600 feet) to two blocks (1,200 feet) away.

Figure 11: Northeast Side (Districts 20 and 24) Distance From Elevated Station by Number of Incidents for 1993-1994

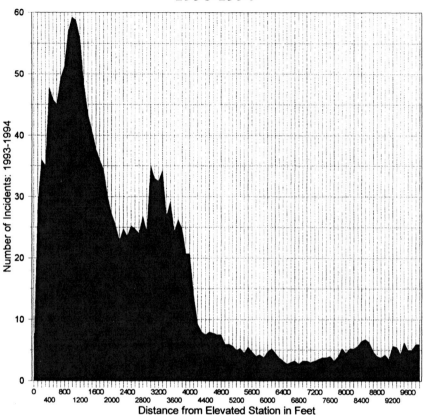

(There is also a secondary peak at about 3,600 feet, which reflects the secondary line of high-risk places along Clark Street.) Block (1995c) concludes that surveillance is a key issue here (see Felson, 1987). The highest risk seems to occur not at the station itself, where there are likely to be other passengers and the ticket-taker, but after the victim has walked a block, where presumably the crowd, if any, has thinned out. The fact that the peak occurs after the first block may reflect the decreasing surveillance after victims turn the corner.

FINAL WORDS

Recent research (Berry et al., 1993) suggests that, contrary to conventional wisdom, strong neighborhood participation in local problem solving does not produce more conflict or delay in policy making. Decentralization is built on the assumption that the most efficient way to define local problems and to develop solutions may be to provide information to local decision makers. This is because the boundaries and concerns of a community do not necessarily coincide with the arbitrary boundaries defined by Census tracts or police districts (Suttles, 1972), and the problems and resources of a local community do not necessarily correspond with citywide definitions and priorities.

But decentralization of problem solving cannot occur without decentralization of access to information. If problem-oriented community policing is to be built upon community and police collaboration in problem solving at the local level, it must also be built upon access to and control of information at the local level. In other words, successful community policing must be built upon a foundation of information that is address-based and focused on the neighborhood-level, that contains both community and law enforcement data, and that is organized so as to be accessible for local problem solving. This chapter has described such an "information foundation for community policing" and has detailed practical suggestions for developing such a GeoArchive.

NOTES

1. This paper is based in part on the experience of the Early Warning System for Street Gang Violence project of the Illinois Criminal Justice Information Authority and the Chicago Police Department (CPD) Area Four Detective Division, which was partially supported by the Bureau of Justice Statistics (BJS). Many Authority analysts, including Robert Whitaker, Lynn Higgins, Anthony Mata, Graham Taylor and Michael Maly, helped with the Early Warning System project in its early stages, but the most crucial persons were the project manager, Lynn A. Green, and CPD Area Four personnel Sgt. Ronald F. Rewers, Det. Richard Respondi and James Elliot. In addition, the project would not have been possible with-

out the advice and support of Paul White of BJS. Richard Block, who pioneered automated crime mapping in Chicago (see Block, 1977), was instrumental in developing the GeoArchive and continues to create innovative applications for community problem solving. Currently, Daniel Higgins, Teresa Hirsch and Ayad Jacob support STAC, the Early Warning System and the GeoArchive at the Authority, and are responsible for many of the ideas and some of the analysis described here.

2. A database (or data table) is a set of information, including an identifier, that is organized in a file structure with fields (variables) displayed in columns and types of information such as offense, date, address or offender's street gang displayed in rows.

3. For a discussion of community policing, problem-oriented policing, and their combination, see the upcoming "Theory Overload" section.

4. Many of these mapping entrepreneurs participated in the Workshop on Crime Analysis through Computer Mapping held in August 1993, and contributed to the proceedings of that seminar (Block et al, 1995.) Sponsored by the Illinois Criminal Justice Information Authority and Loyola University Chicago, with support from the Innovations in State and Local Government program of the Ford Foundation and the JFK School of Government, Harvard University, the theme of the workshop was "more than just a pretty map" (Rengert, 1995a).

5. STAC is a toolbox of spatial analysis statistics designed to support practical law enforcement decisions. STAC is a stand-alone spatial analysis package, not a mapping package. It was developed by the Illinois Criminal Justice Information Authority with the collaboration of STAC users around the world, and is available from the Authority at no cost to law enforcement agencies (Higgins et al., 1995).

6. Spatial analysis is "a general ability to manipulate spatial data into different forms and extract additional meaning as a result" (Bailey, 1994:15). Statistical spatial analysis uses statistics to this end, and consists of spatial *summary* statistics and spatial *analysis* statistics.

7. For more information about the GeoArchive in the Early Warning System for Street Gang Violence Project, see Green and Whitaker (1994), Block and Green (1994), and Rewers and Green (1995). For details about the Chicago Alternative Policing Strategy (CAPS), see Rodriguez (1993), Lewin and Morison (1995), Chicago Community Policing Evaluation Consortium (1994, 1995) and Rich (1995). For reviews of ICAM, see Smith and Eglowstein (1993) and Rich (1995; 1996).

8. In a *digitized* map, features such as streets, rivers or political boundaries have x-coordinates and y-coordinates that place them on the map. A file of such features may be called a *street* file or a *map data* file.

9. Goldstein (1990) defines and explains the steps of problem solving in more detail, including the following: grouping incidents as problems, labeling the problems, analyzing the relevant interests in the problem, critiquing the current response, searching for innovative responses, establishing accountability, implementing solutions, and measuring their impact.

10. "Individual characteristics" here include characteristics of individual persons, places, and situations.

11. For discussions of some deficiencies of and problems with current GIS and spatial statistical packages, see Levine (1996), Levine et al. (1995) and Block (1995).

12. GIS stands for Geographic Information System. Geographical information systems, which by definition are capable of storing and manipulating point, line and area data (Guptill, 1988:3), are database management systems specifically developed to handle spatial data in an efficient relational database system. Database management systems are "normally designed to handle numeric and textual information and are not capable of manipulating spatial data" (Guptill, 1988:2). See the essays in Fotheringham and Rogerson (1994) for more detail.

13. *Geocode* means (1) to assign x- and y-coordinates (e.g., longitude, latitude) to an address; (2) to assign an event, incident or map feature to an area; or (3) the x- and y-coordinates corresponding to a given address. The elements of a *geocoded dataset* are related to x- and y-coordinates so that they may be placed on a map that has the same coordinate system.

14. In "thematic maps" of area data, each area is categorized on a scale, represented on the map by different colors or shading or by an icon (symbol) placed within the area. In thematic point maps, categories of events or places are represented by an icon located at the x- and y-coordinates of that event or place.

15. Even when area information is linked to a central point (*centroid*) or an intersection within the area, the spatial unit of analysis is still area, not point. "Map data" is a drawing of features such as streets, bodies of water or landmarks, with no information behind the drawing other than the location on the map.

16. Figure 5 was produced by Antigone Christakos; Figure 6, by Ayad Paul Jacob.

17. The Hot Spot ellipses in Figure 6 do not represent clusters of homicides, but rather clusters of non-lethal violence or drug offenses. To locate the Community Areas mentioned here, see Figure 5.

18. For a discussion, see Chicago Community Policing Evaluation Consortium (1995).

19. Area dataset boundaries usually do not change as frequently, though the information behind the areas often does.

20. Since 1992, Richard Block has geocoded the approximately 50,000 criminal incidents occurring each month in Chicago, with a "hit rate" (incidents placed on the map) of 97% completely automated and close to 99% after hands-on geocoding. This is possible because of a street file that has been corrected and enhanced with places appropriate to police work, and a program that corrects misspellings and non-standard street name references (R.L. Block, 1995a). The Chicago Police Department's ICAM system achieves an automatic 96% hit rate (Rich, 1996). Again, the high rate is due to improved street files and an address-correction program.

21. See Block (1995a) for a discussion of errors in the TIGER files and how to correct them.

22. In contrast, see the discussion in Guptill (1988) of conducting a User Requirement Analysis to determine user needs, an example of control from the top down rather than from the bottom up.

23. In addition to ICAM and the Loyola Community Safety Project, the new Hartford, CT Comprehensive Communities Program, a collaboration of Hartford, the U.S. National Institute of Justice and Abt Associates, plans to provide mapping capability and training to the 17 neighborhood "problem-solving committees" in the city, in the hope that the organizations will use mapping to increase the effectiveness of their community problem-solving.

24. This map was created by Daniel F. Higgins.

25. For more details of the problem and how to solve it, see Block and Block (1995).

26. Figures 8 and 9 were created by Ayad Paul Jacob.

27. This system is not only quick, but because data are entered only once (traveling to both ICAM and the central repository) it is also accurate and relatively inexpensive.

28. In ICAM II, the capabilities and level of detail in ICAM are being expanded (Rich, 1996).

29. For an innovative approach to this problem, see Kennedy and Braga (this volume).

30. A standard deviational ellipse rotates two axes around the cluster of points, until the variance of the $X_i s$ are maximized along one axis and the variance of the $Y_i s$ are maximized along the other axis (see Stephenson, 1980; LeBeau, 1987; Ebdon, 1985; Levine et al., 1995).

31. Though cognitive maps and expert opinion can provide other valuable information (see Maltz et al., 1991; Weisburd et al., 1993; Buerger et al., 1995), they are not objective, automated analysis tools.

32. For a review of other problems encountered in using frequency across specific addresses to define dense areas, see Buerger et al. (1995).

33. STAC can handle much larger datasets (up to 16,000) than most other point pattern analysis programs.

34. Figure 10 was created by Richard L. Block.

35. For detailed advice and examples on mapping count data, see Monmonier (1993.)

36. Manhattan distance measures the distance "around the block"; Euclidean distance, "as the crow flies."

37. Sean Davis calculated the distance data represented in Figure 11.

REFERENCES

Anselin, L. (1989). "What Is Special About Spatial Data? Alternative Perspectives on Spatial Data Analysis." Paper presented at the spring 1989 symposium on Spatial Statistics, Past, Present and Future, sponsored by the Syracuse University Department of Geography, Syracuse, NY.

Amandus, H.E., D. Zahm, R. Friedmann, R. B. Ruback, C. Block, J. Weiss, O. Rogan, C. Wellford, W. Holmes, T. Bynum, D. Hoffman, R. McManus, J. Malcan, and D. Kessler (1996). "Employee Injuries and Convenience Store Robberies in Selected Metropolitan Areas." *Journal of Occupational and Environmental Medicine* 38(7):714-720.

Bailey, T.C. (1994). "A Review of Statistical Spatial Analysis in Geographical Information Systems." In: S. Fotheringham and P. Rogerson (eds.), *Spatial Analysis and GIS*. London, UK: Taylor and Francis Ltd.

Baladad, R. B. (1996). "Getting the Scoop: For Community Programs, Information Means Crime-Fighting Power. How Has Community Policing Affected Community Access to Information?" *Neighborhoods* 2(2):1-11.

Berry, J.M., K.E Portney and K. Thomson (1993). *The Rebirth of Urban Democracy.* Washington, DC: Brookings Institution.

Block, C.R. (1989). "The Application of Statistics to Criminal Justice Policy: A Populist Experiment." Paper presented at the annual meeting of the American Association for the Advancement of Science, San Francisco, January.

—— (1995). "STAC Hot-spot areas: A Statistical Tool for Law Enforcement Decisions." In: C.R. Block, M. Dabdoub and S. Fregly (eds.), *Crime Analysis through Computer Mapping.* Washington, DC: Police Executive Research Forum. (Proceedings of the 1993 Workshop on Crime Analysis Through Computer Mapping, Illinois Criminal Justice Information Authority and Loyola University Chicago.)

—— M. Dabdoud and S. Fregly (eds.), *Crime Analysis through Computer Mapping.* Washington, DC: Police Executive Research Forum. (Proceedings of the 1993 Workshop on Crime Analysis Through Computer Mapping, Illinois Criminal Justice Information Authority and Loyola University Chicago.)

—— and R. Block (1993). *Street Gang Crime in Chicago.* Research in Brief. Washington, DC: U.S. National Institute of Justice, U.S. Department of Justice

—— and L. Green (1994). *The GeoArchive Handbook: A Guide for Developing a Geographic Database as an Information Foundation for Community Policing.* Chicago, IL: Illinois Criminal Justice Information Authority.

Block, R.L. (1977). *Violent Crime: Environment, Interaction and Death.* Lexington, MA: Lexington-Heath.

—— (1995a). "Geocoding of Crime Incidents Using the 1990 TIGER File: The Chicago Example." In: C.R. Block, M. Dabdoub and S. Fregly (eds.), *Crime Analysis through Computer Mapping.* Washington, DC: Police Executive Research Forum. (Proceedings of the 1993 Workshop on Crime Analysis Through Computer Mapping, Illinois Criminal Justice information Authority and Loyola University Chicago.)

—— (1995b). "Spatial Analysis in the Evaluation of the 'CAPS' Community Policing Program in Chicago." In: C.R. Block, M. Dabdoub and S. Fregly (eds.), *Crime Analysis through Computer Mapping.* Washington, DC: Police Executive Research Forum. (Proceedings of the 1993 Workshop on Crime Analysis Through Computer Mapping, Illinois Criminal Justice Information Authority and Loyola University Chicago.)

—— (1995c). "Effects of Rapid Transit Stations on Patterns of Street Robbery in Chicago." Paper presented at the annual meetings on Crime Prevention Through Environmental Design, Cambridge, MA.

—— and C.R. Block (1995). "Space, Place and Crime: Hot-spot areas and Hot Places of Liquor-Related Crime." In: J.E. Eck and D. Weisburd (eds.), *Crime and Place*. Crime Prevention Studies, vol. 4. Monsey, NY: Criminal Justice Press.

—— T. Fuechtman and K. Vates (1993). "Loyola Community Safety Project: A Tool for Neighborhood Planning." Paper presented at the annual meeting of the Urban Affairs Association, New Orleans, LA.

Bobrowski, L.J. (1988). "Collecting, Organizing and Reporting Street Gang Crime." Chicago Police Department, Special Functions Group. Paper presented at the American Society of Criminology meetings, Chicago, IL.

Boots, B.N. and A. Getis (1988). *Point Pattern Analysis*. Scientific Geography Series, vol. 8. Newbury Park, CA: Sage.

Brantingham, P.J. and P.L. Brantingham (1984). *Patterns in Crime*. New York, NY: Macmillan.

Brantingham, P.L. and P.J. Brantingham (1981). "Notes on the Geometry of Crime." In: P.J. Brantingham and P.L. Brantingham (eds.), *Environmental Criminology*. Beverly Hills, CA: Sage.

Buerger, M.E., E.G. Cohn and A.J. Petrosino (1995). "Defining the 'Hot Spots of Crime': Operationalizing Theoretical Concepts for Field Research." In: J.E. Eck and D. Weisburd (eds.), *Crime and Place*. Crime Prevention Studies, vol. 4. Monsey, NY: Criminal Justice Press.

Canter, P. (1995). "State of the Statistical Art: Point Pattern Analysis." In: C.R. Block, M. Dabdoub and S. Fregly (eds.), *Crime Analysis through Computer Mapping*. Washington, DC: Police Executive Research Forum. (Proceedings of the 1993 Workshop on Crime Analysis Through Computer Mapping, Illinois Criminal Justice Information Authority and Loyola University Chicago.)

Chicago Community Policing Evaluation Consortium (1994). *Community Policing in Chicago, Year One: An Interim Report*. Chicago, IL: Illinois Criminal Justice Information Authority.

—— (1995). *Community Policing in Chicago, Year Two: An Interim Report* Chicago, IL: Illinois Criminal Justice Information Authority. Also see the short summary under the same title, published as an National Institute of Research Bulletin in October 1995 (NCJ 157273).

Choldin, H.M. and D.W. Roncek (1976). "Density, Population Potential and Pathology: A Block-Level Analysis." *Journal of Public Data Use* 4:19-29.

Cressie, Noel (1991). *Statistics for Spatial Data.* New York, NY: John Wiley and Sons.

Curry, G. David (1995). "...And the Disciples Left the Hood: An Application of GIS Analysis to Inter-Gang Conflict." Paper presented at the American Society of Criminology meetings, Boston, MA.

Curtis, L.A. (1974). *Criminal Violence: National Patterns and Behavior.* Lexington, MA: Lexington Books.

Ebdon, D. (1977). *Statistics in Geography.* Oxford: Basil Blackwell.

—— (1985) *Statistics in Geography,* 2nd ed. Oxford: Basil Blackwell.

Felson, M. (1986). "Predicting Crime Potential at any Point on the City Map." In: R.M. Figlio, S. Hakim, and G.F. Rengert (eds.), *Metropolitan Crime Patterns.* Monsey, NY: Criminal Justice Press.

—— (1987). "Routine Activities and Crime Prevention in the Developing Metropolis." *Criminology* 25(4):911-932.

Fisher, R. (1994). *Let the People Decide: Neighborhood Organizing in America* (updated edition). New York, NY: Twayne.

Florence, R. (1995). Guardianship and Tavern Violence: An Exploratory Analysis. Master's thesis, University of Maryland College Park.

Fotheringham, S. and P. Rogerson (eds.) (1994). *Spatial Analysis and GIS.* London, UK: Taylor and Francis.

Goldstein, H. (1977). *Policing a Free Society.* Cambridge, MA: Ballinger.

—— (1990). *Problem-Oriented Policing.* New York, NY: McGraw-Hill.

—— (1993). *The New Policing: Confronting Complexity,* Research in Brief. Washington, DC: U.S. National Institute of Justice.

Green, L.A. and R.B. Whitaker (1994). *Early Warning System Geo-Archive Codebook: Area Four Project.* Chicago, IL: Illinois Criminal Justice Information Authority.

Guptill, S.C. (1988). *A Process for Evaluating Geographic Information Systems.* Washington, DC: U.S. Geological Survey.

Hasson, S. and D. Ley (1994). *Neighborhood Organizations and the Welfare State.* Toronto, CAN: University of Toronto Press.

Higgins, D., C.R. Block and J. Spring (1995). *Manual for Spatial and Temporal Analysis of Crime: 1995 Revision.* Chicago, IL: Illinois Criminal Justice Information Authority.

Hirschfield, A., K.J. Bowers and P.J.B. Brown (1995). "Exploring Relations Between Crime and Disadvantage on Merseyside." In special issue on: Crime Environments and Situational Prevention. *European Journal on Criminal Policy and Research* 3(3):93-112.

Jacob, A.P. and C.R. Block (1995). *The Chicago Early Warning System for Street Gang Violence: Can We Predict Areas at High Risk for a Crisis of Street Gang Violence?* (Manuscript.) Chicago, IL: Illinois Criminal Justice Information Authority.

Kennedy, D.M. (1993). *The Strategic Management of Police Services*, Perspective on Policing. Washington, DC: U.S. National Institute of Justice.

—— A.A. Braga and A.M. Piehl (1996). *The (Un)Known Universe: Mapping Gangs and Guns in Boston.* (Manuscript.) Cambridge, MA: Program in Criminal Justice Police and Management, Harvard University.

Langran, G. (1993). *Time in Geographic Information Systems.* London, UK: Taylor and Francis.

LeBeau, J.L. (1987). "The Methods and Measures of Centrography and the Spatial Dynamics of Rape." *Journal of Quantitative Criminology* 2 (2):125-141.

—— (1995). "The Temporal Ecology of Calls for Police Service. In: C.R. Block, M. Dabdoub and S. Fregly (eds.), *Crime Analysis through Computer Mapping.* Washington, DC: Police Executive Research Forum. (Proceedings of the 1993 Workshop on Crime Analysis Through Computer Mapping, Illinois Justice Information Authority and Loyola University Chicago.)

Levine, N. (1996). "Spatial Statistics and GIS: Software Tools to Quantify Spatial Patterns." *Journal of the American Planning Association* 62 (3, Summer):381-391.

—— K.E. Kim and L.H. Nitz (1995). "Spatial Analysis of Honolulu Motor Vehicle Crashes: I. Spatial Patterns." *Accident Analysis and Prevention* 27(5): 663-674.

Lewin, J. and K. Morison (1995). "Use of Mapping to Support Community-Level Police Decision Making." In: C.R. Block, M. Dabdoub and S. Fregly (eds.), *Crime Analysis through Computer Mapping.* Washington, DC: Police Executive Research Forum. (Proceedings of the 1993 Workshop on Crime Analysis Through Computer Mapping, Illinois Justice Information Authority and Loyola University Chicago.)

Maltz, M.D., A.C. Gordon and W. Friedman (1991). *Mapping Crime in its Community Setting: Event Geography Analysis.* New York, NY: Springer-Verlag.

Maltz, M.D., A.C. Gordon, R.K. Lebailly, W. Friedman, M. Buslik and M. Casey (1987). "Crime Statistics in the Small: Mapping Individual Events." Paper presented at the annual meeting of the American Society of Criminology.

Manning, P.K. (1992). "Information Technologies and the Police." In: M.Tonry and N. Morris (eds.), *Modern Policing*. Chicago, IL: University of Chicago Press.

Mattson, M. and G. Rengert (1995). "Danger, Distance, and Desirability: Perceptions of Inner-City Neighborhoods." In special issue on: Crime Environments and Situational Prevention. *European Journal of Criminal Policy and Research* 3(3):70-78.

Miller, T. (1995). "Integrating Crime Mapping with CAD and RMS." In: C.R. Block, M. Dabdoub and S. Fregly (eds.), *Crime Analysis through Computer Mapping*. Washington, DC: Police Executive Research Forum. (Proceedings of the 1993 Workshop on Crime Analysis Through Computer Mapping, Illinois Criminal Justice Information Authority and Loyola University Chicago).

Monmonier, M. (1993). *Mapping It Out: Expository Cartography for the Humanities and Social Sciences*. Chicago, IL: University of Chicago Press.

Moore, M.H. (1992). "Problem Solving and Community Policing." In: M. Tonry and N. Morris (eds.), *Modern Policing*. Chicago, IL: University of Chicago Press.

—— and R.C. Trojanowicz (1988). "Corporate Strategies for Policing." *Perspectives on Policing* no. 6, Harvard University. Washington, DC: U.S. National Institute of Justice.

Openshaw, S. (1994). "Two Exploratory Space-Time-Attribute Pattern Analysers Relevant to GIS." In: S. Fotheringham and P. Rogerson (eds.), *Spatial Analysis and GIS*. London, UK: Taylor and Francis.

Pyle, G.F., E.W. Hanten, P.G. Williams, A.L. Pearson II, J.G. Doyle and K. Kwofie (1974). "The Spatial Dynamics of Crime," Research Paper No. 159. Chicago, IL: Department of Geography, University of Chicago.

Rengert, G. (1995a). "More Than Just a Pretty Map: How Can Spatial Analysis Support Police Decisions?" In: C.R. Block, M. Dabdoub and S. Fregly (eds.), *Crime Analysis through Computer Mapping*. Washington, DC: Police Executive Research Forum. (Proceedings of the 1993 Workshop on Crime Analysis Through Computer Mapping, Illinois Criminal Justice Information Authority and Loyola University Chicago.)

—— (1995b) "Comparing Cognitive Hot Spots to Crime Hot Spots." In: C.R. Block, M. Dabdoub and S. Fregly (eds.), *Crime Analysis through Computer Mapping*. Washington, DC: Police Executive Research Forum. (Proceedings of the 1993 Workshop on Crime Analysis Through Computer Mapping, Illinois Criminal Justice Information Authority and Loyola University Chicago.)

—— and J. Greene (1994). "Knowledge and Perception of the Inner City: The Case of Community Service Aids." In: D. Zahm and P. Cromwell (eds.), *Proceedings of the International Seminar on Environmental Criminology and Crime Analysis*. Tallahassee, FL: Statistical Analysis Center, Florida Department of Law Enforcement.

Rewers, R.F. and L.A. Green (1995). "The Chicago Early Warning System GeoArchive." In: C.R. Block, M. Dabdoub and S. Fregly (eds.), *Crime Analysis through Computer Mapping*. Washington, DC: Police Executive Research Forum. (Proceedings of the 1993 Workshop on Crime Analysis Through Computer Mapping, Illinois Criminal Justice Information Authority and Loyola University Chicago.)

Rich, T.F. (1995). *The Use of Computerized Mapping in Crime Control and Prevention*, Research in Action Series. Washington, DC: U.S. National Institute of Justice.

—— (1996). *The Chicago Police Department's Information Collection for Automated Mapping (ICAM) Program: A Program Focus*. Washington, DC: U.S. National Institute of Justice.

Rodriguez, M.L. (1993). *Together We Can: A Strategic Plan for Reinventing the Chicago Police Department*. Chicago, IL: Chicago Police Department.

Roncek, D. W. and P.A. Maier (1991). "Bars, Blocks, and Crimes Revisited: Linking the Theory of Routine Activities to the Empiricism of 'Hot Spots.'" *Criminology* 29(4):725-753.

Rossmo, D.K. (1995). "Overview: Multivariate Spatial Profiles as a Tool in Crime Investigation." In: C.R. Block, M. Dabdoub and S. Fregly (eds.), *Crime Analysis through Computer Mapping*. Washington, DC: Police Executive Research Forum. (Proceedings of the 1993 Workshop on Crime Analysis Through Computer Mapping, Illinois Criminal Justice Information Authority and Loyola University Chicago.)

Sadd, S. and R.M. Grinc (1996). *Implementation Challenges in Community Policing*. Research in Brief. Washington, DC: U.S. National Institute of Justice.

Sanford, R. (1995). "How to Develop a Tactical Early Warning System on a Small-City Budget." In: C.R. Block, M. Dabdoub and S. Fregly (eds.), *Crime Analysis through Computer Mapping*. Washington, DC: Police Executive Research Forum. (Proceedings of the 1993 Workshop on Crime Analysis Through Computer Mapping, Illinois

Criminal Justice Information Authority and Loyola University Chicago.)

Smith, B. and H. Eglowstein (1993). "Solutions Focus/ Desktop Mapping Software: Putting Your Data on the Map." *Byte* (Jan):188-200.

Sparrow, M. (1994). *Imposing Duties*. Westport, CT: Greenwood.

Spelman, W. and J.E. Eck (1987). *Problem-Oriented Policing*. Washington, DC: U.S. National Institute of Justice.

Spergel, A. (1984). "Violent Gangs in Chicago: In Search of Social Policy." *Social Service Review* 58(2):199-226.

—— (1986). "The Violent Gang Problem in Chicago: A Local Community Approach. *Social Service Review* (Mar):94-130.

Spergel, I.A., P. Colson, F. Atwell and S. Dinguss (1984). "Reduction of Gang Violence: A Community Development Approach." Paper presented at the Second Annual Symposium on Street Work, University of Tubingen, West Germany.

—— and G.D. Curry (1990). "Strategies and Perceived Agency Effectiveness in Dealing with the Youth Gang Problem." In: C. Ronald Huff (ed.), *Gangs in America*. Newbury Park, CA: Sage.

Stallo, M. (1995). "Mapping Software and its Value to Law Enforcement." In: C.R. Block, M. Dabdoub and S. Fregly (eds.), *Crime Analysis through Computer Mapping*. Washington, DC: Police Executive Research Forum. (Proceedings of the 1993 Workshop on Crime Analysis Through Computer Mapping, Illinois Criminal Justice Information Authority and Loyola University Chicago.)

Suttles, G. D. (1972). *The Social Construction of Communities*. Chicago, IL: University of Chicago Press.

Stephenson, L.K. (1980). "Centrographic Analysis of Crime." In: Daniel E. Georges-Abeyie and K.D. Harries (eds.), *Crime: A Spatial Perspective*. New York, NY: Columbia University Press.

Ward, R.H., N.J. Taylor and P. Fanning (1995). *Community Policing for Law Enforcement Managers*. Chicago, IL: Illinois Criminal Justice Information Authority.

Weisburd, D., L. Maher, L. Sherman, M. Buerger, E. Cohn and A. Petrosino (1993). "Contrasting Crime General and Crime Specific Theory: The Case of Hot Spots of Crime." In: F. Adler and W.S. Laufer (eds.), *New Directions in Criminological Theory*. Advances in Criminological Theory, vol. 4. New Brunswick, NJ: Transaction Publishers.

USING GEOGRAPHICAL TOOLS WITH INTERAGENCY WORK GROUPS TO DEVELOP AND IMPLEMENT CRIME CONTROL STRATEGIES

by

Faye S. Taxman
University of Maryland — College Park

and

Tom McEwen
Institute for Law and Justice

Abstract: *To address crime-related problems in their communities, police departments are increasingly involved in interagency work groups. As community policing and problem-oriented strategies are implemented, these groups are likely to include businesses, community organizations, and non-governmental agencies. Because these partnerships strive to reduce crime and disorder and to promote public safety, they often rely on police agencies for guidance. One of the tools that has promoted successful collaboration among the partners is geographical information, which focuses attention on the problems and needs of a particular neighborhood or community and uses the target area to garner community and government agency support for new initiatives.*

Maps provide a visual tool for displaying crime data that consist of events (criminal activities) and places (crime locations). Police departments are increasingly using maps to understand crime and de-

Address correspondence to: Faye Taxman, University of Maryland, Departmer.t of Criminology and Criminal Justice, 2220 LeFrak Hall, Suite C, College Park, MD 20770.

velop solutions. At the same time, the approaches of community and problem-oriented policing have led police to act with interagency work groups to develop crime prevention and control strategies. The work groups are likely to include government agencies, businesses, and community and other nonprofit and non-governmental organizations. These partnerships strive to reduce crime and disorder by providing a more comprehensive approach to problem solving. Police agencies are now bringing both of those efforts together by using maps and geographical information in their collaborations with interagency work groups.

This chapter explores the critical role of mapping in police departments and work groups, particularly as it relates to successful development of work products. The chapter begins with an overview of mapping as a problem-solving tool and then explores how mapping can contribute to the development of an interagency work plan. Many of the examples are from the sites participating in the Drug Market Analysis Project (DMAP)[1] of the U.S. National Institute of Justice. The experience of those five jurisdictions[2] provides valuable insights into how maps and information can foster collaboration among groups with varying perspectives. Finally, two case studies illustrate how police departments, government agencies, and communities can use crime data and maps to develop systematic responses to crime. The case studies illustrate the importance of full support from the members of the interagency work group. Without their full involvement in all phases, the efforts will be only partially successful.

MAPPING: AN APPROACH TO PROBLEM SOLVING

Recent developments in criminological theory focus on the importance of places, paying special attention to "attributes of places and... routine activities combined to develop crime events" (Eck and Weisburd, 1995:21). Essentially, this has led to an examination of both place and offenders. Research on place has focused on clustering (the location and frequency of crime events), features (the unique social and physical characteristics of places), and facilities (special-purpose structures that operate in a given area). Research on people in places provides insight into how offenders select crime places (Eck and Weisburd, 1995). Crime place research is a growing body of literature that provides a new approach to developing crime prevention and control strategies.

The attention on places, people, and events has renewed interest in the use of geographical information and mapping to understand crime and responses to it. Maps present complicated, detailed data in a way that makes it easier to conceptualize crime problems. Computerized mapping facilitates the process by providing more expeditious methods of producing maps (McEwen and Taxman, 1995). Computerized mapping also contributes to user-friendliness by using symbols, colors, and time lines (Cohen et al., 1993).

McEwen and Taxman (1995) discuss how computerized mapping facilitates the understanding of crime problems. Three types of computer mapping techniques have evolved. *Descriptive mapping* is used to illustrate crimes, calls for service, traffic accidents, and other data in pin-map style or shaded area formats. *Analytical mapping* begins with the analysis of data and then displays the results. The identification of places and crime events is a favored analytical technique. Finally, *interactive mapping* provides the opportunity to make queries and then map the results. These techniques help police agencies identify crime problems and develop solutions that are sensitive to people and place issues. Each of these different mapping techniques can lead to a different understanding of the crime problem and recommended solutions.

Mapping provides the opportunity to be proactive in developing solutions to crime problems. By mapping people and place data, it is possible to discern patterns, and using a variety of data from different sources should enrich the detection of patterns. Researchers have noted that the traditional use of law enforcement data (on arrests or calls for service) can be supplemented with data on such incidents as violations of fire, health, building, or school codes (Maltz, 1995). Problem-solving approaches can then be used to develop a comprehensive solution. As Eck (1996) discusses, mapping should also be driven by theories about crime. Theory-driven mapping will confirm or refute theoretical predictions, thereby altering crime control strategies in the future.

INTERAGENCY WORK GROUPS: ANOTHER APPROACH TO PROBLEM SOLVING

Work groups are often called upon to address critical social problems. These work groups may include the police, government health and social service agencies, businesses, and community and other nonprofit, non-governmental organizations. Work groups provide a forum in which interested parties can join together on common issues and develop a strategic plan of action. Through the efforts of a work group, immediate and continuing attention is given to pressing issues. The Program for Community Problem Solving, a joint effort of five national associations, notes the following:

> Efforts to solve community problems seldom fail because reasonable solutions are not available. Programs are far more likely to run into difficulty because key parties are not included in the decision making or the methods used to identify solutions are not productive [Carpenter, 1990:2].

A work group brings difficult issues to the table and ensures that the forces resisting change are present for problem solving and negotiation. To ensure cooperation, the work group must assemble all parties with a vested interest in the problem. Often the selection is based on geographical area or community. The group, which has diverse and often conflicting interests, then assumes responsibility for defining the problem, developing solutions, and implementing responses. During this process, the partners address controversies and reach a consensus. The goal is to formulate strategies for issues that demand continuing action. Over time, the work group upholds its initial commitments and ensures implementation of appropriate responses.

Work groups are organized in several different ways. The most common approach is to have one agency (the police) take lead responsibility. The "lead agency" approach manifests itself in one of four ways: (1) the agency decides to "solve" the issue itself; (2) the agency stakes out its own position; (3) the agency sets up a committee composed of members with similar perspectives; or (4) the agency "consults" with others and then crafts a plan for the best solution. In each of these scenarios, the lead agency assumes responsibility for the agenda, the definition of the problem, and the definition of "acceptable and workable" solutions. That approach often fails because all participating groups are not fully committed to solving the problem. More importantly, this approach often fails to use data from various sources to fully understand the problem. Solutions may instead evolve from mere perceptions of the problem.

Another approach is consensus building. Here, each member of the work group participates in all phases of the project, such as the definition of the problem and its solutions. Data sharing is an important factor in fostering the consensus process. It also contributes to an understanding of the problem from different perspectives by empowering the members to become active participants. Carpenter (1990:3) describes the process:

In a consensus building process different interests work together to identify issues, to educate each other about their respective concerns, to generate options, and then to reach agreements that all sides can accept. This does not mean that all sides will be equally enthusiastic about a solution; rather, participants will recognize that it is the best solution available.

In a change from the conventional committee approach, representatives of all major interests are involved in developing the process as well as formulating solutions. Representatives can participate in a planning committee, or their advice can be sought in interviews about appropriate issues to address logical components of a program, and who should participate and how. A successful consensus process can be more work to coordinate than other approaches, but will result in a workable solution that all parties can accept—implementation will not be impeded by a dissatisfied interest group.

Through the consensus-building process, interagency work groups reach agreement on issues affecting crime and social disorder in the community, and they take "ownership" of the problem and its solutions. It is a continuing process that requires each participant to value the input and commitment of the other members.

Work groups that strive to build a consensus recognize that no agency is solely responsible for the action or products of the group. The process requires the participants to be equally committed to identifying the problem, defining the target issues, developing effective solutions, and monitoring the implementation. The four stages of problem solving frequently used by police agencies are represented in the SARA model, which contains tasks similar to those of a consensus-building work group (Eck and Spelman, 1987):

(1) *Scanning:* identifying the problem, especially the focus on places and events.
(2) *Analysis:* learning the causes, scope, and effects of a problem.
(3) *Response:* acting to alleviate the problem.
(4) *Assessment:* determining whether the response worked.

The consensus-building approach begins with the identification of stakeholders. As defined by Rossi and Freeman (1990:424), a stakeholder is "concerned with the efficacy and efficiency of efforts to improve social conditions" and generally "has a stake in the outcome." The stakeholders typically have different perspectives on the meaning and importance of the group's efforts. They may be policy makers and decision makers, program sponsors, agencies offering services in an area, persons receiving various services in an area, citizens' and community groups, groups that compete for resources, or organizations that play a leadership role in the community. Contextual stakeholders, or those organizations or individuals located in the immediate area, are also important actors in the consensus-building process. It is imperative that stakeholders participate in the work group to ensure full representation of the issues. This joint effort makes certain that the recommendations are implemented and the outcomes are meaningful.

The selection of work group participants is an important component in the consensus-building process. Contextual stakeholders are critically important to ensure that the group fully represents varying perspectives. However, in some situations the inclusion of these group members presents problems. Weisburd (1996) notes the potential for confidentiality problems or conflicts of interest. The stakeholders may have friends or relatives who will be targeted by law enforcement or other strategies. For example, if gambling, prostitution, or drug dealing occurs at the neighborhood bar, and the work group makes recommendations against those illegal activities, a member may be placed in a delicate situation. However, it may also be possible to develop more effective strategies and a fuller assessment of the net effect of the responses.

Applying the consensus-building approach to crime problems requires law enforcement agencies to be team players. Traditionally, law enforcement personnel have been asked to define and "solve" the crime problem. Although the police agencies may consult with other agencies and citizens' groups, they ultimately have sole responsibility for the response. By contrast, in an interagency collaboration, the police department is a partner in the process and must recognize that other players have equal roles in the achievement of the outcomes. Webster and Connors (1993:81-82) note that involvement of the police and community in consensus-based interagency efforts may result in the "inclusion of many community problems that, in the past, technically have not been the responsibility of the police. These problems are appropriate . . . because they contribute to a crime, disorder, or fear of crime problem." Although the role of law enforcement may shift, the net effect is to motivate all partners to commit to the outcomes.

SUCCESSFUL WORK GROUPS: USING MAPS AND GEOGRAPHICAL DATA

Information is the binding force in interagency collaboration. Police data on such matters as calls for service and numbers of arrests are often relevant to the group's activities. That information, along with other pertinent data sources, forms the work group's foundation because it unites government agencies, businesses, and community groups in a common understanding of the problem. Each member of the work group can contribute data that assists in reaching an understanding the problem. Maps and other data provide a basis from which to develop solutions that are pertinent to the problem, and a focus on places and events helps in defining its characteristics.

Maps play a key role in an interagency project. Maps narrow the scope of the work group and inform the partners of the characteristics of the problem. Maps can also be used to develop action steps. For example, the distribution of crime events around places (such as bars or fast-food restaurants) gives the work group different information than mere knowledge that crime is rising in a particular neighborhood. Solutions can then be tailored to the specific nature of the problem. As noted by Harries (1990:38):

> A geographical perspective can greatly aid problem solving. It can be used to identify problem locations that can then be subjected to a more detailed analysis. During the analysis of a problem a geographical perspective can be used to develop detailed understanding. Like the problem solving approach, a geographical perspective is comprehensive, including the cultural environment (attitudes, values, and learned behavior), the physical environment or context in which human activity takes place (the layout of the city, the influences of the weather, for example), and the social characteristics of people: the patterns of their demographics, including their age, sex, wealth and poverty, racial characteristics, lifestyles (including housing types), and so forth.

The focus on a neighborhood, community, or jurisdiction defines the parties that have a stake in the results of the initiatives and targets the discussion and initiatives on places that affect the quality of life. During the consensus-building process, members are sensitized to the mutual advantages of their efforts. The following discussion, modeled after the SARA process, relates how mapping and geographical information play a key role in each phase of an interagency project.

Scanning: Identification of the Problem

Law enforcement information that is location-oriented, such as call-for-service and arrest data, is invaluable to community work groups because it helps participants identify the problem and how it affects the community. As Eck and Weisburd (1995) note, the focus on "crime place" then leads to consideration of facilities, features of the place, and clustering of events. These three components provide important information on maps that the work groups can use. The more specific the map information, the better the group can identify the unique nature of the problem. Maps help work groups identify crime event locations, crime frequencies, and unique features of the sites (such as alleyways, schoolyards, or abandoned houses).

Several jurisdictions have used call-for-service data to identify locations that have repeat calls. In Houston, the police and Hispanic citizens were concerned about violence in cantinas. Through repeat-call analysis, the police found that 3% of the cantinas in the city were responsible for 40% of the violence. The police then narrowed the scope of the problem and developed a special liquor control team to target the hot spots. In Baltimore County, MD, the domestic violence unit used repeat-call locations to identify areas where domestic violence calls were prevalent. The unit, which included police officers, mental health officials, and community leaders, targeted those areas for preventive actions that included the distribution of fliers on community resources for domestic violence victims (Webster and Connors, 1993). For its problem-oriented policing (POP) projects, the crime analysis unit in San Diego used repeat-call analysis and arrest data to target geographical areas with recurring problems (San Diego Police Department, 1992).

In DMAP, all five sites relied on call-for-service and arrest data to identify the locations of drug markets: Hartford used narcotic arrest data (Tien et al., 1993), Kansas City and Pittsburgh used call-for-service data (Sherman and Rogan, 1993; Cohen et al., 1993), and San Diego and Jersey City used call-for-service and arrest data (San Diego Police Department, 1992; Weisburd et al., 1992). Both call-for-service and arrest data have valuable features. First, they identify the addresses or locations where events tend to occur (the point data) and the spatial distribution or clustering of the points; consequently, it is possible to determine places that are hot spots for certain activities. Second, the data reveal the timing of the events (the hours of day or days of the week), which is a critical factor in understanding the pattern of occurrence. By examining the data, the work groups can assess the factors that make an area attractive for crime and disorder. Mapping the data provides the visual picture that allows the work group to scan the problem and identify its key characteristics.

Analysis of the Problem

The second interagency task involves analyzing information, an important step in the process of gaining commitment from community stakeholders. Before the participants can take ownership of the problem, they must be informed about its causes, scope, and effects. Only a shared understanding leads to a shared commitment to action. Mapping is a tool for analyzing the problem. Harries (1990:27) comments:

> Maps provide ways of dealing with complex data so as to reduce complexity and increase understandability. A map, like a picture, is worth a thousand words. Maps can provide lots of analytical power, reducing confusion and increasing the clarity and certainty of our analyses. This, in turn, allows us to communicate more effectively with others — to be more persuasive — as long as the technique is used appropriately.

Maps relate information in an easy-to-understand manner by making tabular information visual. In the Pittsburgh DMAP (P-DMAP), researchers at Carnegie-Mellon University shared maps on drug markets and other crime events with the Weed and Seed work group. These maps were useful to the project because they identified neighborhoods and communities in which different incidents were likely to occur.

In San Diego, maps supported the POP projects by providing patrol officers with information that could be used to analyze crime events in their beats and to identify crime patterns. Those patterns often were not evident until the data were mapped. The maps could identify when, how often, and where crime events tended to occur. For example, locations for drug dealing were of obvious interest under the department's DMAP program. Figure 1 shows drug dealing locations for a group of four beats in the city. Prior to this map, officers were aware of a few locations, but the map clearly shows clusters of blocks that had high-volume sales. Eck (1993) notes that the use of mapping resulted in a proactive, rather than reactive, approach to policing.

Figure 1: Drug Dealing Locations in Four Beats in San Diego

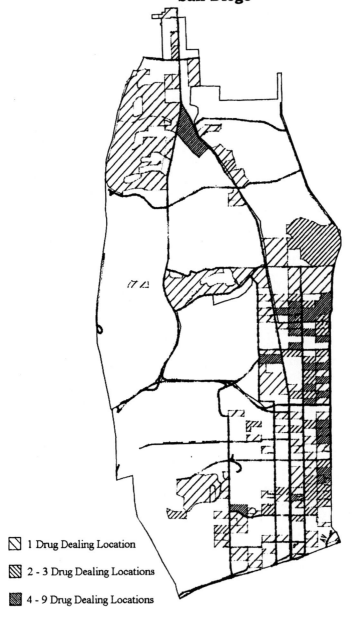

◨ 1 Drug Dealing Location

◩ 2 - 3 Drug Dealing Locations

◼ 4 - 9 Drug Dealing Locations

For the Pittsburgh project, Carnegie-Mellon University developed maps that use colors and symbols to describe various crime events, including type, location, and frequency — information that helps work groups understand the problem in a neighborhood. For example, pin maps showed 1990 call-for-service data in one community (Middle Hill) in order to identify the locations from which citizens called the police to report drug sales, overdoses, and weapons.[3] Each event is a different color on the map: blue for drug sales, green for overdoses, and pink for weapons. The researchers also used different-sized circles to dramatize the clustering of events —the larger the circle, the more calls for service. A different mapping technique, shading, showed changes in the frequency of events during a particular period. Levels of pink indicated areas where activity was "heating up"; levels of blue, where activity was "cooling off." By mapping the change in the extent of the problem over time, the police department and community detected the displacement of drug market activities to nearby neighborhoods. Such a technique can be useful in showing the impact of different responses over time.

The Pittsburgh project also used automated pin maps effectively to indicate drug market areas. The drug markets shown in Figure 2 are based on drug calls and indicate 13 different areas of the city with concentrations of drug activities.

Analyzing the timing of crimes is also a critical step for a community work group. The evaluation of the Tactical Narcotics Teams (TNT) in New York City, for example, emphasizes how crime data based on different times of the day or days of the week will direct the strategy of the group. The timing of crime events also affects neighborhood quality of life. According to Sviridoff et al. (1992:77):

> TNT's presence clearly made drug buyers and sellers more cautious.... [S]ellers shifted their working hours to periods when they thought TNT was not likely to be around.... For example, many participants in the research area crack markets felt it was safe to operate around "dinner time"—between 5 p.m. and 6 p.m. They believed that TNT officers would be eating, changing shifts, or processing people who had been arrested.

Although the preceding examples used police information only, other data may be helpful in analyzing a problem. These data might be provided by housing agencies, social service agencies, fire depart-

Figure 2: Pittsburgh Drug Market Areas

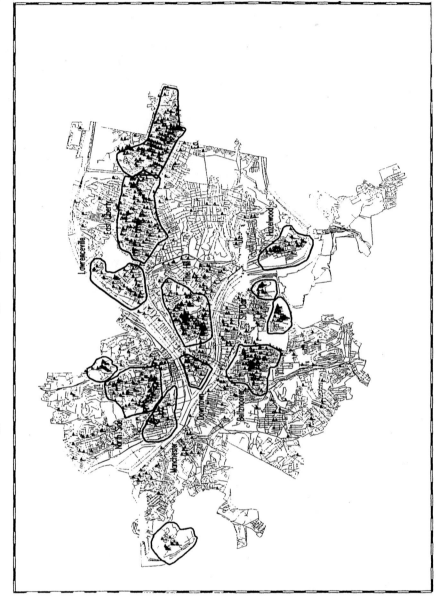

ments, schools, building inspectors, or other sources. Data from those sources may help work groups understand the person (Maltz, 1995) and the place (Eck, 1993), including a place's unique features and crime-proneness. For example, information on street lighting or the types of buildings surrounding the convenience stores might contribute to a better understanding of the robberies in San Diego. The maps in Pittsburgh could be enhanced by showing the types of buildings where drug sales, overdoses, and weapons are reported. It is critical that the work group analyze information from varying perspectives to ensure that a comprehensive response is implemented. The analytical stage lays the foundation for work group participants to recognize their roles in problem solving, commit resources, and develop an effective response.

Response to the Problem

In the response stage, the work group members must develop strategies that address the agreed-upon problem. The response should reflect their roles in the community. Maps are particularly useful for developing responses. The maps provide information about the community that might be useful in developing crime prevention strategies. For example, maps might display a community's natural boundaries (rivers, blocked alleys, buildings, other structures); pertinent facilities (schools, hospitals, clinics, businesses, commercial enterprises); and other neighborhood characteristics. The work group may find this information pertinent to the development of different responses from different agencies. For example, police departments could use law enforcement activities; religious organizations could use houses of worship to hold workshops; social and health organizations could be asked to use mobile vans to reach residents; and businesses could provide financial and administrative support to different target initiatives.

As noted by Eck and Spelman (1987), responses vary, depending on the nature of the problem and the type of solution desired. After analyzing the elements of the problem, the work group must determine a solution. Solutions range from eliminating the problem in its entirety to removing the problem from police consideration. The responses must support the desired solution, and must be realistic enough to obtain continued support and assistance from the community. The maps assist the work group in determining whether the problem is spatially distributed, concentrated, or epidemic. The extent of the problem may lead to the choice of solution. In Table 1, Eck and Spelman provide some guidance in matching solutions to different types of problems.

Table 1: Matching Solutions to Different Types of Problems

Type of Solution	Types of Problems
Eliminate the problem.	Small, simple problems that have recently occurred. Problems that are not persistent. Problems that affect a relatively small group.
Substantially reduce the problem.	Neighborhood crime and disorder problems. Persistent problems. Problems that affect the quality of life.
Reduce the harm created by the problem.	Problems that are prevalent, and when it is almost impossible to reduce the number of incidents. Problems that have characteristics and unintended harmful effects that can be altered. Problems that involve multiple solutions.
Deal with the problem more effectively.	Problems that are jurisdiction-wide and involve larger social issues. Problems needing short-term solutions that involve changes in the way the problem is handled. Problems needing long-term solutions that involve social changes.
Remove the problem from police consideration.	Problems that are created by specific groups as a by-product of their ways of operating. Problems where law enforcement has only minimal impact on the likely outcomes.

Many of the solutions to crime problems add new dimensions to the roles of government agencies, communities, and businesses as these entities forge new relationships to fight crime. For example, police agencies in several jurisdictions have joined forces with correctional agencies to monitor high-risk offenders who are under some type of supervised release. The Redmond, WA, and Madison, WI police departments have initiated efforts to monitor the activities of probationers or parolees and provide feedback to correctional officers (Morgan and Marres, 1994; Balles, 1993). There is a formal exchange of information between the two partners. The correctional agencies inform police officers of the high-risk offenders in their communities, and the police agencies send copies of field investigation or arrest reports to corrections officials immediately after an event occurs. Law enforcement agencies often have timely information on the activities of offenders, which facilitates correctional decisions about technical violations. The Redmond and Madison partnerships resulted in greater cooperation among public safety agencies that had not collaborated in the past even though their missions are closely related. While this solution does not eradicate the crime problem, it does provide an opportunity to substantially reduce the crime problems caused by unsupervised probationers and parolees.

The Police Assisted Community Enforcement (PACE) program in Norfolk, VA is an "interagency support structure [designed] to focus problem solving in neighborhoods and to advance citywide partnership efforts" (PACE, 1993). PACE developed the following initiatives to respond creatively to the problems in six districts, based on place and offender issues:

- Spiritual Action for Empowerment, a coalition of religious organizations that sponsor neighborhood block parties, music, and inspirational speakers for youths.

- Athletic League, which involves youth in recreational activities.

- Nighthawk Basketball, which includes programs for older teens and younger adults in the evening.

- Action Leadership for Empowerment and Resource Training, which uses training to develop community leadership.

The districts implement responses based on the "strength and needs of neighborhoods" (PACE, 1993) and the available resources.

In an extensive review of the results of community involvement in policing efforts to reduce crime and disorder, Grinc (1994) found that implementation is often problematic because of the "fleeting nature of 'projects' to help poor communities," projects that often have short-lived responses but no long-term commitments. One example is the tendency to rely on strong enforcement efforts for an immediate response to a crime problem. Without the commitment of other organizations, the impact of law enforcement efforts is generally short-lived.

When the intensive enforcement ceases, the community is often left without the resources to maintain the newly reduced levels of criminal activity and to develop long-term solutions to the problem. As a result, law enforcement loses credibility in the eyes of the community.

Interagency work groups must take a twofold approach to avoid the typical pattern of short-term responses. First, because many community problems are complex and persistent, the strategy must include short- and long-term efforts that address the different facets of the problems. Second, the group must develop ways to motivate the partners to stay committed to the plan. Ongoing evaluation of the responses creates a role for each member and encourages commitment to long-term solutions.

Assessment of the Response

Assessment is the final stage of the work group process, during which the group develops mechanisms to critique and monitor its responses. This feedback helps to pinpoint needed revisions, such as changing the response, improving the analysis, gathering more information, or redefining the problem. In addition, assessment is a tool that keeps the group committed to the task throughout the implementation. Because community problems often are complex and change dramatically over time, and because work group responses often involve multiple initiatives, it is necessary for the members to monitor the progress of each component and make appropriate adjustments.

Mid-course corrections are used to ensure that the response is a good fit, and to improve the linkages among the program participants. During the Jersey City DMAP, for example, narcotics detectives discovered that they needed to assign aliases to neighborhood street names because the drug organizations were monitoring police radio channels for advance information on enforcement activities. The detectives used the mapping tool to develop code names for the streets and then distributed the revised maps to the field officers. If the drug sellers monitored police channels, they would be unable to determine which street was targeted because of the coding system. Jersey City detectives told their research partners that thinking in terms of place (the neighborhood) rather than person (the suspect) provided them with an effective front-line response tool that facilitated solutions (Gajewski, 1993).

Work groups can also use maps and other informational tools to assess the results of the community initiatives. As previously discussed, P-DMAP used colored maps to show the "heating up" and "cooling off" of problem areas during the course of the project. The Eastside Substance Abuse Awareness Program, a comprehensive, community-based effort to reduce illicit drug activity in one Wilmington, DE, neighborhood, used assessment techniques to improve its responses. As in many interagency work groups, the strategic plan initially involved increased law enforcement to reduce drug activity. Following the police response, the "focus shifted away from law enforcement and more towards community participation and initiative" (Harris and O'Connell, 1994:53). The advisory council that oversees the project includes 38 members, representing state and local governments, schools, social service providers, the police department, churches, and area residents. The council meets monthly and is staffed by a program coordinator funded by the police department. This multi-agency group was instrumental in ensuring that the community was actively involved in the assessment phase, which resulted in solution as to the following problems:

- A continuing issue is irresponsible landlords. Many of the landlords fail to screen potential tenants, some of whom contribute to the neighborhood's drug problems. The advisory council staff asked 85 landlords in the neighborhood to participate in a special program designed to select appropriate tenants for their housing. The program developed screening and referral mechanisms for the landlords.

- Public telephones are often used by drug dealers to arrange transactions. The advisory council worked with the telephone company to remove several public telephones, and to modify telephones so that they could no longer accept incoming calls.

- One neighborhood bar and liquor store was a constant object of complaints from residents in the area. The advisory council met with the owner of the establishment, who subsequently agreed to hire an off-duty police officer. The presence of the officer reduced the loitering, drug dealing, and disorderly behavior that occurred outside the bar.

CASE STUDIES OF WORK GROUP MAP USE

The following case studies illustrate how work groups in two DMAPs used geographical information to reduce such problems as drug trafficking, social disorder, and prostitution in their communities. The case studies also discuss the different types of groups and how the work group process affected the development of effective responses.

COMPASS Project in Hartford, CT: Four Community Organization Groups

The Cartographic Oriented Management Program for the Abatement of Street Sales (COMPASS) in Hartford, CT, provided a new approach to improving the quality of life in areas that were highly affected by crime and drugs. A two-pronged approach — reclamation and stabilization — was undertaken involving interagency work groups led by the police department and a representative from the city manager's office.

COMPASS work groups were formed in four target communities. The groups were developed on a community level because of the unique features of each community. It was anticipated that this might lead to different responses. The organization along community lines also resulted in the inclusion of different partners in the work groups. The following target communities participated:

- Charter Oak Terrace, a small area with numerous public housing buildings. The area is geographically isolated and bounded by a river, a railroad, and an interstate highway. The residents are among the poorest in Hartford, and everyone lives in the same housing project.

- Milner, a 16-block area in the north-central part of Hartford. A highway bisects the area. Housing consists of a mix of multifamily apartment buildings and houses.

- Frog Hollow, located at the south end of the city. It is six times larger than Charter Oak Terrace and three times larger than Milner. It is also located near a congested commercial street.

- Asylum Hill, which is about the size of Frog Hollow but has one-third the residents. It is a diverse neighborhood that includes residential and commercial areas. One-fifth of its families live below the poverty level.

The neighborhood work groups comprised a variety of community organizations, citizens' groups, and businesses; one goal of the project was to include more citizens' groups than government agencies or quasi-governmental organizations. The membership of each group, as shown in Table 2, varied according to the characteristics of the community and the types of drug activity that occurred.

The work groups were charged with developing a reclamation and stabilization plan — a comprehensive strategy to thwart the drug market activities in their communities. The police had primary responsibility for the reclamation efforts, while the stabilization activities involved "a variety of groups in the target area, including target area residents, community groups, institutions, businesses, and city agencies" (Tien et al., 1992:ix). Community support was available for the reclamation, but support for longer-term stabilization was hindered by a budget crisis and turmoil in the city government. Eventually, COMPASS became primarily a police initiative.

Although COMPASS attempted to integrate the work groups in the stabilization efforts, the police department served as the lead agency, and the stabilization revolved around the police community service officer assigned to each target area. That officer assisted target-area residents, businesses, institutions, and organizations by facilitating communication among the police department, city agencies, and work group members. As a result of the role of the police in both reclamation and stabilization, through the use of patrol and community service officers, the process implicitly discouraged other work group members from assuming responsibility for components of the stabilization plan.

Recognizing the need for greater involvement by the city agencies, Hartford formed a Reclamation Steering Committee, coordinated by the Office of Human Services. The committee, which included representatives from the city agencies and community groups, established the following goals:

- Reduce the incidence of drug-related crimes.

- Empower residents to take control of their own neighborhoods, make decisions, and set priorities.

- Increase the ability of residents to become economically self-sufficient.

- Enable service providers and residents to collaborate and negotiate services and strategies.

The work groups in each neighborhood would have responsibility for designing, implementing, and monitoring stabilization efforts. The steering committee desired a "bottom-up" approach, whereby it would act as an advocate for the neighborhood efforts. The committee also developed some tactics that would help the groups achieve their objectives, as shown in Table 3. The work groups would then develop the plans for implementing the tactics. As noted by the evaluators, "the target areas had to have active and well-organized community

Table 2: Agencies Represented in the COMPASS Work Groups

Work Group Members	Charter Oaks Terrace	Milner	Frog Hollow	Asylum Hill	Steering Committee
Community Organization					
Tenants Association	X			X	
Health Council	X				
Recreation Center		X			
Boy Scouts	X				
Church		X	X	X	
Block Watch Group			X	X	
Business Group			X		
Other	X	X	X	X	X*
Government or Police Agency					
City Executive				X	X
Adult Probation	X	X		X	X
Prison Association	X	X	X		
Human Services	X	X		X	X
School		X			
Office of Substance Abuse		X			
Quality Neighborhood Task			X	X	
Drug Enforcement Agency			X	X	
FBI	X				
Alcohol, Tobacco & Firearms	X				
Housing Authority	X				
City Employment Resources					X
Hartford Inst. for Criminal & Social Justice					X
Mayor's Crime Commission					X
Police Department	X	X	X	X	X

*The Hartford Areas Rally Together community group was represented on the steering committee.

Table 3: Overview of COMPASS Approaches and Stabilization Tactics*

	Primary Objectives of Tactic			
Tactic:	Increase Citizen Participation	Improve Physical Condition	Increase Delivery of Services	Deter Drug Activity
Organize block watches in target area	X			X
Forge alliances between target area residents and institutions	X			X
Conduct community organizing forums	X			X
Improve physical condition of private or public property		X		
Enforce housing and public health regulations in target area		X	X	
Expand youth programs, human services, and education			X	
Implement crime prevention programs	X			X
Pressure city agencies to deliver services	X	X	X	X
Conduct neighborhood cleanups	X	X		X
Conduct citizen rallies	X			X

*Tien et al., 1993

groups to facilitate defining the needs and setting the priorities" (Tien et al., 1993:2, 13-14).

Although COMPASS was initially designed so that each of the target neighborhoods would be involved in the design and implementation of the reclamation and stabilization efforts — such as identifying the problem, developing the strategic plan, and assessing the responses — the structure of the work groups did not support such an approach. The tendency was to operate "as usual," which meant that the heads of city agencies had to pledge their commitment and resources. From its inception, COMPASS was perceived more as a police program than a citywide or neighborhood effort. Residents' groups and business associations were not involved early enough in the consensus-building process to take ownership of the problem or the proposed solutions. In addition, the steering committee was unsuccessful in nurturing support on behalf of the neighborhoods.

COMPASS was a valiant attempt at consensus building, but the government, business, and community participants were not sufficiently empowered to assume responsibility. The evaluation of the project identified three features that are necessary for successful neighborhood work groups. First, jurisdictions should consider "neighborhood viability and geography in the selection of anti-drug target areas" (Tien et al., 1993:xvi).Second, the efforts need to be "city," not police, programs. That is, the efforts should proceed by consensus and not be led by a single agency. Third, "detailed program plans, and in particular stabilization or 'seeding' plans, must be developed prior to the start of the reclamation or 'weeding' efforts" (Tien et al., 1993:xviii). The maps and information that the work groups used were based on police call-for-service data only, not data from other agencies. This constrained the work groups from developing realistic stabilization techniques.

The Hartford experience with COMPASS illustrates the importance of the process used in developing work groups and obtaining government, business, and citizen participation in solving complex social problems. COMPASS did not fully engage in a SARA-type process. In the COMPASS project, the stabilization efforts were not developed by consensus or by participants empowered for the implementation. The police took sole responsibility for coordinating the reclamation efforts, which included deciding where the drug markets were and how to change the nature of those markets. Although the police did share information with the community about drug arrests, the information was provided after the reclamation activities. By that time, consensus or momentum for addressing difficult social problems was difficult to build. Consequently, the reclamation efforts succeeded only partially.

COMPASS also dramatizes the importance of providing a full range of data to the community to develop effective responses. The work groups had maps of calls for service in each community, but they did not have geographically based data on human and social services resources and physical conditions. The initiatives they developed, therefore, could not be as specific as those developed by the Eastside Substance Abuse Awareness Program in Wilmington, DE. In that jurisdiction, the responses were driven by problems with specific landlords, public phones, neighborhood bars and liquor stores. In COMPASS, the responses were more generic. The groups identified the need to enforce housing and public health regulations and to expand youth programs, human services, and education in target *areas*, but not in specific sites.

The San Diego Prostitution Task Force

Prostitution is a persistent problem in many communities. In San Diego, several agencies were concerned about the involvement of youth in prostitution. To coordinate an interagency response to thwart those activities, a task force was formed. The task force included representatives from the police department and social service and health agencies; business owners; citizens; and outreach workers specializing in efforts to assist prostitutes. As the task force formulated a comprehensive strategy, it assessed the problem geographically because different areas of the community experienced different problems with prostitution.

The police department provided the task force with the following types of information on arrests in different areas of the county:

- Number of prostitution and related arrests in the past year.
- Number of other arrests in different geographical areas (police beats) of the city.
- Number of prostitution arrests occurring on different streets of the city.
- Characteristics of offenders arrested for prostitution (juvenile or adult, gender, ethnicity, military status).

The review of the arrests focused on the geographical aspects of prostitution. By examining arrest locations, the task force could consider reasons why certain neighborhoods or streets invited this activity, especially prostitution that involved young runaways. There was also concern about other criminal behavior, such as drug sales, that occurred in the areas where prostitutes operated.

The police department provided the task force with a map denoting the locations of arrests and citations for prostitution and the frequency distribution of the street addresses. The task force focused on three geographical areas where prostitution was likely to occur, based on analysis of the official data. Maps showed that prostitution and related arrests were more likely to occur along major thoroughfares in one section of the jurisdiction. Supporting information revealed that the western part of that section accounted for 624, or 46%, of the 1,359 prostitution arrests in the city; nearly a third of those arrests were located on a major street. The map also illustrates that prostitution was concentrated in just a few areas.

By examining the various streets and locations where arrests were made, the task force identified geographical boundaries or features that contributed to the congregation of prostitutes. Some of the task force members had difficulty evaluating tabular data, but maps helped them visualize the frequency distribution of the prostitution arrests. When the members could "see" where the events occurred, they could make more informed decisions about their strategy.

After reviewing the characteristics of arrestees, the police department determined that the prostitution trade differed across the city. The western area attracted younger prostitutes; 65% of the arrestees were 18 to 29 years old; in other areas of the city, less than 47% of arrestees were in that age group. In the central and western parts of the county, prostitutes were just as likely to be males as females; in the eastern part of the city, prostitutes were more likely to be females. The ethnic trends showed that Hispanic prostitutes frequented the central area, while Caucasian prostitutes usually operated in the eastern and western parts.

The analysis also revealed that juveniles accounted for only a small number of the total arrests for prostitution. Only 15 of the 1,359 arrestees were under 18 years old. The police explained, however, that juvenile prostitutes are handled in a different manner than adults. Juveniles are likely to be treated as runaways or to be charged with status offenses instead of criminal charges (e.g., prostitution and loitering), a practice that accounts for underreporting in official statistics on juvenile prostitution.

The geographical information was critical to the task force's development of a comprehensive strategic plan. Health care workers, for example, used the street-location information to target their activities, such as distributing AIDS literature and condoms near the locations where prostitution arrests occurred. In addition, outreach workers made more informed decisions about the placement of "safe houses" for prostitutes. Although the workers already knew many of the prostitution areas, the maps identified new locations.

The task force recognized that the response of multiple agencies was necessary to address the problem of prostitution. As a result, the work group recommended a strategic plan to the legislative body that included the following initiatives:

- Case managers should be assigned to areas of the city where prostitutes work. The managers should provide services for minors, coordinate transitional living facilities and support groups, and assist prostitutes in crisis situations.

- A 24-hour crisis intervention line should be available to prostitutes.

- The Social Services Subcommittee should issue a resource card that directs prostitutes to available services within the community.

- Arrestees for prostitution or solicitation should be required to attend an educational course on health and safety issues, including AIDS, drugs, and sexually transmitted diseases.

- Arrestees for prostitution should be required to attend support group meetings and perform community services through the direction of these support groups.

- An awareness program is needed to educate community members, businesses, and the public about prostitution.

- Prostitution should be added to the criteria for designating extra lighting in high-crime areas.

- A database should be established to track prostitutes, pimps, and factors associated with prostitution. The system should be available to law enforcement agencies in the region.

Without the maps and the data on arrestees, San Diego would have responded with the typical police procedure — arrest. Instead, the city recognized prostitution as a social and crime problem that required an interagency response with long-term solutions. The plan calls for arrest only as a secondary response, with the primary emphasis on prevention and intervention. The police are a part of the solution, as are citizens, businesses, and social service and health agencies. Using community policing and problem-oriented strategies, work group members can respond collectively to address the unique issues of prostitution in different parts of the community.

CONCLUSION: BENEFITS OF MAPPING FOR WORK GROUPS AND PROBLEM SOLVING

Crime problems are often considered too large in scope for anyone to solve. Community policing and problem-oriented policing strategies are currently being used by many police departments to provide a law enforcement response. However, both of those strategies recognize that many crime control initiatives are essentially community initiatives. Without the participation of many different types of organizations and community groups, it is likely that the police can only bring about short-term relief for crime and disorder problems. The involvement of stakeholders is important in developing collective responses, and the use of consensus-building strategies has been shown useful in developing feasible responses to problems that often appear too large for any single agency, acting alone, to solve.

Critical to the development of effective responses is the use of good data to guide the consensus-building process. Maps and geographical data provide work groups with fruitful information. The maps are helpful in identifying and understanding the problem, developing appropriate responses, and monitoring successes. However, the data must be sensitive to the unique features of both places (features, clustering, facilities) and offenders (target selection, mobility). Place and people data can be combined in many different ways, as is shown by the different techniques developed in the Jersey City, Pittsburgh, and San Diego DMAP projects.

Relevant data guide work group decisions by giving the members a broader perspective on a problem. The case studies used in this chapter demonstrate the differences in responses based on the information that the groups used to scan and assess the problem. In COMPASS, the data consisted solely of information on calls for service, while San Diego used place- and offender-oriented data (age of offenders, location of activity, clustering of activity). The results were dramatically different. More specific, long-term solutions evolved from understandings based on the wider range of data.

Interagency work groups offer promise for future efforts to reduce crime and social disorder in neighborhoods. The complexity of social problems requires that all participants assume responsibility and be committed to the process. Using geographical tools and the SARA model for problem solving, all participants can contribute to the definition and analysis of the issues and the development of appropriate responses. That process then leads to a commitment to achieve long-term solutions.

DMAP has demonstrated how geographical tools can be the cornerstone of crime control initiatives in communities across the nation. While DMAP was primarily interested in using geographically based police data, the experience suggests that other geographically based data will contribute to the development of different solutions. The focus on mapping arrest and call-for-service data implies law enforcement solutions. However, by adding other pertinent information (on, for example, school attendance or building code violations), it is possible for work groups to perceive the problem differently and develop different solutions. Mapping has been shown to be critical to targeting problem-solving strategies, uniting stakeholders of varying perspectives, and assisting in assessment of collaborative efforts.

Acknowledgments: This project was funded by a grant from the U.S. National Institute of Justice to the Institute for Law and Justice (Grant number 92-DD-CX-K031). The authors wish to thank NIJ and three anonymous reviewers for their helpful comments in furthering the concepts developed in this paper. The authors would also like to thank Dr. David Weisburd for his helpful comments.

NOTES

1. Overall, DMAP had a three-stage approach: (1) jurisdictions were assisted in the development of information delivery systems that integrated data on address or street locations, (2) the jurisdictions were assisted in the development of strategies for crime control problems, and (3) evaluations were conducted on the success of these new strategies.

2. The five sites and research organizations participating in DMAP were the San Diego (CA) Police Department with the Police Executive Research Forum; the Pittsburgh (PA) Police Department with Carnegie-Mellon University; the Hartford (CT) Police Department with the Queues Enforth Corporation; the Jersey City (NJ) Police Department with Rutgers University School of Criminal Justice; and the Kansas City (MO) Police Department with the Crime Control Institute. The Institute for Law and Justice was provided with a grant to conduct a multi-site evaluation of the DMAP project.

3. The maps developed in P-DMAP use various techniques to present the data. The researchers use a mixture of colors, symbols, and symbol sizes to characterize crime problems. Copies of the maps can be obtained from Dr. Jacqueline Cohen at The Heinz School, Carnegie-Mellon University, Pittsburgh, PA. Maps could not be included in this article due to use of color.

REFERENCES

Balles, J. (1993). "Organizing Government Services at the Neighborhood Level: Putting All the Pieces Together." Paper presented at the Community Policing for Safe Neighborhoods — Partnerships for the 21st Century conference, sponsored by the National Institute of Justice, U.S. Department of Justice, Washington, DC.

Carpenter, S. (1990). *Community Problem Solving by Consensus.* Washington, DC: The Program for Community Problem Solving.

Cohen, J., W. Gorr, and A. Olligschlaeger (1993). *Computerized Crime Mapping: Pittsburgh Drug Market Analysis Program (P-DMAP).* Pittsburgh, PA: Carnegie-Mellon University.

Eck, J. E. (1993). "Drug Market Analysis." Paper presentation at the Community Policing For Safe Neighborhoods — Partnerships for the 21st Century conference, sponsored by the National Institute of Justice, U.S. Department of Justice, Washington, DC.

—— (1996). "Prospective Mapping: Using Theory to Guide Geographical Analysis of Crime Data." College Park, MD: University of Maryland.

—— and W. Spelman (1987). *Problem Solving: Problem Oriented Policing in Newport News.* Washington, DC: Police Executive Research Forum.

—— and D. Weisburd (1995). "Crime Places in Crime Theory." In: J. E. Eck and D. Weisburd (eds.), *Crime and Place.* Crime Prevention Studies, vol. 4. Monsey, NY: Criminal Justice Press.

Gajewski, F. (1993). "Drug Market Analysis and Problem-Oriented Policing." Paper presented at the Fourth Annual Evaluation Conference on Evaluating Crime and Drug Control Proceedings, sponsored by the National Institute of Justice, U.S. Department of Justice, Washington, DC.

Grinc, R. M. (1994). "'Angels in Marble': Problems in Stimulating Community Involvement in Community Policing." *Crime & Delinquency* 40(3):437-68.

Harries, K. (1990). *Geographic Factors in Policing.* Washington, DC: Police Executive Research Forum.

Harris, R.J., and J. O'Connell (1994). *Eastside Substance Abuse Awareness Program Evaluation*. Dover, DE: Delaware Statistical Analysis Center.

Maltz, M. (1995). "Criminality in Space and Time: Life Course Analysis and the Micro-Ecology of Crime." In: J.E. Eck and D. Weisburd (eds.), *Crime and Place*. Crime Prevention Studies, vol. 4. Monsey, NY: Criminal Justice Press.

McEwen, J.T., and F.S. Taxman (1995). "Applications of Computerized Mapping to Police Operations." In: J. E. Eck and D. Weisburd (eds.), *Crime and Place*. Crime Prevention Studies, vol. 4. Monsey, NY: Criminal Justice Press.

Morgan, T. and S.D. Marres (1994). "A Partnership Program Worth Emulating." *Police Chief* May:14-19.

PACE (1993). *Police Assisted Community Enforcement*. Norfolk, VA: author.

Rossi, P.H., and H.E. Freeman (1990). *Evaluation: A Systematic Approach*. Newbury Park, CA: Sage.

San Diego Police Department (1992). "Grant Proposal: San Diego DMAP Phase II." Unpublished paper.

Sherman, L., and D. Rogan (1993). "Raiding Crack Houses: The Kansas City Experiment." Unpublished paper.

Sviridoff, M., S. Sadd, R. Curtis, and R. Grinc (1992). *The Neighborhood Effects of Street-Level Drug Enforcement: Tactical Narcotics Teams in New York: An Evaluation of the TNT*. New York, NY: Vera Institute of Justice.

Tien, J.M., T.F. Rich, M. Shell, R.C. Larson, and J.P. Donnelly (1993). "COMPASS: A Drug Market Analysis Program (DMAP)." Unpublished paper.

—— T.F. Rich, R.C. Larson, and J.P. Donnelly (1992). "On Neighborhood-Oriented Anti-Drug Programs: The Hartford Experience to Date." Unpublished paper.

Webster, B. and E. F. Connors (1993). "Police Methods for Identifying Community Problems." *American Journal of Police* 12(1):75-101.

Weisburd, D. L. (1996). Personal communication to the co-author.

—— L. Green, and D. Ross (1992). "Crime in Street Level Drug Markets: A Spatial Analysis." Unpublished paper.

POWER TO THE PEOPLE: MAPPING AND INFORMATION SHARING IN THE CHICAGO POLICE DEPARTMENT

by

Marc Buslik
Chicago Police Department

and

Michael D. Maltz
University of Illinois at Chicago

Abstract: Community policing is intended to change the way police officers at all levels work. In support of these changes, the police department's information system should also be modified, in ways that may not be immediately apparent; if it is not modified, the full benefits of community policing may not be realized. This chapter describes the way the Chicago Police Department has reorganized its information system, and, more to the point, has changed its policies regarding the sharing of information, in support of a full implementation of community policing.

As Chicago Police Officers Gail Hagen and Margred Colon prepared for their monthly meeting with residents on their beat, they sat in front of a personal computer at the department's 25th District. While one worked the mouse and picked criteria for their search, the other reviewed the previous month's products. The Information Col-

Address correspondence to: Marc Buslik, Chicago Police Department, Internal Affairs Division, 1121 South State St., Chicago, IL 60605.

lection for Automated Mapping (ICAM) system computer provided the officers with access to data on reported crime and community data for the district. By choosing the type of information that was discussed by them and members of the community at the last beat meeting, the officers created a series of maps showing problem areas on the beat and how conditions had changed after they began addressing issues identified at the meetings. After selecting the categories of robberies, burglaries and narcotics-related incidents, the officers prepared maps and listings for each category. They were quite pleased when they were able to see that since they had begun foot patrols on several side streets, all three groups of incidents had decreased in those areas. They knew, too, that the community would be pleased with their efforts and that all parties could see real results from using technology to support community-based policing services. Figures 1 through 3 depict the types of output that are done routinely and easily by police officers using the ICAM system.

ICAM represents, as of 1996, the latest point in an evolutionary process in the use of computerized information systems by the Chicago Police Department (CPD). The department and its community partners have, since the early 1980s, amassed considerable hands-on experience with using computers to interpret crime and community-based data and to create maps. These efforts have helped them to understand how people use these tools cooperatively to better enable the police and the community to "serve and protect." These experiences illustrate how all organizations' information systems need to change, and how police departments can respond to the changes required of them.

In this chapter we review the way the CPD has changed its policies with respect to information, and especially with respect to information sharing, in some fundamental ways. We should point out that this represents our own views of what has happened over the past few decades; others, both within and outside the department, have very different views of what the CPD is now doing and whether it should be doing it. In fact, one of the issues that any police department must face is determining to what extent its information should be shared, with whom and under what circumstances, and the political consequences, both internal and external. While this chapter does not directly address these questions, it does describe how and why the CPD has dealt with information sharing.

Figure 1: "Top Ten List" of Most Active Crime Types for the Beat

Primary	Totals
Burglary	22
Theft Of Auto	13
Theft	13
Robbery	9
Recovered Motor Vehicle	6
Battery Simple	3
Battery	3
Prostitution	2
Liquor Law Violations	1
Narcotics	1

TOP TEN ON 2515

From: 02/22/1996 To 03/20/1996
From: 00:00 To 23:59 Hours

TOTAL: 73

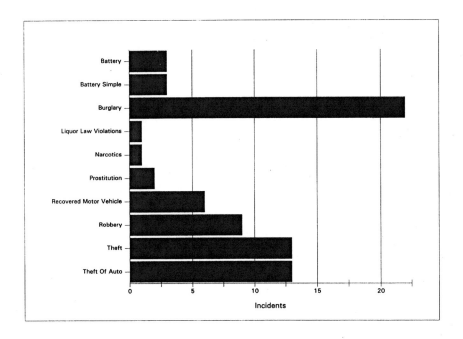

*These data reflect initial case classification based on facts known at the time the incident was reported. They may be revised at a later time.

Figure 2: Typical Map Prepared for a Beat Meeting

BURGLARY OFFENSES IN BEAT 2515   (17)*

ALL LOCATIONS

◊	Liquor License Estab.
⌂	Vacant Buildings
▴	Schools

*These data reflect initial case classification based on facts known at the time the incident was reported. It may be revised at a later time.

The next section examines early modernization efforts of the CPD with respect to information systems. We subsequently explore the CPD computer mapping project, "Mapping Crime in Its Community Setting" (Maltz et al., 1991; see also Rich, 1995), that was the precursor to ICAM, and, in fact, to a great many police computer mapping efforts. The last section discusses some of the choices open to police departments in terms of information policies, and what we see as the advantages of the route chosen by the CPD, that of sharing information with the community.

Figure 3: Listing of Incidents Displayed on the Map

Address	Hse_Apt	Date	Time_1	RD_no	IUCR	Secondary	Location
21 N Mango Av		02/26/1996	1915	A-124857	0610	Forcible Entry	Residence
25 N Major Av		03/03/1996	0110	A-233172	0610	Forcible Entry	Residence Garage
52 W Altgeld St		03/04/1996	2000	A-161545	0610	Forcible Entry	Residence Garage
23 N Lockwood Av		03/04/1996	0630	A-216466	0610	Forcible Entry	Residence Garage
24 N Marmora Av		03/04/1996	0001	A-160204	0610	Forcible Entry	Residence Garage
25 N Marmora Av		03/06/1996	1315	A-164317	0610	Forcible Entry	Residence
29 N Parkside Av		03/06/1996	1400	A-164134	0610	Forcible Entry	Residence
20 N Latrobe Av		03/11/1996	1500	A-219049	0610	Forcible Entry	Residence Garage
22 N Long Av		03/12/1996	1600	A-174711	0610	Forcible Entry	Residence Garage
22 N Major Av		03/14/1996	2200	A-220402	0610	Forcible Entry	Residence Garage
23 N Austin Av		03/15/1996	1800	A-220477	0610	Forcible Entry	Residence Garage
24 N Menard Av		03/17/1996	2100	A-221460	0610	Forcible Entry	Residence Garage
53 W Deming Pl		03/17/1996	0930	A-183240	0610	Forcible Entry	Residence Garage
25 N Menard Av		03/17/1996	0001	A-183051	0610	Forcible Entry	Residence Garage
58 W Grand Av		03/18/1996	0615	A-222386	0610	Forcible Entry	Residence Garage
21 N Laramie Av		03/20/1996	1700	A-223289	0610	Forcible Entry	Residence Garage
24 N Luna Av		03/20/1996	0900	A-188832	0610	Forcible Entry	Residence

THE CPD AND TECHNOLOGY

As police departments go, the CPD was an early adopter of so-phisticated automated information systems. In the late 1950s the department installed an IBM model 407 accounting machine. Several years later, in 1962, the department became the first police agency to install the IBM 1401 mainframe. Two years later, an upgrade brought in an IBM 1410 system. This push toward automation and moderni-zation came primarily at the instigation of a new police superinten-dent, Orlando W. Wilson, who had been brought in to the CPD to clean house in the wake of a department scandal. In addition to com-puterization, a state-of-the-art radio dispatching system was installed at police headquarters, one that was much imitated throughout the world. And in the early 1970s, the department became one of many users of the City of Chicago's IBM System 370 mainframe.

These computing platforms, their applications, and the necessary support systems were adopted to accommodate the information needs of the department as they were then seen: information was collected at the bottom of the hierarchy, and then centralized and summarized so that decisions and policies could be made at the top. As early as 1969, the department had recognized the need to develop new policies for satisfying the growing information needs of all units within the department. At that time, a high-level committee consist-ing of the first deputy superintendent, the four deputy superinten-dents, and the director of the data systems division was created to set policy for information systems use.

In the early 1980s, as computer technology changed, the department introduced personal computers to satisfy specialized automation needs on a limited basis. The ability to input and manipulate data of localized concern and then produce information for decision making closer to the "problem" was the impetus for a de facto change in information system procedures, if not formal policy. One of the primary motivations for this activity was the fact that, as first the Apple II and then the (IBM) personal computer and Macintosh hit the market, police officers throughout the department, on their own initiative, started putting their home computers to work on their own units' problems. One of the authors, then a district tactical officer, created a database of field contacts on his own personal computer (PC); a sex crimes detective developed a database of his own; and spreadsheets and databases of every stripe, on every conceivable platform, could be found in different units throughout the department.

While these local computer applications permitted their developers to deal more effectively with isolated problems, there was no coordination to allow different officers' pet applications, addressing similar needs, to effectively share successes and useful data. This was as much an organizational issue as it was a technical one. As a consequence, in the mid-1980s the department no longer had to be able to interpret reams of data to support its decision making. The creation of sophisticated graphs and charts became easier for the information user, and made data analysis possible for people without extensive training in statistics. Becoming informed became a matter of looking at a picture of the data and being able to visualize trends, rather than having to do this by scanning tables that summarized the data.

Besides the variety of bar charts, time-series plots, and other similar graphics, it became possible to represent data spatially using the computer. Both simple mapping programs and more complex geographic information systems could place location-based data onto a map. Using either separate or integrated data manipulation tools, relationships between the data took on new perspectives. Simply by looking at the resulting map images, an analyst, an internal user or a person from outside the organization could detect spatial patterns in the data.

Also in the late 1980s, the CPD was given access to the computerized map resident on the information system of the Chicago Planning Department. This system permitted location-specific data residing on the city's mainframe computer to be plotted on maps of the city and the various community areas. Officer Larry Bobrowski, a computer-literate gang crimes detective, received permission to experiment with the department's data and mapping software. Utilizing case report information, he was able to generate maps with incident data marked on them. Essentially, he had automated the process of creating the typical police "pin map." This activity was soon superseded by a more ambitious mapping project sponsored by the National Institute of Justice (NIJ), the research arm of the U.S. Department of Justice.

COMMUNITY AND POLICE CRIME MAPPING IN CHICAGO

As we describe below, the Chicago crime mapping project was a rudimentary realization of a mapping system. It did, however, convincingly demonstrate the potential applicability to the day-to-day planning and resource allocation activity of urban police. Moreover, because of the special circumstances of its birth, the project also underscored the benefits that could accrue when the police and community work jointly to employ them. This section explains why community organizations were so heavily involved, the organization of the mapping project, and some of the broader lessons that resulted from the project — lessons that should be of use to any police department interested in developing or improving its crime-mapping activity.

As the crime rate rose in the mid-1980s, various communities were getting organized and making greater demands on the police for relevant information to aid in protecting themselves. With help from Northwestern University, these Chicago-area community organizations also began using data maps to visualize crime and its effects. The Chicago Alliance for Neighborhood Safety (CANS), a consortium of local community groups, had been using maps to show how community development investment in Chicago varied from community to community, and how some communities were shortchanged compared to others.

Finding the maps useful for this purpose, the community organizations wanted to use crime data in the same way. With political support from the late Mayor Harold Washington, they hammered out an agreement with Police Superintendent Fred Rice to receive tapes from the city's mainframe computer containing basic offense data. Even though the data were often over a month old,[1] they helped the community organizations understand what was happening within their communities. CANS created maps from the tapes, first using Apple II computers and later Macintosh computers, that provided a means of integrating different types of data: the location of various crimes, community data such as abandoned buildings and taverns, and more static geographic data such as schools and parks — that is, the contextual milieu of the criminal activity. Each different type of crime was represented on the map with a different symbol or icon. Although users of the maps were not highly skilled in data analysis, they could easily determine patterns related to location. Thus, a successful information system had been created, taking different types of data, combining and analyzing them, and producing output of practical use.

Subsequently, the University of Illinois at Chicago, which had initiated a mapping project of its own, joined forces with these three organizations and obtained a grant from the U.S. National Institute of Justice to evaluate the effectiveness of crime mapping with respect to crime prevention and control (Mapping Crime in Its Community Setting, Grant No. 86-IJ-CX-0074). Through the grant from NIJ, and an accompanying one from the Apple Corporation for hardware and software, the project began to take shape.

Although the Chicago Police Department was the grantee, the project director was an academic (MDM), and all four entities — a police department, two universities, and a consortium of community organizations — were effectively equal partners. It was (and still is) quite unusual for a police department to work directly and on an equal basis with community organizations, some of which had in the past been confrontational with the police. Not only did this arrangement work, but it produced some results that are still worthy of being replicated. One of the main reasons for the project's unique configuration was that, although the police were the custodians of the data, the ones with the most experience in using crime data on maps were the community organizations.

It was decided to implement the project in one police district, District 25. One of the authors (Buslik), then a tactical officer in this district, was assigned by District Commander Mathias Casey to work with the other three organizations on a day-to-day basis. It soon became clear that the standard evaluation that the academics on the team had envisioned — taking stale crime data and seeing if mapping would illuminate patterns in the data — was not going to go over well with this district commander. He had current problems and wanted to use the mapping system to help him immediately and with current data. Therefore, a system was developed whereby his officers would enter the previous day's Uniform Crime Reports Part I offense activity into the computer every morning, by hand.[2]

This is when we ran up against the limitations of the hardware and, more acutely, the software. Computer mapping was then truly in its infancy. None existed for PCs, which had very limited graphics capability at the time. The mapping that was available for the Mac, while of great utility for real estate and business purposes (the applications for which it was developed), had severe limitations. For one, it did not automatically geocode the data: placement on the map of icons representing events had to be done manually, which just delayed the process — but not as much as the earlier delay that the community organizations experienced when the crime data came from the mainframe. For the experimental project, the district commander provided CANS with a diskette every few days, containing the district's criminal activity,[3] and CANS staff and interns placed the icons on the maps.

Despite the patchwork nature of the project, it produced some findings that are still worth underscoring, primarily because some of the current realizations of police computer mapping projects do not seem to take advantage of them. They can be summarized under the following rubrics: institutional memory, power to the people, and cognitive data analysis (Maltz et al., 1991).

Institutional Memory

Police officers who have spent a great deal of time on their beats often feel that they know their beats pretty well — who the bad actors are, what to watch out for, how and when things happen. What is more likely the case is that they know what goes on only during their specific tours of duty. An officer who works during the days sees a different set of activity and actors than does an officer employed evenings or on the graveyard shift. Moreover, on busy beats only half of the activity may be handled by the beat officer, who may be dispatched to assist in a neighboring beat and whose beat also may be covered at times by neighboring officers. So no one single person really knows what's going on in a beat.[4]

Detective activity is even further compartmentalized, since detectives may not deal directly with beat officers (and robbery detectives may not even deal with burglary or narcotics detectives). Much investigative and arrest activity, therefore, is hidden from the view of the officers who supposedly "own" the beat. Therefore, it is often the case that the only place where a person can get an overview of all activity on a beat is on a computer-based map; it serves as the *institutional memory* for the beat. The map provides beat officers with a convenient way to see what happened during the time they were not there.

Power to the People

Information is power, perhaps more so in police work than in other spheres of activity; and the "people," in this case, are those closest to the street who can benefit most directly from this power. In most police departments, information processing was developed for the managers, who have the authority to allocate resources. But it is the beat officer who needs detailed current information about beat activity, and the map provides it in a way that is readily assimilable.[5]

The word "people" also refers to members of community organizations, who also have a need to know what is happening in their neighborhoods and when and where it is happening — and who can provide the police with detailed information about the context of the activity. In fact, this sharing of information leads to "data fusion," whereby information from disparate sources is combined to aid in developing patterns and relationships in the data. Data fusion confirmed the value of the "co-production" of public safety through an improved relationship between the police and the community they serve. This information exchange led to a greater openness and facilitated the development of problem-solving strategies.

"People" also refers to the district commander, who before the project began could only base deployment of personnel on statistics that were at best weeks old, by which time new crime patterns had emerged. With the advent of the computer mapping system, all this changed. Current information, in a form more usable than merely a list of crimes, dates, and addresses, was made available to the district commander, permitting him to allocate patrol resources more rationally. Instead of waiting for the patterns to emerge, this "proactive management" permitted the commander to nip incipient patterns and trends in the bud. Moreover, he took this information, often in the form of maps, to the community and enlisted their support in providing the contextual information to supplement the police information.

Cognitive Data Analysis

Inferring patterns from data is usually left to the "experts," the statisticians who deal with data professionally. But it was our opinion that the true experts were not the data manipulators so much as those who knew the local scene. Statisticians are very helpful in spotting *known* patterns, and finding them in data when they repeat. But if there happens to be a rash of commercial burglaries where the mode of entry is through the roof, it really isn't necessary to program the computer to recognize this "pattern." If all such unique patterns were programmed into the computer, so that it would search for them all the time, the computer would very quickly become filled with algorithms that were no longer of any use.

A canny analyst, on the other hand, doesn't need a computer to analyze the data so much as he or she needs to present the data in a form suitable for pulling out patterns — which is exactly what crime maps excel at. We called this "cognitive data analysis" to distinguish it from statistical data analysis, and in recognition of the fact that the most useful "computer" for such analyses is the non-linear computing device behind the analyst's eyes. The addition to the map of symbols representing parks, schools, abandoned buildings, railroads, and highways facilitates the task of inferring patterns, while a computer would have difficulty in including these features in an algorithm.[6] Our goal was to use the computer not as an "autopilot," wherein the computer algorithm make the analytic decisions, but as "power steering," where the analyst chooses what data to analyze and how to analyze them.

Other Mapping Efforts

The Chicago project was the forerunner of the NIJ Drug Market Analysis Program (Maltz, 1995), some of whose projects are described in this volume. It was also contemporaneous with mapping activity in other Chicago-area (mostly suburban) police departments, implemented by the Illinois Criminal Justice Information Authority, during which time the map-based statistical program STAC (Spatial and Temporal Analysis of Crime) was developed and refined (C.R. Block, 1995). Coupled with a subsequent federally sponsored mapping project aimed at gang-related violence (Rewers and Green, 1995), and a community-based crime mapping project in the neighborhood of Loyola University of Chicago (R. Block, 1995), the foundation was laid for the CPD's ambitious ICAM project — the technical arm of its citywide community policing program, CAPS (Rich, 1996).

The CPD's community policing initiative, the Chicago Alternative Policing Strategy (CAPS) program, was pilot tested in 1993 in five police districts, and has now been implemented throughout the city (Rich, 1996; Chicago Community Policing Evaluation Consortium [CCPEC], 1995). More than most other community policing programs, it relies on computerized mapping through its Information Collection for Automated Mapping (ICAM) system. The mapping system has been specifically designed for ease of use, so that officers who have little experience with computer software can produce maps showing different kinds of activity for different periods of time at the beat, sector, or district level — all according to the officers' needs. Different overlays — vacant buildings, schools, establishments with liquor licenses, locations of Chicago Transit Authority "el" stops — can be put on the maps.

As described in the example at the start of this chapter, beat officers routinely call up maps and print them out. No keyboard entry is needed; this was a requirement put on ICAM by the deputy superintendent in charge of CAPS. Officers can specify the area, the time interval, the types of incidents to be displayed, and the overlays to be included merely by manipulating and clicking the computer mouse. Furthermore, these maps are routinely presented to community groups by the officers when they meet with the groups. Whereas in the past the primary contacts between community organizations and police were made by the district commander or the neighborhood relations sergeant, under CAPS the responsibility has been shifted to the patrol officers.

Moreover, one of the primary goals of this system is, in the words of the CPD superintendent of police, to "provide community members with up-to-date statistical information to help them in identifying and targeting problems" (Rodriguez, 1993). So ICAM was specifically designed to not only support the beat officer, but the neighborhood residents as well. The ICAM system is still in the process of being improved (i.e., ICAM II), and is being evaluated by the CCPEC as part of the overall CAPS evaluation (CCPEC, 1995). Although the evaluation is not complete, at this point it appears that the ICAM system is providing police officers with the information they need to patrol and plan more effectively, and residents with the information they need to gain an understanding of crime problems in their communities. In fact, there are plans to increase public access to crime maps by making them accessible to residents at public information kiosks throughout the city and on the Internet.

However, the use of ICAM has not been without problems. While assigned to patrol districts, one of the authors observed deficiencies in its use, as has the ICAM project development team leader, Sgt. Jon Lewin. Perhaps because both are rather enthusiastic believers in this use of technology, they were surprised and perplexed that it was not being used by the average police officer to a greater extent. Officers were encouraged to use ICAM in thinking about what was happening in their particular venue and in preparation for the community beat meetings. But most merely printed out a map of their beat and make it available to residents.

Why was ICAM not so readily assimilated into the officers' regular activities? Lewin believes that even though ICAM became a good source for information about what was taking place in terms of incident data, most officers felt that they didn't have enough information for the system to be useful to them in "policing" their beat, and believed that it was "just a map" (Lewin and Morrison, 1995). Perhaps training is the problem: Although every officer was shown how to produce the information and most are adept at using the system (in great part due to its ease of operation), there has been no real training in how to use the information. While certainly more intuitive than a typical listing of incidents, even this tool should be supported by some guidance as to its utility. Pattern development with even a trained eye is not easy (Ruiz, 1996). The range of experiences and skills in a police force makes assumptions as to an officer's ability to effectively use any tool suspect. All police recruits know how to drive a car, yet due to a variety of backgrounds, high speed driving is taught from a beginning level to all officers. The same should apply to the use of maps and other information tools as well. As the department has recognized these needs, changes have been made. With a recent police department written directive on the patrol officer's specific duties in providing community-based policing, the utilization of the ICAM maps and reports has been explicitly established. This will partially answer the question of what to do with this information.

The next generation of ICAM (tentatively called "ICAM2") is planned to address both the issues of quantity and quality. Under the category of "citizen information," the current ICAM products will be generated along with information on cleared crimes. This will provide the missing back-end to incidents and answer the question, "what did the police do after the report was made?" Under the menu selection "Crime Conditions," which will be available only for police officer use, both short- (weekly up to several months) and long-term (up to a year) trends can be developed. To make ICAM more useful as an analysis tool, training will address two levels of police user: the general field patrol officer and the specialist analysis officer. Additionally, problem-solving features are being tested, including the ability to generate "hot spots" by offense type and location using criteria set by the user. From this, the ICAM development team foresees that once field officers see what is available beyond the basic map and statistics, they will want to use all the features to better arm themselves in providing service to the community.

While other police departments are also providing maps to the public, many do not show the details but rather an average offense rate for an area. And many also do not show current maps. In our opinion, the more information (and the more detailed the information) given citizens, the better, as Tufte (1983) has also argued. Residents can do more with maps that depict specific incidents — that show, for example, that a specific bar or fast food outlet is surrounded by many incidents — than they can with a choropleth map indicating that Beat 105 has 16.8% more robberies per year (but why per year — why not per resident or per business?) than Beat 106.

INFORMATION POLICY CHOICES IN POLICE DEPARTMENTS

From the above descriptions, it should be clear that restructuring the organization of information is an important aspect of the CPD's community policing initiative, and should be so in any community policing program. What information is provided; to whom; in what form; and with what delay are all important features of an information system. The CPD has addressed these issues by developing an information system that provides (a) detailed crime incident information (b) to patrol officers and community organizations as well as to supervisors (c) in map form with ancillary lists describing the incidents (d) within a day or two of the incident report's filing.

But this is not the norm; many departments maintain a centralized approach to mapping and information management, providing maps for the most part to the command staff and not to those who work the street, let alone to community organization. And even these maps are often choropleth maps rather than incident maps, used primarily for resource allocation and not for crime pattern analysis. Moreover, the maps often summarize a month's worth of data, and so are not very useful in tracking crime patterns that are often transitory. In such departments, information tends to flow from the lower levels of the hierarchy to the middle or highest levels of the organization and eventually resides in a centralized database; it does not flow back to the lower levels to provide the patrol officer with information he or she needs. Centralization of the information in a single database is certainly useful, permitting the integration of data from all sources, but it does not have to be at the expense of getting information back out to the field. When this occurs, many street-level decisions may be made in an information vacuum.

One of the key elements of problem-oriented policing is the greater inclusion of the individual officer in the formal decision-making process. In order to do this, he or she must have access to some of the same information as management personnel. Thus, we need to have a new definition of "management information systems," one in which the beat officer is recognized as an information manager, a client of the information system, at a new level of decision making.

In virtually all realizations of community policing, street officers require more (and different) information because they are responsible for more of their environment. To support them in this responsibility, police departments must recognize that their information systems must change. This does not mean that the information systems need be decentralized; what it does mean is that access to that information must be distributed throughout the organization, since local decisions require local information.

The information needs of the operational level become redefined as we change the locus of decision making in a police agency. Processing of the data must be done in a manner that supports the kind of questions that are asked of the data. When crime data are seen only at the upper levels of the hierarchy, there is too much for managers to comprehend and the data must be summarized. This means that decisions are made in terms of resources provided to districts. However, when crime data are seen at the beat level and cover relatively short periods of time, there are sufficiently small numbers of crimes so that they need not be summarized. This means that beat officers can focus on individual crimes, crime patterns, or offenders. One of the ancillary benefits of an information system geared to the beat officer is that the input data can be expected to improve. As officers realize that the information they provide is of use to them, and they can see the results of their reports ending up on maps that they themselves use, we expect that they will improve the quality of their reports.

The most controversial aspect of the CPD's ICAM project is not just its provision of (very detailed) crime information to the public, but its *institutionalization* of providing this information. Many police departments are concerned about this, and it may be a mixed blessing. Different departments have different relationships with community organizations. Moreover, different community organizations may react differently to police-provided information. Some may see it as useful and are inclined to work with the police cooperatively, others may use it against the police, and still others may try to hide it so the true state of affairs is not known to the public at large. Yet in order for community policing to work, it is axiomatic that decentralization of the dissemination of information must take place, and this requires police departments to think hard about the way they deal with information.

The opinions expressed herein are those of the authors and do not necessarily express those of the Chicago Police Department, the University of Illinois at Chicago, or the U.S. Department of Justice.

NOTES

1. At that time, District Commanders had essentially two sources of data on crime: monthly statistical breakouts of the districts' activity, unavailable until weeks after the month ended; and 24-hour activity reports — daily compilations of incidents occurring over the past 24 hours, prepared at 6 a.m. (using a typewriter) based on a manual review of incident reports.

2. This was done at virtually no labor cost. Since the district commander was already provided with a typed "24-hour activity report" every morning, all we did was arrange to have the report typed into the Macintosh computer, and make sure that the form we provided on the Mac to enter the data would also generate this report.

3. For the purposes of maintaining an acceptable level of confidentiality while at the same time providing useful data, the last two digits of the address were excised.

4. This set of circumstances is being addressed in the CPD's community policing implementation (Chicago Alternative Policing Strategy, or CAPS) by having patrol officers handle virtually all the incidents on their beats, so as to develop their own feel for the beats.

5. Of course, during the project not all officers appreciated the maps. Many saw them as superfluous, because they "knew" their beats. Others saw them as just another form from the top that they had to deal with, and there were doubtless others who were simply "spatially challenged" when it came to reading maps.

6. This raises the question of whether expert system, neural net, or artificial intelligence approaches would provide a better means of inferring

patterns from such spatial data. We doubt it; these approaches may be very useful when trying to look for patterns of, for example, a disease, where the essential aspects of the disease manifest themselves in different cases in similar ways. This is not the case in crime analysis, unfortunately, because each burglar may have a radically different modus operandi (MO). Training a computer algorithm to recognize burglary patterns from the MOs of burglars 1 through 99 will probably not be of much benefit in having it recognize burglar 100. In other words, to a computer analyst a "pattern" is a condition to be diagnosed (like jaundice) while to a burglary detective a "pattern" is not so much a condition (like burglary) but an MO that relates to a specific offender.

REFERENCES

Block, C.R. (1995). "STAC Hot-Spot Areas: A Statistical Tool for Law Enforcement Decisions." In: C.R. Block, M. Dabdoub and S. Fregly (eds.), *Crime Analysis Through Computer Mapping*. Washington, DC: Police Executive Research Forum.

Block, R. (1995). "Spatial Analysis in the Evaluation of the 'CAPS' Community Policing Program in Chicago." In: C.R. Block, M. Dabdoub and S. Fregly (eds.), *Crime Analysis Through Computer Mapping*. Washington, DC: Police Executive Research Forum.

Chicago Community Policing Evaluation Consortium (1995). "Community Policing in Chicago, Year Two: An Interim Report." Chicago, IL: Illinois Criminal Justice Information Authority.

Lewin, J. and K. Morrison (1995). "Use of Mapping to Support Community-Level Police Decision Making." In: C.R. Block, M. Dabdoub and S. Fregly (eds.), *Crime Analysis Through Computer Mapping*. Washington, DC: Police Executive Research Forum.

Maltz, M.D. (1995). "Crime Mapping and the Drug Market Analysis Program (DMAP)." In: C.R. Block, M. Dabdoub and S. Fregly (eds.), *Crime Analysis Through Computer Mapping*. Washington, DC: Police Executive Research Forum.

—— A.C. Gordon and W. Friedman (1991). *Mapping Crime in Its Community Setting: Event Geography Analysis*. New York, NY: Springer-Verlag.

Rewers, R.F. and L. Green (1995). "The Chicago Area Four Geo-Archive: An Information Foundation for Community Policing." In: C.R Block, M. Dabdoub and S. Fregly (eds.), *Crime Analysis Through Computer Mapping*. Washington, DC: Police Executive Research Forum.

Rich, T.F. (1995). *The Use of Computerized Mapping in Crime Control and Prevention Programs.* Research in Action. Washington, DC: U.S. National Institute of Justice.

—— (1996). *The Chicago Police Department's ICAM Program: A Program Focus.* Cambridge, MA: Abt Associates.

Rodriguez, M.L. (1993). *Together We Can.* Chicago, IL: Chicago Police Department.

Ruiz, M. (1996). "Health Statistics Mapping Software." *Geo Info Systems* 6(6):52-55.

Tufte, E.R. (1983). *The Visual Display of Quantitative Information.* Cheshire, CT: Graphics Press.

CRIME MAPPING IN POLICE DEPARTMENTS: THE CHALLENGES OF BUILDING A MAPPING SYSTEM

by

Lorraine Green Mazerolle
University of Cincinnati

Charles Bellucci
and
Frank Gajewski
Jersey City Police Department

Abstract: *This paper identifies the challenges facing police departments that seek to implement computerized crime mapping systems. The first part of the paper highlights the importance of police departments identifying primary "end-users" and then designing systems that accomplish the tasks specific to the needs of their end-users. Data transfer, geocoding, data integration, system customization, and confidentiality issues are discussed. The second part of the paper illustrates the practicalities of implementing geographic mapping systems drawing from our experiences with the Drug Market Analysis Program. We profile the Jersey City, NJ crime mapping system to highlight some of the*

Address correspondence to: Lorraine Green Mazerolle, Division of Criminal Justice, University of Cincinnati, PO Box 210389, Cincinnati, OH 45221-0389 (e-mail lorraine.Mazerolle@uc.edu).

difficulties encountered in implementing a computerized crime mapping system for street-level use. The paper concludes that police departments planning to implement computer crime mapping capabilities need to think carefully about who, what, where, when and how the system will be used and then design the system data sources and interfaces accordingly.

INTRODUCTION

Mapping crime in police departments has emerged as a popular means to display, analyze, and understand the distribution of crime problems (see McEwen and Taxman, 1995; Maltz et. al., 1991; Rich, 1995). Crime analysts and police department planners use computerized maps to examine crime trends, identify emerging crime patterns, and present graphic representations of crime data to management, line officers, and the community. Street-level problem-solving officers use computerized crime mapping capabilities to map out the locations of specific crime problems on their beat, search the regularity of locations where a suspect is arrested, and display patterns of crime activity at the local level.

For many types of inquiries, crime analysts and street problem-solvers need similar computerized crime mapping systems: they both merge Census data and land use data (such as percent of residential properties versus business properties) with police calls, arrests, and field investigations. Crime analysts and problem-solvers also use computer maps to identify emerging patterns of crime activity. In many ways, however, crime analysts and street-level problem-solvers demand different types of inquiry systems for their different purposes. Crime analysts typically create thematic maps that help them to analyze the distribution of crimes against important population, land use, and household data at the Census-tract level. By contrast, street-level problem-solvers typically create point maps that plot the exact locations of arrests, for example, against specific types of environmental characteristics such as the locations of bars, pay phones, and video arcades on a beat.

This paper examines the challenges that confront police departments in designing and implementing computerized crime-mapping capabilities. The paper begins by identifying some of the factors that police departments need to consider when they decide to build a crime mapping system. We contrast the different needs of crime analysts and street-level problem-solvers, the needs of rural versus city police departments, and the capabilities of mainframe versus personal computer (PC)-based mapping systems. The second part of the paper discusses the specific challenges confronting departments that plan to implement PC-based crime mapping systems. In the third section we profile the Jersey City (NJ) Drug Market Analysis System as an example of a PC-based computerized mapping system that was designed and implemented for operational use by street-level problem-solving officers.

DIFFERENT SYSTEMS FOR DIFFERENT PURPOSES

Crime mapping systems provide police departments with a powerful tool with which to examine a vast array of data. Police data (arrests, calls for service, and crime incidents) can be mapped with Census data and any other information for which an address is available (e.g., bars, fast-food locations, pay phones). While the opportunity to map crime appeals to many police agencies, the practicalities of purchasing, installing, customizing, and using crime mapping systems are far from straightforward. Moreover, without having a clear picture of who (in the department) is going to use the system, many enthusiastic ventures into crime mapping end up as frustrating experiences that fail to live up to early expectations. We propose that different police agencies need different types of crime mapping systems. Moreover, even *within* a police agency, different police functions will most likely demand different types of applications. Consistent with this proposition, we examine several factors that police agencies may want to consider in building their crime mapping systems.

Mapping Systems for Crime Analysts and Problem-Solvers

In this section we identify and discuss two primary crime mapping system "end-users": crime analysts and street-level problem-solvers.[1] These end-users have different interests and functions within the police organization. As such, their respective demands of a crime mapping system can be divergent. This section contrasts some demands of crime mapping systems that are typical from crime analysts and street-level problem-solving officers.

Computerized crime maps provide crime analysts and departmental planners with a means to spatially relate crime conditions, patterns, and trends. For example, an analyst can search for places where high levels of crime correlate with relatively low levels of patrol assignments. Patterns can be explored within a mapping system by searching places with elevated levels of crime against patrol deployment patterns across temporal dimensions. Trends can be uncovered by using past patterns to predict the locations of emerging hot spots of crime.

Graphic presentations of search findings provide a powerful medium to communicate conditions, patterns, and trends, often creating an avenue for analysts to bring about significant policy changes. In Jersey City, for example, computerized crime mapping capabilities have been used by departmental planners to develop beat boundaries and to help match community service officers with particular ethnic and racial neighborhoods. In another project, the Jersey City Police Department crime mapping system was used to merge crime data with neighborhood characteristics. Boundaries were created to match Census data with police data aggregated to the beat level of analysis. In this project, workload data were merged with indicators of crime (such as emergency calls and arrests) and then mapped along with Census data showing population densities, proportions of youths by district, and other community-level factors that correlated with high or low work loads. Using these maps, the police department embarked upon a restructuring project that precipitated widespread changes to the organizational structure and function of the department.

While police department planners and crime analysts are typically interested in using computerized crime mapping systems to answer broad-based policy questions, street-level problem-solvers use crime mapping to answer different types of questions. Street officers still require mapping tools to examine conditions, patterns and trends in crime problems, but the units of inquiry and their data needs are often quite different from crime analysts' demands. For example, street-level officers tend to explore crime maps to identify the environmental features that are consistent with different types of problems. Bars are often found to be focal points for open-air drug sales (Eck, 1994; Roncek and Maier, 1991; Weisburd and Green, 1994); assault and robbery problems tend to occur along main throughways and, in particular, near bus stops; and prostitution problems are often found along main throughways. Knowing the unique distributions of crime problems for specific categories of crime is critical for street-level problem-solving officers.

While crime mapping systems can be used by both street-level officers and citywide crime analysts, many police departments customize their inquiry system to meet the specific demands of one group over another. For example, crime analysts will typically demand a mapping system that can routinize the creation of thematic maps describing the changing patterns of crime across the city over the last six months. By contrast, beat officers will typically demand that their mapping system help them to pinpoint crime patterns for specific categories of crime. For example, the Jersey City Violent Crimes Unit used their mapping system to identify robbery incident patterns over a two-week period when they suspected that one particular group was involved in a spate of crimes.

A mapping system designed to routinize thematic maps using six-monthly or yearly blocks of data will frustrate a beat officer asking very different questions and needing more specific time-frame data. Therefore, we suggest that police departments need to identify the primary end-user from the outset, and then prioritize the customization of crime mapping systems accordingly.

Rural, Suburban and City Crime Mapping Systems

Crime mapping systems will be used differently depending on whether the police department is a rural, suburban, or city department. Rural departments face very different crime problems than suburban and city jurisdictions. As such, crime mapping systems need to be customized around the types of questions that are most pertinent to particular departments. For example, rural departments may want to search for a stretch of road where most traffic infringements are given against the locations of traffic accidents by time of day and day of week. By contrast, city departments may want to search for drug-selling clusters or pinpoint the exact locations of robberies by bus stop locations.

The geocoding challenges of rural, suburban, and city departments are also quite different. For rural departments, pinpointing the exact location of an incident may be impossible for many incidents due to vague location descriptions within the data, as well as the existence of roads that do not exist in the map files. Therefore, thematic mapping may be more pertinent at the block-group level of analysis for rural departments. By contrast, pinpointing crime locations and identifying clusters of crime activity (hot spots) will be highly relevant for city and possibly suburban departments.

Over all, finding solutions to geocoding problems and developing customized mapping systems are very different processes for city, rural, and suburban police departments. Therefore, a crime mapping system that may be useful for a city agency may have limited relevance for a suburban department and even less applicability for a rural department.

Different Platforms

Some police departments have purchased sophisticated mapping systems (such as ArcInfo) that run off UNIX or VAX systems. Others have purchased less expensive mapping software (such as MapInfo and Atlas) that can be easily installed and run off PCs. While software is available that allows for easy conversion of files back and forth between different platforms (e.g., ArcLink), police departments need from the outset to make up-front commitments regarding which platform they wish to "house" their mapping system. The following issues are raised regularly while police department are choosing between different mapping platforms:

(1) *Cost*: PC mapping software such as MapInfo, ArcView or Atlas are considerably cheaper than mainframe mapping software systems such as ArcInfo.

(2) *Training*: PC mapping software such as MapInfo is generally regarded as requiring considerably less training than mainframe software such as ArcInfo. ArcInfo systems are often dependent on specialized computer personnel to produce maps, whereas MapInfo requires a shorter learning curve and less start-up expertise to produce useful maps.

(3) *Capabilities*: One question often raised by police departments centers on the relative capabilities of different mapping software. While most police departments tend to underutilize their system capabilities, ArcInfo generally provides more analytic capabilities than MapInfo. However, for thematic mapping and basic crime analysis in police departments, PC mapping systems will provide most of the capabilities needed by police.

(4) *Technical Support*: One question that is raised by many police department personnel is access to (or lack of) technical support. Police departments need to talk with other departments that have recently purchased similar software to ensure that they will have adequate access to technical assistance.

PC MAPPING SYSTEMS: THE CHALLENGES

The power of computerized crime mapping is the ability to draw from and organize a vast array of data in a form that can be quickly digested and understood. Graphic presentation of various types of information on a map allows the user to easily convey a story. However, many police departments become frustrated when they attempt to implement crime mapping systems. This section surveys some of the typical problems encountered by departments in their efforts to implement PC computer mapping systems.

Real Time Versus Archive Data

One technological challenge facing police departments interested in crime mapping is making call, arrest, incident, and other routine sources of police data accessible to the police on a "real-time" basis. As emergency calls are logged, arrest reports typed and investigations recorded, line officers need access to these data. Failure to integrate these data with mapping systems on a real-time basis can lead to officers developing negative opinions of crime mapping systems and perceptions that the systems cannot aid in their problem-solving activities. (See a later section for a discussion of this issue.)

One solution to a demand for "real-time" police data is applying global positioning systems (GPS) technology to policing. This involves installation of receivers in moving vehicles,[2] on people,[3] or on animals[4] that then transmit information to satellites that pinpoint the position of the receiver at routine or specific points in time. Satellite information is then transmitted to a computer terminal (PC or mainframe) that then uses the real-time data to track the locations of the moving objects.

In policing, GPS systems could be used[5] to track police vehicle locations periodically throughout a shift, relay arrest locations, identify arrival times at crime scenes, track police responses to emergency calls for service, or pinpoint the locations of police vehicles closest to an emergency call for service. The obvious problem with GPS technology applied to policing, however, is the specter of surveillance by supervisors over line officers (also see Sorensen, this volume).

Data Transfer

Many police departments have opted to purchase and install PC mapping systems. One of the first challenges confronting police departments that have invested in these systems is the retrieval of police data. The problem is that police department data are often stored on UNIX or VAX systems. While the transfer of these data is relatively straightforward,[6] modifications to the main system interfaces are generally necessary to facilitate easy transfer of the data into the PC environment. For example, system managers often need to install a menu option and programming routine to retrieve sets of data (by crime type and time period), size the retrieved data sets, and then save the data as transferable ASCII files.

Geocoding

Police departments generally confront many problems in merging police data with computer maps. Even when data transfer problems are solved, police data often comes in a form that is difficult to clean and prepare for mapping. While most police computer-aided dispatch (CAD) systems contain "geofiles" (master lists of addresses linked to a location identifier) that are designed to automatically check and prompt call-takers to enter addresses accurately, incoming police data must still be processed (or geocoded) within the mapping system to enable cases to be mapped. Those departments that do not have address-checking procedures set up at the call-taking stage confront numerous cleaning and geocoding problems when they bring the data into the mapping environment.

There are many ways that police departments can improve their geocoding "hit" rates. Methods to improve the integrity of incoming data include training call-takers, blocking incorrect addresses from entry to the system until they have been checked against the geofile, implementing E-911 systems that automatically record the location of the emergency call,[7] regularly updating geofiles, and making geofiles fit the format of the mapping system street files.[8] Other ways to enhance the geocode rate of incoming data are to write routine cleaning programs to process incoming data before geocoding is attempted, and to permanently alter street files to match the form of incoming police department data. One final way to increase the geocode rate of police data is to purchase mapping utilities that attempt to geocode data to a range of alternatives, and then provide "out files" to identify the final match that was made (e.g., MapMarker). Overall, the time taken to retrieve, download, clean, and geocode police data presents challenges for implementing street-level mapping systems whose users often demand real-time data for problem-solving activities.

Managing Data Files

Another challenge for those implementing PC crime mapping systems relates to developing procedures for managing large and evolving data files. PC crime mapping systems have to be set up in a way that provides system managers with automated and routine procedures that allow for accurate, convenient, and easy methods to: clean incoming data; append new data to master data files; re-index files; purge old data; and allow room on PC environments to store large amounts of data. Investments in automating these procedures at the start of building a crime mapping system will increase the integrity of the data used in the system for street-level problem-solving officers.

Customizing the System

Over the last five years, PC mapping software companies have introduced more user-friendly, windows-based mapping systems that offer easier and more sophisticated inquiry options than older, DOS versions. However, police departments need to either hire outside consultants or develop in-house expertise to take advantage of the programming options of the software to allow users to customize mapping environments, and to allow officers to easily access data and conduct common types of inquiries. The easier the access to system queries, the more often officers will use the system for problem-solving activities.

Personalizing the System

Once a mapping system is customized, another challenge to police departments is to build mapping systems that allow officers to introduce new, idiosyncratic data and personalize existing data. For example, some beat officers collect data on the home or business addresses of community members who are cooperative with their problem-solving activities. Others collect information about, and monitor the locations of, vacant lots, abandoned buildings, and other types of environmental factors that they believe contribute to emerging crime problems. These types of data need to be readily accessible to beat officers, and system enhancements must be routinely made to allow for new, idiosyncratic and personalized data to be integrated into the main mapping system.

Documentation

The need for careful documentation on the uses, available data, and typical search routines included in a customized crime mapping system is not usually regarded as a priority for departments building crime mapping systems. However, careful documentation of a mapping system can greatly enhance its use and provide access to it by a greater number of people.

Confidentiality

The confidentiality of maps that pinpoint crime locations is an area of concern that is typically neglected in discussions regarding the development of crime mapping systems.[9] Anytime data are mappable to the address-level of analysis, police departments need to concern themselves with issues of confidentiality. For example, police need to proceed with caution when creating maps that reveal addresses of community members who facilitate problem-solving activities; home addresses of people that have been contacted, but not arrested, in the field; or locations of people calling the police about particularly sensitive crime problems. The problems of confidentiality cannot be easily resolved. Beyond setting up password protections and creating search and query options that block the display of some particularly sensitive fields, police departments need to think carefully about circulating maps that may raise confidentiality concerns.

In sum, building computerized crime mapping systems requires a considerable amount of forethought and planning to ensure both the integrity of the system and its long term usability. Ideally, police departments should consider building in-house skills for system design, creation, and management rather than relying on external consultants. Initial investments in police department personnel will allow departments to develop their systems over time, resolve data problems as they arise, and keep abreast of new technological advances as they emerge.

THE JERSEY CITY DRUG MARKET ANALYSIS SYSTEM: THE PRACTICE OF BUILDING A PC MAPPING SYSTEM

In 1989, the U.S. National Institute of Justice (NIJ) funded five cities (Jersey City, Kansas City, Pittsburgh, Hartford, and San Diego) to be part of the Drug Market Analysis Program (DMAP). DMAP comprised three broad objectives: to develop a systematic process for identifying drug markets (see Weisburd and Green, 1994); to develop a computerized crime mapping system for operational drug enforcement purposes; and to develop, implement, and evaluate an innovative enforcement strategy targeting street-level drug markets (see Weisburd and Green, 1995). This section examines the second objective of the Jersey City DMAP: building a computerized crime mapping system that was developed as an operational tool for the project.

Building the DMA System

The DMA computer system was envisioned as an independent micro-computer network to be linked to the main computer system in Jersey City through a complex set of mini/micro computer interfaces. The configuration utilized the department's CAD system minicomputers that acted as host servers for seven 386 PCs: one at each of the four police districts located throughout the city, two at the narcotics unit (one for the experimental team and one for the control team) and one at the Center for Crime Prevention Studies at Rutgers University in Newark. The mini-computers were capable of storing data files in MS-DOS format, which assured compatibility with the remote PCs. All PCs were remotely linked to the mini computers via 9600-baud modems utilizing dedicated telephone lines, except for the Rutgers University link that used a 2400-baud call guard dial-up modem with a password and call back feature for security reasons. The DMA system used FoxPro for database management and MapInfo (for DOS) for geographic data analysis.

One of the first major problems encountered was the accuracy of the street files supplied by MapInfo. While MapInfo correctly states that its Topologically Integrated Geographic Encoding and Referencing (TIGER) files are 85% accurate (or better), there was no way of telling which street coordinates were inaccurate or missing. To identify inaccurate location information, we created a database with all the street addresses and intersections in the jurisdiction and then geocoded call and arrest databases in MapInfo. The unmatched locations were then checked and corrected. In Jersey City, the police department's geofiles along with databases from other city agencies (Traffic Engineering and the Department of Urban Research and Design) allowed for accurate construction and checking of all addresses in Jersey City. We also spent time driving the streets of Jersey City and checking the addresses on new streets and on some segments that consistently generated unmatchable addresses during geocoding attempts. With these early efforts to correct the map files we estimate that the Jersey City map files are now about 99% correct.

In the early stages of DMAP, it became apparent that the police department's investigation and arrest data would present a problem for geocoding in MapInfo. The Electronic Data Processing (EDP) Unit keyed arrest and investigation information into a Local Area Network (LAN) system directly from hard copy reports. Since EDP's needs for

these data concerned only Uniform Crime Reports reporting requirements, exact location information was not a priority. Therefore, location information was not standardized, nor was it even considered
important. We identified thousands of common names, variations on
street extensions, and other idiosyncratic ways of entering incident
locations.

Initially, we thought that implementation of the new Management
Information System (MIS) would supersede the LAN system of recording arrest and investigation data. Unfortunately, the department
was unable to install the MIS during the operational period of DMAP,
and we were compelled to correct the problems of the local area network reporting system to gather arrest and investigation data.

To overcome this problem, we wrote a series of programs to
"parse-out" location information. These data were then matched to a
master street name file or a common place name file. Locations that
were unable to be corrected ultimately had to be reviewed one at a
time and manually adjusted. Needless to say, this was a very time
consuming and tedious task. Initially, locations were successfully
geocoded in about 40% of cases. After running through the "cleaning
programs," the match rate reached 85%. Finally, after manually correcting the incoming data, over 90% of the arrest and investigation
data were geocoded. At times, a 96% match rate was possible. At the
same time, a training program was undertaken to impress upon EDP
personnel the importance of entering location data in a correct and
standardized way. Afterward, the geocode match rate improved substantially.

The CAD data were less complicated. With the geofiles integrated
with the CAD system, the match rate for the call data was generally
98%. The two percent errors occurred when the Communication Bureau's call-takers "forced" location information into the system, even
though the CAD geofile indicated that the address was not valid.

One of the problems that plagued the DMAP was the lack of ability
to transfer arrest and investigation in a timely manner. For the operational component of the DMAP, the lag time in transferring data
seriously undermined the perceived worth of the system (see a later
section for further discussion of this issue). EDP was responsible for
keying information into the LAN system after receiving the hard copies from the various divisions and units throughout the department.
The hard copies were prepared by these units and then reviewed by
clerical personnel before being delivered to the EDP. This initial process took about five days. It took another two days for EDP to key the
information into the LAN. By this time, the data were already seven

days behind. Moreover, the design of the LAN databases made it difficult to download data for DMAP purposes on a daily basis. The central problem revolved around the lack of assigning a case control number to individual records. To guard against downloading duplicate records, we had to wait until the tenth of each month before retrieving the prior month's data. This resulted in the DMA system regularly being at least one month behind in arrest and investigation records.

A second problem emerged when we tried to update data on the DMA system. After the data were retrieved, cleaned, and formatted to fit the DMA system file structures, the master data files had to be updated on a routine basis with new, incoming data. Once again, this required human intervention and time scheduling to ensure data integrity in updating master files.

Experiences with the Jersey City DMA System

The Jersey City DMA system was designed to be an operational tool for the narcotics detectives responsible for carrying out the DMAP experiment (see Weisburd and Green, 1995). For 20 years before the start of the DMAP experiment, the Jersey City Police Department narcotics squad had used traditional drug enforcement tactics to tackle the drug problem in the city. These tactics included surveillances, arrests, search warrants and "street pops." The information that the narcotics squad had about drug activity in the city derived primarily from personal observations, common knowledge about "hot" drug locations, and information gleaned from background checks that could be done manually from the Bureau of Criminal Intelligence suspect files. The detectives tended to think about their jobs in terms of the number of people they could arrest. They spent their time cruising popular drug spots, making arrests, and figuring out ways to get at middle-level suppliers. In this way, narcotics detectives thought of their jobs in a suspect- or people-oriented way rather than in a place- or community-oriented way.

From the very beginning of the DMAP in Jersey City, we wanted to develop a computerized crime mapping system that would become an operational tool for narcotics detectives during the experimental phase of the project. The experimental team of narcotics detectives were to follow a stepwise problem-solving strategy to control drug activity at their allocated drug hot spots (see Weisburd and Green, 1995). The crime mapping system was an important information tool to help them analyze drug activity in their designated hot spots.

The first step taken to design the Jersey City DMA system was to interview every member of the narcotics squad. We asked detectives for their ideas in developing an inquiry system that would help them to control drug market activity. When we examined the detectives' responses, their requests clearly fell into three categories. First, detectives provided logistical requests about the computer system. For example, they requested that the system not be locked up overnight, and indicated that up-to-date information was essential.

Second, detectives wanted the DMA system to allow them to make various types of "suspect-specific" requests. They wanted to review suspects' prior arrest histories, car registration details, vehicle type preferences, social security numbers, employment histories, and aliases and nicknames. Detectives also needed information on whether suspects had registered firearms and names of co-offenders. They also wanted to be able to search for names of people meeting particular profiles.

Finally, several detectives wanted the DMA system to allow for "place-specific" requests. While clearly in the minority of requests compared to person-specific requests, some detectives wanted the system to help them identify the hours of operation at drug markets, the common methods of sales, the type of drugs sold, and the physical layout of a specific drug market area. They also wanted the DMA system to provide general information about the types of clientele who frequented particular drug markets and to generate lists of places where suspects had been known to sell or buy drugs.

Detectives could easily list the types of inquiries that they wanted to generate about a suspect. Most detectives could identify five or six "wish-list" items relating to the types of suspect information they wanted to build into the DMA system. By contrast, when it came to listing information needs about a place, detectives were not so clear about the sorts of information they might need. For example, detectives did not request that the DMA system provide information about community members who might help them to clean up drug problem areas, nor did they request information about block watch groups or other community organizations in a problem area. They also did not request information about other agencies working in problem areas that they could coordinate their enforcement efforts with.

The difficulty that detectives had in thinking of place-specific and community-related information derived from one central issue: in the past detectives had been driven by informal department policy that rewarded those who made the most arrests. From the detectives' point of view, getting specific information about particular suspects was going to facilitate their work in the short term much more than general place-specific information that could facilitate their problem-solving activities. From the detectives' perspective, working in non-traditional ways to reduce the level of drug activity at problem places was not going to give them visibility or maintain their arrest quotas. Moreover, narcotics detectives in Jersey City felt that non-traditional drug control tactics that decreased their monthly arrest rates would subsequently reduce their overtime payments. These structural factors severely limited our efforts to impress upon the detectives the worth of problem-solving activities.

The DMA system was designed by the Jersey City Police Department and by staff from the Center for Crime Prevention Studies at Rutgers University. The system was driven entirely by the DOS version of MapInfo, with Mapcode applications written to customize inquiry options.[10] The DMA system was programmed by Lieutenant Charlie Bellucci of the Jersey City Police Department, and was built around a series of custom-designed, pull-down menus that provided a series of search facilities designed to focus detectives on activities within drug market boundaries (see appendix). Our system provided an inquiry system that was designed to make users think about drug problems and possible solutions from a geographic perspective. For example, the system would prompt users for a drug market number, zoom on the market and then allow users to display counts of calls and arrests. DMA system users could request searches by market, police district, or for the entire city on the locations of suspects by age, race, gender, aliases, or crime involvements. For each drug market, users could search for information on the type of drug sold, the times of most activity (for arrests or calls), and the hottest corner inside a drug market.

The DMA system allowed detectives to identify the exact locations of drug market activity. It also allowed them to examine the proximity of drug markets to other places of interest such as bars, schools and highway exits, and to undertake inquiries about arrest histories, citizen complaints and social characteristics of drug markets. The detectives could build custom-designed maps of areas of interest where stores, schools and community group locations could be highlighted on the maps, and print out hard copies of maps of any portion of Jersey City.

Before the start of the DMAP, every narcotics detective participated in a series of DMA system training sessions. In groups of three or four, every detective received hands-on training that taught the basics of turning on a computer and the steps involved in each DMA system module. Many detectives had no experience with computers, and a handful were excited to have the computer age brought to their work environment; others were more skeptical.

To generate at least a base-level of expertise in the DMA system, we initiated a "specialist program" where one detective in each squad self-selected themselves to become the "computer expert" for the squad. In the past, a squad member was designated the "surveillance man," the "sweep man," or the person who generated informants. Selecting one member of the squad to learn the features of the computer system fit well with past task specializations within each squad.

The Jersey City DMA system included several important features. For example, the system was built to be "police proof." Lieutenant Bellucci, understanding the frustrations that narcotics detectives would go through in learning the way the system worked, created a "reset data" feature that allowed a detective who had "zapped" all data from the system to regain control over the computer, reset all the data and maps to the default setting, and begin the search procedure again.

Since the inception of the Jersey City DMA system, problems arose in keeping data up-to-date. This difficulty proved to be a significant drawback for the operational dimension of the DMA experiment, leading to many frustrations among narcotics squad detectives. Although the DMA system allowed detectives to search for suspects, they felt that the geographic overlay of the system merely "cluttered" their inquiries. For example, one detective stated, "We only need to get information about the [suspects]... why are you making me look at this map?" Another commented, "Why do I need to use this map? I know where every street in the city is already." Yet another said, "I can't really see the point of the map — we go where the action is and that means tracking down a suspect, not looking at a map." Apart from highlighting the difficulties of introducing computer technology into police operational units, these comments illustrate the frustrations felt by detectives in changing the focus of their mode of operation. The Jersey City DMA experiment sought to change detectives' activities from being arrest-oriented to being more focused on the problems of a place. The DMA system was the tool of a new approach for controlling drug problems in specific hot spots. As such, the new "tool" was seen as symbolic of change and became a focal point of detective resistance to implementing problem-solving approaches to controlling drug problems.

During the course of the experiment, however, some detectives came to appreciate the system. Some officers offered suggestions as to how the DMA system could be improved. Some of the specific requests from the narcotics officers for DMA system enhancements included adding more custom information to the maps, such as drawing the directions of one-way streets; identifying whether a particular street was one or two lanes; and drawing buildings of choice on the maps.

DMA System Usage

We conducted two surveys, in May and December 1992, of narcotics detectives in Jersey City to determine the usage level and perceptions of the DMA system. A selection of the results appears in Table 1.

Table 1: DMA System Usage

Selected Response	Wave 1 May, 1992 N = 28	Wave 2 December, 1992 N = 29
Never use computer?	10	1
Use it several times a week?	8	12
Use it everyday?	3	3
Used before going out on shift?	11	10
Used to check market boundaries?	12	7
Used to check specific addresses?	10	13
Used to gather information on suspects?	11	24
Print out maps?	2	6
Satisfied with the DMA system?	10	19
Need up-to-date data?	2	10

Table 1 suggests that the DMA system served an important function during the project, at least for some of the detectives. The level of use increased between the first survey, conducted two months after the start of the experiment, and the second survey, undertaken eight months after the initiation of DMAP. The DMA system was both used more frequently and seen as more helpful as the experiment proceeded. At the start of the experiment, ten officers never used the computer system. By December, only one detective claimed to never use the computer. It was disappointing, however, to note that by December 1992 only six persons were actively printing out maps. This result is most likely because across the six squads of officers, only one person received in-depth training on the DMA system.

Nineteen officers were satisfied with the DMA system by December, compared to only ten in May. An increase, however, was seen in the number of detectives who used the DMA system to gather information about suspects — from 11 detectives in May to 24 by December. There are two possible explanations for this increase: the detectives became more suspect-oriented, or they simply found the information helpful. Based on our monitoring of the DMA experiment activities (see Weisburd and Green, 1995), it is suggested that the latter proposition is the more likely.

Over all, these results are consistent with our field observations of the narcotics detectives' activities during the course of the DMA experiment. One of the biggest hurdles that we had to overcome during the DMA project in Jersey City was coercing narcotics detectives to think more in terms of targeting and cleaning up drug hot spots rather than "bouncing" around the city and targeting the people involved in the drug trade. The DMA system provided a constant reminder and an inquiry tool that encouraged narcotics detectives to think about the problems associated with drug hot spots and the patterns of drug activity within market boundaries. This was in stark contrast to the way they had previously thought about the drug problem in Jersey City.

CONCLUSION

Building a computerized mapping system in police departments presents many challenges. The first challenge concerns the decision whether to build a mapping system for crime analysts and police department planners, or to invest resources into building a tool for street-level problem-solving officers. While there is overlap in the system needs of both "user-groups," many system demands, including data needs and types of inquiries, will be different for these two different end purposes. As such, police departments need to decide where they want to invest their energies and then build their mapping systems accordingly.

A second challenge concerns the ability of police departments to integrate PC mapping capabilities within mainframe computing environments. This requires investments to build links between the storage systems at the mainframe level with the data requirements for mapping purposes. Some problems include timely download capabilities; building "blocks" in the system to guard against overlapping downloading; and building PC protocols to accept, clean, and append new, incoming data with the existing master files at the PC level. Automatic cleaning, appending, archiving and re-indexing are essential features that must be created to ensure the integrity of the data being mapped.

Building custom menus that are user-friendly and that enable officers to undertake searches and inquiries that fit with their problem-solving activities is a third challenge to police departments contemplating building crime mapping systems for street-level use. Common types of inquiries, that can be easily built, must fit with the types of information that line officers need to facilitate their problem-solving efforts. Custom-built systems must accommodate changes from time to time and be adaptable across a range of problem-solving efforts. For example, detectives in a violent crimes unit need to make different types of inquiries of a mapping system than narcotics detectives.[11] Similarly, a beat officer is interested in undertaking searches of quite a different kind from either narcotics detectives or violent crime squad detectives.

Computerized mapping systems have a lot to offer police departments. Whether a police department chooses to implement PC-based crime mapping capabilities for street-level use or to develop more thematic mapping capabilities for crime analysis or policy planning purposes, graphic presentation of crime data provides a means to identify, analyze and communicate problems, priorities and plans in a quick and easy manner. The power of mapping crime, however, is greatly enhanced when police departments invest resources in planning, pilot testing, and solving logistical problems from the outset.

This paper was supported under awards 90-IJ-CX-K004 and 91-MU-CX-K005 from the National Institute of Justice, U.S. Department of Justice. Points of view in this document are those of the authors and do not necessarily represent the official position of the U.S. Department of Justice.

NOTES

1. There are many other end-users in a police department. For example, specialized detectives will have different demands than street-level problem-solvers; housing unit officers demand a different type of analytic capability than detectives; and district captains are interested in different types of maps compared to headquarters planners.

2. Taxicabs are being fitted with GPS to locate them when a driver is in danger; cars are being fitted with GPS to locate them if they are stolen); and the MacMahon Productivity Monitoring System in Australia is using GPS to track and monitor payloads in earth-moving vehicles.

3. Proposals have been put forth to install GPS receivers rather than electronic monitoring devices on parolees.

4. An application that won the GPS world application of the year was tracking sheep around Chernobyl to determine radiation levels.

5. GPS are currently being pilot tested in several jurisdictions. One department on Cape Cod, MA, for example, is testing a GPS.

6. Some of the problems encountered in building a link between a mainframe system and a PC include: installing the software on the mainframe to create files that may be downloaded, building the physical connection between the PC and mainframe, installing "dial-up" software that is compatible with the mainframe system, and creating data files in the PC-database form that "fit" the records downloaded from the mainframe system.

7. E-911 systems enhance the integrity of the location from where the call is made. However, it does not help to enhance the integrity of the dispatch location (or the location where the event is occurring) if this location is different from the call location.

8. For example, ensure that the geofile and the street files record addresses in the same way (e.g., Ave not Av; E Third Street and not E 3rd or Third Street E).

9. Two important exceptions include an NIJ-sponsored conference held in May 1994, and the NIJ Center for Crime Mapping roundtable discussions in February 1997, where the issue of confidentiality in mapping was the topic of roundtable discussions.

10. The mapping capabilities of MapInfo have evolved tremendously since the original DMA system was created. For instance, MapInfo no longer supports, to any great extent, the DOS version of MapInfo. Instead, it now focuses its support on the Windows-based mapping environment, which includes many features that were unavailable at the time the DOS version of the Jersey City DMA system was created.

11. Since the conclusion of the DMAP experiment in Jersey City, NIJ has funded two additional projects in Jersey City that build upon our experience with implementing computerized crime mapping capabilities at the street level. First, NIJ funded a problem-oriented policing project with the Violent Crimes Squad. As with the DMA project, we built an inquiry system to facilitate their problem solving efforts. One of the interesting features of this new system was the aggregation of data within the violent crime places to enable detectives to "assess" the changes in calls and arrests over the life course of a problem "case." This process follows very closely the recommendations of Eck and Spelman (1987) in their plea for officers to be more sophisticated in their assessment phase of the SARA problem solving model. Second, NIJ recently funded a project to tackle drug and violent crime problems in public housing. This project aims to build a mapping system that allows for apartments and common areas to be systematically linked to police department data.

REFERENCES

Eck, J. (1994). Drug Markets and Drug Places: A Case Control Study of the Spatial Structure of Illicit Drug Dealing. Doctoral dissertation, University of Maryland, College Park.

—— and W. Spelman (1987). *Problem Solving: Problem Oriented Policing in Newport News*. Washington, DC: Police Executive Research Forum and U.S. National Institute of Justice.

Maltz, M., A. Gordon and W. Friedman (1991). *Mapping Crime in Its Community Setting: Event Geography Analysis*. New York, NY: Springer-Verlag.

McEwen, J.T. and F.S. Taxman (1995). "Applications of Computer Mapping to Police Operations." In: J.E. Eck and D. Weisburd (eds.), *Crime and Place*. Crime Prevention Studies, vol. 4. Monsey, NY: Criminal Justice Press.

Rich, T. (1995). *The Use of Computerized Mapping in Crime Control and Prevention Programs*. Research in Action (July). Washington, DC: U.S. National Institute of Justice.

Roncek, D. and P. Maier (1991). "Bars, Blocks and Crimes Revisited: Linking the Theory of Routine Activities to the Empiricism of 'Hot Spots.'" *Criminology* 29(4):725-754.

Weisburd, D. and L. Green (1995). "Policing Drug Hot Spots: Findings from the Jersey City DMA Experiment." *Justice Quarterly* 12(4):711-735.

—— (1994). "Defining the Drug Market: The Case of the Jersey City DMA System." In: D.L. MacKenzie and C. Uchida (eds.), *Drugs and Crime: Evaluating Public Policy Initiatives*. Thousand Oaks, CA: Sage.

APPENDIX:
The Jersey City Drug Market Analysis System Menus

Main Menu

Drug_mkt
Count
Search
Info_map
View
Magnify
Zoom User
Reset Data

Inquiry Options

Drug_Mkt	Enter the drug market number

Count	Provides an aggregate count of narcotics arrests and calls occurring within the drug market boundary

Search		
	Find Addr	Enter the address you want to locate
	Make Fltr	Enter the details of a person or place that you want to get information on Some of the search options include: first name, last name, nick name, age, sex, race, location type, drug type, time of day, day of week.
	Delete Fltr	Remove the filter that was created for a special search.
	Arrest	Display the (purple) arrests on the map
	Calls	Display the (green) calls on the map
	Streets	Display the (white) street lines on the map
	Report — Arrest	Display the full arrest reports for people arrested at the defined arrest location.
	Calls	Display the full CAD system call reports for calls made about the defined location.

Options for Building a Crackdown Map

Info_Map	Boundary	Label the map with the market boundary number or district name.
	Point	Label an arrest point with the arrestee's last name.
	Street	Label a street.
	Address	Label the address range on a street.
	Clear Labels	Clear all the labels that you put on the map.
	Image Clear	Clear all the labels that you put on the map.

View Options

View		
	City	Click on here and you will see a map of the whole city.
	North	Click on here and you will see a map of the North District.
	East	Click on here and you will see a map of the East District.
	South	Click on here and you will see a map of the South District.
	West	Click on here and you will see a map of the West District.
	Magnify	Click on here and the cross hairs will appear so that you can magnify a target area.
	Zoom User	Click on here and you can change the view (measured in inches per mile) to a size that you want.
	Last View	Click on here and the map goes back to the previous size that you had it.
	Redraw	Click on here and you will get a refreshed picture of the map.
	Printer	Click on here and you can print out a copy of your map.

Magnify	Click on here and you can magnify a part of the map to the size that you want.

Zoom User	Click on here and you can change the view (measured in inches per mile) to a particular size

Reset Data	If you zap the data, or do something where you lose all of the information of the map, click on here and it will put it all back for you.

GEOGRAPHIC INFORMATION SYSTEMS AND CRIME ANALYSIS IN BALTIMORE COUNTY, MARYLAND

by

Philip R. Canter

Baltimore County Police Department

Abstract: *Analytic mapping and geographic databases are being increasingly recognized by police departments as an important tool in crime analysis, crime prevention and program evaluation. Improvements in technology, reasonably priced computer-based geographic information systems (GISs), and the availability of geographic data sources make it possible for law enforcement agencies to use analytic mapping. Police departments using automated mapping systems largely rely on attribute data associated with point locations to produce computer pin maps based on a variety or combination of crime event features. GISs can be used as a tool to identify factors contributing to crime, and thus allow police to proactively respond to the situations before they become problematic. This article will explore the use and possibilities of GIS by Baltimore County Police in describing and analyzing crime activity. Examples are included that demonstrate the potential of GIS in analyzing crime, developing interdiction strategies, and evaluating the effectiveness of prevention strategies. As this technology gains greater acceptance and use within police departments, it will become clear that the ability to produce automated pin maps is only one of many possible applications. Ultimately, GIS should be viewed as a tool for which police analysts could obtain a better understanding of criminal activity from a geographic perspective.*

Address correspondence to: Philip R. Canter, Baltimore County Police Department, 400 Kenilworth Drive, Towson, MD 21286.

CRIME ANALYSIS IN BALTIMORE COUNTY, MARYLAND

Baltimore County Police Department's Crime Analysis Unit

The primary objective of Baltimore County's crime analysis unit is to provide information that can make the police department more efficient in carrying out its universal mission: to prevent and suppress crime. Crime analysis influences policy, helps justify budget requests, and assists in identifying or defining a problem for further study. While the purpose of crime analysis in some police agencies can vary, it is generally recognized in Baltimore County that competent analysis provides important input to decision makers.

Baltimore County Police Department created its Crime Analysis Unit in the late 1970s during a time of rapidly escalating crime. The unit's mission was to identify crime patterns (cluster analysis) and trends (time series), relate known suspects to crime incidents (linkage analysis), provide information needed to deploy police resources in response to an identified crime problem, and evaluate the effectiveness of crime prevention/suppression strategies. Since its inception, Baltimore County's Crime Analysis Unit has strongly emphasized case and suspect information.

Data are the foundation of any crime analysis unit. Analysts in Baltimore County developed a special coding form called the Crime Analysis Worksheet to collect information needed to identify attributes associated with criminal incidents. The Crime Analysis Worksheet contains information about the crime such as modus operandi, location of crime, actions taken by an offender to commit the crime, property taken, and suspect/vehicle information. The investigating officer circles the appropriate response to each category on the worksheet, and then forwards along with a copy of the offense report to the Crime Analysis Unit. Police officers are required under Rules and Regulations to complete a Crime Analysis Worksheet for any robbery or burglary in Baltimore County. The crime analysts initially focused on robberies and burglaries because it was believed that either crime would be responsive to a police strategy such as directed patrol, tactical deployment, or surveillance. Eventually the Crime Analysis Worksheet was converted to a bubble scan format, allowing analysts in Baltimore County to add motor vehicle theft and drugs to the crimes analyzed.

Once a Crime Analysis Worksheet is received by an analyst, information contained on the form is checked against police reports associated with the incident and then entered into a computer for subsequent analysis. Because the department's first computer system — an IBM System 3 — was equivalent to a low-end 8088 microcomputer system, the amount of information and type of analyses was limited to pre-designed summary statistical reports with some cross-tabulation of pre-selected categories. Eventually crime analysts were able to use statistical software, spreadsheets, and database management systems as advancements occurred in microcomputers and software.

One method used by crime analysts to determine locations containing a high concentration of incidents is a pin map. Crime locations, usually represented by a pin, are placed on a map containing all of the streets for an area of interest such as a police precinct or a municipality. The size and area of the map used for pin mapping will depend on its scale. Map scale relates and adjusts a mapped distance to the actual geographical distance. The map scale is important because it will determine the area of study, and the relationship between a particular point location such as a street robbery to other geographic features such as a bus stop or shopping center. The map scale also influences an analyst's ability to determine through visual inspection whether the areal distribution of crime constitutes an unusually high concentration of points.

Police analysts in Baltimore County originally used 2,000 scale base maps developed by the Maryland State Highway Administration for their pin mapping. Analysts needed to assemble and join twelve 2,000 scale maps to cover the entire 610-square-mile area of Baltimore County. Each map of the County required 70 square feet of wall space. Any other geographic features of interest, such as police reporting areas, precincts or posts, were drawn by analysts on each countywide map. Since police reporting areas are subdivided police precincts delimited by streets or other geographic features such as railroad tracks or power lines, it was important that the base maps used for pin mapping be continuously updated to reflect changes in land use and development. Consequently, paper base maps were constantly being printed and assembled by police analysts. The process of continually updating these maps was labor intensive given that there are over 1,200 reporting areas in Baltimore County.

Pin maps can be useful in displaying the location of crime for a large geographic area such as a county or police precinct. Some Baltimore County crime analysts have also maintained that the act of reading a report and physically placing a pin on a map helps them to retain information about the crime. As the number of crimes increased in Baltimore County, however, the amount of effort required to manually maintain pin maps became problematic. The ability to accurately place a pin on a map that represented the actual crime location required a considerable amount of effort by the analyst. Obvious limitations associated with manual pin mapping also compromised the geographic accuracy associated with crime locations. In addition, the amount of information associated with a case and represented by a pushpin was limited to a few characteristics, like time of day or modus operandi. Consequently, there was a possibility that an analyst could miss an active crime pattern. Furthermore, the geographic location of an incident represented by a pin on a map is not quantifiable, so analysts were prevented from testing hypotheses about the spatial distribution of crime. Finally, the base maps needed to be constantly updated as new roads or other geographic features in Baltimore County changed over time. It became apparent that county police needed to use a geographic information system to assist in the mapping and analysis of crime.

GEOGRAPHIC INFORMATION SYSTEMS

Geographic information systems (GISs) use computers to represent and analyze spatially related phenomenon. All GISs have two functions: (1) to display maps or geographic features such as crime locations (points), streams (lines), or census tracts (polygons); and (2) to use a database manager that organizes and relates attribute data to various map features. A GIS uses a digital map database to link spatial data to descriptive information.

Several types of matching algorithms enable a GIS to link and maintain spatial relationships between geographic and descriptive information. The ability to link and maintain spatial relationships between data sets defines a GIS. As an example, suppose two data sets exist for a city: number of robberies by reporting area, and population by reporting area. These two data sets can be either mapped individually or combined to show a robbery rate. Now increase the number of data sets from two to six. The number of different map combinations increases to over 60. Increase the number of data sets to 10, and you have over 1,000 possible combinations.

A GIS can combine data using either spatial or tabular file attributes. The ability to combine data collected for different boundary layers addresses a problem analysts often confront: examining relevant data collected by other agencies which, for a variety of reasons, are unable or incapable of matching police geography. One recent example in Baltimore County involved the need for various local government agencies participating in a community conservation program to identify deteriorating urban communities targeted for intervention strategies. Each county agency used either its own geographic unit such as a school district, or census geography such as a tract to collect data used to identify deteriorating urban communities. The different boundary layers used by various county agencies, including reporting areas (police), census tracts (planning), and school districts (education), had to be combined to form a composite layer showing the location of deteriorating communities. Digital map files representing the various boundary layers were already available and used in a countywide GIS, so combining information associated with the different geographic boundaries to form a composite layer was fairly routine. While one has to be cautious about making inferences for small areas based on statistics collected for larger, overlapping geographic areas, the fact remains that most government agencies collect data at different geographic levels and scale. The ability to combine information associated with different geographic boundaries, a process sometimes referred to as "fuzzy" matching, is a powerful descriptive tool.

Geographic Information Systems and Baltimore County Police Department

The location of a crime is an important attribute feature, and is included along with law, offender, and target as a dimension of a criminal event (Brantingham and Brantingham, 1991) . Crime location, and any other geographic information associated with a criminal event, can provide clues about the identity of suspects, assist in the design of prevention or apprehension strategies, aid in the evaluation of programs, and help gain a better understanding of environmental factors that may be associated with crime.

Analysts interested in identifying areas containing a high concentration of crime need to know the location of incidents. As noted earlier, there are several issues associated with manual pin maps that limit their value as an analytical tool. Baltimore County police analysts spent a large amount of time determining the placement of pushpins representing an offense location. As caseload increased analysts became more interested in the number of incidents by reporting area, and not necessarily by point location. Yet, there was a recognition that the point locations, particularly relative to other map features, were an important part of crime analysis. There was a strong need, therefore, to determine the accurate placement of incident locations in a cost-effective and efficient manner.

By the mid-1980s there were several events that moved the Baltimore County Crime Analysis Unit into a microcomputer-based GIS environment. These events included a centralized records management system that allowed crime analysts to download significant amounts of information on crime, such as an incident location represented by a street address and the last known home address of an offender associated with a criminal incident. Other events involved: improvements in microcomputer processing and storage systems needed to use and manipulate large database files; the availability of microcomputer software needed to synthesize and analyze large quantities of data; and cost reductions for computers and peripheral equipment such as printers and plotters. In addition, the redesign of Baltimore County's communication system used for dispatching calls received by the 911 center to police, fire, and emergency medical services was particularly important in influencing Baltimore County police to use a GIS.

Baltimore County's communication system had a number of problems, including limited voice transmission and inaccurate geographic reference tables needed to associate call locations to a dispatch plan. Limited voice transmission would be addressed by broadcasting over a new 800 Mhz system paid for by a voter-approved bond referendum. A problem remained with the geographic reference tables, collectively called a geofile, because attempts to internally maintain these files to reflect changes in land use and new development were too numerous and technically challenging given the equipment and resources available at the time. It was recognized that improvements to the 911 communication system provided an excellent opportunity to improve the geofile used by the computer-aided dispatch (CAD) system.

It was known that the Baltimore Region Metropolitan Planning Organization (MPO) had been maintaining and updating a digital map file for Baltimore County based on the 1980 census GBF/DME file. It became necessary to convince county government to use some of the bond funding for updating or replacing the 911 CAD geofile. This was not an easy task since project costs had already exceeded budgeted amounts. Furthermore, individuals responsible for maintaining the 911 CAD geofile believed that any problems with the file were being exaggerated.

To demonstrate that problems existed in the 911 geofile, a GIS was used to construct a map showing discrepancies between the 911 CAD geofile and the MPO digital map file. The map convincingly showed that streets in the 911 geofile had inaccurate address ranges, and were in many cases assigned to the wrong police reporting area. The map also demonstrated the utility of a GIS. As a result, the MPO was contracted to update the 911 CAD geofile, and to supply quarterly updates reflecting changes in land use and street topology.

One issue associated with digital map files concerns their geographic accuracy; that is, how closely geographic features such as roads or streams represented as x,y coordinates in a digital map file relate to the earth's surface. Since the geofile provided by the MPO was to be used for geographically tracking police cars via an automated vehicle locator (AVL) system, it was important that the file be geographically accurate. A third party vendor, ETAK, was subsequently contracted to adjust and calibrate the digital map files so that they were positionally accurate to within 50 feet. In summary, Baltimore County was not only able to improve the accuracy of its 911/CAD geofile, but was also able to obtain geographically accurate digital map files that could be used by a GSI. The digital map files provided by the MPO not only included maps of all county streets, but also various boundary files such as police reporting areas, zip codes, Census tracts, Census-designated places, Census block groups, and transportation zones. The digital map files and accompanying boundary layers were subsequently exported for use by MapInfo, a GIS selected by Baltimore County police for computer mapping.

The Baltimore County Police Department was the first county agency to use a microcomputer-based GIS. To demonstrate the potential of computer mapping within the department, in conjunction with the MPO police analysts used MapInfo to geocode drug arrest locations coded by drug type and action (sales/possession). The same demonstration maps were included in an application to the Bureau of Justice Assistance's Byrne Memorial Grant Program. The proposal was funded and the department was able to purchase additional hardware and software needed to track and identify drug markets in Baltimore County.

During this time, a number of other county agencies were actively exploring the use of microcomputer-based GISs. With the coordination of Baltimore County's Office of Planning and Zoning, several other county agencies purchased MapInfo for computer mapping. These county agencies entered into a site license agreement with the

MPO to provide quarterly updates to MapInfo mapfiles. The site license purchase agreement allowed county agencies to obtain updated mapfiles at a reasonable cost. It also ensured that geographically coded data used by other agencies were based on the same coordinate system.

Most Baltimore County agencies are now using MapInfo for microcomputer mapping. A County MapInfo Users Group was formed to provide training and assistance in mapping applications. In addition, a newsletter called "MapInformation" is produced quarterly for county agencies using MapInfo. The newsletter contains articles contributed by user group members, as well as suggestions on using computer mapping applications. The introduction of a countywide microcomputer-based GIS has prepared many agencies for an upcoming migration to a wide-area GIS network. Using a RISC-based GIS/RDBMS called ArcInf/ArcInfo and Oracle respectively, county agencies will eventually be able to access and process most geographic information maintained at one location.

Applications of Geographic Information Systems by Baltimore County Police Analysts

GISs have three broad applications: (1) forward data mapping; (2) backward data mapping; and (3) interactive data modeling (Levine and Landis, 1989). The design and respective cost of a GIS will depend on a system's ability to perform each of the three applications. A powerful GIS system will be capable of performing all three operations, while a lower-cost GIS may be strong in forward and backward data mapping, but less capable of performing interactive data modeling. A police department will need to determine how the system is to be used before making a decision as to which system to purchase. For this reason, it is recommended that an agency perform a comprehensive review of user needs and expectations prior to purchasing a GIS.

Forward Data Mapping

A common GIS application involves the ability to map point locations, and to shade areas reflecting the presence and intensity of a variable. Both applications are referred to as "forward data mapping." Forward data mapping is used to map attributes contained in the database files that are linked by a GIS to a geographic location. The process of forward data mapping is analogous to descriptive mapping, since some type of geographic information and its respective attributes are being described on a map. Forward data mapping involving point locations is also referred to as automated pin mapping because maps closely resemble the types of maps used by police analysts for pin mapping. For this reason, most police agencies use a GIS almost exclusively for their forward data-mapping abilities.

Most of the maps produced by crime analysts in Baltimore County, particularly those presented to the community or to police commanders, involve forward data mapping. The maps produced by police analysts show the location of crime represented by one or more case attributes. For example, a robbery location will appear as a triangle, and color coded according to type of location (convenience store, bank, street, etc.). Color intensities associated with each robbery location will vary to represent day or night offenses. Police analysts also have greater flexibility in manipulating mapped data through database commands that select and map information based on user-provided criteria.

The ability to relate attribute data to a geographic location is useful in determining when and where to deploy police resources in response to a particular crime problem. Patrol officers have commented that these types of descriptive maps have been helpful in problem solving and for directed patrol. Police analysts also use forward data mapping to determine the effects that a particular strategy, such as increased police visibility in a community, may have on the number and location of crimes observed over time.

Figure 1 is an example of forward data mapping. Police analysts were confronted with an increase in robberies reported in the Towson area of central Baltimore County during August 1995. An examination of the attributes associated with these robbery cases revealed that a large number involved either a black male or pair of black males using a blue steel automatic handgun. Most of these cases occurred along major arterials, and were close to the city-county line. Based on the location of these robberies, it appeared that major arterials were being used as escape routes and that the offenders were destined for the city. This is usually enough information to: (1) identify the type of problem occurring, (2) determine which locations were victimized by the same offenders, and (3) develop a tactical strategy, in this case resource deployment for use in areas likely to contain target locations and escape routes.

Forward data mapping also allows an analyst to assign attributes associated with a file record and represented geographically by an x,y coordinate pair to a polygon like zip code or Census tract. Once attri-

Figure 1: Robberies Reported in the Towson Area
August, 1995

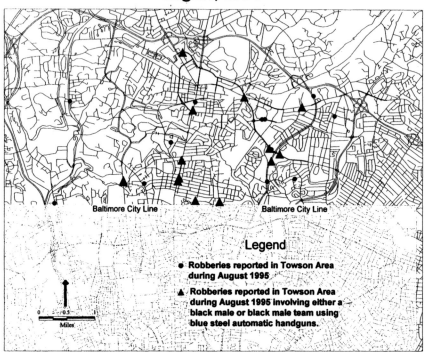

Note: Shows how forward data mapping is used to identify attributes associated with robbery cases in Baltimore County.

butes are associated to a polygon they can be further represented on a map by a color or thematic pattern. For example, communities experiencing a high number of residential burglaries may appear as a bright color compared to a community experiencing a fewer number of cases. A GIS could also use a color corresponding to a range of counts such as all communities containing between 5 and 10 residential burglaries. Police analysts in Baltimore County usually use thematic maps to display information based on a large number of records, such as burglaries over a one-year period or average police response times calculated from over 300,000 CAD data records. While the tactical value of thematic boundary maps may be limited, these types of maps are useful in quickly conveying the frequency and intensity of crime to police precinct commanders and the public.

The ability of a GIS to perform forward data mapping is the most basic of the three applications. Yet, the ability to quickly and accurately show point locations and any attribute data associated with an incident using thematic mapping is a tremendous benefit to a police department. Since computers are being used to manipulate digital data in a computer mapping environment, the analyst can easily instruct a GIS to display information based on pre-determined criteria. The analyst is still required, however, to make conclusions about the information being displayed, and any interpretations will be based on the analyst's subjective judgment.

Forward data mapping will allow an analyst to display all robbery locations on a computer map, but it will not identify for the analyst areas constituting a high concentration of incidents. The analyst will intuitively identify areas containing a high number of robberies based on a visual inspection of the map in a manner similar to that used with pin maps. Nevertheless, the obvious difference between manual pin mapping and a GIS from a forward data mapping perspective includes: improved accuracy in identifying the location of incidents such as crime; the ability to associate and display multiple attributes to any given incident location; the ability to quickly display information using a variety of medium (such as acetate transparencies for overheads, different-size paper, or a computer screen); the ability to display mapped information at different scales; and the reduced time and concomitant reduction in operating costs resulting from having a computer rather than an analyst construct a map.

Backward Data Mapping

Backward data mapping differs primarily from forward data mapping in that selection criteria used to construct a map are based on geographic, rather than tabular, information. In forward data mapping, an analyst will rely on the attribute information to determine how incidents are to be displayed. In backward data mapping, an analyst will have a GIS display information based on the relationship between an incident's location and geography. An analyst, for example, may believe that a high concentration of robberies are determined by incidents located within one half-mile of one other. The GIS would first determine the geographic location of each robbery, and then compute the distance from one robbery location to all other robbery locations. After this operation is performed for all such locations, a map would display only those robbery cases whose closest neighboring robbery location was within a half-mile. The result would be a map displaying a group of cases constituting a high concentration of robberies based on the distance criteria provided by an analyst.

As in forward data mapping, points representing discrete crime locations can be aggregated to a polygon and then thematically mapped. In backward data mapping, a GIS can be used to determine the size of each polygon such as acres or square miles to compute a crime density for each polygon. One polygon, for example, may have more incidents than a neighboring polygon, but it also may be twice as large in land area. A crime density map would allow an analyst to consider the effect a polygon's size may have on the number of incidents. Polygons with small areas and a higher number of incidents may require more attention than a larger polygon with the same number of incidents.

Backward data mapping is the first step in gaining a better understanding of the relationship between crime and geography. The ability to analyze data is enhanced in two ways: first, by associating a map feature such as a road, transit station, or school to an incident location; and second, to relate incident locations to a geographic component, such as longitude and latitude, size, or distance. Rather than relying largely on nominally scaled attribute data, analysts can test hypotheses based on ratio-scaled data such as distance. Backward data mapping is used for spatial analysis such as cluster analysis, quadrat analysis, or nearest neighbor analysis. For this reason, backward data mapping is needed to perform analytical mapping. Backward data mapping also introduces a proactive component to crime analysis by enabling an analyst, for example, to develop models based on relationships between crime and census information; or by marketing crime prevention information to households located in potentially criminally active communities.

Figure 2 shows the distribution of residential burglary incidents occurring within a community located in northwest Baltimore County. Police analysts noted that these cases were occurring within a relatively short time period, involved a particular modus operandi, and were located within close proximity of each other. Analysts concluded that these cases probably involved one or more suspects working together, and that the pattern would likely continue if left unabated. This is an example of how forward data mapping is used to subjectively identify high-crime areas.

Police analysts were interested in using an auto-dialing system to contact and alert households in this community about the burglary problem, and in providing advice to households as to how to prevent their homes from being victimized. A GIS was used to reduce the list of all households in Baltimore County with published phone numbers to only those located within the zip code containing the burglaries. As an example of backward data mapping, police analysts used a GIS to extract published phone numbers for households located within the criminally active area shown in Figure 3.

Figure 2: Residential Burglary Cases in Randallstown Community

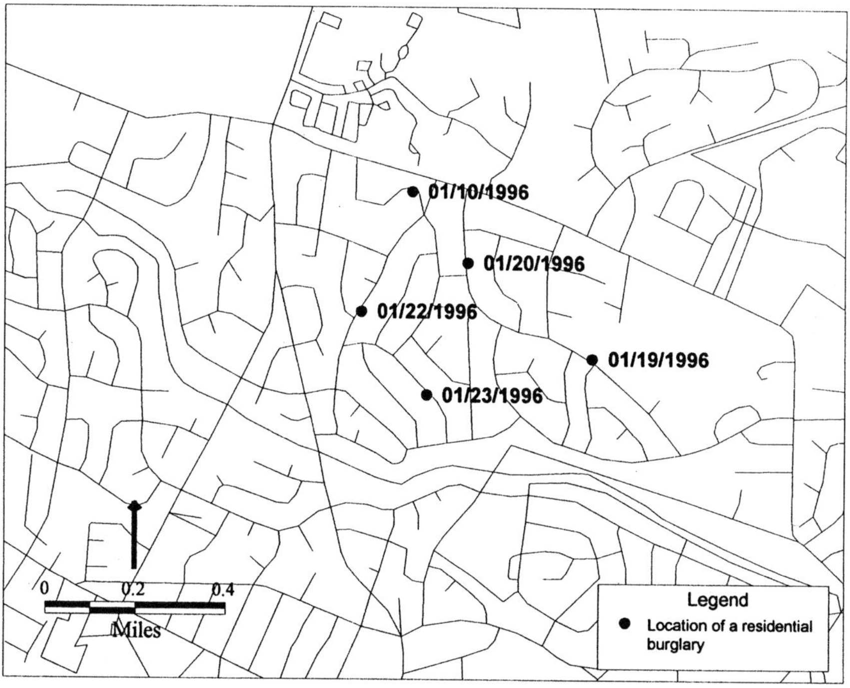

Note: Distribution of residential burglary incidents occurring within a community located in northwest Baltimore County. Police analysts noted these burglaries probably involved one or more suspects working together because the cases were similar.

Figure 3 shows the location of burglaries occurring after the auto-dialing system was used. The additional burglary cases are largely occurring outside of the initial target area, and appear to have been displaced possibly as a result of the auto dialer. At the time, it was

Figure 3: Residential Burglary Cases Before and After Autodialing

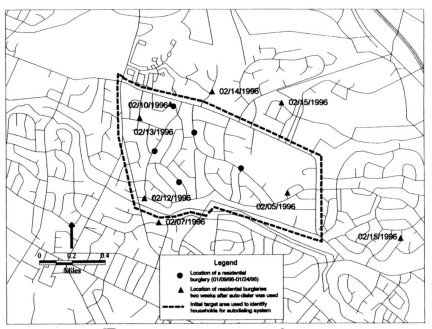

Note: Distribution of residential burglary incidents after the autodialing system was used (02/02/96-02/03/96). Note that the additional burglary cases are largely occurring outside of the initial target area, possible due to a displacement effect.

not known whether this displacement occurred as a result of target hardening, increased vigilance by the community, increased police presence, or the burglary suspect being alerted by the auto dialer because he or she lived within the community. In response to the apparent displacement of burglaries, analysts redefined the target community by expanding the area delimited by a new polygon.

Additional studies of similar situations and applications will determine whether decisions used to define the target community for an auto dialer strategy are accurate. At this time, preliminary findings suggest that some displacement of crime is occurring after a community is targeted by an auto dialer message. It is possible that displacement may be an anticipated reaction by the offender, and that surveillance should be concentrated in areas contiguous to an auto-dialer target community during and immediately after the initial contact period. Most recently, police analysts in anticipating a possible displacement of crime resulting from use of the auto dialer system expanded a target area to include neighboring communities not yet impacted by a residential burglary problem. In the process, one of the people contacted by the auto dialer who had resided in one of the neighboring communities called 911 when noticing two "suspicious" individuals walking down the street. These two individuals were attempting to burglarize a residence in the neighborhood when caught by police.

Interactive Data Modeling

Interactive data modeling involves using a GIS to predict or simulate some phenomenon such as crime. Once models are developed, a GIS can be used to vary and assess conditions influencing expected outcomes. Analysts may have a GIS estimate response times as police post sizes change, or a GIS may be used to determine the number and types of calls for police service given changes in an area's land use. The ability to test and evaluate different simulations can have a significant influence on police operations and policy. Determining, for example, relationships between police response times and the size of a post could influence the number of patrol cars put into service during a shift. Alternatively, changes in land use due to subdivision activity and the concomitant increase in demand for police service may justify a developer impact fee. It is the ability to perform interactive data modeling that makes a GIS such a powerful tool.

Figure 4 is an example of how police analysts in Baltimore County use interactive data modeling to test the effects different boundary realignments have on balancing work load within police posts. Each call for police service is weighted by call type or workload unit, with calls involving a serious offense such as a violent crime assigned a higher value or weight compared to a less serious offense. Weights assigned to each call-for-service record are subsequently summed by reporting area, and then further aggregated into a fixed number of posts for each eight-hour shift. The objective is to balance work load among posts within each precinct, while maintaining adequate response time.

The precinct shown in Figure 4 is Wilkens, located on the southwest side of Baltimore County. There are a total of seven posts or beats assigned to the Wilkens precinct during the midnight shift. Analysts use a redistricting method in MapInfo to create police posts by aggregating a reporting area's work load to form seven districts. Since there are seven posts during this shift, each post should contain approximately 14% of the precinct's total work load. Initially the precinct is considered as one large post containing 100% of the work load equal to 278,131 units. Analysts start by aggregating reporting areas and their respective work load to form the first post. As the first post is being created, the percentage assigned to the first district is reduced by the amount added to the first post. This process continues until all seven posts have been created. Analysts use interactive modeling to add or subtract reporting areas and their respective work load to balance call types among the entire police precinct, while at the same time considering the effect these changes may have on police service to the community.

Most of the interactive data modeling performed by a GIS has occurred in the physical sciences and urban systems. Examples include environmental impact assessments, network modeling, Universal Soil Loss Model, hydrologic models, and land-use suitability modeling. There is a significant amount of interest in interactive data modeling for the social sciences, including the ability to geographically predict crime.

The spatial distribution of crime has been extensively studied over the decades, particularly in respect to either the socioeconomic conditions of neighborhoods in which the criminal lives or a crime occurs (Bursik, 1988; Harries, 1974; Shaw and McKay, 1969). Crime as it relates to the built environment has also received considerable attention, notably through the works of C.R. Jeffery (1971) and Oscar Newman (1972). The development of interactive models to geographically predict crime will likely be influenced by social disorder theories, which use socioeconomic conditions as explanatory factors, combined with information on the environment in which crime occurs. Socioeconomic data is readily available, and the ability to link it to crime and/or arrest locations requires a standard matching procedure used by all GISs. Data on the built environment is routinely collected and used as part of a comprehensive GIS.

Figure 4: Police Posts Based on Workload Assignments by Reporting Area

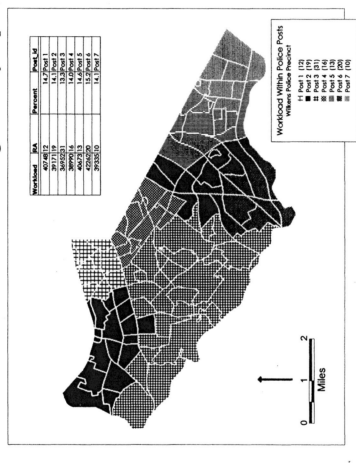

Workload	RA	Percent	Post_Id
40748	12	14.7	Post 1
3917	19	14.1	Post 2
3695	31	13.3	Post 3
3899	16	14.0	Post 4
4067	13	14.6	Post 5
4226	20	15.2	Post 6
3933	10	14.1	Post 7

Workload Within Police Posts
Wilkens Police Precinct

⊦⊣ Post 1 (12)
■ Post 2 (19)
‡‡ Post 3 (31)
▨ Post 4 (16)
▥ Post 5 (13)
▦ Post 6 (20)
▒ Post 7 (10)

0   1   2
Miles

Note: Police use interactive data modeling to test the effects different boundary alignments have on balancing workload within posts. Table at upper right shows Post 1 consists of 12 reporting areas totaling 40,748 workload units or 14.7% of the precinct's workload.

173

While ecological data allude to important social issues such as the possible effects of poverty and unemployment on crime, the problem of spatial contiguity and spatial scale that can influence the outcome of statistical tests cannot be ignored. These problems are further complicated by variant factors like opportunity, behavior, and motivation that influence the occurrence of crime. Interactive data modeling based on tangible variables pertaining to land use or the built environment, in combination with information on an area's socioeconomic-demographic status, will provide a better understanding of crime. Police analysts will eventually be able to: describe what impact land use changes may have on demand for police service in economically depressed areas; determine why some locations are repeatedly victimized; or study the relationship between features such as transit stops or public housing and crime. As analysts gain additional experience with GIS, the opportunity to develop and refine predictive models will increase.

Using Geographic Information Systems for the Spatial Analysis of Crime

Police analysts in Baltimore County, by studying the geographic and temporal dimensions of crime, can gain a better understanding of the environmental factors that may be influencing criminal behavior. Analysts in Baltimore County use information obtained from the spatial analysis of crime to: identify areas that may likely be targeted by an offender; determine whether common attributes exist among a group of reported cases; explore relationships between crime and other geographic features such as land use and the built environment; investigate relationships between criminal residence and ecological data; and study the movement of offenders to predict the location of future targets and to establish interdiction points along escape routes. Police analysts are particularly interested in identifying crime patterns and determining whether these patterns are randomly distributed due to chance, or if there is a tendency for a set of cases to statistically group or cluster. Once an analyst identifies a spatial cluster, information is disseminated to patrol and specialized units for subsequent action.

Spatial Clustering

Police analysts in Baltimore County continually monitor the geographic distribution of crime for the purpose of identifying high-crime areas or "hot spots." A high-crime area is defined by three criteria:

crime frequency, geography and time. These areas contain at least two criminal incidents of the same crime type. Sometimes the crimes have similar characteristics, such as modus operandi or type of weapon, suggesting one or more offenders working together may be responsible for the pattern; other times the only similar characteristic associated with a crime pattern may be the crime type. A high crime activity area is usually small in size, but may become larger the longer a problem continues. In addition, a high-crime area is usually identified as such based on the number of offenses reported over the most recent one- to two-week period. Once a high-crime area is identified, the analyst will continue to monitor the pattern over time until it abates. In some situations, high-crime areas in Baltimore County have continued for several weeks.

One method used by police analysts in Baltimore County to identify a high-crime area is a standard deviational ellipse. The standard deviational ellipse is computed using the Illinois Criminal Justice Authority's Spatial and Temporal Analysis of Crime (STAC). Input includes x,y coordinate pairs for each crime location, a search radius, and a set of parameters used to define the search area. Baltimore County crime analysts compute a search radius based on approximately twice the size of the area per point (Boots and Getis, 1988). Assuming that a map of the search area, or precinct, was overlaid with a square grid, the length of a grid's side would be determined by (2A/N) where A= the size of the search area and N= the number of crimes. The next step would be to circumscribe a circle around a square grid by finding the point at which the diagonals of the square intersect. The diagonals are equal to ([2A/N])/cos 45°), with the radius equal to one-half of a diagonal's length. As an example, suppose a total of 30 burglaries occurred in the Wilkens precinct over a two-week period. The Wilkens precinct has an area equal to 24.79 square miles. The length of a grid's side, (2A/N), would be equal to (49.58/30), or 1.29 miles. The search radius, 0.91 miles, is equal to one-half of a grid's diagonal, or (1.29/cos 45°)/2.

Figure 5 shows standard deviational ellipses for motor vehicle thefts occurring in the Wilkens police precinct during the last two weeks of September 1995. In an attempt to address boundary issues for cases occurring in a neighboring precinct, the search area defined by the STAC's SPACE parameter file overlapped approximately ½ mile into the precinct contiguous to Wilkens. The search radius, 0.63 miles or 3,339 feet, was based on the 62 cases of motor vehicle theft occurring within the study area and the size of the precinct (24.79 square miles). Four ellipses or hot-spot areas were identified and mapped; three of the ellipses were relatively small in area, averaging 0.36 square miles, while the fourth ellipse contained 38 cases in an area of 6.6 square miles. With the possible exception of the second ellipse, a casual examination of the map suggests that the hot-spot areas produced by SPACE and delimited by the standard deviational ellipses do contain a high concentration of cases. There also appears to be some clustering of motor vehicle thefts among the cases contained within the fourth ellipse. The null hypothesis that complete spatial randomness exists for cases located within the fourth ellipse can be tested using a two-dimensional nearest neighbor analysis.

The longitude/latitude coordinates associated with each motor vehicle theft location are first converted to state plane coordinates. These coordinates are used in a spreadsheet as shown in Table 1, with each cell in the spreadsheet containing the distance from one theft location to all other theft locations. Note that the number of cases has been reduced from 38 to 33 because several locations represented by identical coordinates experienced multiple thefts over the two-week period. The coordinates associated with multiple theft locations were subsequently reduced to one coordinate pair since it is the relationship between locations, and not time, which is of interest. Also note that the diagonal shown in the distance matrix, which is the distance between one location and itself, was assigned a high value so that any other nearest neighbor distance wouldn't be excluded. The @MIN function in Lotus 1-2-3 was used to identify the nearest neighbor coordinate and distance, and the @AVG function was used to average the observed nearest neighbor distances. The observed average distance is compared against an expected value of the average nearest neighbor distance for a random sample of points approximated by the formula $(d_I)=0.5(A/N)$ and a standard deviation of $0.0683A/N^2$ (Boots and Getis, 1988). A z-statistic of -2.0, significant at the .025 level (two-tailed test), tends to confirm that the distribution of motor vehicle thefts within the fourth ellipse is not random. The negative z-statistic results from closer-than-expected average nearest neighbor distances, further suggesting that the distribution of motor vehicle cases is clustered.

The nearest neighbor analysis confirmed that the overall distribution of motor vehicle thefts within the fourth ellipse was not randomly distributed. Of particular interest to police, however, is identifying the location of cases that contributed to the apparent clustering effect.

Figure 5: Baltimore County, Maryland Motor Vehicle Thefts in Wilkens Police Precinct Last Two Weeks of September, 1995

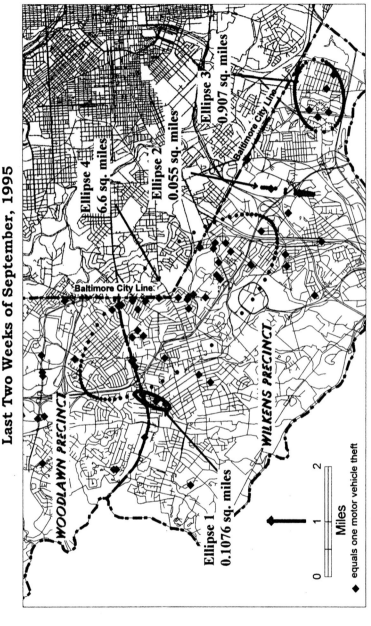

Note: Shows four standard deviation ellipses for motor vehicle thefts. Standard deviational ellipses were developed by STAC available from the Illinois Criminal Justice Information Authority SPACE Analyzer program.

Table 1: Motor Vehicle Thefts in Wilkins State Plane Coordinates

Distance To		ID	1	2	3	33
		YCOORD	517336.0	518309.0	520276.0	531823.0
Distance From		XCOORD	888245.0	885012.0	886280.0	880665.0
ID	YCOORD	XCOORD	1	2	3	33
1	517336	888245	999999.0	3376.2	3536.2	16350.2
2	518309	885012	3376.2	999999.0	2340.3	14195.9
3	520276	886280	3536.2	2340.3	999999.0	12839.8
⋮						
33	531823	880665	16350.2	14195.9	12839.8	999999.0

Note: Longitude/Latitude coordinates translated to Maryland State Plane Coordinates using BLMSPC27 coordinate conversion program. The Pythagorean theorem was used to compute distances from one coordinate pair to all other coordinate pairs.

178

These cluster "cells" are used by police analysts to identify areas targeted for directed patrol, surveillance, and crime prevention. The state plane coordinates used for the two-dimensional nearest neighbor analysis can also be used as input to a statistical clustering program. A cluster analysis procedure detects case groupings based on the closest case distances within a group and the largest distances between groups.

Five clusters, shown in Table 2, were selected using SYSTAT's K-means clustering procedure. Four of the five clusters within the fourth ellipse as well as the area delimited by the third ellipse, were targeted for directed patrol. Figure 6 shows the distribution of motor vehicle theft cases over a two-week period following the directed patrol strategy. The number of motor vehicle thefts dropped by 55%, from 62 cases to 28 cases during the first two weeks of October 1995. Most of the target areas identified during the last two-week period of September 1995 no longer existed during the first two weeks of October. Two notable exceptions, which were identified as hot-spot areas during the first two weeks of October, included additional motor vehicle thefts in an area originally located in ellipse 2, and a growing number of cases within the first cluster cell of the fourth ellipse. It is interesting to note that ellipse 2, while identified by STAC's SPACE program as a hot-spot area during the last two weeks of September, was not originally identified as a target area because it consisted of two cases. The number of cases located around ellipse 2 increased and spread geographically over the following two-week period. Most of the activity formerly located in the cluster cells associated with ellipse 4 ceased, the one exception being cases located in the first cluster cell which continued to occur and spread north of the precinct boundary possibly, as a result of displacement.

Space-Time Interactions

In some situations, police analysts in Baltimore County have noted that multiple offenses involving the same offender have a tendency to occur in the same communities over a relatively short period of time. For this reason a space-time interaction could suggest an association between a group of cases and an offender. In August 1995 a series of robberies began to occur in a 21-square-mile area of Baltimore County. The attributes associated with these cases were similar, but not identical, so it was initially difficult to determine whether the increase in robberies was due to a particular offender. For example, in some cases the robberies were committed by an individual and other times in pairs, there was no apparent type of location preferred, and the days of week varied. The only common case attributes, other than space and time, were race, gender, and type of weapon used by the offender to commit the crime. It was believed that any tendency for cases to cluster over time and space might support the possibility that these crimes were related to a common offender.

Analysts use the Knox method to detect simultaneous clusters in both time and space (Armitage, 1971). Based on known temporal and spatial characteristics of past robberies occurring within the 21-square-mile target area, analysts determined that on average a robbery occurs every one to two days and that the distance between sequentially occurring robberies averaged 10,732 feet, or about 2 miles. Eight robbery cases suspected of being caused by the same offender were paired and tabulated according to adjacency in time and space. The total number of paired cases is equal to $N(N-1)/2$, or 28 cases. Case pairs occurring within two days of one other were identified as being close in time, while those occurring under two miles were counted as close in space. A Poisson distribution was used to test whether the observed frequency differed significantly from a mean equal to the expected frequency. Table 3 shows counts associated with the observed and expected frequencies, as well as the probability associated with observing at least the number appearing in each cell.

Although the probabilities associated with each cell are not considered to be particularly significant, it is interesting to note that frequencies associated with cells close in time had the lowest chance probabilities. In fact, it was later determined that the eight robbery cases were committed by the same offenders.

Spatial Proximity and Diffusion Analysis

Police analysts in Baltimore County are frequently asked to examine relationships between crime and some geographic feature such as a school, transit station, or apartment complex. The ability to relate map features to some dependent variable is called spatial proximity analysis (Garson and Biggs, 1992). It presumes that a relationship exists between the map feature and the dependent variable. For example, Figure 7 shows robbery locations in proximity to a known drug market located in a low-income apartment complex in northwest Baltimore County. The map shows that robberies, as the dependent variable, tended to cluster within and around the drug market area. Police analysts have noted that an increase in street robberies located in and around high-density residential areas tends to correlate with

Table 2: Point Clusters (Motor Vehicle Thefts) Located Within the 4th Standard Deviational Ellipse Using SYSTAT's k-means Program

Summary Statistics for 5 Clusters						
Variable	Between SS	DF	Within SS	DF	F-Ratio	Prob
YCOORD	.494574E +09	4	.652590E +08	28	53.050	0.000
XCOORD	.435254E +09	4	.301599E +08	28	101.021	0.000

Members		Statistics				
Case	Distance	Variable	Minimum	Mean	Maximum	St.Dev.
Cluster Number :1						
19	1971.74	YCOORD	527255.00	529974.00	531823.00	1438.17
20	1037.29	XCOORD	880665.00	881199.50	881818.00	381.47
22	572.49					
26	267.16					
30	659.14					
31	660.37					
32	877.36					
33	1360.97					
Cluster Number: 2						
5	1861.04	YCOORD	521275.00	523516.25	525360.00	1373.23
7	1827.54	XCOORD	880796.00	882256.25	884039.00	993.87
10	613.07					
13	276.16					
14	1191.47					
15	648.41					
16	788.68					
17	1332.91					
Cluster Number: 3						
12	1299.14	YCOORD	523341.00	525004.00	526667.00	1663.00
18	1299.14	XCOORD	874552.00	875333.00	876114.00	781.00
Cluster Number: 4						
1	2636.38	YCOORD	517336.00	520641.75	523269.00	1840.07
2	1964.44	XCOORD	885012.00	886520.75	888245.00	974.56
3	309.62					
4	408.24					
6	1062.48					
8	908.46					
9	925.97					
11	1859.82					
Cluster Number: 5						
21	1135.65	YCOORD	528762.00	529568.29	529890.00	379.49
23	1345.26	XCOORD	875290.00	876836.00	878723.00	1324.25
24	1093.30					
25	666.47					
27	885.00					
28	779.75					
29	715.26					

Figure 6: Baltimore County, Maryland Motor Vehicle Thefts in Wilkens Police Precinct Case Displacement/Relocation

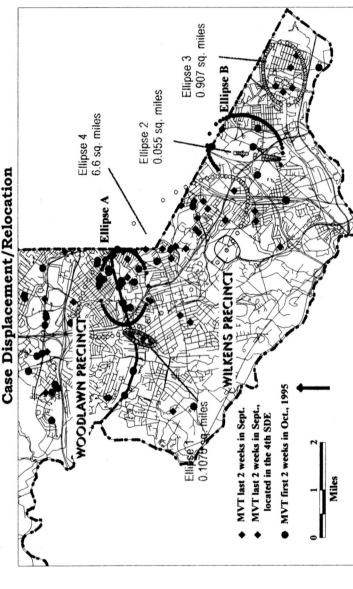

Note: Auto theft cases dropped 55% over a two week period following directed patrol strategy. Note change in the shape of ellipse 2 due to an increase in auto thefts (ellipse B). Also note change in cases near the precinct boundary (ellipse A).

Table 3: Counts Associated with Observed and Expected Frequencies, Along with Probabilities Associated with Observing At Least the Number Appearing In Each Cell

		TIME			
		Close	Not Close	Total	
S	Close	8	3	11	Observed
P		(8.25)	(2.75)		Expected
A		0.139	0.221		Probability
C					
E					
	Not Close	13	4	17	Observed
		(12.75)	(4.25)		Expected
		0.109	0.194		Probability
	Total	21	7	28	

drug activity. In Baltimore County, police analysts use a GIS to establish buffers or polygons around locations having a history of drug activity. Analysts can quickly monitor robberies occurring in and around drug market areas to determine whether a market is becoming active.

Using Geographic Information Systems to Develop Predictive Models: Baltimore County's Spousal Abuse Study (1989)

Between 1980 and 1989 the number of spouse assault cases in Baltimore County was increasing at an average rate of 6% per year, with a 78% increase in the number of spousal assaults per 100,000 people during the same period. In response to a growing number of domestic violence cases, Baltimore County Police started a Spouse Abuse Unit whose responsibilities included the collection of victim and suspect data that enabled police to identify and aggressively prosecute repeat offenders. Using the data collected by the Spouse Abuse Unit, police analysts in Baltimore County conducted a study with two objectives: (1) to identify locations and areas within the county that were experiencing a high number of spousal assault cases, and (2) to develop a model that could be used to identify areas where spouse assault cases were being underreported.

The first objective involved identifying spouse assault locations based on the incident address. Nine police reporting areas were subsequently identified as having a high number of spouse assault cases. A list of attributes including demographic, social, economic, and case information was associated to each area. It was noted that most of the incidents were located in areas with a high unemployment rate and a low median household income. This information was forwarded to precinct commanders for further attention as part of their strategic planning efforts.

The second objective, developing a model to predict areas containing underreported cases, used 76 variables relating to income, employment, housing, population, drugs and alcohol abuse. Information was collected from a variety of sources, including the U.S. Census Bureau, the Baltimore County Department of Economic Development, the Baltimore County Office of Planning and Zoning, and the Baltimore County Office of Substance Abuse. Since most data was available by Census tract, police analysts used a GIS to aggregate point data such as arrests for driving while intoxicated (DWI) to Census tracts. A stepwise regression identified three variables that related to spouse assault: drug-alcohol charges (log), renter population (log), and unemployment rate (log). The three variables accounted for 64% of the variation in the dependent variable, or number of spouse assault victims.

The model produced a list of residuals or differences between the actual number of reported cases and the number expected given the values associated with each independent variable. The residuals were mapped and visually inspected for spatial autocorrelation. Although there was a tendency for residuals to group in areas that were predominantly African-American, a formal test for spatial autocorrelation using Dacey's test for contiguity revealed that the residuals were not spatially autocorrelated. In summary, the model was reliable in predicting Census tracts with a lower-than-expected number of reported spousal assault cases. Once these Census tracts were identified, precinct commanders used their community outreach officers to circulate information to residents about domestic violence.

Using Geographic Information Systems to Develop Crime Rate Denominators

Crime analysts in Baltimore County rely primarily on the number of incidents occurring within a particular area over a given time period to identify high-crime areas. In the process of studying the location of crime over a period of several years, analysts have noted that a small number of communities have a disproportionate number of crime. Upon closer examination, it appears that other factors like environmental risk or opportunity are influencing the number of crimes within these high-crime communities. For example, some po-

Figure 7: Robberies Located in Proximity to Drug Market

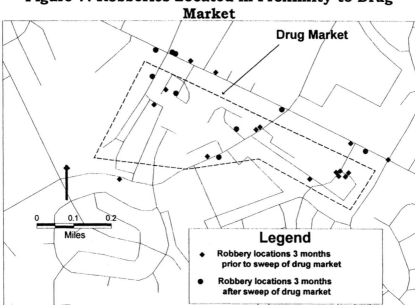

Note: Robbery locations in and around a known drug market area. Analysts have noted increases in robberies as drug activity in emerging markets increases. Note the decrease and apparent displacement of robberies after a sweep of drug market.

lice reporting areas in Baltimore County consistently have a high number of residential burglary cases, but these reporting areas also have a high number of residential dwellings. As expected, there is a strong statistical correlation (0.675, n=524) between the number of residential burglaries and the number of residential dwelling units within Census block groups, suggesting that the number of dwelling units is a direct indicator of residential burglary opportunity. Police analysts in Baltimore County use a crime rate denominator to provide an adjustment for opportunity.

Most of the data used to develop opportunity measures are contained in tabular files collected by other government agencies. Many agencies use a GIS to manipulate and map data contained in these files. For example, Baltimore County Police initially obtained information on the number of dwelling units by Census block from the U.S. Census Bureau's Topologically Integrated Geographic Encoding and Referencing System (TIGER). Census and crime data were subsequently aggregated to Census block groups using a GIS. Baltimore County's Office of Planning and Zoning is required under its Basic Services Legislation to monitor subdivision activity relative to critical services areas, so that the number of dwelling units is constantly updated to reflect changes in land use and growth. In this manner, police analysts have access to an opportunity measure such as the number of dwelling units that is updated and current.

Figure 8 shows two thematic maps of residential burglaries in Baltimore County by Census block group. A natural break method was used to define the five thematic class ranges for each map. The first thematic map shows the number of residential burglaries reported in 1995 by Census block group. A total of 15 Census block groups were classified as having a high number of residential burglaries. Nearly all of these Census blocks were rental developments, having a high percentage of rental units and a high number of dwelling units. For example, each Census block group in Baltimore County has, on average, 537 dwelling units. The 15 Census blocks classified as having a high number of residential burglaries averaged 1,353 dwelling units. Since we know that the number of residential burglaries tends to increase as the number of dwelling units increases, one can see why these 15 Census block groups would have a high number of cases.

The second thematic map was based on a residential burglary rate, or number of residential burglaries per 1,000 dwelling units. Using a natural break method to construct the thematic map revealed only two Census block groups as having a high number of residential burglaries relative to the number of dwelling units. Furthermore, the second map identifies some areas of the county as having a greater-than-expected number of residential burglaries given the number of dwelling units contained within the Census block group. This is apparent in some of the predominantly rural areas of Baltimore County.

Figure 8: Thematic Maps of Residential Burglaries

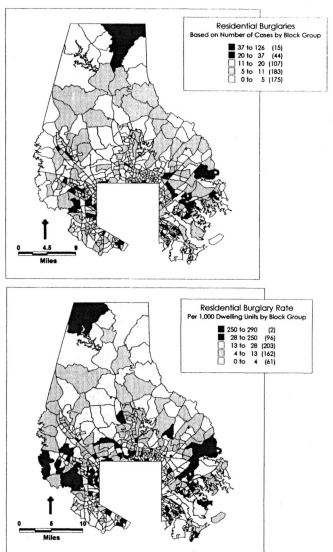

Note: The two thematic maps show the effect a risk measure, such as number of dwelling units, has on pattern and interpretation of a residential burglary problem.

Using a Geographic Information System for Community Policing in Baltimore County

One of the advantages of using a GIS is the ability to use and display large amounts of data. Information appearing on a map can be quickly synthesized and understood by a police officer, police commander, and, perhaps most important, the public. Most community meetings with Baltimore County police now include computer-generated maps of crime, with incident locations represented by colors and symbols corresponding to various types of criminal offenses. Maps can effectively communicate to the public that either a crime problem exists, or reassure a community that a problem may not exist. Overall, these maps are generally well-received by the public, primarily because there are usually significant differences between how the public perceives crime in their community compared to the reported crime displayed on the map.

It is apparent that in addition to other factors that may be contributing to problems in a community, data and information from a variety of government sources are needed by an officer as part of his or her problem-solving efforts. Crime remains an important measure of a community's health and well-being. Crime that is consistent and increases in frequency will negatively effect the viability of a community. Providing timely information about a community's crime problem is needed for a quick and effective response to the problem. Crime information at the community level must be available to police officers, and it must be in a format that can be quickly understood.

Over the last several months the Baltimore County Police Department has tied each of its eight precincts into the crime analysis database. Police officers now have the ability to access information on burglaries, motor vehicle thefts, robberies, drug activity, and field intelligence reports within 24 hours of the incident. Funded by the Maryland Governor's Office on Crime Control and Prevention, the department's Street Level Access Program (SLAP) contains the same databases and computer mapping features used by the crime analysts. Patrol officers can sit at a microcomputer and within one minute produce a map showing crime by precinct, post or community.

The SLAP system also has a report generator and a search utility that were designed by police and precinct commanders involved in community policing. Information about crime trends and patterns are electronically communicated to each precinct by the crime analysis unit, and, in return, field intelligence information on drug activity is communicated from patrol officers to the unit. This information will eventually allow analysts to identify surrogate indicators of drug activity in Baltimore County communities. Eventually, additional data collected by other government agencies will be available to patrol officers through the SLAP system, including the Drug Awareness Warning Network (DAWN), treatment data by Census tract, and other community viability measures.

CONCLUDING REMARKS

Law enforcement agencies have an established history of using innovative technologies to assist in suppressing and preventing crime. A majority of police agencies use computers and information systems for crime analysis and crime investigation. The location of crime and the use of geographic space by offenders are important components of the criminal event. There is, therefore, general agreement that information collected for the purpose of analyzing and identifying crime patterns and trends should include mapped crime locations.

GISs are designed to integrate and view descriptive information about phenomenon such as a crime in a spatial context. The ability of a GIS to map criminal incidents has enabled analysts in Baltimore County to effectively identify areas experiencing high-crime activity. Once high-crime areas are identified, computer mapping assists in the development and evaluation of interdiction strategies. Further, analysts can gain a better understanding of the relationships among crime, target, and offender patterns by relating incidents to geographic criteria. The ability to associate criminal incidents to other spatial information has allowed analysts in Baltimore County to explore a variety of factors influencing crime. Eventually, geographic models based on spatial attributes associated with factors influencing crime will be developed.

The multidisciplinary approach to the geographic study of crime has helped to identify concerns about assumptions used in spatial analysis. One could conclude that more study is required to gain a better understanding of crime within the dimensions of space/place and time. The use of GISs will undoubtedly be an important part of these studies. Theory not withstanding, there are practical applications in having police use GISs to assist in the prevention and suppression of crime. Foremost is the ability to use geographic information to efficiently and effectively allocate police resources.

This chapter is dedicated to the memory of Kai Martensen whose tireless devotion and work in policy and management contributed to the advancement of the police profession nationwide. The Baltimore County Police Department is grateful to Kai for his vision and commitment to professionalism in law enforcement. We believe Kai would be pleased to see the technological advances in geographic information systems and crime analysis.

REFERENCES

Armitage, P. (1971). *Statistical Methods In Medical Research*. New York, NY: John Wiley and Sons.

Boots, B.N. and A. Getis (1988). "Point Pattern Analysis." In: G.I. Thrall (ed.), *Scientific Geography Series*. Newbury Park, CA: Sage.

Brantingham, P.J. and P.L. Brantingham (eds.) (1991). *Environmental Criminology*. Prospect Heights, IL: Waveland Press.

Bursik, R.J. (1988). "Social Disorganization and Theories of Crime and Delinquency: Problems and Prospects." *Criminology* 26:519-551.

Garson, D.G. and R.S. Biggs (1992). *Analytic Mapping and Geographic Databases*. Newbury Park, CA: Sage.

Harries, K.D. (1974). *The Geography of Crime and Justice*. New York, NY: McGraw-Hill.

Jeffery, C. R. (1971). *Crime Prevention Through Environmental Design*. Beverly Hills, CA: Sage.

Levine, J. and J.D. Landis (1989). "Geographic Information Systems for Local Planning." *Journal of the American Planning Association* 55:209-220.

Newman, O. (1972). *Defensible Space*. New York, NY: Macmillan.

Shaw, C. and H.D. McKay (1969). *Juvenile Delinquency and Urban Areas* (rev. ed.). Chicago, IL: University of Chicago Press.

Crime Mapping
in Research

COGNITIVE MAPPING OF THE CITY CENTER: COMPARATIVE PERCEPTIONS OF DANGEROUS PLACES

by

George F. Rengert

and

William V. Pelfrey, Jr.
Temple University

Abstract: *Preconceived notions can affect the job performance of community service recruits. In this investigation, the knowledge and perception of relative safety of recruits being trained to patrol central Philadelphia are compared with actual locations and safety levels of these neighborhoods to determine which communities were not perceived accurately. Results demonstrate that knowledge of the area did not translate into perceptions of safety. Rather, preconceived notions of the ethnic composition of the neighborhoods translated into notions of relative safety. These faulty impressions need to be corrected before recruits are assigned to serve this community.*

The ability to store and access information about the environment generally is taken for granted. We also take for granted that our perceptions of the environment are correct. After all, we perceived them — that is, we saw, heard, touched, or smelled them. Or, we heard others we trust describe the environmental elements to us. Therefore, we feel we have a good idea of what varying places we have experi-

Address correspondence to: George F. Rengert, Department of Criminal Justice, Gladfelter Hall, Temple University, Philadelphia, PA 19122.

enced either first or second hand are like. But do we?

There is a vast literature on how we perceive the environment centered in the multi-disciplinary field of environmental cognition. This focus can be traced back to cognitive psychology (Tolman, 1948), from which geographers developed much of their pioneering work (Downs and Stea, 1973; Golledge, 1976; Golledge and Spector, 1978; Gould and White, 1974; Lloyd, 1976). From geography, several environmental criminologists have applied this research to the study of crime and fear of crime (Brantingham et al., 1977; Carter and Hill, 1979; McPherson, 1978; Pyle, 1980). One of the key questions asked by these scholars is, How accurate are our perceptions of crime and how justified are our fears of crime (Pelfrey and Pelfrey, 1995)?

These are important questions since our behavior is governed not by what objectively exists in the environment, but by what we perceive to exist. Therefore, environmental perception governs our day-to-day behavior. For example, Pyle (1980) points out that lack of use of the shopping, cultural, and recreation facilities within central parts of Akron, OH by suburban residents may be due to an unjustified fear of crime. Not all parts of central Akron are high-crime areas, although most suburban residents perceive them as such. Pyle (1980) demonstrates that, objectively, certain suburban locations have a more serious crime problem than central Akron.

In a study of two neighborhoods in west Philadelphia, Mattson and Rengert (1995) demonstrated that residents perceived actual distances as longer in neighborhoods perceived as dangerous than in those perceived as safe. Since one of the determinants of whether we use a facility is perceived distance from the potential user, a desirable facility located in an environment viewed as dangerous (a public zoo) was not only underutilized because of the perceived danger, but also because of the inaccurately perceived distance from potential users. In fact, the perception of danger was so pervasive that objectively experienced problems did not add to the distance perception in the perceived dangerous neighborhood, but significantly increased perceived distance in the relatively safe neighborhood. In other words, bad experiences did not add to the perception of fear and distance in the neighborhood perceived as dangerous to begin with, while they did in the neighborhood perceived as safe. Quite clearly, the perception was more important than the objective reality in determining the use of the contrasting environments. This is just another example of the relationship between environmental perception and individual behavior, there are many more. This chapter illustrates how environmental cognition and spatial behavior are related in conceptual terms. We begin with a discussion of the formation of mental maps.

MENTAL MAPPING

Golledge (1987) provides an extensive review of this field. He interprets the relationship between environmental cognition and spatial behavior as follows:

> While rejecting environmental determinism as a major underlying theory, researchers admit that many behaviors are place specific — that is, behavior plans are devised not necessarily just on the basis of the nature of the currently occupied environment, but perhaps also on the image of other places with which one has to interact. This image is based on information previously obtained from both primary and secondary sources. Thus an arrival at a particular place is usually accompanied by some a priori expectations about the type of behavior that could take place in such a place.... Information from the "a priori given world" [is] mediated by sets of values, beliefs, and meanings that had both idiosyncratic and general significance and that heavily influence[s] the probability that a bit of information emanating from an element or thing was received, stored, and potentially used by people [p. 132].

Behavior, then, is the result not only of referencing past events, but also of expected outcomes. Therefore, interpretation of the environment is a function of social and cultural values and constraints. That is, emotion, fears, beliefs, prejudices, and misconceptions interact with the objective environment to form our image of the environment. This image of the environment is termed our "mental map."

The process of mental mapping consists of a set of operations designed to code environmental information in such a manner that it can later be decoded to allow spatial behavior to take place. The process of acquiring spatial knowledge is termed the "cognitive mapping process." The environmental information stored in memory is termed a cognitive, or mental, map.

The process of cognitive mapping has four elements: an actor, an external environment, a set of outputs from environment to actor called "environmental cognition," and a set of outputs from actor to the environment called "environmental response behavior." Therefore, spatial behavior cannot be explained in terms of stimulus and response alone. Rather, the environmental stimulus is recoded and reordered in the mind in a way that is unique to the actor. Therefore, no two persons' mental maps of the same environment are exactly alike, and no two people can be expected to react to a given environment in exactly the same manner. However, there are generalities according to age, sex, ethnicity and regional characteristics (Golledge, 1987).

As the accuracy of mental maps vary, so also do individual behaviors depart from what one might objectively consider normal. Therefore, in order to understand relations between persons and environment, one needs to discover the information base on which behavior is overlaid. This study is an examination of how central Philadelphia is perceived by two groups: a class of cadets being trained to serve the city; and a class of students enrolled in a criminal justice class at Temple University in 1994. The image of central Philadelphia not only will effect how the public service cadets perform their job, but also how students, visitors, and residents make use of and behave within this environment. Both factors are of concern to those who have a stake in the economic and social viability of city centers in the U.S. Certainly, civic leaders and government officials have concerns for the future viability of central Philadelphia.

CHANGING THE IMAGE OF CENTRAL PHILADELPHIA

Like many old East Coast cities, Philadelphians are concerned about their city center. Many feel it is not clean. There are many homeless people on the streets. Many users feel that it is no longer a safe place to work, shop, or entertain their friends. In fact, CIGNA insurance corporation has capitalized on this perception by offering a $100,000 insurance policy to any businessperson in central Philadelphia to compensate him or her for assault, robbery, or kidnapping while not on the job (Wedo, 1994). Several long-time businesses closed, and many others were contemplating a move to a suburban mall (Liedman, 1991). In other words, central Philadelphia was losing its economic and social base.

Others feel that the city center can be revived. In the early 1990s, business and civic groups in central Philadelphia organized themselves and held many strategy sessions to identify solutions to their problems (Liedman, 1991). One of the foremost problems facing them was the perception that center-city Philadelphia was no longer safe. They wanted to change this perception by making it a cleaner, friendlier, and safer place that would attract customers, tourists and businesses. The question turned on how to improve the quality of life in this area for day and nighttime users.

It was decided that one should not turn to the traditional source of community service — the police department — to reconstitute this area of the city. First, the Philadelphia police were already spread thin because of recent cutbacks eliminating 8,000 to 6,000 officers. Secondly, equity considerations argue against powerful business and civic organizations consuming more than their fair share of scarce police resources needed in other parts of the city. Finally, the police may not be the best vehicle for improving the overall quality of life in the city center. Community policing concepts are just beginning to diffuse through the Philadelphia Police Department, and not all officers embrace these concepts wholeheartedly.

The business and civic organizations decided to supplement the already existing police detailed to the city center with a private force of their own. In order not to confuse the private force with the Philadelphia police, private officers were termed "community service representatives." They would be a sort of para-police, calling in the city police in critical situations requiring immediate response and providing a uniformed presence that deters opportunistic street crime. The private force would be trained from the beginning to embrace a "problem-solving" approach in order to better the quality of life in center-city Philadelphia. This idea is not unique. There are several other public-private forces throughout the U.S. from Portland and Denver to New York and New Orleans (Liedman, 1991). The business and civic communities of central Philadelphia decided to fund this project with private monies contributed by their constituents. The training of these community service recruits is the focus of this analysis; their perception of central Philadelphia will be compared with that of a class of students at Temple University. In this manner, we gain insight into the perceptions of those hired to change the image of the city, and of potential users of the city. First, we will consider the importance of area perception to the community service recruits.

At the outset, it became apparent that the preconceived notions these community service recruits might have could affect their job performance, since effective community service entails an accurate, intimate knowledge of the community the officer is assigned to serve. The heart of modern community service is not only the effort, but the desire of a community service officer to become familiar with the special problems faced by the residents and users of their assigned community. This accumulation of knowledge is an ongoing process that requires persistent interaction of the officer with the community.

Also important is the baseline the prospective community service officer is starting from. As has been well-documented in the psychology of dissonance and consonance (Festinger, 1957), preformed opinions of new recruits are often difficult to erase. Once a person has made up his or her mind about the characteristics of an area, it is more difficult to correct faulty impressions than to teach correct opinions in the first place. This is due to the fact that the faulty impressions may have reached a state of consonance that is difficult to erase. For example, if a person thinks of an area of the city as unsafe, this impression tends to persist and impact the manner in which public service representatives approach a problem situation located within that area.

Newman (1972) illustrates the manner in which perception can effect public service by the reaction of New York City police to two contrasting public housing projects located across a highway from each other. One is a high-rise public housing project, and the other is composed of three-story walkups. The police perceived the high-rise projects as dangerous. In answering calls for service in the high rise, the police were relatively authoritarian, which resulted in hostile responses from the residents. These hostile responses created greater perceptions of danger and more authoritarian responses on the part of the police. Thus, the police and the community were in a vicious cycle downward.

In the walkup projects, on the other hand, the residents had a positive relationship with the police. This resulted in friendly, cooperative encounters that produced more effective police work. Since the socioeconomic characteristics of the residents in the two projects were similar, the question of which came first, the chicken or the egg, arises. Clearly, if public service representatives have a preconceived notion of the relative safety of an area, it will impact their approach to community problems.

In any case, public service representatives must use care in clearly dangerous situations no matter where they are situated spatially. In a study of police officers killed in the line of duty, Davis and Pinizzotto (1993) noted that slain officers tended to use less force than other officers in similar circumstances, and often considered force only as a last resort. Slain officers were more service oriented and tended to gravitate toward the public relations aspects of law enforcement work. Since this is exactly the approach we wish the Philadelphia public service representatives to use, they must be realistic in evaluating areas and situations in their work and not base their reactions on faulty impressions.

Faulty impressions may arise from a variety of theoretical bases (Golledge and Stimson, 1987). The most important for our purposes is the principle stating that the less well-known an area is, the more likely it is that negative connotations are ascribed to it (Kaplan and Kaplan, 1982). For example, subjects nearly always rate their own cities as safer than other cities, and their own residential neighborhood as safer than less well-known surrounding neighborhoods (Mattson and Rengert, 1995). Therefore, the level of knowledge is believed to be an important determinant of the positive or negative perception of an area. The people assigned to train these community service recruits became concerned with their preexisting knowledge and perception of center-city Philadelphia.

A second basis of faulty impressions of the environment arise from how people are socialized, especially in their formative years. Early studies held that women are socialized to be more fearful of strange environments (Macoby, 1966). On the other hand, women are socialized to be less confrontational and more supportive in problem situations. More recent studies cast doubt on these early findings (Adler, 1975; Golledge et al., 1995). In either case, evaluations of the performance of women police officers in the Metropolitan Police Department of Washington, DC by The Police Foundation found that women officers were more likely than their male colleagues to receive support from the community, and were less likely to be charged with improper conduct (Bloch and Anderson, 1974). In New York City, female officers were perceived by civilians as being more competent, pleasant, and respectful, and their performance seemed to create a better civilian regard for police (Sichel, 1978). Since these are important considerations for our community service recruits, we decided to evaluate differences between male and female recruits in Philadelphia.

Data

In the following analysis, recruits being trained to serve center-city Philadelphia and a control group of students at Temple University are examined to determine whether their level of knowledge of this region of the city is indeed related to their perception of its relative safety. Data were collected during a training session conducted by one of the authors, and later in a classroom at Temple University. Data were of two types: (1) information on the knowledge the recruits and students possess of the location of important landmarks of center-city Philadelphia; and (2) information on the perception the recruits and students have of the communities composing the city.

In order to record each student and community service recruit's knowledge of center-city Philadelphia, each was handed a base map of this area with the major streets recorded on it. The subjects also received a list of 32 major landmarks located within this area. Then they were asked to place a dot on the base map where they believed each landmark is located, and to number this dot with the corresponding number of each landmark. This resulted in a map of 32 dots corresponding to where the recruits and students believed each landmark to be located.

It is possible that recruits and students could have knowledge of the location of landmarks without having other knowledge of the area. For example, this knowledge could come from studying a map of central Philadelphia that depicts the major streets and tourist attractions (Golledge et al., 1995). In this case, the subjects would have map knowledge without the accompanying real-world experience of the area. In the present study, however, all the community service recruits and Temple students stated that they had been to the city center many times. It is the hub of public and private transportation in Philadelphia. There were no subjects without first-hand knowledge of this area. We have no information on the degree of map knowledge the subjects may have obtained. We are proceeding under the assumption that most spatial knowledge of the center of Philadelphia was obtained through observation of this environment rather than from maps or other printed materials.

The perception of center-city Philadelphia was recorded on a second base map. In this case, the map of the city is divided into 16 units of equal size. The recruits and students were asked to identify that unit or sub-area of the map containing the most dangerous neighborhood to walk through in the daytime, and to give it a score of zero. They were then asked to locate the safest neighborhood to walk through in the daytime, and to record a 10 for the sub-area contained within this community. Given these anchors, the recruits and students were then asked to scale all remaining 14 sub-areas between zero and 10 with regard to whether they were similar to the most dangerous or the safest neighborhoods in center-city Philadelphia.

This same scaling routine was used to gather information on where the subjects perceived various ethnic communities to be concentrated. They were asked to pick the area among the 16 possible that contains the greatest concentration of white residents and label it a 10. They were then asked to pick the area that contained the smallest concentration of white residents and label it a zero. They were then asked to scale the remaining 14 areas between these two extremes, depending on whether they were more like the area with the greatest concentration or the least. This procedure was subsequently followed for black, southeast Asian, and Hispanic populations. Therefore, each subject had five maps, one of perceived safety and four of their perception of concentrations of ethnic populations. This information formed the basis of the cognitive maps we later constructed.

The Analysis

We begin with an examination of the relationship between knowledge of an area and its perceived safety using the data described above. Later in our analysis we will examine the relationship between the perceived location of various ethnic groups and perceived safety. In each case, we begin with the community service recruits and then repeat the exercise for the students at Temple University.

Knowledge of the area is assumed to be directly related to the ability of each recruit to accurately locate major landmarks on the base map, since there is no evidence that subjects had studied maps of central Philadelphia extensively. The level of knowledge is measured by determining how many inches on the map their plotted location is in a straight line from the actual location of each landmark. This measurement of error is summed over the 32 landmarks, and then divided by 32 to determine the average error per landmark for each recruit. This average error is our measure of the relative knowledge of each community service recruit of center-city Philadelphia.

The perception of relative safety is measured in a slightly different manner. Since each community service recruit is compared with all others, the first task is to determine the norm with which to make this comparison. In this case, the perceived level of safety is summed over all community service recruits for each sub-area and divided by 24 (the number of recruits) to obtain the average value for each sub-area in center-city Philadelphia. Then, the score each recruit placed within a sub-area has this average subtracted to obtain a measure of deviation from the mean for each neighborhood for each recruit. Finally, this deviation is summed over all sub-areas and divided by 16 to obtain the average deviation from the mean for each recruit. This average deviation is our measure of the relative perception of safety of center-city Philadelphia. The higher the score, the safer the recruit perceives the overall city center to be relative to his/her fellow recruits.

Finally, we use nonparametric measures of statistical association due to the small sample size and since we cannot assume a normal distribution of the data. Spearman rank order correlation coefficients allow for the statistical test of association of whether a significant relationship exists between knowledge and perception of safety among the community service recruits. This analysis was repeated in a class of 34 students at Temple University and compared with the original analysis.

RESULTS

Table 1 lists the landmarks of center-city Philadelphia ranked in the order of how well-known their locations are to the community service recruits and students. Notice that the students were much less accurate in identifying the locations of these major landmarks than the recruits, even though we might assume that the students are much more likely to have studied maps of Philadelphia in their formal education at Temple University. This is an encouraging finding, since the level of responsibility is higher for the recruits who are hired to serve this area than the students who are potential consumers. Notice that City Hall is the best known landmark in center-city Philadelphia for both groups. Notice also that the two landmarks that are least known are religious centers. One might speculate that these subjects know government centers better than religious centers. However, it is surprising that the Police Administration Building ranked 21 out of 32 sites for the community service recruits. In general, centrally located sites were more accurately located than those found toward the edge of the map.

Figure 1 portrays the average perceived daylight walking safety of center-city Philadelphia by the community service recruits. Figure 2 portrays perceived daylight walking safety for the students. Isolines have been drawn to highlight the perceived relative safety of each area. This is one method of presenting a mental map by interpolating values between two sub-areas. For example, if two contiguous sub-areas have values of 3.5 and 4.5, respectively, then an isoline depicting the value of 4.0 is drawn an equal distance between the centers of the two sub-areas. Isolines depicting values of the nearest whole number are drawn on each map.

Table 1: Major Landmarks and Error in Their Location

Landmarks	Cadets	Students	Weighted Mean
City Hall	0.26	0.30	0.28
Gallery Shopping Plaza	0.50	0.70	0.62
Hahneman Hospital	0.98	1.50	1.31
Penns Landing Stage Area	0.89	1.60	1.34
Independence Hall	0.54	1.90	1.39
Chinese Arch	0.81	1.80	1.47
Academy of Music	0.73	2.00	1.62
Betsy Ross House	1.05	2.20	1.72
Philadelphia Community College	1.37	1.80	1.72
Franklin Institute	0.87	2.40	1.77
Police Administration Building	1.46	2.00	1.78
Jefferson Medical College	0.99	2.40	1.82
Reading Terminal Market	1.00	2.50	1.88
Main Branch of the Free Library	0.88	2.60	1.89
Rittenhouse Square	0.95	2.80	2.03
Hershey Hotel	0.83	3.00	2.10
Society Hill Towers	1.53	2.50	2.10
Art Museum	1.13	2.90	2.17
Cathedral of St. Peter and Paul	1.14	2.90	2.17
Ben Franklin Bridge	2.30	2.30	2.30
Jefferson Hospital	2.20	2.40	2.32
Academy of Fine Arts	1.53	2.90	2.33
Natural Science Museum	1.32	3.20	2.42
Logan's Circle	0.98	3.50	2.46
Masonic Temple	0.88	3.70	2.53
TLA Cinema	2.19	3.20	2.78
City Tavern	1.79	3.80	2.97
Ben Franklin Museum	1.92	3.90	3.08
Graduate Hospital	2.03	3.90	3.13
Washington Square	2.48	3.90	3.31
Friends Meeting House	3.43	3.70	4.60
Christ Church	4.74	4.50	4.60

These maps are similar to contour maps used to illustrate elevation on topographic maps. Notice that the map of the community service recruits is much simpler than the map for the students. Yet, there is general agreement between the two groups that central Philadelphia is safest in the middle and becomes less safe toward the

Figure 1: Average Perceived Daylight Walking Safety of Cadets

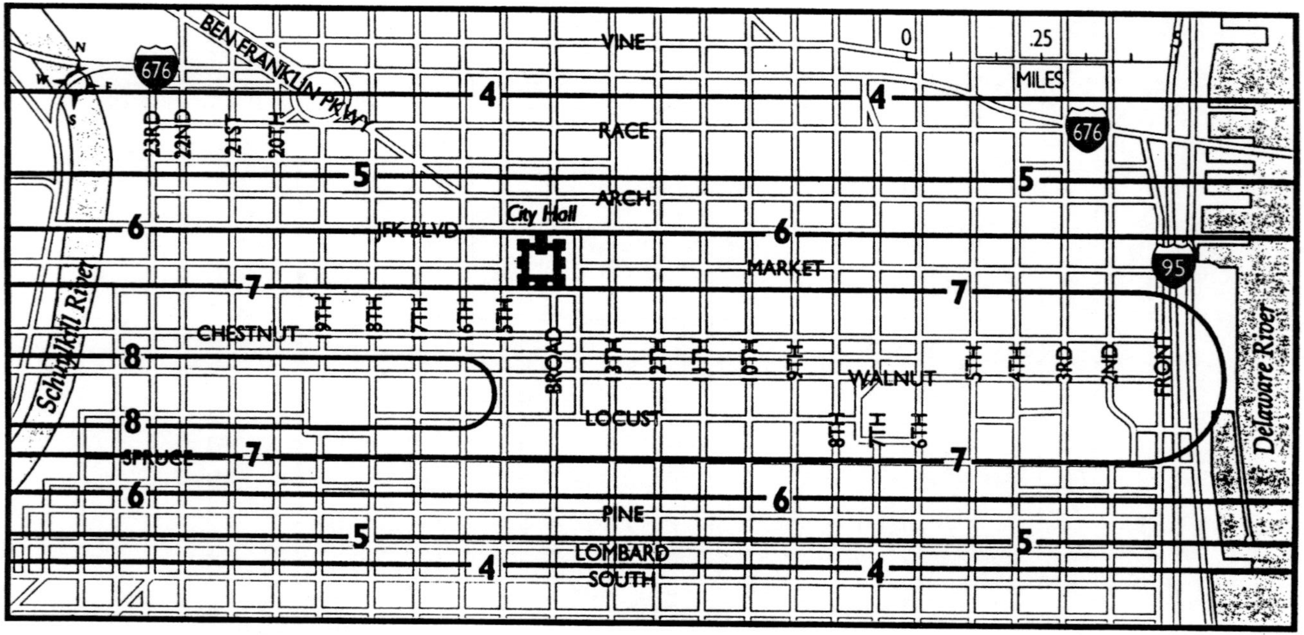

Figure 2: Average Perceived Daylight Walking Safety of Students

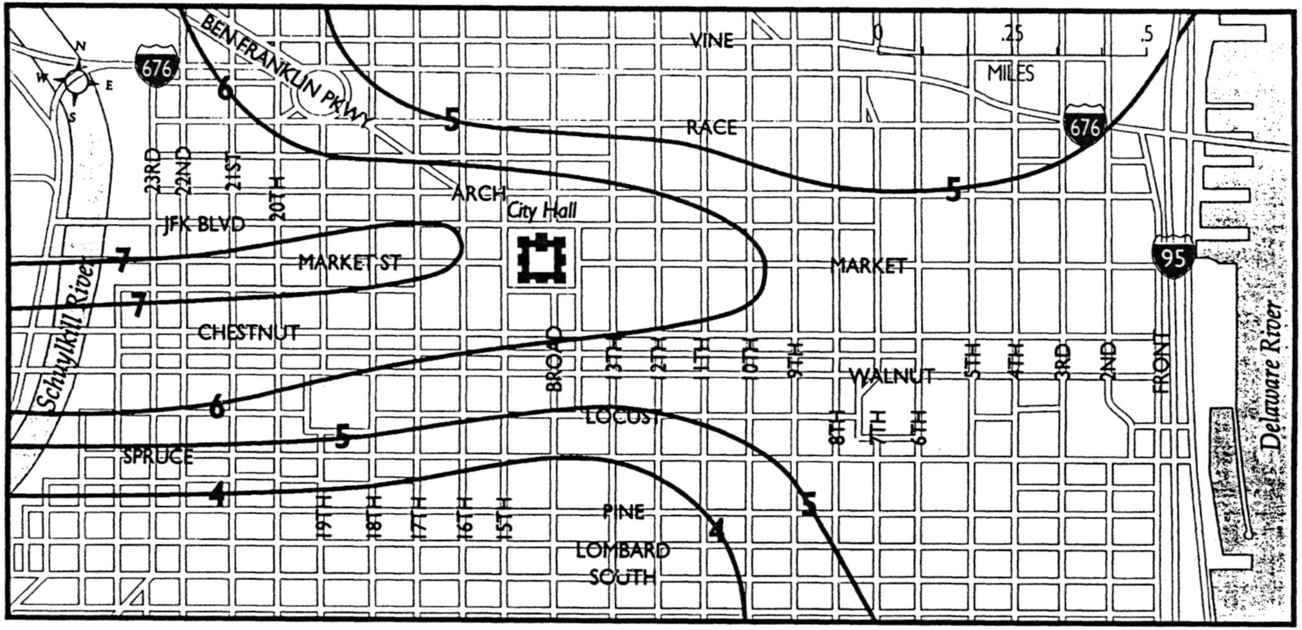

edges of the maps. Table 2 lists the deviation of each recruit's safety perception from the average of the entire group summed over all sections of center-city Philadelphia. Table 2 also lists the average knowledge of the location of the landmarks for each recruit, as measured by a straight line from the plotted locations to the actual locations. The ranks of each recruit on each measurement are also given in Table 2. Table 3 portrays this information for the students.

Table 2: Knowledge and Perceived Danger — Cadet Data

Recruit	Perceived Safety	Rank	Knowledge of Landmarks	Rank
1	-.68	10	.43	2
2	-24.68	24	1.06	18
3	-12.68	21	.65	3
4	4.32	9	.90	12
5	20.32	3	1.76	21
6	-6.68	15	1.91	22
7	-8.68	16	2.20	23
8	-11.68	20	.80	9
9	-9.68	17	.38	1
10	-13.68	22	.79	8
11	-.68	11	.98	15
12	26.32	1	1.18	19
13	-3.68	12	1.01	16
14	-14.68	23	.94	13
15	14.32	4	.78	7
16	-4.68	13	.64	5
17	5.32	7	.65	6
18	7.32	6	.80	10
19	-10.68	19	3.17	24
20	5.32	8	1.06	17
21	23.32	2	.95	14
22	-6.68	14	.88	11
23	-9.68	18	.62	4
24	13.32	5	1.43	20

Table 3: Knowledge and Perceived Danger — Student Data

Student	Perceived Safety	Rank	Knowledge of Landmarks	Rank
1	1.18	17	2.92	13
2	-3.82	21	3.39	10
3	2.18	16	1.87	24
4	17.18	4	2.85	15
5	24.18	2	2.28	20
6	16.18	5	4.88	2
7	-29.82	34	5.15	1
8	-14.82	29	3.34	11
9	-.82	20	2.26	22
10	15.18	6	2.74	17
11	-6.82	24	4.04	6
12	-5.82	22	3.41	9
13	-13.82	28	1.26	31
14	14.18	7	2.26	21
15	20.18	3	1.58	28
16	-29.82	33	2.39	19
17	-15.82	30	1.89	23
18	-12.82	26	3.01	12
19	30.18	1	2.88	14
20	6.18	13	1.51	29
21	-13.82	27	3.90	7
22	10.18	10	.79	34
23	13.18	8	2.63	18
24	11.18	9	1.68	27
25	-16.82	31	4.07	5
26	-6.82	23	1.85	25
27	6.18	12	1.17	32
28	2.18	15	4.22	3
29	.18	18	1.33	30
30	-.82	19	1.80	26
31	-18.82	32	3.71	8
32	9.18	11	1.13	33
33	-9.82	25	4.09	4
34	4.18	14	2.76	16

As can be seen at the outset, our initial proposition that the better known the center of Philadelphia is to a community service recruit or to a student, the safer he/she will perceive the area does not hold up for either group. A Spearman rank order correlation produces a coefficient of knowledge of .112, which is not significant (.611) for the community service recruits, and -.332 which is significant at the .055 level for the students. For this group of recruits and students, relative knowledge of the city center does not translate into perceived safety. In fact, the relationship is inverse for the Temple students. The better they know the area, the less safe they perceive it to be. Since this finding runs counter to previous research (Mattson and Rengert, 1995), we must ask why this is the case. Could it be that the city center is indeed dangerous, and the more familiar one is with that danger, the more accurately they perceive it? This question could be addressed by scaling the actual crime occurring within the 16 center-city areas between zero and 10, and testing whether those recruits and students who have the most accurate knowledge of the location of major landmarks also have the most accurate knowledge of the relative safety of different parts of the center-city.

In this analysis, we scaled only the violent crimes of robbery, assault, homicide, and rape — crimes that instill the most fear in users of the center-city. This was accomplished by dividing the center-city into 16 areas of equal size, and counting the number of these crimes (unweighted for severity) that occurred in each area in 1992. These values were divided by the largest value evident, so that the area with the highest number of violent crimes has a value of 1 and all other areas are measured by the proportion they are of this value. These numbers were then subtracted from 1 so that the highest crime area has the lowest value (zero), as is the case when the recruits and students scaled the areas. The numbers were then multiplied by 10 so that the possible range is zero to 10. This resulted in a range of values from zero to 8.4, with five values above the midpoint of five and seven values below. In other words, it is nearly a normal distribution with few areas clustering about any value. Center-city Philadelphia is not a uniformly dangerous or safe area. there is considerable variation between sub-regions.

A Spearman rank order correlation coefficient is calculated using the following variables. The first variable is the deviation when the actual level of safety is subtracted from the perceived level of safety for each recruit or student, and the absolute values summed over the areas to provide a measure of how far from reality each recruit or student views the various sub-areas in either a positive or a negative direction. The second variable is the difference resulting when the actual locations are subtracted from the perceived locations for the 32 landmarks of center-city. When the two variables are ranked across all recruits, the Spearman rank order correlation coefficient is

.336, which is significant at the .109 level for the community service recruits, and a -.330 correlation coefficient which is significant at the .057 level for the students. In neither case, do we find a highly significant relationship between knowledge of the city center and the accuracy of perceived safety of the area. Again, in the case of the students, the relationship is in the opposite direction from that expected.

Finally, we ask if we can identify by personal characteristics who is most likely to accurately identify the location of landmarks; and who is most likely to rate center-city Philadelphia as safe or unsafe. In other words, is there a type of recruit or student who does not know the city center but rates it as a safe area or vice versa? Past research is not consistent on this topic. For example, early psychological research held that women tend to have poorer spatial skills than men (Macoby, 1966). However, more recent geographic investigations find no statistical differences in spatial skills based on sex. In fact, some evidence points to a higher performance overall by geographically trained females on spatial tasks (Golledge et al., 1995). Therefore, we are not sure whether to expect the females or the males to be more accurate in locating landmarks in central Philadelphia on a base map.

Our results are as contradictory as the results of previous studies. When we summed the distance that each male recruit had plotted the location of major landmarks from their actual locations and divide by the number of male recruits, we obtain an average value of 1.48 inches. When we compute the mean for the ten women recruits, it is a slightly larger 1.63 inches on average. For the control group of students, the respective values for men are 2.77 inches and for women 2.51 inches on average. So the women are slightly less knowledgeable and/or accurate in locating major landmarks in center-city Philadelphia than their male counterparts for the community service recruits, but the opposite is true of the control group of students.

Next we consider feelings of safety during the daytime. When we sum their mean deviation from the average perceived safety level, we find a surprising result in the case of the community service recruits. The average deviation from the mean for the 14 male recruits is -39.20, the average deviation for the 10 female recruits is +19.88. In other words, the women recruits perceived center-city Philadelphia to be much safer than their fellow male recruits. The magnitude of the difference is a surprising finding. In the case of the students, the average deviation from the mean for the 22 males is -2.2, the average deviation for the 12 females is 24.6. In this case, we find that the students support the findings based on the community service recruits in that the females perceive central Philadelphia as safer than the males. If the perception of safety on the part of the female recruits translates into less authoritarian behavior, they may be able to function more satisfactorily as community service agents. On the other hand, if the center city is an unsafe area perceived more accurately by the males, the female recruits may be in a very vulnerable position.

This proposition is difficult to test. Some evidence is provided by observing how accurately the men and the women recruits and students estimated the actual relative crime rates of each of the 16 locations in central Philadelphia. The actual violent offenses are scaled between zero for the most dangerous location and 10 for the safest location.. Then, these values can be subtracted from each recruit's and student's perceived level of safety for each location. These absolute values are then summed over the 16 locations and divided by 16 to obtain an average value for each recruit and student. This will be a measure of how accurately each recruit and student estimated the actual safety level of each center-city location. If the male community service recruits and students are more accurate in this exercise than the female recruits and students, then we might argue that they have a better knowledge of the relative safety level of the city center as a whole and the greater care they are expected to exercise may be justified.

Since there is considerable variation in the violent offenses between sections of the center city, the question turns on who can most accurately identify this variation — the men or the women. The results do not demonstrate much difference between the men and women recruits. When the actual safety level is subtracted from the perceived safety level, the mean absolute deviation is 46.76 for the women recruits and 45.55 for the men recruits. The men are a bit more accurate in perceiving the safety level than the women. But the difference is too small to be significant. In the case of the students, the values are 85.58 for the women and 84.50 for the men; again, no significant difference. In other words, neither the men or the women are very accurate in identifying the relative level of safety in center-city Philadelphia. The question now turns on which areas are causing the errors in the recruits' and students' perceptions of relative safety.

Three maps were constructed in which the isolines of the perceived and of the actual safety are portrayed (Figures 1 to 3) to partially answer this question. Notice that there are extreme differences between Figures 1 and 2 and Figure 3. The community service recruits and students perceived the center of the city to be the safest,

Figure 3: Actual Violent Crime in Central Philadelphia

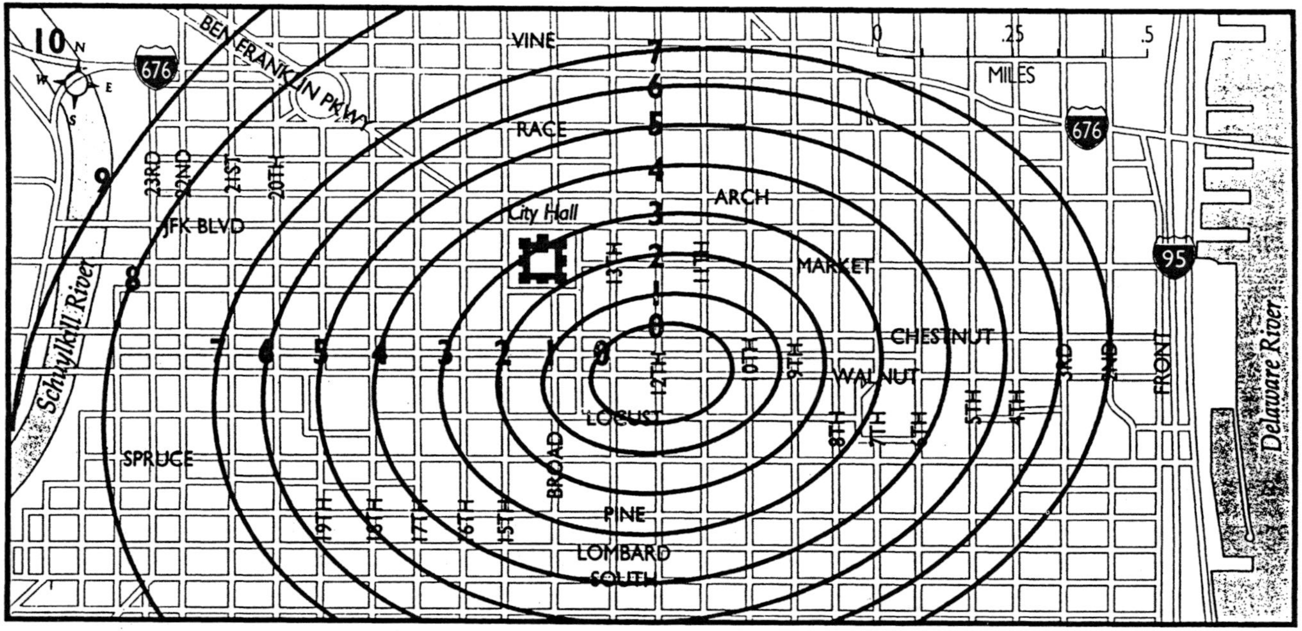

with a ridge of decline in either direction away from the center of Philadelphia. In actuality, violent crime in Philadelphia is spatially arranged as a "hot spot" centered just to the southeast of the center of the city. In other words, the community service recruits and students incorrectly perceived crime to increase toward the edge of the city center where low-income residential areas begin. In reality, violent crime decreases in these directions. In fact, the safest area in the center city is the Logan Circle area to the far northwest of the city center — an area the community service recruits rated as one of the least safe in the center-city.

The reason there is so much variation between perceived and actual safety in the case of these recruits and students may revolve around a conceptual problem. What they may have been scaling is "potential safety" rather than "actual safety." In other words, an area may be relatively safe in actuality because people avoid the area. Both routine activity theory (Cohen and Felson, 1979) and Jacobs' (1961) critical intensity theory of land use explain that a potential victim must be present for a crime to take place.

We are left with the question of whether an area is unsafe if people avoid it, so few if any crimes take place there. In actuality, it is not unsafe if people avoid the area so that no crimes take place, but it is potentially unsafe if one were to wander into the area. Therefore, the actual safety level is lower in parts of the city center that are heavily utilized; actual safety is higher in areas less used. What we are missing is a measure of the "population at risk." Again, is it safe if no one goes into an area? This does not seem to be the case: the most heavily used part of Philadelphia is the central section of the city center that has the highest number of violent crime incidents. We do not know the relative crime *rates* since we have no measure of the relative use of each sub-area. In other words, we have no measure of the population at risk of violent crime.

A better approach may have been to ask each recruit and student where the most violent crime occurs rather than where the safest areas in the central city are located. As long as we have no statistics on how many people use each area of the city center so that we can measure the population at risk, we cannot compute an accurate measure of the actual safety level of each area. We are left with a measure of how much violent crime takes place, and of the recruits' and students' perceptions of where it is the most and least safe to walk in the city center. With regard to potential safety, the recruits and students may be more accurate than the violent crime statistics.

On the other hand, perceived safety may not be an accurate measure of the risk of violent crime. A perceived unsafe area may not be an area within which violent crime is likely to take place. For example, when people first visit the observation deck of the Empire State Building in New York City, they tend to be fearful. The fear may not be a rational response to the actual safety of standing on this spot. Likewise, the outer regions of the city center may be perceived as unsafe because of the proximity of a lower income minority community a few blocks away. This fear also may not be rational and could negatively impact how the community service representatives respond to problems within the surrounding neighborhoods. This is a serious issue, since city officials want the community service recruits to treat all residents and all neighborhoods in center-city Philadelphia in a manner that is fair and not tainted by preconceived notions of their relative safety.

This issue can be tested using additional data collected during the training sessions. In order to measure how accurately each recruit estimated the location of ethnic populations in central Philadelphia, each was asked to scale a map of center-city Philadelphia divided into 16 equal-sized areas between zero and 10 with respect to which area contained the highest proportion of black households. The recruits were then asked to assign a 10 to the area they believed to contain the highest proportion of black households and a zero to the area they believed to contain the lowest proportion of black households. Then the other 14 areas were scaled between zero and 10, depending on whether the recruit believed it to be most like the highest or the lowest rated neighborhood. The same task was completed for white, Hispanic, and southeast Asian populations.

The issue now is whether perceived safety is related to where the recruits believed different ethnic groups to be located. This issue can be tested by estimating Spearman rank order correlation coefficients between perceived daytime walking safety and perceived ethnic population concentrations.

Table 4 lists the correlation coefficients when perceived daytime walking safety is correlated with the perceptions of where ethnic communities are concentrated in center-city Philadelphia for the cadets. Table 5 lists the same data for Temple students. Notice that there is general agreement between the cadets and the Temple students. Perceived safety is positively correlated with the perceived concentration of the white population, and negatively correlated with the concentration of ethnic minority populations. The southeast Asian population is weakly negatively correlated and very insignificant statistically. Only the perceived concentration of the white population was correlated positively with perceived safety. These findings highlight an issue in police training: if police are to obtain community cooperation, they cannot let preconceived faulty notions of the relative safety of a neighborhood impact their approach to localized problems. If police behave in an authoritarian manner because they perceive black and Hispanic neighborhoods to be dangerous, they will initiate the vicious cycle downward described earlier, as the residents will respond hostilely to this approach. Trainers of recruits must develop techniques to instill a realistic perception of danger rather than one based on the easy preconceived notions of who lives in a particular community.

Table 4: Correlation Coefficients Between Ethnic Communities and Perceived Safety by Cadets

Variable	Coefficient	Significance
White	.8511	.000
Black	-.5596	.058
Hispanic	-.7825	.003
Southeast Asian	-.3363	.285

Table 5: Correlation Coefficients Between Ethnic Communities and Perceived Safety by Students

Variable	Coefficient	Significance
White	.5928	.016
Black	-.4161	.109
Hispanic	-.7060	.002
Southeast Asian	-.2167	.420

The ethnic characteristics of the recruits (over half of whom were black or Hispanic) made no difference in how they perceived safety in the various ethnic communities. This point is highlighted by the November 27, 1993 statement of leading black civil rights leader, Jesse Jackson, as quoted by Glastris and Thornton (1994:38): "There is nothing more painful for me at this stage in my life than to walk down the street and hear footsteps and start to think about robbery and then look around and see it's somebody white and feel relieved. How humiliating."

The perception of the characteristics of different ethnic groups seems to permeate most members of society, including community service recruits. For their own safety, police must use care in dangerous confrontations. For effective community policing, police must not base their perceptions of safety on the ethnic composition of a neighborhood. Otherwise, the community cooperation so necessary in modern community policing will not be forthcoming; the coproduction of safety between the community and the police will be short-circuited.

REFERENCES

Adler, F. (1975). *Sisters in Crime*. New York, NY: McGraw Hill.

Bloch, P and D. Anderson (1974). *Policewomen on Patrol: Final Report*. Washington, DC: Police Foundation.

Brantingham, P.J., P.L. Brantingham, and T. Molumby (1977). "Perceptions of Crime in a Dreadful Enclosure." *Ohio Journal of Science* 77: 256-261.

Carter, R.D. and K.Q. Hill (1979). *The Criminals' Image of the City*. New York, NY: Pergamon Press.

Cohen, L. and M. Felson (1979). "Social Change and Crime Rate Trends." *American Sociological Review* 44:588-605.

Davis, Ed and Anthony Pinizzoto (1993). *Killed in the Line of Duty*. Washington, DC: Uniform Crime Reporting Section, U.S. Federal Bureau of Investigation.

Downs, R.M. and D. Stea (eds.) (1973). *Image and Environment: Cognitive Mapping and Spatial Behavior*. Chicago, IL: Aldine.

Festinger, Leon (1957). *A Theory of Cognitive Dissonance*. New York, NY: Harper and Row.

Glastris, P. and J. Thornton (1994). "A New Civil Rights Frontier." *U.S. News and World Report* 2:38-39.

Golledge, R.G. (1976). "Method and Methodological Issues in Environmental Cognition Research." In: G.T. Moore and R.G. Golledge (eds.), *Environmental Knowing*. Stroudsburg, PA: Dowden, Hutchenson, and Ross.

—— (1987). "Environmental Cognition." In: D. Stokols and I. Altman (eds.), *Handbook of Environmental Psychology*. New York, NY: John Wiley & Sons.

—— V. Dougherty and S. Bell (1995). "Acquiring Spatial Knowledge: Survey Versus Route-Based Knowledge in Unfamiliar Environments." *Annals of the Association of American Geographers* 85:134-158.

Golledge, R.G. and A.N. Spector (1978). "Comprehending the Urban Environment: Theory and Practice." *Geographical Analysis* 10:403-426.

Golledge, R. and R. Stimson (1987). *Analytical Behavioral Geography*. New York, NY: Croom Helm.

Gould, P. and R. White (1974). *Mental Maps*. Harmondsworth, UK: Penguin Books.

Jacobs, Jane (1961). *The Death and Life of Great American Cities*. New York, NY: Vintage Books.

Kaplan, S. and R. Kaplan (1982). *Cognition and Environment*. New York, NY: Praeger.

Liedman, J. (1991). "If You Clean It They Will Come." *Business Philadelphia*, November, pp.33-35.

Lloyd, R. E. (1976). "Cognition, Preference and Behavior in Space: An Examination of the Structural Linkages." *Economic Geography* 52: 241-253.

Macoby, Eleanor (1966). *The Development of Sex Differences*. Stanford, CA: Stanford University Press.

Mattson, M. and G. Rengert (1995). "Danger, Distance, and Desirability: Perceptions of Inner City Neighborhoods." *European Journal of Criminal Policy and Research* 3:70-78.

McPherson, M. (1978). "Realities and Perceptions of Crime at the Neighborhood Level." *Victimology* 3:319-328.

Newman, Oscar (1972). *Defensible Space: Crime Prevention Through Urban Design*. New York, NY: Collier Books.

Pelfrey, Sr., W.V. and Pelfrey, Jr., W.V. (1995). "Fear of Crime and Victimization: Changes Over Time in Age and Gender Relationships." Paper presented to the Academy of Criminal Justice Sciences, Boston, March.

Pyle, G.F. (1980). "Systematic Sociospatial Variation in Perceptions of Crime Location and Severity." In: D. Georges-Abeyie and K. Harries (eds.), *Crime: A Spatial Perspective.* New York, NY: Columbia University Press.

Sichel, J. (1978). *Women on Patrol: A Pilot Study of Police Performances in New York City.* Washington DC: U.S. National Criminal Justice Reference Service.

Tolman, E.C. (1948). "Cognitive Maps of Rats and Men." *Psychological Review* 55:189-208.

Wedo, B. (1994). "Insurance For Crime Victims: CIGNA Offers Coverage of Up to $100,000." *Philadelphia Daily News,* August 27, p.A87.

THE (UN)KNOWN UNIVERSE: MAPPING GANGS AND GANG VIOLENCE IN BOSTON

by

David M. Kennedy
Anthony A. Braga
Anne M. Piehl
Harvard University

Abstract: The experience, observations, local knowledge, and historical perspective of working police officers and others with routine contact with offenders, communities, and criminal organizations may represent an important underutilized resource for describing, understanding, and crafting interventions aimed at crime problems. Mapping and other information-collecting and -ordering techniques, usually aimed at formal police data, can also be used to good effect to capture and organize these experiential assets. This chapter describes one such exercise carried out as part of a project to apply problem-solving techniques to youth gun violence and gun markets in Boston. A working group comprised of Harvard University researchers, police officers from the Boston Police Department's Youth Violence Strike Force, probation officers covering high-risk neighborhoods, and city-employed gang-mediation "street workers": estimated the number and size of the city's gangs; mapped their turf; mapped their antagonisms and alliances; and classified five years of youth victimization events according to their connection (or lack thereof) to this gang geography. The products of these exercises provide: a "snapshot" of Boston's gang turf; an estimate of gang involvement in high-risk neighborhoods; a sociogram of gang relationships; and an estimate of Boston gangs' direct contribution to youth homicide victimization.

Address correspondence to: David M. Kennedy, Program in Criminal Justice Policy and Management, John F. Kennedy School of Government, Harvard University, 79 John F. Kennedy Street, Cambridge, MA 02138 (e-mail: David Kennedy@harvard.edu).

INTRODUCTION

The experience, observations, local knowledge, and historical perspective of working police officers and others with routine contact with offenders, communities, and criminal organizations may represent an important underutilized resource for describing, understanding, and crafting interventions aimed at crime problems. Mapping and other information-collecting and -ordering techniques that are usually aimed at formal police data can also be used to good effect to capture and organize these experiential assets. These possibilities include, but are not limited to, "hot-spot" mapping and place-focused intervention. In particular, the identification and analysis of networks hold promise. This paper describes one such exercise carried out as part of a U.S. National Institute of Justice (NIJ)-funded project to apply problem-solving techniques to youth gun violence in Boston.[1] A working group comprised of Harvard University researchers, police officers from the Boston Police Department's Youth Violence Strike Force, probation officers covering high-risk neighborhoods, and city-employed gang-mediation "street workers": estimated the number and size of the city's gangs; mapped their turf; mapped their antagonisms and alliances; and classified five years of youth homicide victimization events according to their connection (or lack thereof) to gangs. The products of these exercises provide: a "snapshot" of Boston's gang turf; an estimate of gang involvement in high-risk neighborhoods; a sociogram of gang relationships; and an estimate of Boston gangs' direct contribution to youth homicide victimization. These products can be combined powerfully with more traditional mapping and network analysis tools and approaches. Such "knowledge-based mapping" is arguably an important contribution to understanding and intervening in crime and public safety problems.

The Current State of Mapping in Police Departments

Crime mapping and spatial analyses have existed in police departments since the beginning of modern policing (Durbak and Rengert, 1993). Manual pin maps of crime and traffic accidents have a very long history. Automated or computerized mapping has developed over the past 25 years in police agencies. In the last few years it has expanded substantially due to: the growing movement toward a more analytic "problem-solving" style of policing; academic interest in hot spots of geographically concentrated crime; the support of the federal government; and significant advances in microcomputer technology (McEwen and Taxman, 1995). A recent poll by the International Association of Chiefs of Police revealed that 30% of 280 police departments in its Law Enforcement Management Information Section regularly use mapping software (Rich, 1995).

Academics have been instrumental in the proliferation of crime mapping and spatial analysis within police departments, as researchers have formed partnerships with police agencies to use mapping to better understand and respond to urban crime problems. Toward this end, the NIJ has funded partnerships between researchers and police departments to implement and assess map-based crime analysis systems such as the Microcomputer-Assisted Police Analysis and Deployment System in Chicago (Maltz et al., 1991), and the five-site Drug Market Analysis Program (DMAP) in Jersey City, NJ, San Diego, Pittsburgh, Kansas City, and Hartford (U.S. National Institute of Justice, 1989; Maltz, 1993).

Applications of mapping and spatial analyses to decision making within police agencies vary depending upon the role of the user. Planners and administrators use maps to inform decisions on deployment, such as determining the number of officers or patrol cars to assign to a certain district or a particular shift (Durbak and Rengert, 1993). Detectives and police investigators use mapping techniques to analyze crime location patterns and to solve complex serial crimes (see Rossmo, 1995). As police departments move toward a problem-solving model of policing, patrol officers can use maps to good effect in identifying trouble spots on their beats and the times of the day these locations are likely to be most active. The Chicago Police Department's Information Collection for Automated Mapping (ICAM) program is an important part of the department's community policing program known as the Chicago Alternative Policing Strategy program. ICAM displays current crime and community conditions, and allows police officers to design custom crime maps and obtain lists of the top crime problems within a specific beat (Rich, 1995).

MAPPING TECHNIQUES AND THE IDENTIFICATION OF URBAN PROBLEMS: A FOCUS ON PLACES, AND PLACE-FOCUSED INTERVENTIONS

Computerized mapping is valued by practitioners and scholars as a powerful tool for identifying crime problems and developing crime control and prevention programs. To date, mapping has been utilized almost entirely in support of place-focused diagnoses and interventions. Maps' innate geographic character have combined with the recent academic interest in hot spots to generate this result. Research on the distribution of crime across city landscapes has revealed that crime does not occur evenly; rather, it is concentrated in relatively small places or hot spots that generate more than half of crime events (Pierce et al., 1988; Sherman et al., 1989; Weisburd et al., 1992). Place-focused interventions based on this insight have demonstrated impressive crime-control results. As part of the Jersey City DMAP a randomized experimental evaluation of a place-oriented drug enforcement strategy found significant reductions in disorder-related calls for service in the target areas, with little evidence of displacement (Weisburd and Green, 1994). The Minneapolis Hot Spots Patrol Experiment revealed that 250% more police presence in the treatment locations produced a 13% overall reduction in reported crime, and a 50% reduction in researcher observations of disorder when compared to control locations (Sherman and Weisburd, 1995).

Geographic mapping applications, particularly when linked to other law enforcement databases, and their associated statistical tools can identify hot-spot locations and generate a wealth of valuable information on their temporal variations, offender characteristics, and victim characteristics. Early geographic analyses of offense locations organized street addresses by the frequency of activity, such as calls for service (see Pierce et al., 1988; Sherman, 1987), and distinguished hot spots by identifying those addresses that produced the highest number of events. Although such analyses were appropriate for certain types of interventions, they did not define hot-spot areas, as a single address may or may not be located within a high-density crime area (Block, 1993). Further, address-level analyses are sensitive to coding errors and short movements of offenders around a specific area (Weisburd and Green, 1995). Crime analysts and researchers sought more sophisticated ways of analyzing their data.

The development of such mapping techniques has progressed immensely over the past ten years. Since the mapping of a large number of data points typically results in a cluttered, uninterpretable map (Maltz et al., 1991), different methods of distinguishing clusters of crime events have developed. Data-driven techniques to identify hot spots of crime range from thematic mapping to very complex point-pattern analyses. Thematic mapping, also known as areal analysis, identifies the density of crime events within arbitrary boundaries such as police reporting areas or Census tracts (Block, 1993). Although policy makers can distinguish areas that experience disproportionate numbers of crimes and target these areas for interventions, areal maps suffer from interpretation problems such as aggregation bias (see Brantingham and Brantingham, 1984). The crime within a "hot" arbitrary areal unit can be concentrated within a very small area, such as a street block. Alternatively, the actual dense area can be divided by boundary lines, diluting the magnitude of the crime problem across areas. These limitations can cause interventions to be mistakenly applied to whole neighborhoods when, in fact, the reality of crime clustering would suggest a much more geographically focused application. Conversely, the limitations can cause actual hot spots to be diluted and therefore missed entirely.

In an effort to better find and describe hot-spot areas, the Illinois Criminal Justice Information Authority developed a software package called Spatial and Temporal Analysis of Crime (STAC). Regardless of artificial boundaries, this program provides a quick way to summarize point data, via complex algorithms, into ellipses drawn around the densest clusters of crime on the map (Block and Block, 1993). STAC is currently being used by at least 69 police departments and continues to be developed (Rich, 1995).

Whatever the means used to identify hot spots, the resulting intervention strategies have almost invariably been place-focused. This is sufficiently true that place-focused strategies have been treated both in practice and in the literature as the only ones feasible. According to Spelman (1995), much of the concentration of crime — for instance, youth crime — at specific places is due to random and temporary fluctuations; police can therefore control about 50% of crime at a particular place through focused problem-solving interventions. "[O]perational personnel need specific objectives that can be reasonably achieved, and at least a rough idea of when to quit. For example, if problem-solving can realistically reduce crime by, say, 40% in some locations, then line officers and neighborhood organizations err if they quit after a 10% reduction — there are many gains left on the table. They also err if they persist after a 38% reduction — there is little left to accomplish, and they could probably achieve more if they took on a different problem" (Spelman, 1995:135-137).

This logic, particularly the last statement, makes sense only as long as the problem-solving strategies in question are focused on the characteristics of the particular places in question. A problem-solving strategy with a different frame of reference could have a much more profound impact (or, of course, one much less profound). An effective youth strategy combining, for example, recreation programs with a curfew might reduce all youth misbehavior, and would therefore necessarily reduce youth misbehavior in hot spots, perhaps beyond what could be achieved through place-focused strategies. At the same time, hot-spot analysis, including mapping, could be an important input into the design and implementation of such strategies.[2] It is important to remember, therefore, that there is no logical reason why hot-spot problems should necessarily be addressed through place-focused interventions.

Neither is there any logical reason that mapping applications should be limited to geographic phenomena, hot-spot analysis, or hot spot/place-focused intervention strategies. For example, many cities have problems with delinquent groups, particularly youth violence fueled by conflicts between gangs (Curry et al., 1994). The resulting crime and disorder problems often exhibit geographic concentration, and mapping can identify hot spots of youth violence. However, such analyses reveal nothing of the violent youth groups, or their conflict networks, that exist across the city. Identifying gangs and understanding the nature of their conflicts could be instrumental in preventing or responding to flare-ups of violence. Interventions focused on serious offenders, violent groups, patterns of conflict, and weapons all hold promise and could reduce violence, including violence concentrated in hot spots.

Criminal network maps and analyses are obvious alternative applications of mapping technology in the problem-solving process. Criminal networks can range from local youth gangs to narcotics organizations to terrorist groups; all represent significant challenges to federal, state, and local law enforcement agencies. A variety of analytic tools and concepts — Anacapa charting systems, computerized link analyses, template matching, event flow charts, and telephone toll analyses — are currently used to examine criminal organizations (Sparrow, 1991). These techniques can be potent tools for combating criminal groups, but are currently utilized primarily by federal law enforcement agencies with respect to more or less traditional organized crime and narcotics trafficking problems. They are underutilized by police agencies with regard to other crime problems. Further, the current state of the art is relatively unsophisticated. Criminal intelligence analysis can be improved by the developing field of structural network analysis, and computerized network analysis programs hold much promise in identifying vulnerabilities, such as central players and weak links, within criminal networks (see Sparrow, 1991).

Other possibilities include the use of mapping to monitor parolees, probationers, and repeat sex offenders (see Rich, 1995) and victims and victim locations (Farrell, 1995). Police agencies have creatively used mapping to solve specific, and often uncommon, problems such as serial murder and rape (Rossmo, 1995; LeBeau, 1992), but rarely use such applications systematically to track potential or more routine existing problems. Mapping can provide an opportunity for technological support for these other problem frames, but the problem-solving frameworks and supporting computer applications both need additional development.

DATA AND INFORMATION RESOURCES

Along with the focus on hot spots and place-focused interventions, mapping has to date relied largely on formal police data. For example, the designers of the Repeat Call Address Policing experiment in Minneapolis avoided using police officers to identify persistent problem addresses for three reasons: "(1) the potential criticism as discriminatory law enforcement; (2) its susceptibility to police officers' pet peeves to the exclusion of major consumers of police resources or major sources of bloodshed; (3) the potential for selection bias in evaluations, resulting from the picking of easier to solve problems" (Buerger, 1994: footnote 3). The result of approaches such as these has been that mapping techniques have been almost totally reliant on official police data. However, such data are known to have important shortcomings. Arrest and investigation data are subject to both underreporting and enforcement bias (Black, 1970). While citizen calls for service are not as affected by police discretion, these data are also subject to both underreporting and overreporting (Pierce et al., 1988; Sherman et al., 1989). No currently available routine reporting systems are good sources of information on disorder and fear (Kennedy and Moore, 1995). Therefore, mapping techniques that rely exclusively on the analysis of official data have their own inherent biases and limits. They also run, to some extent, against the tide of community and problem-solving policing, which seek to manage officer discretion rather than deny it and to promote and benefit from line officers' creativity and problem-solving capacity (Goldstein, 1990; Sparrow et al., 1990; Kennedy and Moore, 1995).

There has been some expansion of mapping analyses to include data from non-police sources. The Illinois Criminal Justice Information Authority developed an extensive geographic database of both community and law enforcement data known as the GeoArchive. The Authority suggests that when combined with a community/problem-solving policing program, a GeoArchive can become "an information foundation for community policing" (Block and Green, 1994:1). A variety of data are collected: street map data; official crime data (calls for service, arrests, offender characteristics, victim characteristics); corrections data (the addresses of persons released on probation or parole); landmark data (parks, schools, public transportation); and population information (Block and Green, 1994). The Chicago Police Department's ICAM system is connected to the city's mainframe computer and provides police officers with the locations of abandoned buildings, businesses, and liquor stores (Rich, 1995). Several multi-agency task forces, such as Denver's PACT (Pulling America's Communities Together) program, have integrated and mapped data to identify risk factors for delinquency in crafting broad, multi-disciplinary solutions to reduce violence (Rich, 1995). These types of information-gathering efforts can be invaluable to police officers and others analyzing urban crime problems and developing appropriate interventions at the local, district, or citywide level.

Even these efforts rely almost entirely on official data collected by public agencies. There have been some exceptions to this rule. For example, in Jersey City, the police department's Planning and Research Bureau and Rutgers University researchers "counted," or assigned, official data to street segments or intersection areas, rather than at specific addresses or larger "areal" units such as police reporting areas. Once the initial counting was complete and the top crime intersection areas were established, these researchers consulted other data sources in determining the groupings of these units into the boundaries of high-activity crime places. In the DMAP, community survey responses and phoned-in citizen tips on narcotics trafficking were used to supplement official data in the identification of drug markets (Weisburd and Green, 1994). Jersey City's pilot problem-oriented policing program to control high-activity violent crime places made use of the observations of Rutgers researchers and the Jersey City Police Department's Violent Crimes Unit officers to identify place boundaries. A wide array of intersection area-level data were considered in defining high-activity crime places, including officers' perceptions of violent crime problems, community perceptions of violent crime problems, physical characteristics, and social characteristics (Braga et al., 1995).

However, some of the richest information for describing public safety problems and driving problem-solving efforts simply is not available from any official data systems. The "experiential assets" of practitioners and community members can make potentially powerful contributions to identifying and understanding crime problems. In particular, qualitative methods such as ethnography, interviews, focus groups, and survey research can supply valuable information.

For communities suffering from violence involving delinquent groups, for example, intelligence on the social networks within groups and the antagonisms between rival groups is important for addressing violent crime in affected neighborhoods. Qualitative methods are appropriate and desirable techniques to collect the relational data on contacts, ties, connections of groups, and group attachments of individuals within networks (Scott, 1991).

Particularly closely linked to crime mapping and hot-spot approaches is cognitive mapping. Cognitive maps represent perceptions of spatial reality (see Smith and Patterson, 1980; Gould and White, 1974) by individuals on such dimensions as street gang territories, drug market areas, and other geographic phenomena. Criminologists have advocated the use of cognitive maps based on the perceptions of law enforcement personnel and community members to enhance community problem-solving efforts within neighborhoods and specific places (see Block and Green, 1994). A key notion in cognitive mapping is that it is the perception of an individual (or the perceptions of individuals) that is being mapped; the resulting construct may or may not have anything meaningful to say about reality. New knowledge, however, can sometimes be gained from the mapping exercise itself, and also from important consistencies and discrepancies between qualitative and official data (Rosenbaum and Lavrakas, 1995). These concepts have been sparsely used in support of crime control and problem-solving exercises; some notable exceptions include the mapping of gang turf based on police officer perceptions in Chicago (Block and Block, 1993), and the identification of problem locations within buildings and common areas by housing project residents in Jersey City (Terrill and Green, 1995).

Both academics and police practitioners have been reluctant to incorporate these methods into easily used mapping approaches and computer applications. Some argue that the subjective assessments of practitioners are not accurate; for example, psychiatrists' ability to predict "dangerous" persons has been found to be minimal (Monahan, 1981; Ennis and Litwack, 1974). Mainstream police administration, and many academic approaches to police and public safety research, have long discounted the views of line police officers as partial, biased, and of no great utility (Goldstein, 1990; Sparrow et al., 1990; Braga et al., 1994). At the same time, many police officers feel that their knowledge and expertise are essentially ineffable — that, in the words of James Fyfe, "It's just something you learn over time, is all" (as quoted in Toch and Grant, 1991:41). Neither attitude — that police officers know nothing, and that police knowledge is irredeemably particular and uncommunicable — lends itself to collecting, testing, and analyzing practitioner knowledge.

However, others feel that practitioners, particularly police officers, develop rich pictures of their environment and can provide accurate and valid assessments of area characteristics, crime problems, and criminal activity (Bittner, 1970; Braga et al., 1994). In Egon Bittner's classic phrase, some officers know "the shops, stores, warehouses, restaurants, hotels, schools, playgrounds, and other public places in such a way that they can recognize at a glance whether what is going on within them is within the range of normalcy" (1970: 90). These perceptions sharpen and improve as police mature in their careers and gain experience (Rubinstein, 1973; Muir, 1977). A rigorous examination of the assessments of experienced narcotics officers relative to other, more formal, measures of drug activity found that the officers were highly capable of identifying street drug activity based on quite brief exposures (Braga et al., 1994). To date, though, most mapping exercises, geographic/hot-spot focused or otherwise, do not rely heavily on the systematic gathering, analysis, and application of information from practitioner or community sources. This is an important, but largely unexplored, frontier (Toch and Grant, 1991).

THE BOSTON GUN PROJECT

The authors have been exploring ways to capture the experiential assets of practitioners, and to incorporate them in the design and implementation of problem-solving interventions, as part of the Boston Gun Project. The Boston Gun Project is a problem-solving exercise aimed at preventing youth violence in Boston by: convening an interagency working group; performing original research into Boston's youth violence problem and illicit gun markets; crafting a citywide, interagency problem-solving strategy; implementing that strategy; and evaluating the strategy's impact. Key participants in the project have included gang officers from the Boston Police Department, probation officers whose jurisdictions incorporate those Boston neighborhoods at high risk for youth gun violence, and city-employed "streetworkers" — outreach specialists focused on preventing and mediating gang disputes and diverting youths from gangs.

It was evident from the beginning of the project that these practitioners knew a great deal about kids, gangs, and youth violence in Boston. In ride-alongs with probation officers through high-risk neighborhoods, for example, the officers could point out gang turf with great specificity, describe how turf and turf patterns had changed over time, trace the history of specific gangs and gang members, describe the criminal activities of particular gangs, and trace the emergence and decline of particular gang-related activities such as wearing particular colors and marking turf with sneakers. Boston Police Department gang officers had a vivid sense of current and historical patterns of gang criminality and conflict, and of gangs' responses to particular police strategies. Streetworkers had insight into all these matters, plus perspective on how gang members and other youths experienced life in their neighborhoods. This included gang members' experience of the threat of other gangs, and how they regarded police and other authorities.

These different groups of practitioners were focused on the same basic issue — in essence, serious youth offending and serious youth offenders — and had a certain amount of experience working with one other. Therefore, their sources of information overlapped to some degree. However, the groups worked from bases of experience that were meaningfully different. Probation officers worked with the courts and convicted offenders, and to some extent with offenders' families, employers, and other community contacts. The probation officers we worked with had also recently begun to "patrol" certain communities at night in conjunction with Boston Police Department gang officers in an effort to control the behavior of high-risk youth offenders in the community. Police gang officers primarily worked the streets, primarily in an adversarial relationship with youth offenders, and had access to police department information. Streetworkers worked closely with individual youths and groups of youths, both in the street and through city-sponsored diversion and recreation programs.

As the project progressed, several key questions emerged regarding the role of gangs and gang conflict in Boston's youth homicide problem. Practitioners felt strongly that several things were true. They believed that Boston had youth gangs, which had identifiable turf and were violent. They believed that the youth homicide problem was almost entirely a gang problem, that essentially all youth homicide offenders were gang members and that essentially all youth homicide victims — excluding innocent bystanders — were gang members. They believed that the basic dynamic that produced gang violence was a vendetta-like "beef" between gangs that was sometimes but not always initiated by drug trafficking or some other instrumental issue, but that once initiated took on a life of its own and could continue indefinitely and even intergenerationally. The authors, in response to this, framed the following essential questions. What was the contribution of gangs to youth homicides in the city? How many gangs and gang-involved youths were there in Boston? Where were gangs' turfs? What were the patterns of conflict and alliance among gangs?

We worked with our practitioner partners to answer these questions in a structured way that would both bring rigor to the analysis and be of utility in designing and implementing a problem-solving response. The following sections describe some of the methods used and the results obtained. We present our various research activities in their proper order of *logical* precedence; the actual research was a bundle of overlapping and simultaneous tasks conducted over roughly the summer of 1995.

Did Boston Have a Gang-Related Youth Homicide Problem?

The central matter was clearly whether youth gangs were important contributors to the city's youth homicide problem. We began, therefore, by addressing this question.

It is noteworthy that this was a question that simply could not have been answered by examining official police records. The Homicide Bureau of the Boston Police Department records as little as possible about the motive in the cases it investigates in order to prevent creating documentation that would be discoverable and of potential use to the defense at trial. The Homicide Bureau has, quite recently, begun issuing annual reports of how many of the previous year's homicides were gang-related, drug-related, domestic, and the like. It does not identify which particular cases belong in these categories, however, and it compiles the reports by polling homicide investigation teams about their previous year's caseload. The bureau's reports, in other words, are themselves based on qualitative methods.

We assessed the contribution of gangs to Boston's youth homicide problem by assembling a group comprised of Boston Police Department gang officers; probation officers; and streetworkers. This group met in three sessions of approximately four hours each.[3] Those participating changed somewhat from session to session, with constant participation by four police officers, one streetworker, and two probation officers, and episodic participation by approximately half a dozen police officers, two streetworkers, and one probation officer.

The authors provided documentary support and kept records of the proceedings.[4] Documentary support consisted of an annualized, alphabetized list of 155 gun and knife homicide victims (that is, each calendar year's victims arranged in alphabetical order) age 21 and under for the years 1990-1994.[5] The list included the names of associated cleared offenders where those names were available; a separate list featured incident locations arranged by victims' names in alphabetical order. Both lists were prepared by the authors using information furnished by the Planning and Research Office of the Boston Police Department. Each participant was provided with this package of documents.

The group examined and discussed each incident of victimization, beginning with the 1994 list and proceeding backward in time. The discussion ranged quite freely but was structured by the authors. For each victimization, the following questions were addressed in roughly the following order. Do you (the group) know what happened in this homicide? Was the victim a gang member? Was the perpetrator (or perpetrators) a gang member (or members)? What was the killing about, and was it gang-related?

As these questions suggest, it took more than gang involvement on either the victim's or perpetrator's part for the incident to "count" as gang-related. The authors did not provide, or press, any particular definition of "gang-related" on the group, though they did sometimes make the formal disposition based on the group discussion. For the most part, however, the practitioners participating had a strong and shared, though often not previously articulated, sense of what it meant for an incident to be gang-related, and this sense was allowed to emerge inductively through the process.

Gang-related, as the group understood it, meant in practice that the incident was either the product of gang behavior such as drug dealing, turf protection, or a continuing "beef" with a rival gang or gangs, or a product of activity that was narrowly and directly connected with gang membership such as a struggle for power within a particular gang. Not all homicide involvement by gang members counted under this definition. A homicide committed by a gang member in the course of an armed robbery of a store, with no other indication of gang-relatedness, would not have been classified as gang-related. The homicide victimization of a gang member, for instance during a street robbery, with no other indication of gang-relatedness, would also not have been classified as gang-related.[6]

The authors also did not provide, or press, a definition of gang on the group.[7] It was clear that violent behavior was central to the conception the practitioners in fact used; during the gang-mapping process, described below, much the same set of participants not infrequently made remarks such as "[group in question] isn't a gang any more, they just sell drugs." In practice, all practitioners used a definition that could be reduced to "self-identified group of kids who act corporately (at least sometimes) and violently (at least sometimes)." "Gang" has much the same place, therefore, in this process that "crime report" has in more traditional mapping operations: though the extent of the connection between the referent and reality is difficult to determine, all participants agree that it has meaning and what that meaning is.

It is worth dwelling on this point. Our process was not intended to, and could not, answer the question "Does Boston have a gang problem?" To do so would have required coming up with a workable definition of gang; ascertaining whether Boston had, by this definition, gangs; and then determining whether Boston's gangs were a problem, with "problem" defined in some way that was independent of the existence of gangs as such. This last step is particularly difficult conceptually; since criminal and violent activity is generally part of the definition of a gang (see, e.g., Miller, 1975), it is hard even in principle to sort out how to differentiate description from diagnosis when discussing "gang violence."

This was not the subject of our inquiry. Though the definition of gang actually used by practitioners is well within the bounds of standard police and academic practice, it is here used essentially as a placeholder conveying no additional information about the nature of gangs in Boston. Our main question could be reframed equally well as "Does Boston have a homicide problem connected to [this youth group phenomenon we have agreed to call gangs]?" We were interested in whether Boston's gangs — gangs as defined by those who worked with them — were an important contributor to the city's youth homicide problem.

Of the 155 victimizations, 107, or 69%, were "known": that is, practitioners could provide an account of what happened. Ninety incidents, or 58% of the total 155 victimizations, were classified by the group as gang-related. All "unknown" incidents were classified as non-gang-related. Seventeen, or 11%, were known but not classified as gang-related. Thus, nearly three-quarters of the incidents classified as non-gang-related were so classified because they were unknown, suggesting that our estimate of the incidence of gang-related homicide is a conservative one.

Certain aspects of this process were noteworthy and shed some light on the validity of the outcomes. There was nearly total consensus across the various practitioner participants concerning what should be classified as known and unknown. There was also nearly total consensus as to what had actually happened in known incidents. These broad agreements could be construed as an unhappy, and falsifying, unwillingness to disagree. We are inclined to construe it otherwise. First, the process itself ran counter in important ways to representations practitioners had already made. They had argued that virtually all youth homicides were gang-related, and that they were familiar with the background of virtually all youth homicides. When the process showed neither proposition to be entirely accurate, the practitioners neither fought it nor indulged in obvious opportunities to "game" the process, for instance, by misclassifying incidents. We are therefore inclined to believe that the various practitioners did in fact know what they said they knew about particular incidents; that there was a genuinely high degree of agreement among members of different agencies, who relied to some extent on different sources of information; and that the results of the process are reasonably reliable.

This exercise therefore produced an assessment that at least 60% of Boston's gun and knife youth homicides over five years were gang-related. In our view, that was sufficient to constitute a gang-related youth homicide problem.

Mapping Gangs and Gang Turf, Estimating Membership, and Identifying Antagonisms and Alliances

Next, we wanted to know how many gangs there were in Boston; what their names, sizes, and turfs were; and what antagonisms and alliances they had. We worked with much the same set of practitioners to answer these questions.

This exercise took three sessions, totaling some ten hours. The first session included only police officers; the second two also included probation officers and streetworkers. The process was extremely straightforward. The practitioners were assembled around a 4'x 8' street map of Boston and asked to identify the territories of individual gangs. As each gang territory was identified, practitioners would draw the territory's boundaries on the map, and one of the authors would number it and record the name of the gang on a separate document.[8] When the territory had been defined, the practitioners were asked to estimate the number of members belonging to the gang. Last, a circle enclosing the numerical gang identifier was drawn on a sheet of flip-chart paper, and the practitioners were asked to name any gangs with whom the instant gang had antagonisms or alliances. These "vectors" were drawn on the flip chart paper, with one color representing antagonisms and another alliances. Antagonisms that were at the time particularly active were so designated.

There was strong agreement among practitioners about what gangs were active in the city. There was a considerable amount of discussion, sparked by examination of the map and the desire to identify enemies and allies, about whether particular gangs that had been historically active were still so. These discussions invariably were resolved in a consensus. There was strong agreement among the practitioners about both turf boundaries and antagonisms/alliances. Police officers and probation officers tended to agree on size estimates, with streetworkers offering marginally higher estimates.

The results produced a geographic territory map for the 61 gangs identified (Figure 1); estimates of membership size; and sociograms of antagonisms and alliances. Membership estimates totaled between 1,100 and 1,300 youths, only about 3% of those in the affected neighborhoods.[9] Only a few gangs reached the 60-100 range, with membership of less than ten not uncommon (see Table 1). The conflict and alliance data were digitized and presented in network form using KrackPlot 1.7 (Krackhardt et al.,1993); this program facilitates the drawing of a network's nodes and lines, and creates a corresponding data matrix of relationships. (The data matrix can then be imported into network analysis software packages such as GRADAP, STRUCTURE, and UCINET for further analyses, as will be treated below.) On quick inspection, there appear to be several noteworthy features of the resulting networks (see Figures 2, 3, and 4). Conflicts outnumber alliances; certain particularly significant "nodes" (Castlegate, Academy) seem evident; and more or less pervasive, but (at any given time) quiescent, rivalries outnumber "live" and active rivalries.

Network Analysis and Computer-Based Network Analysis Applications

The nature of this gang network, and the network as a focus of interventions to reduce serious youth violence, became a central concern as the Boston Gun Project progressed. The research described above, plus other research that showed both homicide victimization and offending to be concentrated among high-rate criminal offenders

Figure 1: Boston Gang Areas

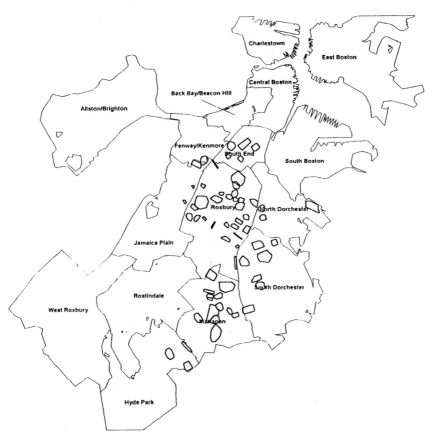

(see Kennedy et al., 1996) made the design of an intervention to reduce gang violence and gang conflict a top priority. Two key ideas emerged: to "tax" gangs for violent activity through focused attention to all their criminal activity, probation and parole conditions, and the like; and to enhance the deterrent impact of this intervention by explicitly communicating the new "rules" in the city to gangs and gang

Table 1: Distribution of Estimated Gang Membership

Range	Number	Percent
Less than 10	11	18.0%
10-19	21	34.4%
20-29	7	11.5%
30-39	8	13.1%
40-49	1	1.6%
50-59	2	3.3%
60-69	2	3.3%
70-79	0	0.0%
80-89	0	0.0%
90-99	1	1.6%
More than 100	1	1.6%
Unknown	7	11.5%

members. The aim was to reduce violence in the community; decrease the fear the kids experience; and throw a "firebreak" across the currently self-sustaining cycle of violence, gun acquisition, and more violence (see Kennedy et al., 1996).

We thus faced two important questions: (1) Which gangs would be the most efficient to target if police agencies wanted to disrupt key sources of conflict? (2) How could we best diffuse the deterrent message across Boston's gang landscape? These are network analysis questions (Sparrow, 1991). We approached them utilizing UCINET IV network analysis software (Borgatti, Everett and Freeman, 1992).

The theoretical concept of "centrality" is clearly important for identifying those gangs that are somehow pivotal or key in the conflict network.[10] "Central" gangs are strategic to target for intervention because their removal will reduce more conflict than targeting peripheral groups. The simplest and most straightforward way to measure centrality is to determine the "degree" of the various nodes in the network. The degree of a point is defined as the number of other points to which it is directly linked (Scott, 1991).

Figure 2: Boston Gang Conflict Network

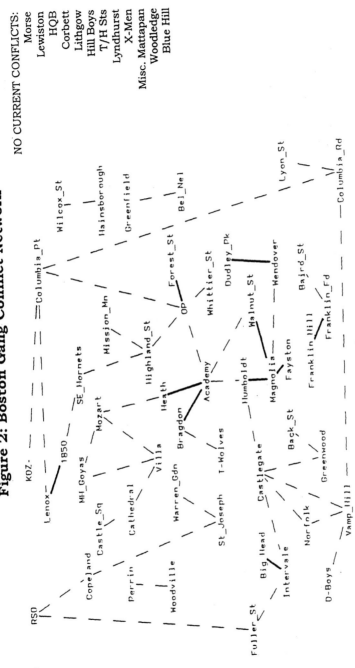

NO CURRENT CONFLICTS:

Morse
Lewiston
HQB
Corbett
Lithgow
Hill Boys
T/H Sts
Lyndhurst
X-Men
Misc. Mattapan
Woodledge
Blue Hill

Key: _ _ _ = conflict
_____ = intense conflict

237

Figure 3: Boston Gang Alliance Network

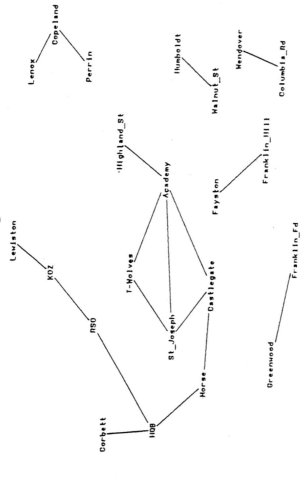

No Current Alliances: Warren Gdn., Woodville, Dudley Park, Lyon St., Back St., D-Boys, Baird St., Wilcox St., Hainsborough, Greenfield, Bel Nel, Lithgow, Mission Main, Hill Boys, T/8 Sts., Lyndhurst, X-Men, Misc Mattapan, Woodledge, Blue Hill, Mozart, Vills, MH Goyas, Heath, Cathedral, Castle Sq., 1 RSO, SE Hornets, Columbia Point, OP, Forest St., Whittier St., Bragdon, Magnolia, Intervale, Fuller St., Big Head, Norfolk, Vamp Hill

238

Figure 4: Boston Gang Conflict and Alliance Network

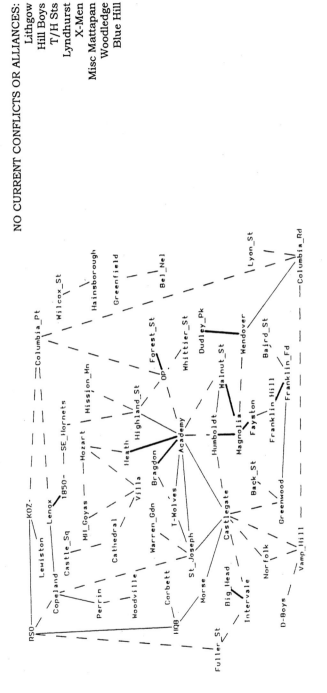

NO CURRENT CONFLICTS OR ALLIANCES:
Lithgow
Hill Boys
T/H Sts
Lyndhurst
X-Men
Misc Mattapan
Woodledge
Blue Hill

Key: — — — = alliance
     - - - - = conflict
     ———— = Intense conflict

239

UCINET and other such programs provide the capacity for quick, easy analysis of such questions. We made some simple judgments in analyzing our gang network. The conflict lines were valued according to the intensity of the conflict (values assigned: intense conflict=2, conflict=1). This allowed the weighting of more violent conflicts to be considered in the identification of central gangs. Conflict lines were also represented as non-directional, as the conflicts were not directed (in other words, a conflict between Heath and Academy is a symmetric negative association). UCINET analysis showed Magnolia, Academy, Orchard Park, and Castlegate as the gangs with the highest centrality in Boston's conflict network (see Table 2).

Degrees are measures of "local centrality": the relative importance of a node within its social neighborhood. A more sophisticated assessment of the importance of a particular gang within the conflict would take into account the centrality of the points to which it is connected (Bonacich, 1972).[11] In other words, certain gangs may be more central or pivotal ("in the thick of things") to youth violence across Boston than other gangs that have the same degree of connections.[12] Network theory uses the concept of "eigenvector centrality" to capture this quality of "centrality of centrality."[13] UCINET analysis of eigenvector centralities reveals Magnolia, Academy, Humboldt, Walnut Street, Fayston Street, Heath, Bragdon Street, Orchard Park, Wendover, and Castlegate to be key players in the conflict network (see Table 3). Probably not coincidentally, these are gangs that consistently come up in conversation with our practitioner partners as the most significant and troublesome. Reducing their violence, and their "beefs" with other gangs, would make sensible first steps in an intervention focused on Boston's gang landscape.

We also used structural network analysis in pursuit of support for an effective communications strategy. Here, UCINET was employed to identify naturally existing subgroups, or "cliques," such that "talking" to one member would effectively be talking to all members.[14] Network theory defines cliques as groups of mutually connected individuals or as pockets of dense connections (Knoke and Kuklinski, 1982). If Magnolia, for example, were subjected to an intensive enforcement effort, or was otherwise communicated with — for instance, through probation officers or formal meetings between gang members and authorities — which other gangs could be expected to be aware of the message being sent by law enforcement agencies?

Table 2: Degree Centrality [a]

Gang	Degree	Normalized Degree[b]
Magnolia	7.00	11.67
Academy	7.00	11.67
Orchard Park	6.00	10.00
Castlegate	5.00	8.33
Intervale Posse	4.00	6.67
Humboldt	4.00	6.67
Columbia Point Dogs	4.00	6.67
Vamp Hill Kings	4.00	6.67
Mozart	3.00	5.00
1850 Building Boys	3.00	5.00
Lenox Hill Smokers	3.00	5.00
Villa Victoria	3.00	5.00
Heath	3.00	5.00
Wendover Falcons	3.00	5.00
Highland Street	3.00	5.00
Walnut Street	3.00	5.00
Columbia Road	3.00	5.00
Bragdon Street	3.00	5.00
Franklin Field	3.00	5.00
Big Head Boys	2.00	3.33
Dudley Park	2.00	3.33
Norfolk Kings	2.00	3.33
Franklin Hill Giants	2.00	3.33
Fuller Street	2.00	3.33
RSO	2.00	3.33
Fayston Street	2.00	3.33
Greenwood Street	2.00	3.33
St. Joseph	2.00	3.33
Forest Street Dodgers	2.00	3.33
South End Hornets	2.00	3.33
Copeland	2.00	3.33
Mission Hill Goyas	2.00	3.33
Cathedral	2.00	3.33
KOZ	1.00	1.67
D-Boys	1.00	1.67
Baird Street	1.00	1.67
Wilcox Street	1.00	1.67
Hainsborough	1.00	1.67
Greenfield	1.00	1.67
Bel Nel	1.00	1.67
Mission Main	1.00	1.67
Back Street Boys	1.00	1.67
Warren Gardens	1.00	1.67
Timberwolves	1.00	1.67

Gang	Degree	Normalized Degree[b]
Whittier Street	1.00	1.67
Perrin Street	1.00	1.67
Woodville	1.00	1.67
Lyon Street	1.00	1.67
Castle Square	1.00	1.67

(a)　The links between nodes were coded as follows: one=conflict; two=intense conflict.

(b)　The normalized degree centrality of each gang is the degree divided by the maximum possible degree (number of connections within the sociogram) expressed as a percentage (Borgatti et al. 1992).

Many different theoretical models exist for identifying subgroups within networks.[15] We explored the n-clan technique for identifying cliques, as it is acknowledged as yielding "the most useful and powerful sociological generalization" of cohesive subgroupings[16] (Scott, 1991:120). The n-clan method is regarded as desirable because it limits the diameter (the path between its most distant members) to be no greater than the value of n which defined the clique. In other words, it ensures relatively close linkages by eliminating outsiders as intermediaries. Two was selected, by convention, as the value of n. Path lengths greater than two risk involving more distant and weak links. As Scott (1991) argues, "Values greater than two can be difficult to interpret sociologically. Distance two relations can be straightforwardly interpreted as those which involve a common neighbor who, for example, may act as an intermediary or a broker" (p.119).

We restricted the algorithm, for convenience, to identify clans that had at least five members; the analysis identified 13 subgroups, with several groupings sharing common members (see Table 4). Each of these cliques would make a useful target for communication strategies since a message to one group would effectively reach at least five groups. Gangs that are common to several cliques, such as Academy, would make particularly useful targets.

Table 3: Bonacich Centrality[a]

Gang	Eigenvector	Normalized Eigenvector
Magnolia	0.509	71.957
Academy	0.437	61.856
Humboldt	0.383	54.117
Walnut Street	0.350	49.512
Fayston Street	0.245	34.629
Heath	0.226	31.969
Bragdon Street	0.223	31.597
Orchard Park	0.186	26.309
Wendover	0.159	22.533
Castlegate	0.135	19.137
Forest Street Dodgers	0.090	12.661
Dudley Park	0.077	10.844
Mozart	0.065	9.148
Columbia Point Dogs	0.060	8.540
Timberwolves	0.054	7.603
Vamp Hill Kings	0.054	7.581
Highland Street	0.052	7.289
Intervale	0.046	6.516
Norfolk Kings	0.045	6.429
Whittier Street	0.045	6.330
Greenwood Street	0.035	4.888
Columbia Road	0.029	4.117
Big Head Boys	0.022	3.136
Villa Victoria	0.022	3.101
Lenox Street Smokers	0.021	3.011
Mission Hill Goyas	0.021	2.947
South End Hornets	0.016	2.232
KOZ	0.015	2.055
1850 Building Boys	0.014	1.986
D-Boys	0.013	1.824
Mission Main	0.012	1.754
Fuller Street	0.012	1.671
Back Street	0.008	1.176
Lyon Street	0.007	0.991
Cathedral	0.006	0.792
RSO	0.003	0.428
Castle Square	0.001	0.191
Copeland	0.001	0.110
St. Joseph	0.000	0.028
Warren Garden	0.000	0.007

(a) The normalized eigenvector is the "scaled eigenvector centrality divided by the maximum difference possible expressed as a percentage" (Borgatti et al., 1992). For more discussion on eigenvector centrality, see Bonacich (1972).

Table 4: N-Clans Cliques

Clique	Gangs
1	Heath, Academy, Orchard Park, Highland St., Walnut St., Bragdon St., St. Joseph, Castlegate, Timberwolves, Humboldt
2	Academy, St. Joseph, Castlegate, Humboldt, Intervale, Norfolk Kings, Vamp Hill Kings, Greenwood, Morse
3	Academy, Copeland, St. Joseph, Castlegate, Timberwolves, Warren Garden
4	Academy, Walnut Street, Castlegate, Magnolia, Humboldt
5	Castlegate, Norfolk Kings, Vamp Hill, Columbia Rd., D-Boys
6	Lenox St., Columbia Point, Orchard Park, Columbia Rod., KOZ
7	Lenox St., Columbia Point, Copeland, RSO, KOZ
8	Lenox St., Copeland, St. Joseph, RSO, Perrin St.
9	Academy, South End Hornets, Orchard Park, Forest St., Highland St., Mission Main
10	Academy, Columbia Point, Orchard Park, Forest St., Highland St., Whittier St.
11	Columbia Point, Vamp Hill Kings, Wendover, Columbia Road, Lyon St.
12	Walnut St., Magnolia, Humboldt, Fayston, Wendover
13	Copeland, Fuller St., RSO, KOZ, HQB

Combining Qualitative and Quantitative Mapping[17]

Having produced the qualitatively-derived map of gang territories, some interesting applications of more traditional mapping techniques became possible. The gang territories were hand-digitized using MAPINFO for Windows. MAPINFO sub-routines allowed us to determine that a relatively small portion of the city of Boston is covered by the 61 gang areas: the sum total geographic expanse of the 61 areas is 1.7 square miles, only 3.6% of Boston's 47.47 square miles. Gang turf makes up only 8.1% of the area of even those Boston neighborhoods — Roxbury, Dorchester, Mattapan, Jamaica Plain, Hyde Park, and the South End — with gangs.

We geocoded 1994 Boston police department data on dimensions that might reasonably be expected to be gang-related: gun assault, weapons offenses, drug offenses, armed robbery, youth homicide and calls for service regarding "shots fired." We then examined what proportion of these reported crimes and calls occurred within and outside gang turf. Gang turf areas experience more than 12% of the city's armed robberies and roughly a quarter of all other categories (see Table 5). Armed robberies are overrepresented in gang areas by a factor of nearly 4:1 relative to the rest of the city as a whole; other categories, by a factor of around 8:1 or more. Relative to the high-crime neighborhoods in which they are found, gang areas experience greater criminal activity in ratios of from nearly 3:1 to nearly 7:1 (see Table 6).[18] Interestingly, drug offenses, which are most open to police discretion and enforcement bias, are only somewhat more overrepresented than serious violent crimes.

Several caveats should be considered in reviewing the findings. We do not take this analysis to suggest that any or all of the gang areas identified are Boston's top crime hot spots; we did not set out to identify crime hot spots in the city. Instead, we identified, for other reasons, areas with youth gangs, and examined certain aspects of those areas. Likewise, we have to date only examined the selected reported crimes noted and cannot speak to other important crimes such as sexual assault.

Nor can it be concluded from this analysis that gangs cause crime and are responsible for the high crime rates in gang areas. While this is likely true in some instances, in others it could well not be. If, for instance, a particular housing project has a high crime rate caused primarily by adults and/or outsiders and a youth gang, it would be a mistake to conclude that the youth gang alone was responsible. More work will need to be done to establish these relationships in particular places.

Nor do our crime data for the most part allow us to distinguish between incidents involving juveniles and those involving adults. This cuts two ways. To the extent that our crime data include offenses committed by adults, any link between youth gangs and crime is *overstated*: controlling gang behavior would not much affect crimes committed by adults. However, if youth gangs are responsible for a disproportionate amount of youth crime committed in the city, and if much of this youth crime is committed in gang areas, then our analysis will *understate* both the importance of gang areas and the potential utility of controlling gang behavior, since gang areas would

Table 5: Selected Crime Incidents and "Shots Fired" Calls in Gang Areas

Incident Type	Gang Areas Total	Percent of City Total	Percent of Neighborhood Total
Gun assault	216	24.1%	28.7%
Weapons offense	121	25.7%	31.1%
Drug offense	1,187	26.0%	36.7%
Armed robbery	292	12.7%	19.6%
Youth homicide*	42	27.1%	28.9%
"Shots fired" calls	789	22.0%	28.0%

*Firearm and knife homicide victims, ages 21 and under, between 1990 and 1994

Table 6: Overrepresentation Ratios of Selected Crime Incidents and "Shots Fired" Calls in Gang Areas

Incident Type	City Ratio	Neighborhood Ratio
Gun assault	8.52:1	4.58:1
Weapons offense	9.28:1	5.13:1
Drug offense	9.40:1	6.58:1
Armed robbery	3.91:1	2.76:1
Youth homicide*	10:1	4.67:1
"Shots fired" calls	7.57:1	4.36:1

*Firearm and knife homicide victims, ages 21 and under, between 1990 and 1994

then represent even more youth crime than our calculated ratios would suggest. In that case, doing something about youth gangs in gang areas would have an even greater impact on *youth* crime. Finally, of course, our data do not allow us to measure neighborhood and community fear, which may well be connected to gang areas (see Katz, 1988).

All that said, there is certainly something going on in and/or around the gang territories we have identified. Whatever it is should get some problem-solving attention, and the mix of qualitatively driven mapping and formal-data-driven mapping is a provocative and potentially useful one.

Figure 5: 1994 Shots Fired Calls for Service
Density of Shots Fired by BPD Reporting Area

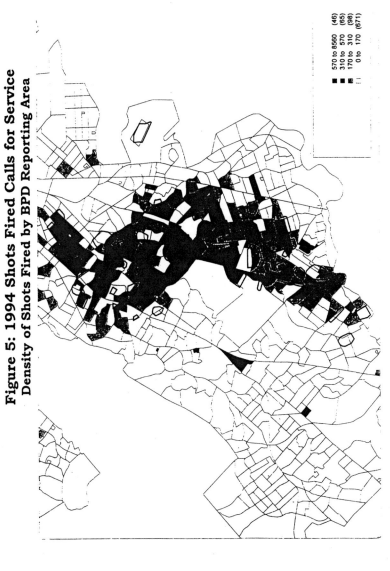

570 to 8560   (46)
310 to 570   (65)
170 to 310   (98)
0 to 170   (671)

Note: Numbers are standardized; Density = Number of shots fired calls by RA Area (Sq. Mi.)

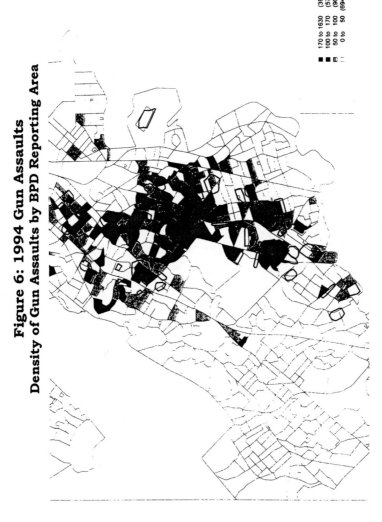

Figure 6: 1994 Gun Assaults
Density of Gun Assaults by BPD Reporting Area

170 to 1630 (39)
100 to 170 (57)
50 to 100 (90)
0 to 50 (694)

Note: Numbers are standardized; Density = Number of gun assaults by area (Sq. Mi.)

Finally, 1994 shots-fired calls for service and gun assault incidents were matched to the Boston Police Department reporting areas (RAs) from which they originated. Since RAs are of varying geographic size, we adjusted the weighting of the RAs by the RA land area in square miles.[19] This process yielded thematic maps of Boston's RAs with the densest concentration of shot-fired calls and gun assault incidents. A comparison of shots fired calls and gun assault incidents to gang areas yields an arc of high-density shots fired areas that appears to correspond almost exactly to the curve of the gang areas, with "hotter" shots-fired areas tending to cluster around gang areas and groups of gang areas (see Figures 5 and 6).[20] As an alternative method of examining the distribution of crime around the gang areas, we used the Illinois Criminal Justice Information Authority's STAC software to identify gun assault incident and shots-fired hot-spot areas.[21] The densest clusters of gun assaults and shots fired fall entirely within the arc of gang territories defined through our qualitative methods (see Figure 7). Recognizing, as always, that correlation is not causation, this is a striking result deserving further attention to assess the role of gangs and consider the possibility of both gang-focused and hot spot-focused interventions.

VALIDITY

The question remains, of course, of the validity of our qualitative methods and the resulting maps and analyses. Two main issues pertain here. One is, *how accurate is the information practitioners provided as inputs to the processes?* Another is, *what distortions might the processes themselves have imposed on the practitioner information, and thus on the products of these processes?*

On these questions, it should be noted first that mapping exercises are not themselves configured as tests of, and cannot in fact answer questions regarding, the validity of the data used as inputs or of the mapping processes themselves. A traditional police data-driven mapping exercise aimed at identifying hot spots of armed robbery is not a test of, and cannot say much regarding, the (for instance) police incident report and call-for-service data used to drive the mapping process. For this, we must turn to other considerations, such as the large body of existing literature on crime reporting and calls for service. This literature says, as we have noted, that these data have strengths and weaknesses that must be attended to in interpreting the results of mapping and other analytic exercises that employ them. But unless the mapping exercise reveals hitherto unknown

Figure 7: Boston Gang Areas: STAC Hot Spot Ellipses

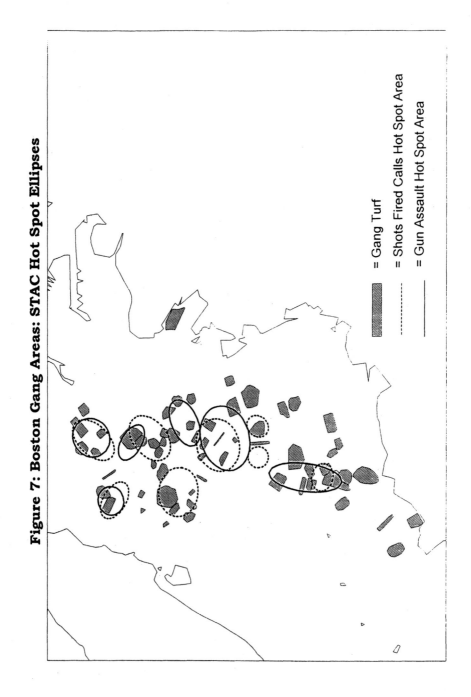

= Gang Turf

= Shots Fired Calls Hot Spot Area

= Gun Assault Hot Spot Area

problems with a particular official-data data set, such as a gross lack of reported crime and calls in an area known for other reasons to have a high crime rate, it can neither add to nor detract from our understanding of the validity of the data used as inputs.

The same is true with our qualitative methods. The structured information-gathering and mapping exercises we employed cannot in and of themselves tell us very much about the validity of the practitioner information that they employed. And since we lack a literature on police practitioner information, knowledge, and perception equivalent to that on reported crime and calls for service, we have considerably less outside theory and analysis to bring to bear on interpreting our results. Nor do we have a literature on the impact various qualitative methods have on the conclusions drawn from practitioner information, knowledge, and perception. It seems to us, in fact, that these are literatures that badly need creating.

There are still some things we can say about these questions. Our results, it seems to us, have face validity. They do not show, for instance, that Boston's youth gangs are responsible for all youth homicide (or no youth homicide); that vast (or tiny) areas of the city are claimed by youth gangs; or that gangs are active in areas with no youth homicide problems (or that there are areas with serious youth homicide and other youth crime problems but no youth gangs). None of the results fall outside the bounds of what one could reasonably expect.

The findings also have a rather high degree of concurrent validity. Inputs to the processes came from, as we have noted, different agencies with different sources of information, organizational cultures, and operational experiences; the results of the processes were credible to both participants from and policy makers in these agencies. Our findings, also as noted herein, fit nicely with official Boston Police Department data on selected reported crimes and calls for service. In addition, they fit nicely with the results of other research on gang size and offending. Further, the findings fit nicely with other research we have done on the criminal histories of youth homicide victims and offenders in Boston.[22] Finally, they were credible to local practitioners not involved in the process who had their own sources of information and knowledge on the dimensions we examined.[23]

None of this, of course, makes our findings true: practitioners could have a shared, but inaccurate, view of reality, and the match between this and other research does not mean that gang realities in Boston in fact resemble those found elsewhere. To actually test the truth of our findings, we need pertinent and independent sources of information. The trouble is that that information is not available from existing official sources, nor from any other readily utilizable sources. We can work with homicide case files and investigators to construct alternative accounts of the incidents we examined, and we are in fact pursuing this avenue. But homicide investigators do not routinely concern themselves with the key gang/non-gang distinction we are addressing. Thus, they do not address this question in each of their cases, nor do they have definitions of gang and gang-related that are consistent and commensurate with those we used. We can work with gang members and community members to address the issues of gang size, gang relationships, and gang connection to homicide events, but the results of these methods, while interesting and informative, would themselves be subject to questions of validity. As with the results of mapping and other similar exercises based on official quantitative data, the rigorous testing of our results lies on the murky border between difficult and impossible.

Happily, for the purposes for which our exercises were designed, this doesn't matter very much. Our answers are good enough to make policy. They tell us with acceptable reliability whether Boston has a youth gang homicide problem — it does; how productive an effective intervention aimed at that problem could be in the context of youth homicide in the city — it could reach more than half and probably not more than 80% of such victimization; and provide some guidance as to how and where to apply group-, hot spot-, and network-focused interventions. Like more traditional official data-driven mapping tools, the answers are intended to help move the problem-solving process along, and this they do.

CONCLUSION

The exercises described in this article — assessing the contribution of Boston's youth gangs to its youth homicide problem; identifying gang territories; estimating gang memberships; identifying patterns of conflict and alliance among gangs; and analyzing the resulting products to help understand and intervene in a serious local crime problem — rely on the structured gathering of information from practitioners. These approaches represent potentially powerful additions to mapping crime and public safety problems, and to supporting the design and implementation of strategies to address those problems. Our findings indicate that alternative sources of information can be used to good effect in diagnosing and responding to crime and public safety problems. These sources include qualitative methods to structure practitioner knowledge, and alternative mapping concepts and applications such as criminal network maps and computer network analysis. These techniques reveal a rich understanding of the social processes underlying the spatial representations of criminal activity. Without the robust qualitative mapping exercises, traditional mapping techniques and the geographic manifestation of youth firearms violence likely would have steered us toward place-focused interventions. Our expanded problem-solving framework has the potential to produce a more refined and possibly more effective intervention.

The mapping applications utilized in this problem-solving exercise also underscore the value of capturing practitioners' extensive experience and knowledge in understanding crime and public safety problems. The considerable expertise and creative potential of line personnel are important, and currently underutilized, assets. The community and problem-solving policing movement seeks to benefit from the creativity and capacity of line officers to respond to crime problems. Structured qualitative information-gathering and mapping exercises incorporating police officers and other practitioners can be an effective tool in collecting and ordering these experiential assets, and, thus, expanding the potential of police departments and other agencies.

Police departments adopting community and problem-solving policing must also foster enthusiasm and promote creativity among line officers and supervisors, in order to develop their organizational capacity to respond to seemingly intractable crime problems such as youth firearms violence or drug markets. "Knowledge-based" mapping can provide an effective vehicle to generate interest and rally support. The products of our mapping exercises were striking to both our practitioner partners and policy-level officials; they recognized that the description and analysis of Boston's gang landscape, the contribution of gangs to the city's youth homicide problem, and the presentation of gang conflict and alliance networks provided tangible starting points to craft appropriate problem-solving responses. At the same time, many participants were surprised by the various findings and maps, indicating that the structured processes added value to the practitioner knowledge used as inputs, and that the exercise of representing, refining, and structuring such knowledge can be useful even to those from whom knowledge is being drawn. The active participation of practitioners in the data-collection process helped bridge the commonplace and stifling "academic-practitioner gap," generated considerable enthusiasm, and lent greater credibility to the research findings among Boston's law enforcement community. This high level of acceptance and interest proved to be a valuable asset in the implementation of an innovative problem-solving approach aimed at controlling serious youth violence in Boston.

Acknowledgments: This project, "Firearms and Violence: Juveniles, Illicit Markets, and Fear," was supported under award #94-IJ-CX-0056 from the National Institute of Justice, Office of Justice Programs, U.S. Department of Justice. Points of view in this document are those of the authors and do not necessarily represent the official position of the U.S. Department of Justice.

NOTES

1. For more on the Boston Gun Project, see Kennedy et al.,1996.

2. One operation fitting this pattern was Tampa PD's QUAD street drug market disruption, which used police officers and community sources to identify and track street drug-dealing hot spots and then used that information as a key input in a strategy aimed at the entire Tampa street market (see Kennedy, 1993.)

3. The authors would like to thank Amy Solomon for her valuable assistance in coordinating these meetings.

4. These records were in the form of written notes only. The possibility of recording the proceedings was taken up, and soundly rejected, by the practitioners involved.

5. This list of victims is the same one being used for other parts of the Boston Gun Project, such as assessing demographic profiles and criminal histories of victims and offenders, and analyzing weapon utilization (see Kennedy et al., 1996). This sample excluded four obviously non-"street" crimes that otherwise fit this profile (one accident, one suicide, and two fetal homicides). Between 1990 and 1994, these 159 youth victims accounted for 30% of the total number of homicides (524) and 37% of all gun and knife homicides (435) in Boston.

6. Law enforcement agencies in different cities use different definitions for "gang-related" crime, and this impacts the amount of gang-related crimes reported. For example, Los Angeles defines crime as gang-related when gang members participate, regardless of motive; Chicago uses a

more restrictive definition, classifying homicides as "gang-related" only if there is a gang motive evident (Maxson and Klein, 1990).

7. Defining "gang" is a core problem in analyzing and understanding gang- and group-related youth crime and violence (see Begall and Curry, 1995). The character of criminal and disorderly juvenile gangs and groups varies widely both within and across cities (see, e.g., Curry et al., 1994).

8. This approach to mapping gang turfs has similarities, but is not identical, to that used in Carolyn and Richard Block's well-known study of gang homicide in Chicago (Block and Block, 1993). The map of gang territories used in that research was provided by the commander of the centralized gang unit of the Chicago Police Department and later digitized by Richard Block. Although the broad turf geographies of the largest Chicago gangs were extremely illuminating for research purposes, the maps, in practice, were not regarded as useful for decision making by Chicago police officers. Apparently, the broad maps lacked the detail necessary to analyze and respond to conflicts between factions of the largest gangs. Further, the maps needed to be updated regularly to reflect the dynamic changes in gang territories and disputes over time, which was not routinely done. Additional research is being pursued by the authors of the original Chicago study to detail these factions, and to include the perceptions of other important stakeholders such as the narcotics unit and community members (Carolyn Block, personal communication).

9. This figure was calculated by dividing the practitioners' estimate of gang members by the total population aged 14-21 in neighborhoods that had gangs (South End, Roxbury, Jamaica Plain, Mattapan, Hyde Park, North Dorchester, and South Dorchester). The small proportion of Boston's youths involved in gangs is consistent with estimates of youth participation in gangs from other cities (see Klein, 1995; Esbensen and Huizinga, 1993).

10. For a discussion of centrality and other key concepts in network theory, see Sparrow, 1991.

11. As Scott (1991) summarizes, "Bonacich holds that the centrality of a particular point cannot be assessed in isolation from the centrality of all other points to which it is connected...that is to say, the centrality of I equals the sum of its connections to other points, weighted by the centrality of each of these other points" (p.91). Degree and Bonacich centrality are two approaches to identifying central points within a network. Theoretically, these measures were most appropriate to answer our questions; however, other measures exist that researchers may want to consider, including: betweenness, closeness, Euclidean centrality after

multidimensional scaling, point strength, and business (see Sparrow, 1991, for a discussion).

12. Our application of a Bonacich centrality is a departure from convention; this measure of centrality is based on a notion of "transmission" or "transmission of influence" between more central players. In most cases, the transmission mechanism is an association or an alliance. In this study, the mechanisms are antagonisms and recurring violence; the Bonacich measure was used to identify gangs that are central to conflict with other very active "beefing" gangs. We are positing that a law enforcement focus on a central gang will disrupt more antagonisms and efficiently reduce the transmission of violence. These gangs are also efficient to target if practitioners are interested in sending a deterrent message to other active gangs; this is discussed further below.

13. Larger eigenvector coefficients indicate increased importance of a node in the network. The Bonacich centrality routine calculates all possible eigenvalues of the relationship matrix (via factor analysis), but only gives the eigenvector corresponding to the largest possible eigenvalue as a measure of centrality (see Borgatti et al., 1992).

14. For clique identification, conflict and alliance networks were combined and analyzed; the assumption was made that information travels equally well through alliance and conflict links. It could well be that it does not; however, field interviews with gang members and Boston Police Department gang officers indicate that gangs pay close attention to the activities of their rivals. The links in these analyses were not valued according to the intensity of the conflict or the presence of an alliance (values assigned: conflict or alliance=1, no conflict or alliance=0).

15. As these analyses were exploratory, we selected a recommended technique. Researchers and practitioners may want to explore other techniques, such as k-cores, m-cores, k-plex, cliques, and n-cliques, to identify cohesive subgroupings within networks (see Knoke and Kiklinski, 1982; Scott, 1991).

16. The interpretation of the n-clan technique and the concept "cohesive subgroupings" is not straightforward when the links between nodes represent hostilities rather than lines of communication or association. The transmission of information in groups is traditionally represented as communication between willing partners, such as brokers or liaisons in a fencing operation. Although a "partnership" does not exist, we suggest that information can also travel through groupings of gangs in conflict due to their sensitivity to the actions of their rivals. It is likely that a deterrent message can diffuse through a clique of gangs when the illicit activities of one gang have been halted by an intensive enforcement effort. Further, the deterrent message can be amplified to other gangs in the identified clique if all are visited by law enforcement officers and edu-

cated on their behavior (violence) that triggered the intervention on the targeted gang.

17. We would like to thank Charles Ellis of MaconUSA for his generous help in facilitating certain of the mapping tasks in this project.

18. In estimating how "overrepresented" crime is in these gang areas relative to the rest of the city, we compared the crime rates in gang areas to what would be expected if crime were evenly distributed across the city. The proportion of the city occupied by gang areas is 3.6%; the neighborhoods in which there is at least one gang area comprise 8.1% of the area of the city. The expected crime rates for the gang areas were calculated by: subtracting the total crime in gang areas from the total crime in the city; multiplying by .036 to estimate the crime that would be expected in the areas if it was not gang turf; adding this estimate of "base" crime in the areas to the total crime in the city; and multiplying by .036. The same procedure was used to estimate the expected crime rates for the 8.1% of the neighborhoods with at least one gang area.

19. The standardization per square mile was necessary to prevent distortions caused by aggregating the data. If the thematic shading of "hotter" RAs was based on raw totals, those areas that had the highest counts would be designated as the "busiest" areas. These findings, however, would necessarily be biased by the size of the RA. Boston's reporting areas are not proportional; certain RAs are more than ten times the size of others. Thus, the greater geographic expanse increased the likelihood of experiencing a gun assault or shot fired, and thematic shading based on raw counts of incidents per RA were more influenced by size than intensity of activity.

20. Areal analyses were used only to exhibit the distribution of gun assaults and shots-fired calls around gang areas. Although thematic mapping was very useful for preliminary research into the relationship between crime and gang turfs, we caution others from making policy decisions or designing interventions on the basis of such techniques. As noted, areal analyses suffer from interpretation problems, such as aggregation bias (Brantingham and Brantingham, 1984) and spatial autocorrelation (Roncek and Montgomery, 1993; Odland, 1988).

21. The STAC analyses were conducted for the entire city of Boston (area=419,676,777 sq. meters), with a search radius of 325 square meters (the minimum search size STAC would allow for a city-wide analysis). Both analyses yielded significant Nearest Neighbor Index scores (shots fired=0.26, gun assault=.30), indicating that clustering exists within the geographic distribution.

22. See Kennedy et al., 1996. Briefly, three-quarters of both youth homicide victims and known youth homicide offenders had at least one arraignment in Massachusetts courts; of those with at least one arraign-

ment, more than 40% had ten or more arraignments, for a wide variety of offense categories.

23. One long-time gang crime prosecutor in the U.S. Attorney's office reacted to the network map of gang antagonisms by leaping to his feet and shouting, "Yes! That's it!"

REFERENCES

Ball, R. and G. D.Curry (1995). "The Logic of Definition in Criminology: Purposes and Methods for Defining 'Gangs.'" *Criminology* 33:225-245.

Bittner, E. (1970). *The Functions of the Police in a Modern Society.* Bethesda, MD: U.S. National Institute of Mental Health.

Black, D. (1970). "The Production of Crime Rates." *American Sociological Review* 35:733-748.

Block, C. R. (1993). "STAC Hot Spot Areas: A Statistical Tool for Law Enforcement Decisions." In: C.R. Block and M. Dabdoub (eds.), *Workshop on Crime Analysis Through Computer Mapping Proceedings.* Chicago, IL: Illinois Criminal Justice Information Authority.

—— and R. Block (1993). *Street Gang Crime in Chicago.* Research in Brief Series. Washington, DC: U.S. National Institute of Justice.

Block, C.R. (1996). Personal communication to the first author from the senior research analyst of the Statistical Analysis Center, Illinois Criminal Justice Information Authority.

Block, C.R. and L. Green (1994). *The GeoArchive Handbook: A Guide for Developing a Geographic Database as an Information Foundation for Community Policing.* Chicago, IL: Illinois Criminal Justice Information Authority.

Bonacich, P. (1972). "Factoring and Weighting Approaches to Status Scores and Clique Identification." *Journal of Mathematical Sociology* 2:113-120.

Borgatti, S., M. Everett and L. Freeman (1992). *UCINET IV Version 1.0.* Columbia: Analytic Technologies.

Braga, A.A., D.L. Weisburd, and L.A. Green (1995). "Identifying Violent Crime Hot Spots in Jersey City." Paper presented at the annual meeting of the American Society of Criminology, Boston, November.

Braga, A.A., L.A. Green, D.L. Weisburd, and F. Gajewski (1994). "Police Perceptions of Street-Level Narcotics Activity: Evaluating Drug Buys as a Research Tool." *American Journal of Police* 13:37-58.

Brantingham, P. and P. Brantingham (1984). *Patterns in Crime*. New York, NY: Macmillan.

Buerger, M. (1994). "The Problems of Problem-Solving: Resistance, Interdependencies, and Conflicting Interests." *American Journal of Police* 13:1-36.

Curry, G.D., R. Ball, and R. Fox (1994). *Gang Crime and Law Enforcement Recordkeeping*, Research in Action. Washington, DC:U.S. National Institute of Justice.

Durbak, A. and G. Rengert (1993). "More Than Just a Pretty Map: How Can Spatial Analysis Support Police Decisions?" In: C.R. Block and M. Dabdoub (eds.), *Workshop on Crime Analysis Through Computer Mapping Proceedings*. Chicago, IL: Illinois Criminal Justice Information Authority.

Ennis, B. and T. Litwack (1974). "Psychiatry and the Presumption of Expertise: Flipping Coins in the Courtroom." *California Law Review* 62: 693-752.

Esbensen, F.-A. and D. Huizinga (1993). "Gangs, Drugs, and Delinquency in a Survey of Urban Youth." *Criminology* 31:565-587.

Farrell, G. (1995). "Preventing Repeat Victimization." In: Michael Tonry and David Farrington (eds.), *Building a Safer Society: Strategic Approaches to Crime Prevention*. Crime and Justice: A Review of Research, vol. 19. Chicago, IL: University of Chicago Press.

Goldstein, H. (1990). *Problem-Oriented Policing*. Philadelphia, PA: Temple University Press.

Gould, P. and R. White (1974). *Mental Maps*. New York, NY: Penguin Books.

Katz, J. (1988). *The Seductions of Crime*. New York, NY: Basic Books.

Kennedy, D.M. (1993). "Closing the Market: Controlling the Drug Trade in Tampa, Florida." Program Focus series, National Institute of Justice, U.S. Department of Justice, Washington, DC.

—— and M. Moore (1995). "Underwriting the Risky Investment in Community Policing: What Social Science Should Be Doing to Evaluate Community Policing." *Justice System Journal* 17:271-291.

—— A.M. Piehl, and A.A. Braga (1996). "Youth Violence in Boston: Gun Markets, Serious Youth Offenders, and a Use Reduction Strategy." *Law and Contemporary Problems* 59:147-196

Klein, M. (1995). *The American Street Gang: Its Nature, Prevention, and Control*. New York, NY: Oxford.

Knoke, D. and J. Kuklinski (1982). *Network Analysis*. Beverly Hills, CA: Sage.

Krackhardt, D., M. Lundberg, and L. O'Rourke (1993). "KrakPlot: A Picture's Worth a Thousand Words." *Connections* 16(1&2): 37-47.

LeBeau, J. (1992). "Four Case Studies Illustrating the Spatial-Temporal Analysis of Serial Rapists." *Police Studies* 15:124-145.

Maltz, M. (1993). "Crime Mapping and the Drug Market Analysis Program (DMAP)." In: Carolyn R. Block and Margaret Dabdoub (eds.), *Workshop on Crime Analysis Through Computer Mapping Proceedings.* Chicago, IL: Illinois Criminal Justice Information Authority.

—— A. Gordon, and W. Friedman (1991). *Mapping Crime in Its Community Setting: Event Geography Analysis.* New York, NY: Springer-Verlag.

Maxson, C. and M. Klein (1990). "Street Gang Violence: Twice as Great or Half as Great?" In: C. Ronald Huff (ed.), *Gangs in America.* Newbury Park, CA: Sage.

McEwen, J.T. and F. Taxman (1995). "Applications of Computer Mapping to Police Operations." In: J.E. Eck and D. Weisburd (eds.), *Crime and Place.* Crime Prevention Studies, vol. 4. Monsey, NY: Criminal Justice Press.

Miller, W.B. (1975). *Violence by Youth Gangs and Youth Groups as a Crime Problem in Major American Cities.* Washington, DC: U.S. National Institute for Juvenile Justice and Delinquency Prevention.

Monahan, J. (1981). *Predicting Violent Behavior: An Assessment of Clinical Techniques.* Beverly Hills, CA: Sage.

Muir, W. (1977). *Police: Streetcorner Politicians.* Chicago, IL: University of Chicago Press.

Odland, J. (1988). *Spatial Autocorrelation.* Beverly Hills, CA: Sage.

Pierce, G., S. Spaar, and L. Briggs (1988). *The Character of Police Work: Implications for the Delivery of Services.* Boston, MA: Center for Applied Social Research, Northeastern University.

Rich, T. (1995). *The Use of Computerized Mapping in Crime Control and Prevention Programs.* Research in Action. Washington, DC: U.S. National Institute of Justice.

Roncek, D. and A. Montgomery (1993). "Spatial Autocorrelation Revisited: Conceptual Underpinnings and Practical Guidelines for the Use of Generalized Potential as a Remedy for Spatial Autocorrelation in Large Samples." In: Carolyn R. Block and Margaret Dabdoub (eds.), *Workshop on Crime Analysis Through Computer Mapping Proceedings.* Chicago, IL: Illinois Criminal Justice Information Authority.

Rosenbaum, D. and P. Lavrakas (1995). "Self Reports About Place: The Application of Survey and Interview Methods to the Study of Small Areas." In: John Eck and David Weisburd (eds.), *Crime and Place.*

Crime Prevention Studies, vol. 4. Monsey, NY: Criminal Justice Press.

Rossmo, D.K. (1995). "Place, Space, and Police Investigations: Hunting Serial Violent Criminals." In: John Eck and David Weisburd (eds.), *Crime and Place.* Crime Prevention Studies, vol. 4. Monsey, NY: Criminal Justice Press.

Rubinstein, J. (1973). *City Police.* New York, NY: Farrar, Straus, and Giroux.

Scott, J. (1991). *Social Network Analysis: A Handbook.* Newbury Park, CA: Sage.

Sherman, L. (1987). *Repeat Calls to Police in Minneapolis.* Washington, DC: Crime Control Institute.

—— and D. Weisburd (1995). "General Deterrent Effects of Police Patrol in Crime Hot Spots: A Randomized Controlled Trial." *Justice Quarterly* 12:625-648.

—— P. Gartin, and M. Buerger (1989). "The Hot Spots of Predatory Crime: Routine Activities and the Criminology of Place." *Criminology* 27:27-56.

Smith, C. and G. Patterson (1980). "Cognitive Mapping and the Subjective Geography of Crime." In: D. Georges-Abeyie and K. Harries (eds.), *Crime: A Spatial Perspective.* New York, NY: Columbia University Press.

Sparrow, M. (1991). "The Application of Network Analysis to Criminal Intelligence: An Assessment of the Prospects." *Social Networks* 13: 251-274.

—— M. Moore, and D. Kennedy (1990). *Beyond 911: A New Era for Policing.* New York, NY: Basic Books.

Spelman, W. (1995). "Criminal Careers of Public Places." In: J.E. Eck and D. Weisburd (eds.), *Crime and Place.* Crime Prevention Studies, vol. 4. Monsey, NY: Criminal Justice Press.

Spergel, I. (1995). *The Youth Gang Problem: A Community Approach.* New York, NY: Oxford University Press.

Terrill, W. and L. Green (1995). "Mapping and Identifying Hot Spots in Public Housing." Paper presented at the annual meeting of the American Society of Criminology, Boston, November.

Toch, H. and J.D. Grant (1991). *Police as Problem Solvers.* New York, NY: Plenum Press.

U.S. National Institute of Justice (1989). *Program Plan.* Washington, DC: Author.

Weisburd, D. and L. Green (1994). "Defining the Street-Level Drug Market." In: D. MacKenzie and C. Uchida (eds.), *Drugs and Crime: Evaluating Public Policy Initiatives*. Thousand Oaks, CA: Sage.

—— (1995). "Policing Drug Hot Spots: The Jersey City DMA Experiment." *Justice Quarterly* 12:711-736.

Weisburd, D., L. Maher, and L. Sherman (1992). "Contrasting Crime General and Crime Specific Theory: The Case of Hot Spots of Crime." *Advances in Criminological Theory*, vol. 4. New Brunswick, NJ: Transaction Books.

MAPPING CRIME FOR ANALYTIC PURPOSES: LOCATION QUOTIENTS, COUNTS, AND RATES

by

Patricia L. Brantingham
Simon Fraser University

and

Paul J. Brantingham
Simon Fraser University

Abstract: *Crime can be analyzed and mapped in a number of different ways. This article compares maps of violent crime across the cities of British Columbia utilizing three crime measures: counts, rates and crime location quotients (LQCs). The LQC, adapted from regional planning, provides views of crime patterns not obtained with the two more traditional measures of crime. When used in conjunction with crime counts and rates, the LQC offers a way of understanding how one area is different from another for purposes of research and deployment of prevention and control resources.*

Crime and its contextual backcloth exist at many spatial and temporal levels of resolution, from the international scene to the individual crime site, from the trends of centuries to the patterns of seconds (Brantingham and Brantingham, 1993, 1984; Brantingham et al.,

Address correspondence to: Patricia L. Brantingham, School of Criminology, Simon Fraser University, Room WMC-1630, Burnaby, BC V5A 1S6, CAN (e-mail: pbrantin@sfu.ca).

1976). That is, crime can be studied, analyzed and dealt with at many different levels of aggregation in time and space. Meaningful crime analysis can be done, for instance, at international levels, at national levels, across smaller areas that range from regions to states to counties to cities, and at detailed levels within a particular city — even down to the street block or individual address level. Temporal analyses can sweep across centuries, can examine a set of years, months, days, hours, minutes or seconds. Over the past decade, mapping has become a key tool for crime analysts seeking to understand the patterns of crime (see, e.g., Block et al., 1995), enabling them to see or visualize differences and similarities across time and space.

Analyses of individual criminal events and of individual person, building or street victimization studies are currently of great interest (Clarke, 1980, 1992), but for practical purposes individual criminal events must be aggregated in order to assess patterns and devise methods for addressing them (e.g., Kohfeld and Sprague, 1990; Kennedy and Forde, 1990; Normandeau, 1987; Brantingham et al., 1991; Cusson, 1983, 1993). The variety of questions open to the crime analyst and the level in the cone of resolution used in analysis will always vary with the type of problem being considered. In addition, the type of crime measure used in analysis will vary with the problem under consideration.

This article explores how questions about crime, measures of crime and levels of resolution are linked conceptually, and how crime analysis can be improved by mapping different measures of crime and comparing the results. The article illustrates this by mapping three different crime measures — the crime count, the crime rate, and the crime location quotient (LQC) — at the interurban level of resolution, utilizing 1994 crime data from the 68 separate municipal policing jurisdictions in British Columbia, CAN.[1]

A particular emphasis is placed on crime location quotients because this is a relatively new technique for criminologists. The LQC will be described in more detail later in this article, but it is basically a method of measuring the relative mix of different types of crimes for a particular area compared to the mix in surrounding areas. For example, a city such as Tucson or Virginia Beach can have a relatively low robbery rate but still have neighborhoods in which robbery makes up a relatively high proportion of all crimes compared to the city as a whole. Robbery is a problem in such neighborhoods even when it is not a problem citywide. Conversely, robbery can make up a very high proportion of offenses in a city such as San Francisco or

Newark, but within such "robbery" cities there will be subareas in which robbery represents a low proportion of crimes. Such proportional mixes are independent of total crimes in an area, and really represent a local crime "specialization."

As will be shown in this article, when used in conjunction with crime counts and crime rates, LQCs offer a way of understanding how one area is different from another for purposes of research and deployment of prevention and control resources. This article focuses on city-level data, but the LQC can be used for comparison of states or nations on the one hand or for comparison of regions, cities or neighborhoods on the other. The LQC can be used for comparison of the crime mix in different decades within centuries in historical research, or for comparison of the crime mix within the different hours of the day in thinking about deployment of police during different shifts. It is a tool that can be used at different levels of spatial and temporal resolution.

STATISTICAL CRIME ANALYSIS

There is a need for constant improvement and innovation in methods of analysis, no matter what questions are being asked or what levels of resolution are being studied. Methods are constantly changing. The methods used by criminologists frequently originate from other disciplines such as sociology, psychology, geography, statistics or mathematics. These are not static disciplines. Interestingly, many currently used techniques had their origins in studies of criminal events. For instance, in statistics both Quetelet (1842) and Poisson (1837) focused on the study of crime. Galton, Pearson and Yule were all concerned, among other things, with developing statistical techniques that could be used to understand crime, as both hereditary and social problems (Stigler, 1986).

This article describes and maps the LQC, a new type of crime measure borrowed from the related disciplines of regional economics and regional planning. The location quotient (LQ) is used in regional planning and regional economics to look at *relative* local economic activity. LQs will be described in some detail after a brief review of crime counts and crime rates.

Crime analysis in the tradition of Guerry (1831) and Quetelet (1842), and as conducted by most criminologists, looks at crime as an aggregate measure for some summary unit. The most common summary measures are crime counts and crime rates based on police-recorded offenses, victimization rates based on survey estimates, and offender rates based on surveys and judicial convictions data.

Crime counts are used to assess the locations of "hot spots," assess police work loads and estimate future resource needs. Police, after all, must respond to discrete events, not estimates or ratios. In Canada, crime counts take the form of "actual crimes." These represent events recorded as crimes following a preliminary investigation that has established that a "reported crime" has in fact occurred. Crime rates, in contrast, are used to assess the risk of crimes occurring to particular types of people in particular locations or at particular times, and to assess trends discounted for changing conditions (such as population growth). Crime rates are particularly useful in planning prevention campaigns and in assessing the impact of changing social conditions of the risk of crime. Crime rates use some measure of crime occurrence as a numerator and units at risk as a denominator. The numbers in the numerator and denominator vary. Ideally the numerator is some measure of events or occurrences, and the denominator is the most direct measure of units at risk. When the numerator is a personal crime, the denominator frequently is the number of people residing in the aggregation area. When the numerator is residential breaking and entering, the denominator frequently is the number of dwelling units.

There are always problems with such crime measures. The count of events, based on official data, is usually an undercount both because some crimes are not reported to police and because counting and recording rules typically record only the most serious offense in any complex criminal transaction. Such counts do, however, appear to be good measures of serious offenses and of offenses involving lost property covered by insurance (Litton and Pease, 1984; Brantingham and Brantingham, 1984; Gove et al., 1985). There are difficulties obtaining reasonable estimates for denominators when the potential "victims" move or are moveable. Boggs' (1960) work began the exploration of how patterns change as the denominator in the ratio changes. For example, an auto theft rate based on a residential population ratio produces a very different picture of high- and low-crime areas in a city from that produced by a rate calculated using the number of automobiles present in the different areas. Boggs' (1960) work has been carried many steps further by Harries (1991); both show the interesting variability in what is "seen" as denominators change.

LOCATION QUOTIENTS

Location Quotients (LQs) are a measure developed in regional planning and economics to try to address questions of the relative structure and importance of local economies, while conceptually avoiding some of the stationarity problems of spatial analysis. Local areas are placed within a wider comparative context for analysis. Regional science has always looked for ways to compare activity at metropolitan or regional levels of aggregation.

LQs were developed to indicate activity in one area compared to its surrounds. For example, within a metropolitan area the city center will contain most of the commercial activities. Rural farming areas also have commercial centers: some small towns provide minimum essential goods and services; slightly larger towns provide a larger array of goods and services for a wider area encompassing a number of the smaller towns and their hinterlands; while finally a major city will provide a much wider range of specialized goods and services to a much larger region encompassing many hinterlands, small towns, and larger towns. Each town, however, is a commercial center, although the volumes of business in the smaller towns make it difficult to see them as commercial centers from the perspective of large cities. Still, the small town commercial centers may provide the same core mix of commercial activities (albeit with less choice of suppliers) provided in the largest cities. When the smaller towns and large cities provide the same mix of goods and services, they may be functionally equivalent even though their volumes of activities are very different. Rural towns attract business from the hinterland; large cities attract business from the hinterland and from the rural towns.

Similar considerations can be seen at work across the neighborhoods and communities within large cities. Bedroom neighborhoods often have small local commercial and entertainment districts; larger subdivisions have local shopping malls, bar clusters, multi-screen theaters; and finally, the urban center has a dense business, entertainment and industrial concentration that attracts people from all parts of the metropolis. Commuting between areas is the modern urban way of life.

Before this article describes the way LQs are calculated, it should start to become clear that such relative measures have a use in crime analysis. Within a country such as the U.S. certain states and cities dominate the total counts of crimes or have the highest crime rates. However, even in lower crime states or cities, there can be certain types of crimes that are disproportionally present compared to their surrounding areas and disproportional compared to the mix in higher-crime-rate cities or states. For example, 40 or 50 robberies in a city in a low-robbery state such as Idaho or Wisconsin may make that a relatively high-robbery city in context. In contrast, a city with 40 or 50 robberies in a high-robbery state such as California would be a relatively low-robbery city. This type of relative specialization can have meaning in crime analysis, particularly when the analysis is related back to the relative mix of other socio-economic conditions.

From the planning perspective, the primary purpose of analysis is often to make predictions about future activity, and to base those predictions on the way the area under study functions in relation to its surrounding area. What happens in one city is seen to depend not only on what happens in other cities but also on what happens or what exists in surrounding resources. For example, what happens in Vancouver or New York or Madrid depends on what happens in other large cities, but also on what happens in the local areas surrounding them. The interrelationship between and within urban areas, and between urban and rural areas, is complex. Relationships can be explored within any particular urban area as well as between urban areas. What happens in one neighborhood can be compared to what happens in surrounding neighborhoods.

Equation 1 presents the basic formula for a Location Quotient in Regional Science (Klosterman et al., 1993). While many economic activity indicators might be used, LQs are frequently calculated on the basis of employment. Employment can be defined in many ways, but is frequently divided into service, manufacturing, secondary and primary extraction groups. Each of these may be subdivided repeatedly, working down to detailed types of employment.

$$(1)\ LQ_{i_n} = \frac{E_{i_n}}{E_{t_n}} \Bigg/ \frac{\sum_{n=1}^{N} E_{i_n}}{\sum_{n=1}^{N} E_{t_n}}$$

Where:

n = small area under study

N = total number of areas

E_i = employment in industry i

E_t = total employment in all industries

The LQ assumes a "normal" distribution in a "standard" area, that is, a "normal" number of jobs in a certain category in a "standard" area. Within regional sciences this normal number is used as a measure of the amount needed to satisfy regional demand (self-sustainability). When the local amount falls below the normal amount, it is assumed that goods (or services) are exported. Equation (1) shows the ratio for importing or exporting. The numerator counts the number of persons employed in a particular type of job in a specific area divided by the total employed in that area. The denominator is a similar ratio for a comparison surrounding area that may be used as the "normal" distribution for the "standard" area. The equation can be formulated for different study areas and different categories of employment, and can involve comparison with different standard areas. While there are obvious problems with this measure in regional science, it does provide the potential for a relative crime measure in criminological studies.[2]

USE OF LOCATION QUOTIENTS IN CRIMINOLOGY

In criminology, of course, Location Quotients would use crimes as the basic unit of count. Equation (2) restates the Location Quotient formula in criminological form:

(2)

$$LQC_{i_n} = \frac{C_{i_n}}{C_{t_n}} \Bigg/ \frac{\sum_{n=1}^{N} C_{i_n}}{\sum_{n=1}^{N} C_{t_n}}$$

Where:

n = small area under study

N = total number of areas

C_i = count of crime i

C_t = total count of all crimes

Using an LQC, some towns and cities would be identified as centers for violent crimes; others, as centers for property crimes. Some are centers for robbery; some for burglary; some for automobile theft. The center in one region might not appear to be a center when compared to centers in other regions. This is similar to a small town being a center of commerce in a rural area but not in a large urban area. It is perhaps more important to note that, since this is a relative measure, a center cannot have high LQs for all crimes. It is a measure that identifies relative area specialty in crimes.

The advantage of an LQC in crime analysis is that there is no need to obtain a count of the number of targets as is necessary in calculating a crime rate. The LQC for robbery would be based on counts of robberies and all crimes,[3] not population or number of target businesses. The LQC for motor vehicle theft would be based on vehicle thefts and total crimes, not the number of people or the number of motor vehicles. In this way, the LQC minimizes the problems highlighted by Boggs (1960) and Harries (1991) in their discussions of which types of denominator variables to use in constructing rates for different types of crimes. Stationarity is still a problem, but can be addressed by recalculations for different time periods.

Table 1 provides a hypothetical example of how LQCs work. In this example there are five states listed (States A to E) as well as a national total for all index offenses and for robbery. As can be seen in the table, robbery makes up 5% of index offenses nationally. State A has a low number of robberies but has the same robbery rate as State B, which has the highest number of robberies and the highest robbery rate. State A has an LQC greater than State B. This means that while these two states have the same robbery rates, State A has a higher proportion of robbery offenses compared to the national proportion than does State B. They are both high rate states, but State A shows a "preference" for robbery compared to State B. Robbery is a larger part of the total crime problem in State A than in State B. State C has the same high robbery rate as State A and State B, but it has a much lower total crime rate than would be expected from the national trend. Consequently, State C has a LQC 7 times what would be expected from the national trend. State D and E both exhibit low robbery rates but have LQCs similar to State A. Although robbery rates are low, they make up a relatively large share of the crime problem in both States D and E. The point is that LQCs do not necessarily "copy" crime rates or crime counts. They are really a dimensionless measure of preference or choice of crime type in the smaller unit compared to a larger trend.

Table 1: Location Quotient Example: Hypothetical States

State	Robbery Count	Total Crime Count	Population	Robbery Rate	Robbery LQC
State A	10,000	150,000	25,000	400	1.4
State B	50,000	1,500,000	12,500,000	400	0.7
State C	25,000	75,000	6,250,000	400	7.1
State D	25,000	375,000	13,000,000	192	1.4
State E	3,000	40,000	1,500,000	200	1.6
USA Total	660,000	14,000,000	258,000,000	256	0.05

The LQC provides an additional, alternative view of crime. It is not a rate and is not a percentage. The LQC is without dimension; it is a relative measure. When a study area (be it a state, a city or a neighborhood) has an LQC equal to 1.00 for a specific crime, that means that it has a proportional mix of that crime similar to the larger comparison area (country, state or city). When the value of the LQC falls below 1.00, the relative proportion of that crime in the smaller study area is below the normal trend in the larger comparison area. When the LQC is above 1.00, the specific crime is above the normal trend. In fact, the amount above 1.00 indicates the percentage above the normal trend. In Table 1, State A has an LQC value of 1.4, meaning that it is 40% higher than the national trend for robbery. State B has an LQC value of 0.7, or is 30% below the national trend. State C has an LQC of 7.1, or is 610 % above the national trend! Robbery is the major crime problem in State C. States D and E both have low robbery rates, but robbery is a relatively greater problem in the latter than in the former.

Statistical models using LQCs are different from the models most commonly constructed by criminologists. LQCs are relative measures and are potentially helpful when analyzing fear or concern about crime. A widespread fear of murder by a stranger can be triggered in a small community by one local crime, while a similar level of fear might require clear evidence that a serial killer is active before being triggered in a large urban center. Similarly, one or two bank robberies might seem like very little in New York City, but a large number in smaller towns like Flemington or Montauk. LQCs may also prove good predictors of local media response to specific reported crimes or even to variations in sentences in different places at different times.

LQCs are also indicators of what attracts people, both locally and from a distance, to a particular location. Some crime sites are crime generators; others are crime attractors. Crime generators are places that attract large volumes of people, generating criminal opportunities in the process. Some of the people attracted to a generator location will notice those opportunities and act on them even though they had not been intending to commit any crime in the first place. Crime attractors are places notorious for providing opportunities for crime. Offenders travel to crime attractors with the preestablished intention of committing some specific crime there (see Brantingham and Brantingham, 1995).

LQCs also have a statistical model-building strength. In many models using crime rates, the independent and dependent variables are both rates based on population. In such instances, the overall strength of the model may be the result of the same numbers being used as the denominators on both sides of the equation. With LQCs, the independent variable would not have the same base. Independent variables may even reflect routine activities in the LQ form. For example, a measure of the number of bars to total number of businesses in a town can be compared to the ratio for the region under analysis. It seems reasonable that as the local ratio begins to exceed the regional ratio, the LQC for violent crime would also increase. This would not necessarily be found in an analysis of violent crime rates when population is used as the denominator. It might not even be found if the number of bars were used as the denominator in constructing crime rates.

It should be noted that LQCs are ratio variables, and, like all ratio variables, can be influenced by substantial changes when the ratios are calculated from very small numbers. LQCs have a numerator and a denominator. The numerator is the only part of the equation that can have small numbers. For example, when the analysis is of areas with low levels of crime, a change from 20 to 25 recorded crimes of a specific type could have an impact on the calculated value of the LQC when the total local-area crime count is also low. Such a substantial impact might be reflected in local-area fear levels in particular. Such a possibility warrants exploration of past reported crimes in small crime-volume areas. It could be that in small areas with low crime totals, such as city blocks or Census tracts, a three-year average of crime counts should replace an annual total to smooth out fluctuations and ensure stability in the LQC. In fact, LQC analysis using moving averages or autoregressive functions may become useful in time-series analyses that examine the evolution of concentrations of specific types of crime in specific areas. This is worth future research. For example, as an area grows or declines the crime rate might not change, but the crime mix might change quite substantially. This would make the crime problem faced by residents and police alike quite different, even though the volume of crime remained the same. LQCs offer a potential for exploring area crime specialization over time.

While LQCs have many strengths, it is worth noting that this measure, like all other measures of crime, is dependent on a classification schema. That is, limits are introduced when crimes are divided into property/violent clusters, or specific criminal code violations or index crime categories. This is another conceptual level of resolution. While not addressed in this article, LQCs could be used in numerous categories initially or could be staged. They could first be calculated for violent and property crimes in two categories. After that, violent or property crimes could be divided into subcategories and LQCs recalculated. Each approach would inform the researcher about something slightly different. For example, which specific crimes are different from the general trends, or, within a category such a violent crimes, which types of violent crimes are different from a restricted comparison to violent crime trends. While it will not be discussed in more detail in this article, the hierarchical nature of classification of crimes may reveal fine but important differences between areas.

It is also important to note that there is value in looking at changes in LQC from one time period to another. A change in a specific crime LQC can signal a dramatic change. If the LQC increases it means that there has been a shift in the local *dominance* of that crime. If the LQC for that crime decreases it means that there has been a decrease in the local dominance of that crime. Unlike crime rates or crime counts, LQCs operate within fixed numeric limits. The set of areas forming the full area under consideration will together account for the full area crime totals. There will be areas with LQCs greater than 1.00, less than 1.00 and equal to 1.00. LQCs may go up when total or specific crimes decrease, and may go down when specific crimes go up. The LQC is a relative measure without a dimension. LQCs are like changes in the proportion of persons who die from a specific disease. All people die. When the proportion goes down for one cause it increases for another cause. These proportional changes, such as an increase in a particular cause of death, may occur whether the death rate increases, decreases or remains stable.

Over all, the LQC offers an additional view on crime and potentially has value in understanding crime patterns. Counts and rates are not sufficient; volume dominates both. LQCs are relative measures of crimes that show how a specific area varies from general trends. Context is imbedded within LQCs.

Mapping Crime Patterns: An Illustration

To illustrate the different things that can be learned from analyzing the patterns of crime counts, crime rates and LQCs, we use 1994 data on crimes known to the police in 65 municipal forces in British Columbia. The basic data are population counts, total criminal code offense counts and total violent crime[4] counts for each city. Data were geocoded to Universal Transverse Mercator (UTM) NAD 27, Zone 10 centroids for each municipality using MapInfo for Windows. Maps presented in this discussion were generated using Stanford Graphics and MapInfo.

The substantially different pictures of crime obtained by looking at counts, rates and LQCs are illustrated in Table 2, which presents the top 15 ranked British Columbia cities in terms of violent crime counts, violent crime rates, and LQCs for violent crime.

Violence counts are, unsurprisingly, tied to city size. Vancouver, the largest city and largest policing jurisdiction in the province, ranked first in violent crime counts. Surrey, the second largest jurisdiction, and Burnaby, the third largest, ranked second and third in violent crime counts respectively. Outside the Greater Vancouver area, the other large population centers — including the provincial capital, Victoria, and three large interior population centers — also ranked highly in terms of violent crime counts. These are the hot spots where police and the rest of the justice system will have to deal with a large number of violent crimes and criminals, and where the medical system and insurance schemes will have to deal with large numbers of victims.

This pattern is mapped in abstract two-dimensional form in Figure 1. The axes plot UTM Northing and Easting coordinates. Cities are positioned in their relative locations in geographic space. The view is from the south, looking due north.. There is a major hot spot in the southern part of the province, anchored by Vancouver, Surrey and Burnaby. The black-and-white depiction does not do justice to warm spots in the Okanagan Valley, where Kelowna is located, and on the southern end of Vancouver Island, where Victoria is located.[5] These are the areas that require resources keyed to volumes of violent victimization.

Crime rates, of course, tell a very different story. In this case, rates are calculated by dividing the violent crime counts for each city by its estimated 1994 population. Rates are expressed as violent crimes per 1,000 population. The British Columbia cities with the highest rates of violent crime are smaller cities in the northern and northwestern parts of the province. These areas are depicted as hot spots in Figure 2. Most of these cities are service and recreation centers for large hinterlands: fishers, forest workers, miners and ranchers come to these cities looking for entertainment.[6] Liquor consumption is high and assaults in particular occur with substantial relative frequency.

These cities characteristically have relatively low volumes of crime, but should concentrate crime prevention planning efforts on violence. People in these cities run a much higher risk of violent attack than residents in the larger cities of the southern parts of the province. The crime-count hot spot centered on Vancouver becomes a crime-rate cold spot once crime per unit volume of population is considered. This pattern is also mapped in Figure 2.

Table 2: Top Ranked Cities for Three Crime Measures

Rank	FORCE	Violent Count	FORCE	Violent Rate	FORCE	Violent LQC
1	Vancouver	8,246	Williams Lake	38.89	North Cowichan	2.96
2	Surrey	4,394	Prince Rupert	35.04	Kitimat	1.95
3	Burnaby	2,216	Quesnel	34.59	Prince Rupert	1.94
4	Victoria	2,041	North Cowichan	33.32	Esquimalt	1.75
5	Prince George	1,961	Dawson Creek	32.78	Mackenzie	1.70
6	Kelowna	1,337	Fort St. John	28.95	Port Alberni	1.65
7	Richmond	1,259	Port Alberni	28.95	Sechelt	1.54
8	Kamloops	1,175	Port Hardy	27.38	Dawson Creek	1.51
9	Chilliwack	1,079	Victoria	27.02	Fort St. John	1.50
10	Coquitlam	952	Prince George	26.12	Smithers	1.43
11	Matsqui	941	Merritt	25.37	Terrace	1.41
12	Delta	858	Langley City	25.33	Kimberley	1.39
13	Langley District	836	Smithers	24.47	Quesnel	1.37
14	Saanich	818	Terrace	22.41	Prince George	1.37
15	Maple Ridge	643	Esquimalt	22.01	Squamish	1.36

Figure 1: Provincial Violent Crime Counts, 1994

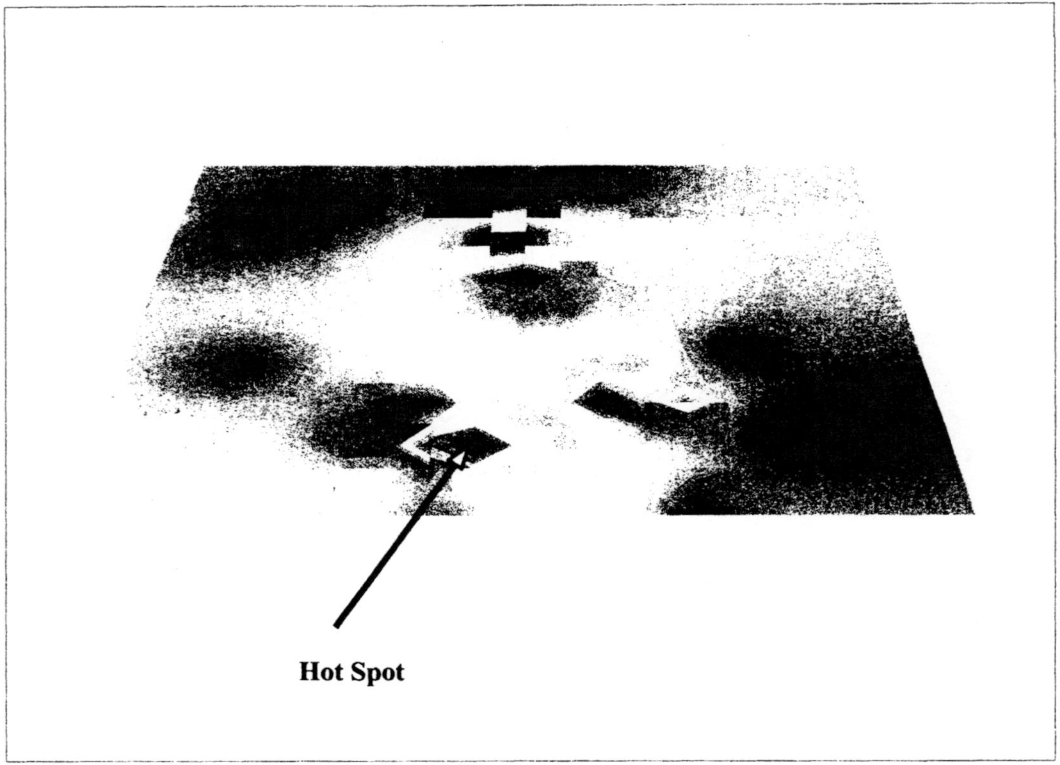

Hot Spot

Figure 2: Provincial Violent Crime Rates, 1994

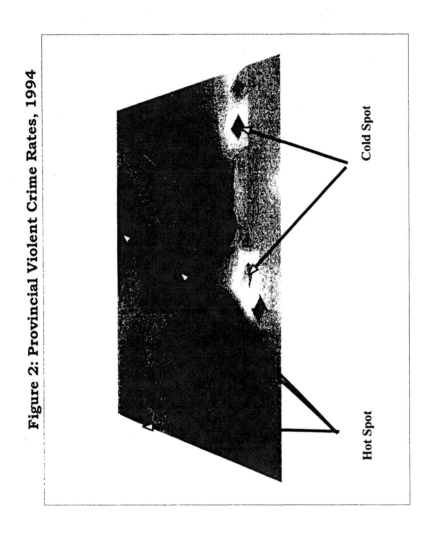

Cold Spot

Hot Spot

LQCs for violent crime across British Columbia cities tell yet another story. Cities with high LQCs for violent crime are those in which violent crime makes up a much higher proportion of the total crime problem than is characteristic of the provincial pattern generally. Although some high-rate cities will also have high LQCs, many will not. Some cities with relatively low total crime counts and relatively low violent crime rates will have high LQCs because violent crime makes up a disproportionate share of all the crimes that occur in that municipality when compared to the provincial pattern in general. Kitimat, for instance, ranks second in LQC, but only 24th out of the 65 cities in terms of violent crime rates. Kimberly ranks 12th in terms of LQC, but only 46th out of the 65 cities in terms of violent crime rate. This means that although the overall risk of crime is relatively low in these cities, those crimes that do occur are much more likely to be violent ones than in most other cities in the province.

The converse can also be true: some cities will have relatively high violent crime rates, but those rates will be embedded in such high overall crime rates that any particular crime is not much more likely to be a violent crime than it would be in other, far less crime-prone cities. Williams Lake is an example of such a place: it ranks first overall in terms of violent crime rate, but 18th in terms of LQC. Williams Lake's LQC of 1.33 for violent crime indicates that its violent crime mix is above the normal pattern for the province as a whole, but not extremely so. Some cities will have high violent crime counts, low violent crime rates and very low LQCs for violent crimes. Burnaby, for instance, ranked third in terms of violent crime counts, 35th in terms of violent crime rates but 54th out of the 65 cities in terms of LQC. This indicates that a substantially smaller proportion of Burnaby's crime mix involves violent crimes than is typical of the crime mix in the province generally. This means that any particular crime occurring in Burnaby would be less likely to be a violent crime than any particular crime occurring in the province at large. That LQCs and rates tell different stories is apparent from regressing rates on LQCs. Violent crime rates explain only about half the variation in the LQCs.

Figure 3 maps the LQCs for violent crimes for British Columbia cities. The North Cowichan area of Vancouver Island stands out as having a much higher proportion of all its crime take the form of violence than is normal for the province as a whole: it is depicted as an LQC hot spot. A northwestern warm spot is also visible. Violent crime makes up a smaller-than-expected proportion of the crime mix in the large population centers in Greater Vancouver and the southern part of Vancouver Island, which generally appear as cold spots.

Violent crime counts, violent crime rates and LQCs for violent crime are mapped across the police jurisdictions of the Vancouver and Victoria metropolitan areas in Figures 4, 5 and 6. Violent crime counts show hot spots in Vancouver and Surrey, the two largest municipalities in British Columbia. These counts are population driven. Violent crime rates show a very different picture, with hot spots in the city of Victoria and in North Cowichan on Vancouver Island, and in Langley City, a small suburban bright-lights district in the metropolitan Vancouver district. LQCs show yet a different pattern to violent crime. The entire Vancouver region has relatively low LQCs, indicating that violent crime makes up less of the crime mix in this region than it does in the province as a whole. North of Vancouver, two resort destinations — Sechelt, a coastal community, and the Squamish-Whistler ski-resort area — show violent LQCs that are substantially above provincial levels. On Vancouver Island, the North Cowichan area and the municipality of Esquimalt, adjacent to Victoria, have very high LQCs. These communities experience substantially more violence per unit of crime than the province as a whole.

A more immediate mapping of the differences in the three crime measures is seen in Figure 7, which focuses on the municipalities of Greater Vancouver. Bar charts present first the violent crime count, then the violent crime rate, then the LQC for violent crime in each municipality.[7] Vancouver, the largest city in the metropolitan area, stands out in the left center of the map. Vancouver displays a very high violent crime count, a substantially lower violent crime rate, and a much lower LQC for violence. Although a large number of violent crimes occur in Vancouver, a much smaller proportion of its total crime mix comprises violence than is typical of the province as a whole. This suggests that Vancouver's crime mix is relatively benign (if such a term can ever be applied to a crime problem), and that the city has a more intense problem with property and other types of crime rather than with violence.

Although a more detailed situational analysis would be necessary, it appears that high priority in crime prevention planning ought to be placed on reduction of property offenses and other nonviolent offenses. In contrast, many of the municipalities adjacent to Vancouver proper have relatively low violent crime counts. But of the few crimes that occur in these municipalities, many more are violent than would be typical of the province as a whole. In these municipalities, crime prevention efforts should focus on the violent crime attractors and generators in an effort to reduce the volumes of situations that support violent crime. Here much can be gained through attention to the problems of violence. This understanding of the need to develop crime prevention programs aimed at reduction of violent crime would be missed if the main focus of crime prevention planning were either the crime counts or the crime rates for these communities. Some of the communities with very low violent crime counts and crime rates would benefit more from attention to violent crime than would other similar-sized communities that have reputations for violence problems but that in fact have relatively low LQCs.

Mapping crime counts and rates and LQCs together can provide very useful visual information that helps identify some important characteristics of local crime problems. It also provides insight into resource needs, crime risks for citizens at large, and the prevention strategies and priorities that could most profitably be pursued.

CONCLUSION

Crimes occur on a backcloth (Brantingham and Brantingham, 1993): at whatever level of analysis is pursued (macro, meso, micro), it is important to see how specific crime type occurrences relate to crime in general. LQCs provide a measure that helps identify whether a specific crime pattern is disproportionately high or low in a particular place or location. While LQCs should not be used without considering counts and rates, they do provide a relative or contextual view of crime and should prove helpful in understanding crime patterns and in developing priorities and approaches in crime prevention.

While not the focus of this article, LQCs should have great value in research into the prediction of crime patterns. Relative socioeconomic and relative activity measures may turn out to be good predictors of crime patterns in ways that more traditional measures have not. The use of LQ measures should make it possible to develop predictor variables that reflect activity, movement and the actual variety in use where different activities occur. Data sources for aggregate analysis can begin to include economic measures, as well as Census and survey information. Mapping relative use measures may prove a particularly useful tool for criminologists and crime prevention professionals alike.

Figure 3: Provincial Violent Crime Location Quotients, 1994

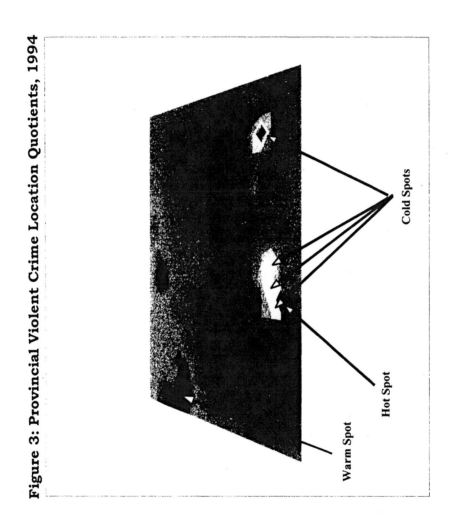

Cold Spots

Hot Spot

Warm Spot

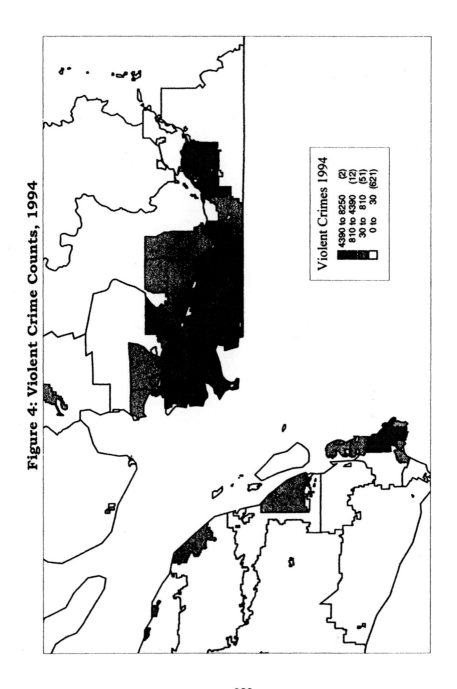

Figure 4: Violent Crime Counts, 1994

Violent Crimes 1994

4390 to 8250 (2)
810 to 4390 (12)
30 to 810 (51)
0 to 30 (621)

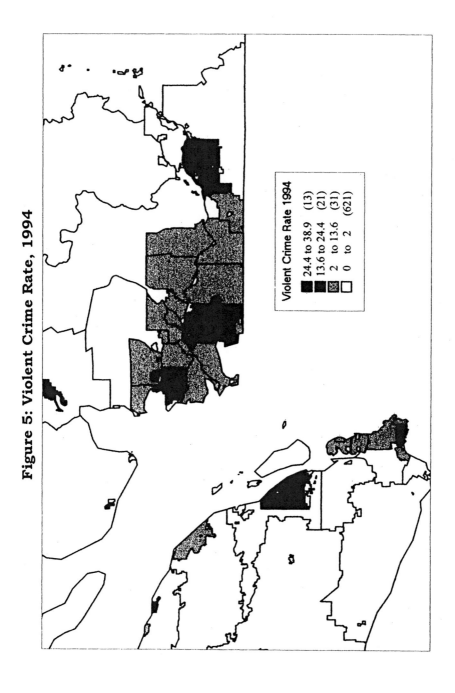

Figure 5: Violent Crime Rate, 1994

Violent Crime Rate 1994
24.4 to 38.9 (13)
13.6 to 24.4 (21)
2   to 13.6 (31)
0   to 2 (621)

283

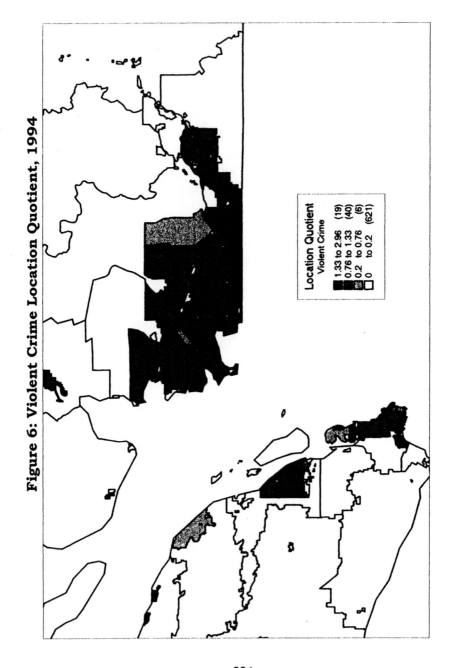

Figure 6: Violent Crime Location Quotient, 1994

Location Quotient
Violent Crime

1.33 to 2.96 (19)
0.76 to 1.33 (40)
0.2 to 0.76 (6)
0   to 0.2 (621)

New measures are always difficult when they are first used, but LQCs offer criminology a technique that should open many new areas of research using existing socioeconomic data. The LQCs should be particularly important when studying crimes that are dependent on movement and activities. It is always important to remember that a low-crime-rate city may be seen by its residents as a high-crime city for specific crimes. For example, a small town that is a commercial center in a rural area may well experience more property offenses than a surrounding area or a nearby center without a commercial component. A large commercial center adjacent to an even larger commercial center may, relatively, have less property crime. Traditional crime rates or analyses of crime volumes will not find the importance of the activities compared to what surrounds them. LQCs and associated socioeconomic LQs may make such contextual analysis much easier.

Figure 7: Relative Violent Crime Counts, Rates and Location Quotients
Greater Vancouver Municipalities, 1994

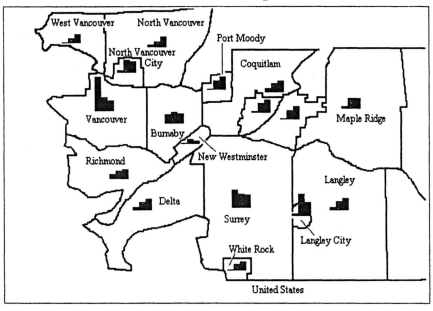

NOTES

1. Twelve jurisdictions maintain independent municipal police forces. The remainder contract with the Royal Canadian Mounted Police, who provide municipal policing services through autonomous municipal detachments. A similar arrangement is found in many American jurisdictions. The Los Angeles County Sheriffs' Department provides contracted municipal policing services to a substantial proportion of the independent cities in the county. Other cities in the county — Los Angeles or Long Beach, for instance — maintain their own independent forces.

2. Clearly, the Location Quotient approach has limitations in regional science. With major cities being linked economically, it is not possible to actually identify what activity in a "standard" area would be. This is similar to identifying what a "standard" crime pattern would be. In actual practice, LQs mean more for their relativity and defined context, which is taken as the "standard" for logical purposes.

3. LQC is a relative measure, so the denominator can be flexible. For instance, with robbery in the numerator, the LQC might be calculated using the count of all violent crimes, the count of all criminal code offenses, or the count of all offenses known as the denominator, depending on the context in which the analyst wished to comprehend robbery centers.

4. Violent crime in Canada includes murder, manslaughter, infanticide, attempted murder, sexual assault, assault, abduction and robbery.

5. Most contemporary mapping packages work in color. This is a problem for presentation in print media.

6. This represents one of the denominator problems with crime rates. The actual usage of a city may greatly exceed the resident population.

7. Note that these three sets of bars represent somewhat different scales, as indicated in Table 1.

REFERENCES

Boggs, S. L. (1960). "Urban Crime Patterns." *American Sociological Review* 30:899-908.

Block, C.R., M. Dabdoub and S. Fregly (1995). *Crime Analysis Through Computer Mapping.* Washington, DC: Police Executive Research Forum.

Brantingham, P.L. and P.J. Brantingham (1984). *Patterns in Crime.* New York, NY: Macmillan.

—— (1993). "Environment, Routine and Situation: Toward a Pattern Theory of Crime." *Advances in Criminological Theory* 5:259-294.

—— (1995). "Criminality of Place: Crime Generators and Crime Attractors." *European Journal on Criminal Policy and Research* 3:5-26.

—— and P.S. Wong (1991). "How Public Transit Feeds Private Crime: Notes on the Vancouver 'Skytrain' Experience." *Security Journal* 2: 91-95.

Brantingham, P. J., D. A. Dyreson and P. L. Brantingham (1976). "Crime Seen Through a Cone of Resolution." *American Behavioral Scientist* 20:261-273.

Clarke, R.V.G. (1980). "Situational Crime Prevention: Theory and Practice." *British Journal of Criminology* 20:136-147.

Clarke, R.V. (ed.) (1992). *Situational Crime Prevention: Successful Case Studies.* New York, NY: Harrow and Heston.

Cusson, M. (1983). *Why Delinquency?* Toronto, CAN: University of Toronto Press.

—— (1993). "A Strategic Analysis of Crime: Criminal Tactics and Responses to Precriminal Situations." *Advances in Criminological Theory* 5:295-304.

Gove, W. R., M. Hughes and M. Geerken (1985). "Are Uniform Crime Reports a Valid Indicator of the Index Crimes?" *Criminology* 23:451-501.

Guerry, A. M. (1831) *Essai Sur la Statistique Morale de la France.* Paris, FR: Chez Crochard.

Harries, K. D. (1991). "Alternative Denominators in Conventional Crime Rates." In: P.J. Brantingham and P.L. Brantingham (eds.), *Environmental Criminology.* Prospect Heights, IL: Waveland Press.

Kennedy, L.W. and D.R. Forde (1990). "Routine Activities and Crime: An Analysis of Victimization in Canada." *Criminology* 28:137-152.

Klosterman, R.E., R.K. Brail and E.G Bossard (1993). *Spreadsheet Models for Urban and Regional Analysis.* New Brunswick, NJ: Transaction Publishers.

Kohfeld, C.W. and J. Sprague (1990). "Demography, Police Behavior, and Deterrence." *Criminology* 28:111-136.

Litton, R. A. and K. Pease (1984). "Crimes and Claims: The Case of Burglary Insurance." In: R. Clarke and T. Hope (eds.), *Coping with Burglary.* Boston, MA: Kluwer-Nijhoff Publishing.

Normandeau, A. (1987). "Crime on the Montreal Metro." *Sociology and Social Research* 71:289-292.

Poisson, S.D. (1837). *Recherches Sur la Probabilité des Jugements en Matière Criminelle et en Matière Civile, Précédés des Règles Générales du Calcul des Probabilités.* Paris, FR: Bachelier.

Quetelet, A.J. (1842). *Treatise on Man and the Development of His Faculties.* Edinburgh, SCOT: W. and R. Chambers.

Stigler, S. M. (1986). *The History of Statistics: The Measurement of Uncertainty before 1900.* Cambridge, MA: Belknap Press of Harvard University Press.

MAPPING IT OUT: REPEAT-ADDRESS BURGLAR ALARMS AND BURGLARIES[1]

by

James L. LeBeau
Karen L. Vincent
Southern Illinois University at Carbondale

Abstract: While the police are trying to cope with large volumes of false-alarm calls, a new direction in crime prevention asserts that preventing repeat victimization of people, property, places, and situations might be more efficient than other traditional crime prevention doctrines. Using graduated circle maps, this study compares the spatial distributions of alarm calls and burglary incidents across Charlotte, NC, during 1990. Specific comparisons are made regarding the spatial distributions and repeat-address natures of all burglar alarms, all burglaries, burglaries without alarms, and places producing both alarm calls and burglaries. Comparisons of tables indicate that burglaries are more of a single-address phenomenon than alarm calls. Map comparisons imply that the spatial distributions of alarms, and burglaries without alarms are different. Inferences are made suggesting that premises with alarms might be responsible for displacing burglars to locations without alarms and that the sheer number of false alarms might subtract from any gains made by targeting places for repeat-burglary victimization.

INTRODUCTION

A new doctrine for enhancing the efficiency and efficacy of crime prevention measures has been to focus on those that have already

Address correspondence to: James L. LeBeau, Center for the Study of Crime, Delinquency, and Corrections, Southern Illinois University, ML 4504, Carbondale, IL 62901-4504.

been victimized, because prior research has indicated they are more likely to be victimized again (Farrell and Pease, 1993). The study of repeat victimization is concerned with precisely identifying the persons, places, properties, and situations that are at higher risk and are more likely to enjoy the benefits of crime prevention measures or techniques.

One of the most popular target-hardening techniques for preventing burglaries has been the installation of burglar alarms (see Reppetto, 1974). This seemingly simple and straightforward way for the public to become more personally involved in the fight against crime has become a nightmare for the police, because alarm calls for service constitute a significant proportion of the total calls-for-service work load. Moreover, what is more problematic is that a majority of the burglary alarm calls are false. Therefore, within a police agency, any improvements in effectiveness and efficiency gained by focusing on repeat-burglary victimizations can be negated by continuously expending the resources for responding to burglar alarms.

The purposes of this study are to numerically examine and cartographically display the relationships among burglar alarms, burglaries, repeat-address alarms, and repeat-address burglaries. The numerical examination involves comparing the magnitudes of the different types of incidents and assessing their degrees of address repetition. The cartographic display involves constructing, interpreting, and comparing maps of the geographic locations of the incidents. This effort will enable one to assess the degree to which the incidents occur in similar or different spaces. This essay demonstrates the first steps one might want to take in conducting a spatial analysis of burglar alarms and burglaries.

THE PROBLEMS WITH BURGLAR ALARMS

Repeat addresses in regard to predatory crime and hot spots have been a research focus for academics and an operational focus for the police (Sherman, 1989; Sherman et al., 1989). In the meantime, the issue of repeat-address burglar alarms has been an operational headache for the police, the private security industry, and the public. Burglar alarm calls cause problems for the police because they are numerous and usually false. Estimates vary from city to city, but one has alarm calls constituting 30% of all police calls with 95% of the calls being false (Daughtry, 1993). Other studies have found similar figures (see Werner, 1993). During the first 11 months of 1994, the Baltimore County (MD) Police Department responded to 63,335 alarm calls, of which 98% were false. The police department estimates the average cost per alarm call is about $67.00, resulting in over $4 million being expended in responding to alarm calls (Funk, 1995). During 1994, the Chicago Police Department, responded to over 300,000 alarm calls, of which only 5,000 were the result of criminal activity. The metric published by the Chicago Police Department to demonstrate cost of responding to false alarms was not an average dollar amount per false alarm, but it was estimated that the equivalent of 195 full-time officers responded to false alarms (Chicago Police Department, 1995). Basically, responding to a large volume of burglar alarm calls is a drain on police resources and essentially makes the police the servant of the private security alarm industry (Moslow, 1994).

Alarms are activated for a variety reasons, besides the obvious one of someone breaking into a building. Weather changes, traffic vibrations, and human errors are three of the general causes of false-alarm activations (see Hakim et al., 1996). Training and technological improvements have been viewed as the potential solutions for reducing false alarms, but these are more long-term in nature. In the meantime, many jurisdictions have sought to partially recover the costs from responding to false alarms by implementing a fine system whereby an alarm user would be charged a certain fee according to the number of false alarms activated during a specified period (see Chicago Police Department, 1995; Werner, 1993). Alarm fines have not been the panacea that its authors had envisioned but rather have created more controversy, pitting the police, public, government officials, and the alarm industry in a never-ending debate.

METHODS

The Data

The alarm and burglary data for this study come from the computer-aided dispatch (CAD) files of the Charlotte, (NC) Police Department for the year 1990. The CAD files are a very rich source of information because recorded with each call for service, when appropriate, is its Uniform Crime Report classification. Therefore, it is possible to ascertain the street-block location and disposition (i.e., false alarm, burglary) for each alarm call. Finally, a great asset of this database is that duplicate calls and multiple calls reporting the same event are eliminated, thus enhancing the reliability that a incident is truly unique and being counted only once.

The pertinent variables for mapping are the total numbers of alarm calls and burglary incidents. The latter is the sum of all forced and attempted burglaries. The variables are modified by ascertaining the number of calls and burglaries at the same address. This produces four different distributions for examining and mapping: (1) repeat-addresses of all alarm calls; (2) the repeat-addresses of all burglaries; (3) the repeat-addresses of all burglaries without alarms; and (4) the repeat-addresses of places producing both alarm calls and burglaries. Therefore, the basic unit of analysis is the incident or call and its street-block address. In this analysis it is not possible to determine the total number of commercial or residential alarms and burglaries.

The Mapping

The addresses for each incident or call are entered into a database manager and the number of repeat calls are assessed for each address, thus creating a new database. The addresses are geocoded using a popular off-the-shelf mapping program's version of the Census Bureau's TIGER (Topologically Integrated Geographic Encoding and Referencing) files (see Garson and Biggs, 1992). Then the database containing frequencies is submitted to the mapping program to produce a graduated circle map. This type of thematic map plots circles according to the value of each point (see Monmonier, 1993). The essence of the analysis involves the interpretation and comparison of the thematic maps.

RESULTS

The Efficacy of Burglar Alarms

During 1990, the Charlotte Police Department responded to 382,923 calls for service. Burglary alarm calls, which numbered 48,622, constitute 12.7% of the total calls-for-service work load. While this percentage is lower than that found in other studies, the proportion of alarms that are false agree (see Table 1). The proportion of false alarms encountered by the police is almost 98%. Nevertheless, the second-highest outcome of alarm activations (1.57%) is burglary. During 1990, there were 10,828 residential and commercial burglaries reported to the police. The alarm data indicate that 1.57%

of the alarm calls accounted for 7% of all burglaries. Furthermore, only 117 on-scene arrests (81 for burglary) were made from alarm activation calls, while 130 on-scene arrests were made during burglaries that did not involve alarms. Basically, from these data it can be construed that alarms are neither effective nor efficient.

Table 1: Outcomes of Burglar Alarm Activations

Outcome	Number	Percent
Assault	15	.03
Burglary	762	1.57
False	47,539	97.77
Larceny	55	.11
Robbery	51	.10
Vandalism	158	.32
Other	42	.08
Total	48,622	100.00

Mapping It Out: The Study Site

Figure 1 shows the study site with its major street and rail routes. The darker roads are interstates that run east-west in the northern portion of the city and from the north to the southwest through the western portion of the city. The oddity of Charlotte's street network is the absence of a beltway or restricted-access highways on the east side connecting or leading to other parts of the city.

Two features of the landscape make the central business district (CBD) very conspicuous. First, the CBD is delineated by the interstate highway loop in the upper central portion of the map. Second, the rail lines all converge or pass through this general area, and there are two large rail yards northeast and west of the CBD. Knowing the position of the CBD and the layouts of the street and rail networks is very important, because many of the businesses and industries that depend on access to transportation networks will site their facilities as close as possible to the transportation network. This basic fact of economic geography influences the spatial distribution of many targets for burglars and likely places for alarms.

Figure 1: Charlotte, NC, 1990: Major Street and Rail Routes

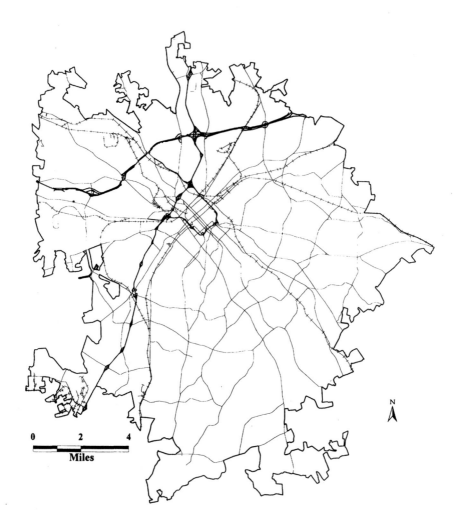

Mapping It Out: Repeat-Address Burglar Alarms

During 1990, 48,622 alarm calls came from 10,641 addresses (see Table 1). The one-time-only or single-address alarm calls (4,568) accounts for 42.93% of the addresses, but only 9.39% of all alarm calls (see Table 2). The maximum number of repeat calls to the same address is 144. But it is important to note that, at 10 calls to the same address, the cumulative proportion of alarm addresses is almost 90% while the cumulative proportion of alarm calls is less than 52% (see Table 2). Therefore, the remaining 9% of the addresses produces about 48% of the calls.

Figure 2 is a graduated circle map showing the distribution of repeat-address alarms across Charlotte. At the outset it might appear that there is too much information on the map to extract a sense of spatial pattern and order. But considering the transportation access need for business and industry, it is possible to see that many of the major street and rail lines are almost completely delineated with the layout of alarm calls. Clearly, the incessant addresses are located along the major transportation routes. The most chronic location in the CBD, with 144 alarm calls, is a bank building that houses other business and commercial offices. The majority of the chronic locations on the north side of the CBD are commercial or business locations. Some of the chronic locations in the southeast are an office building, a string of auto dealerships, and other stores. The chronic location south of the CBD is a mall complex, while the chronic address in the southwest is a large wholesale establishment (Figure 2). The majority of the alarms in the blank areas, we can assume, are residential.

Mapping It Out: Repeat-Address Burglaries

Burglary is primarily a single-address phenomenon since 81.52% of all the victimized addresses and 61.1% of all the burglaries involve just one call to a single address (Table 3). At ten calls to the same address, the cumulative proportion of addresses is 99.8% and the cumulative proportion of total burglaries is 97.30%.

Table 2: Repeat Addresses of Burglar Alarms

N of Calls to Same Address	N of Separate Addresses	% of Total Addresses	Cum. % of Addresses	Total Alarm Calls	% of Alarm Calls	Cum. % Of Alarm Calls
1	4568	42.93	42.93	4568	9.39	9.39
2	1670	15.69	58.62	3340	6.87	16.26
3	942	8.85	67.48	2826	5.81	22.07
4	596	5.6	73.08	2384	4.9	26.97
5	493	4.63	77.71	2465	5.07	32.04
6	370	3.48	81.19	2220	4.57	36.61
7	287	2.7	83.88	2009	4.13	40.74
8	218	2.05	85.93	1744	3.59	44.33
9	203	1.91	87.84	1827	3.76	48.09
10	150	1.41	89.25	1500	3.09	51.17
11	143	1.34	90.59	1573	3.24	54.41
12	110	1.03	91.63	1320	2.71	57.12
13	93	0.87	92.5	1209	2.49	59.61
14	90	0.85	93.35	1260	2.59	62.2
15	93	0.87	94.22	1395	2.87	65.07
16	49	0.46	94.68	784	1.61	66.68
17	47	0.44	95.12	799	1.64	68.32
18	36	0.34	95.46	648	1.33	69.66
19	47	0.44	95.9	893	1.84	71.49
20	43	0.4	96.31	860	1.77	73.26
21	38	0.36	96.67	798	1.64	74.9
22	28	0.26	96.93	616	1.27	76.17
23	34	0.32	97.25	782	1.61	77.78
24	24	0.23	97.47	576	1.18	78.96
25	24	0.23	97.7	600	1.23	80.2
26	28	0.26	97.96	728	1.5	81.69
27	12	0.11	98.08	324	0.67	82.36
28	18	0.17	98.24	504	1.04	83.4
29	14	0.13	98.38	406	0.84	84.23
>30	173	1.63	100	7664	15.76	100
Total	10,641			48,622		

Figure 2: Repeat-Address Burglary Alarms

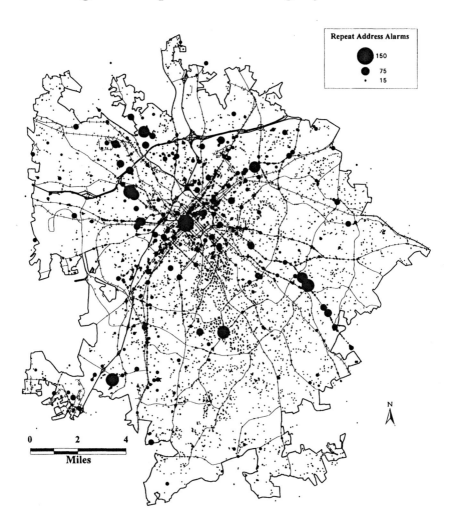

Table 3: Repeat Addresses of All Burglaries

N of Calls to Same Address	N of Separate Addresses	% of Total Addresses	Cum. % of Addresses	Total Burglaries	% of Total Burglaries	Cum. % of Burglaries
1	6616	81.52	81.52	6616	61.10	61.1
2	991	12.21	93.73	1982	18.30	79.40
3	283	3.49	97.22	849	7.84	87.25
4	102	1.26	98.47	408	3.77	91.01
5	45	0.55	99.03	225	2.08	93.09
6	25	0.31	99.34	150	1.39	94.48
7	19	0.23	99.57	133	1.23	95.70
8	6	0.07	99.64	48	0.44	96.15
9	5	0.06	99.71	45	0.42	96.56
10	8	0.10	99.80	80	0.74	97.30
11	5	0.06	99.87	55	0.51	97.81
12	2	0.02	99.89	24	0.22	98.03
13	1	0.01	99.90	13	0.12	98.15
14	2	0.02	99.93	28	0.26	98.41
16	1	0.01	99.94	16	0.15	98.56
17	1	0.01	99.95	17	0.16	98.72
20	1	0.01	99.97	20	0.18	98.90
36	1	0.01	99.98	36	0.33	99.23
40	1	0.01	99.99	40	0.37	99.60
43	1	0.01	100.00	43	0.40	100.00
Total	8,116			10,828		

The burglary incidents appear in Figure 3. This distribution is different from that of the alarms. While both have high concentrations in the CBD, burglaries appear to have higher concentrations in areas contiguous with the CBD in locations to the east, northeast, north, northwest. A rather stark contrast is the relative lower density of burglaries due south of the CBD compared with alarms and the three chronic repeat-addresses east of the CBD (compare Figures 2 and 3). Visually, it appears that while the alarm and burglary distributions overlap in some areas, there are enough departures to feel that the patterns are dissimilar.

Figure 3: Repeat-Address Burglaries

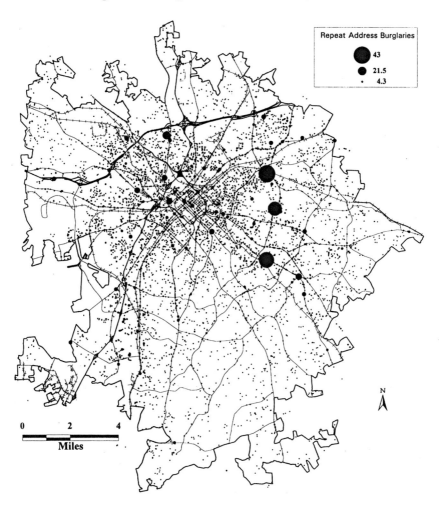

Dissimilarity between the two patterns is tested by using a raster-based geographic information system. In a raster system one can think of a map as a matrix, where the position of each cell represents its relative position in geographic space and the value of the cell corresponds to some feature or phenomenon being mapped. Therefore, it is possible to produce a map or a matrix of alarms and another of burglaries, with the cells in both maps representing the same locations. Therefore, with these matrices it is possible to employ different statistical analyses.

Raster maps of the burglary and alarm distributions are made and subjected to a regression analysis, with burglary serving as the dependent variable. One of the products of this analysis is the coefficient of determination, more commonly known as r square. The resulting r square indicates that 26.9% of the variation of burglaries is explained by the variation of alarms. Therefore, this evidence strongly suggests that the two phenomena only moderately share the same space.

Mapping It Out: Repeat-Address Burglaries Without Alarms

During 1990, there were 9,694 burglaries without alarms across 7,574 addresses (see Table 4). Single-address burglaries account for over 83% of the addresses and over 65% of the incidents. After four burglaries at the same address, 1.00% of the addresses and 3.14% of the burglaries remain. Furthermore, there are three addresses producing 109, or 1.12%, of the burglaries without alarms (see figure 3). These three chronic locations clearly reappear in Figure 4 and dominate the geographic pattern of burglaries, in general, and burglaries without alarms, in particular. Moreover, comparing Figures 2 and 4 reveals that these chronic locations are not in relatively high-alarm activation areas.

Two of the three chronic locations are mini-storage warehouses, while the third is a large apartment complex. All three locations correspond to the routine activity process of suitable targets lacking capable guardianship (Cohen and Felson, 1979). Basically, the storage sites are unattended during the night and the apartment dwellers are absent primarily during the weekdays while pursuing their routine activities. However, these locations must be exceptionally vulnerable

Table 4: Repeat Addresses of Burglaries Without Alarms

N of Calls to Same Address	N of Separate Ad- dresses	% of Total Ad- dresses	Cum. % of Ad- dresses	Total Bur- glaries	% of Total Bur- glaries	Cum. % of Bur- glaries
1	6316	83.39	83.39	6316	65.15	65.15
2	881	11.63	95.02	1762	18.18	83.33
3	224	2.96	97.98	672	6.93	90.26
4	76	1.00	98.98	304	3.14	93.39
5	26	0.34	99.33	130	1.34	94.74
6	16	0.21	99.54	96	0.99	95.73
7	13	0.17	99.71	91	0.94	96.66
8	4	0.05	99.76	32	0.33	96.99
9	2	0.03	99.79	18	0.19	97.18
10	4	0.05	99.84	40	0.41	97.59
11	3	0.04	99.88	33	0.34	97.93
12	2	0.03	99.91	24	0.25	98.18
13	1	0.01	99.92	13	0.13	98.31
14	2	0.03	99.95	28	0.29	98.60
16	1	0.01	99.96	16	0.17	98.77
36	1	0.01	99.97	36	0.37	99.14
40	1	0.01	99.99	40	0.41	99.55
43	1	0.01	100	43	0.44	100
Total	7,574			9,694		

since none of the other high-frequency repeat-addresses are similar types of properties. The other conspicuous repeat-burglary addresses without alarms are spatially arranged along major transportation routes in and around the CBD.

Mapping It Out: Addresses With Alarms and Burglaries

Assessing the relationship between alarms and burglaries becomes more complicated when one examines the addresses producing both phenomena. Table 5 is organized according to the number of burglaries emanating from the same address. Furthermore, within each address-repetition group, it is possible to distinguish the total number of burglaries, the proportion of burglaries with alarms, total alarm activations, the proportion of false alarms, and the range of alarm activations for each group. The result is 542 addresses generating 5,971 alarms and 1,134 burglaries, of which 762 are with alarms. An important fact revealed by Table 5 is that even though 762,

Figure 4: Repeat Burglaries Without Alarms

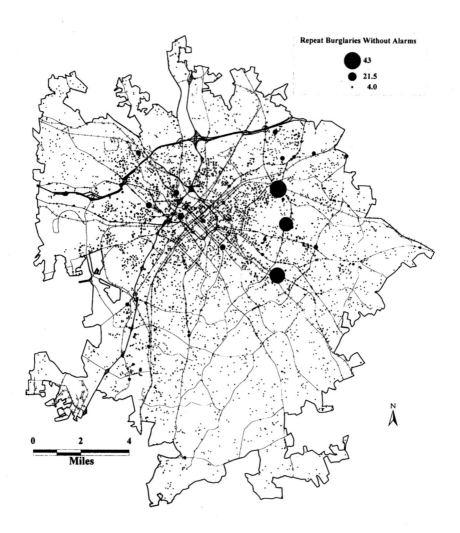

or 67%, of all the 1,134 burglaries are alarm-related, the addresses are still generating very high proportions of false alarms.

Two important facts are not revealed by Table 5. First, 23 addresses have more burglaries than alarms. There are only 46 alarm activations, of which 28 are associated with a burglary, but there are an additional 67 burglaries. The latter group is perhaps an example of those who have recently adopted burglar alarms. Second, there are 61 addresses where all the burglaries (62) are related to alarm activations (62); thus, there are no additional burglaries or alarms. This means, then, that there are only 60 addresses to which the police have been summoned only once for either an alarm or burglary. In other words, 11% of addresses account for 7.8% of the burglaries with alarms and 2.5% of all the alarms, making places with alarms and burglaries more of a repeat-address phenomenon than places without alarms.

Mapping the addresses with repeat alarms and burglaries requires a modification to the graduated-circle technique, since two phenomena are being plotted. Therefore, the ratio of burglaries to alarms is calculated and subjected to a thematic mapping routine that creates graduated circles in the form of pie charts. Moreover, another modification to the mapping methodology, made to enhance visualization, is to remove from the base map the major street and rail routes. After presenting four maps of the same site with the same scale and projection, the reader should now have a mental image or template of the layout of the city.

In Figure 5, the distribution of addresses with repeat alarms and burglaries plainly delineates the CBD and major street and rail routes (compare Figure 1 and 5). Moreover, if a line is drawn from the southwest to the northeast corner of the map, a spatial bias is clearly revealed because a majority of the locations would lie on the northwest side of this line. However, the place producing the most alarms (113) with only five burglaries lies south of this line. This is the same mall complex that appears in Figure 2 and that was mentioned in the discussion of incessant alarm activation places. In Figure 5, there are many isolated repeat-alarm and burglary places or addresses, especially around the periphery of the city. However, the overall impression is that many of the repeat-alarm and burglary places are contiguous, and that their combined experiences and propinquity produce areas or regions of repeat alarms and burglaries.

Table 5: Addresses With Alarms and Burglaries

N of Burglaries at the Same Address	N of Addresses	Total Burglaries	Total Burglaries with Alarms	% Burglaries with Alarms	Total Alarm Calls	% False Alarms	Min. - Max. Alarms
1	300	300	300	100.00	2410	87.55	1-69
2	110	220	150	68.18	1305	88.50	1-52
3	59	177	101	57.06	731	86.18	1-39
4	26	104	58	55.77	473	87.73	2-26
5	19	95	45	47.37	432	89.58	2-113
6	9	54	32	59.26	134	76.11	1-33
7	6	42	22	52.38	170	87.05	1-51
8	2	16	6	37.50	60	90.00	23-37
9	3	27	21	77.78	56	62.50	15-23
10	4	40	13	32.50	73	82.19	3-31
11	2	22	4	18.18	61	93.44	8-53
17	1	17	1	5.88	25	96.00	25
20	1	20	9	45.00	41	78.04	41
Total	542	1,134	762		5,971		

Figure 5: Addresses With Repeat Alarms and Burglaries

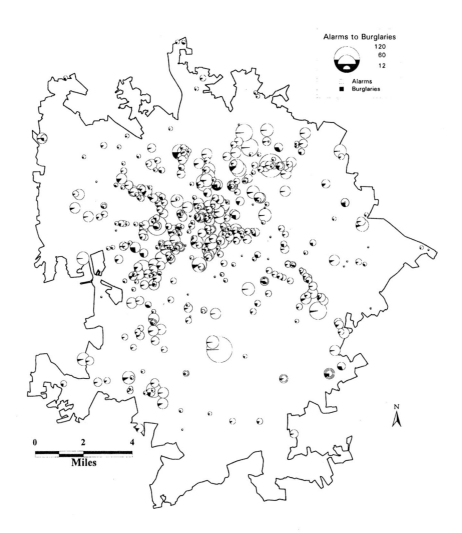

IMPLICATIONS AND NEW DIRECTIONS

What Do The Numbers Tell Us?

If we compare Tables 2, 3, 4, we see that address repetition is more of a problem for alarms and that burglary is mainly a single-address or low-frequency repeat-address phenomenon. As noted earlier, the exceptions are the places generating both alarms and burglaries, but their numbers are minor compared to the places experiencing burglaries without alarms.

Where Do The Numbers Lead Us?

At the citywide level, efforts focusing on reducing repeat victimization might be inefficient since burglary is primarily a single-address crime. Furthermore, the sheer mass of the alarm calls will indirectly subtract from any organizational gains made by focusing on the prevention of repeat burglaries. The direction to take, then, is one of implementing polices for better managing or controlling alarm calls. Levying fines for false alarms has already been discussed; other policies include: lowering the dispatch and response time priority for alarm calls, taking alarms off 911 phone lines, and requiring alarm company personnel to be on the premises of an activation before police respond (see Hakim et al., 1996). Most of these policies have been recently implemented in different cities, thus we can assume that evaluations for their effectiveness are forthcoming. As a matter of fact, Charlotte is in the process of implementing a fine system.

What Do The Maps Tell Us?

The graduated circle maps do an excellent job of highlighting the most chronic addresses and enhancing pattern recognition. Specifically, these maps help delineate the spatial biases of alarms and burglaries, and distinguish between their spatial patterns.

Where Do The Maps Lead Us?

Basically the maps lead us to making more and different maps. The problem with using graduated-circle maps is that they detract the untrained map observer's attention away from what might be the more complex patterns and pertinent problems. Specifically, attention is paid to the large circles aligned along the major street and rail routes, while the vast number of small-repetition addresses scattered across the landscape are ignored. There is a very high probability that these burglaries and alarms activation are residential simply because a vast majority of the land use in an urban area is residential (see Knox, 1994). Therefore, differentiating between residential-commercial alarms and burglaries, and changing the scale of the map to allow for the examination of smaller areas, may provide more insight into the distribution of the phenomena.

Changing the map scale, aggregating the locations of the alarms and burglaries into areal units (i.e., Census tracts and Census block-groups), and defining these areal units in terms of their socioeconomic, demographic, and land-use characteristics may answer questions about the differential effectiveness of alarms and their relationships with burglaries (see Buck et al., 1993). Furthermore, employing socioeconomic and demographic variables allows one to construct residential burglary and alarm activation rates, thus making it possible to compare differential rates by social class.

Making use of the maps, along with incorporating the temporal dimension, have great potential for measuring two properties or outcomes of crime prevention activities, namely, displacement and the diffusion of benefits. It was previously determined that the coefficient of determination between the alarm and burglary distributions is moderate (26.9%). Yet the relationship between the two might be stronger and more interdependent. Recent ethnographic studies have revealed that burglars generally prefer to avoid targets with alarms (Cromwell et al., 1991; Rengert and Wasilchick, 1985; and Wright and Decker, 1994). Therefore, the potential for displacement becomes the focus of the relationship between alarms and burglaries. This proposition might be better tested with different types of data (e.g., interviews with suspects). Nevertheless, there is some cartographic evidence suggesting that the process is taking place.

Comparing Figures 2 and 4, it is possible to observe spaces where repeat-address alarms along major streets are contiguous with areas that have large concentrations of burglaries without alarms. One such area is on the west side of the city, north and west of the CBD. The eastern boundary is the interstate running from north to southwest. The northern boundary is the interstate running from west to east, and the southern boundary is a major street with a parallel rail line originating and lying west of the CBD. The city limit is the western boundary. Figure 2 shows many chronic-alarm addresses along the major street and rail routes. However, spaces between the routes in this area are riddled with burglaries without alarms (see Figure 4). The problem is determining the degree that the alarmed premises influence the victimization of others without alarms. To accomplish this, it will be imperative to incorporate temporal information in order to assess the time order of alarms and burglaries and to determine if there are significant lead lag relationships between the two.

Assessing the diffusion of benefits (Clarke and Weisburd, 1994) or free-rider effects (Miethe, 1991) involves mapping the precise locations of alarms and burglaries on parcel maps. These are maps that delineate the areal extent of specific properties or land holdings. Such a window will allow one to view the spatial relationships among alarmed, burglarized, and non-victimized, or free-rider, premises. This might be a more optimal unit analysis than the Census block (see Miethe, 1991).

DIRECTIONS FOR ETHNOGRAPHIC RESEARCH

Future ethnographic studies of burglars should include questions about the deterrent effect of alarms. If burglars are reluctant to enter alarmed premises then the following questions should be posed: How can you tell that a place has an alarm? If a place has an alarm what are the principle criteria for selecting another? Will a burglar switch to different types of targets? In other words, if a burglar finds that a warehouse or a school has an alarm will he or she switch to a residence?

The Most Difficult Direction To Follow

Finally, there is a need for a comprehensive study of false alarms. Such a study would examine the types of alarms, by function and brand, and the reasons for activation. Such a study would be controversial since it involves grading or evaluating the products and marketing the practices of the private security industry. Presently, the alarm industry is profiting in a product whose purchase provides hope for the consumer, but its high frequency of false activations may lead the police to become dangerously complacent.

◆

NOTES

1. The inspiration for the title of this chapter emanates from *Mapping It Out: Expository Cartography for the Humanities and Social Sciences* by Mark Monmonier, 1993, The University of Chicago Press.

REFERENCES

Buck, A.J., S. Hakim, and G. Rengert (1993). "Burglar Alarms and The Choice Behavior of Burglars: A Suburban Phenomenon." *Journal of Criminal Justice* 21:497-507.

Chicago Police Department (1995). *Silenced Alarms Delight Cops.* Web Page: http:// 199.177.48.2/Community Policing/ MakeTheRight-Call/FalseBurglarAlarms.html.

Clarke, R.V. and D. Weisburd (1994). "Diffusion of Crime Control Benefits: Observations on Reverse Displacement." In: R.V. Clarke (ed.), *Crime Prevention Studies*, vol. 3. Monsey, NY: Criminal Justice Press.

Cohen, L.E. and M. Felson (1979). "Social Change and Crime Rate Trends: A Routine Activity Approach." *American Sociological Review* 44:588-605.

Cromwell, P., J.N. Olson, and D. Avary (1991). *Breaking and Entering: An Ethnographic Analysis of Burglary.* Newbury Park, CA: Sage.

Daughtry, Sylvester, Jr. (1993). "False Alarm Reduction: A Priority for Law Enforcement." *Police Chief* 60(1):14.

Farrell, G. and K. Pease (1993). *Once Bitten, Twice Bitten: Repeat Victimization and Its Implications for Crime Prevention.* Home Office Crime Prevention Unit Series, No. 46. London, UK: Her Majesty's Stationery Office.

Funk, D. (1995). "Merchants Try to Even Odds: Tired of Being Blamed, Retailers Considering New False Alarm Laws." *Baltimore Business Journal* 12(34):9.

Garson, G.D. and R.S. Biggs (1992). *Analytic Mapping and Geographic Databases.* Newbury Park, CA: Sage.

Hakim, S., G.F. Rengert, and Y. Shachmurove (in press). "Estimation of Net Benefits of Residential Electronic Security." *Justice Quarterly.*

Knox, P.L. (1994). *Urbanization: An Introduction To Urban Geography.* Englewood Cliffs, NJ: Prentice-Hall.

Miethe, T.D. (1991). "Citizen-Based Crime Control Activity and Victimization Risks: An Examination of Displacement and Free-Rider Effects." *Criminology* 29:419-40.

Monmonier, M. (1993). *Mapping It Out: Expository Cartography for the Humanities and Social Sciences.* Chicago, IL: University of Chicago Press.

Moslow, John J. (1994). "False Alarms: Cause for Alarm." *FBI Law Enforcement Bulletin* 63(11):1-6.

Rengert, G. and J. Wasilchick (1985). *Suburban Burglary.* Springfield, IL: Charles C Thomas.

Reppetto, T.A. (1974). *Residential Crime.* Cambridge, MA: Ballinger.

Sherman, L.W. (1989). "Repeat Calls For Police Service: Policing the 'Hot Spots.'" In: D.J. Kenney (ed.), *Policing and Police: Contemporary Issues.* New York, NY: Praeger.

—— P.R. Gartin, and M.E. Buerger (1989). "Hot Spots of Predatory Crime: Routine Activities and the Criminology of Place." *Criminology* 27:27-55.

Werner, T. (1993). "Cost of False Security Alarms Prompts Fees and Fines." *Philadelphia Business Journal* 12(15):3b.

Wright, R.T. and S.H. Decker (1994). *Burglars on the Job: Streetlife and Residential Break-ins.* Boston, MA: Northeastern University Press.

Crime Mapping in the Next Decade

ARTIFICIAL NEURAL NETWORKS AND CRIME MAPPING

by

Andreas M. Olligschlaeger
Carnegie Mellon University

Abstract: The recent change in emphasis from reactive to proactive law enforcement, as evidenced by such concepts as community-oriented policing, has resulted in the need for tools to support these efforts. While geographic information systems (GISs) have been very successful at tracking criminal activity, proactive law enforcement requires systems that anticipate the emergence of criminal activity. One such system under development at Carnegie Mellon University and the Pittsburgh (PA) Bureau of Police is an early warning system that incorporates a GIS, previously developed to track criminal activity, and a relatively new technology — artificial neural networks — to predict the emergence or "flare ups" of drug hot-spot areas. The system obtains its input from cell-aggregated GIS-based data, processes the data with a previously trained artificial neural network and outputs the results to a choropleth map indicating those areas for which the network has predicted a relatively high number of 911 calls for service for drugs. The focus of this paper is to describe how the early warning system was developed, and to explain some of the underlying theory behind neural networks. In addition, the performance of the network is compared to some of the more traditional geographic forecasting methods.

INTRODUCTION

Computerized mapping has come a long way since the first mainframe applications (such as SYMAP) produced "maps" on high-speed line printers that shaded choropleth (or thematic) maps using differ-

Address correspondence to: Andreas M. Olligschlaeger, H. John Heinz III School of Public Policy and Management, Carnegie Mellon University, 5000 Forbes Avenue, Pittsburgh, PA 15213.

ent combinations of ASCII characters printed one on top of the other. However, the concept of geographic information systems (GIS) and all that it implies is still relatively new to researchers and practitioners alike. In part this is because people are only just beginning to realize that GIS can be much more than merely an automated mapping system, and in part because the quality of spatial data contained in a GIS can be so high that researchers are continuously finding new uses for it. In fact, it can be a one-stop shopping center for information. GIS is indeed an exciting field, especially within the context of law enforcement.

There is no doubt that GISs have proven themselves to be an invaluable tool for law enforcement. Examples of successful uses of GIS from a research perspective abound for a variety of law enforcement support functions, such as measuring the geographic displacement of drug offenders (see, for example, Green, 1993), monitoring the effects of law enforcement strategies on nuisance bar activity (Cohen et al., 1993), and point pattern analysis of crime locations (Canter, 1993). Other examples of more general purpose crime mapping systems for law enforcement include the Drug Market Analysis Program (DMAP) effort undertaken in Jersey City, Hartford, San Diego, Pittsburgh and Kansas City (McEwen and Taxman, 1994; Maltz, 1993), and PA-LEGIS (Pennsylvania Law Enforcement Geographic Information System), an integrated GIS and police records management system developed for smaller police departments (Bookser, 1991).

The impact of GIS in law enforcement is further illustrated by the fact that today virtually all commercially available police record management and emergency operations systems include a GIS component. As police organizations automate their operations and implement more modern computer systems, taking advantage of advances in information science such as open-architecture database systems, enterprise-wide computer applications and ever-increasing microprocessor and network speeds, more and more information will become available to police officers at the click of a mouse. Moreover, all of this information will be linked together from various sources and organized in ways that were previously unheard of. Police investigators will likely find this wealth of information a boon to their work, but crime analysts may well find themselves faced with information overload.

At the same time that police departments are making greater use of computer technology, they are also undergoing a change in law enforcement philosophy. Evidence of this change can be seen in the fact that many departments are implementing community-oriented policing (COP) in an effort to emphasize proactive rather than reactive law enforcement. While the concept of COP is certainly not new (for a review of early initiatives, see Trojanowicz, 1986), the way in which information is utilized in COP has changed over the years. In many cities, desktop personal computers have replaced the daily log for foot patrol officers, and in some cities the time-honored tradition of a notebook and pencil has given way to hand-held, pen-based mobile computers.

The current decade has shown that providing police officers with automated tools to collect and access information is not a problem. While they will undoubtedly become more sophisticated, such tools already exist in many police departments. Given the right amount of funding, careful planning and proper implementation, there are abundant technical solutions available to those departments wishing to automate information gathering and dissemination. Rather, the challenge in the next decade will be to provide crime analysts and police administrators with the tools to support proactive law enforcement efforts. This, in turn, will require the use of increasingly sophisticated data analysis methods and statistical techniques.

This chapter addresses one way in which GISs can provide such tools in the next decade. Specifically, it describes how another relatively new technology — artificial neural networks — was incorporated into a GIS-based early warning system for street-level drug markets implemented by the Pittsburgh Bureau of Police as part of the MAP. The resulting computer system predicts the emergence, or "flare-ups" of drug "hot-spot" areas. Input for the system is obtained from cell-aggregated GIS-based data that is processed by a previously trained artificial neural network. The output is then displayed on a choropleth map indicating those areas for which a relatively high number of 911 calls for service for drugs are anticipated.

The chapter proceeds in the following manner. First, the existing early warning system used by the Pittsburgh Bureau of Police, as well as some of the pitfalls encountered during its development, is described. Second, a brief overview is given of some of the more prevalent models used in space-time forecasting. The third section provides a brief overview of artificial neural networks. Fourth, an artificial neural network used for space-time forecasting is introduced. The fifth section presents a case study of predicting flare-ups of 911 calls for service for drugs, and describes how the artificial neural network was incorporated into the early warning system. In the conclusion the chapter is summarized and future work is outlined.

THE PITTSBURGH DMAP SYSTEM

The Pittsburgh DMAP computer system is a fully integrated GIS linking a variety of sources of information into a single user interface. Specifically, these sources consist of 911 calls for service, police incident and arrest data, property tax and ownership information, liquor license data, and map sheet coverages from the Pittsburgh-Allegheny GIS (PAGIS). The map sheets include streets, property parcels, building footprints, parks, cemeteries, schools, public housing projects, Census tracts, neighborhoods and police zones.

The DMAP system is designed to provide support for both investigative and administrative police personnel. Users can query the system by any geographic area (such as neighborhood or census tract) or by a single address. Depending on the type of query users can, for instance, map out police or 911 incidents, determine property ownership, produce reports of incidents involving persons residing at a particular address, or map geographic displacement of criminal activities. One component of DMAP that is of particular interest to this chapter is an early warning system that allows administrative personnel to analyze crime pattern trends by geographic area.

Development of the early warning system was possible in part because of a key feature of GISs: the ability to associate xy coordinates with the address of an incident. This concept is known as "geocoding." During geocoding, an address is matched against a known data set (also referred to as an "address coverage") containing the xy coordinates of all addresses located within a particular area. There are two types of address coverages: point-based and line-based. Line-based (or street) address coverages are by far the most commonly used, in part because they are much easier to construct and maintain and in part because they are available at low cost from a variety of sources. Street-address coverages consist of nodes (points in space that can represent either curves or intersections) and arcs. For example, an arc connecting two intersections can represent a street block. Each arc has a number of attributes associated with it, including the street name, street type, street direction, and the left and right beginning and ending address. Geocoding using line-based address coverages proceeds in the following manner: the system locates the arc that not only shares the same street name, type and direction of the address to be matched, but where the street number also falls into the left or right beginning and ending address range. Once the arc has been located, the xy coordinate of the address is determined by interpolation between the beginning and ending node of the arc. For example, if the left address range of an arc is between 100 and

198, and the street number of the address to be matched is 150, then the xy coordinate of the matched address will be halfway between the two nodes.

Point-based address coverages are different in that the xy coordinates of an address are determined not by the street the address is located on, but some other key identifier such as a building footprint or the center of a property parcel. Because one building or property parcel may contain several different addresses, one or more addresses can share the same xy coordinate. In order to match an address, all the system has to do is find an exact match in the address coverage and retrieve the corresponding xy coordinate. Geocoding using point-based address coverages is therefore much faster because the algorithm requires fewer steps. The implementation of a point-based address coverage is more costly and time-consuming than line-based address coverages, but yields a far more accurate data set for geocoding. The Pittsburgh DMAP system uses a point-based address coverage where the xy coordinates of addresses were determined using the geographic centers of property parcels. For each parcel the lot and block number was related to the property tax file, resulting in one or more valid addresses for each parcel. These addresses, along with the xy coordinate, were then added to the address coverage. The final result contains one record for each valid address in the City of Pittsburgh.

Problems arise during geocoding when an address cannot be located in the address coverage. If this is the case, the data are lost and cannot be displayed or located on a map. The two most common causes of unmatched addresses are inaccurate address coverages and inconsistently spelled street names. In Pittsburgh both of these causes were encountered. Most GIS software packages have a component that allows users to manually select an address from a list of candidates in the event that an exact match cannot be found. This is fine when only a few addresses are to be matched, but too time-consuming when hundreds of thousands of addresses are to be matched, as is the case in DMAP. As a result, the Pittsburgh DMAP system utilizes its own geocoding algorithm where addresses are pre-processed to eliminate spelling inconsistencies and candidates are automatically selected according to a specific set of rules. Because of this algorithm DMAP successfully matches about 97% of all addresses.

The accuracy of geocoding in DMAP means that little information is lost in the geocoding process. In addition, the geocoding algorithm ensures that data from various otherwise incompatible sources can be consistently collated via the address, resulting in a large data set that can be aggregated according to any spatial unit.

The early warning system utilizes this data set to provide choropleth maps of changes in criminal activity based either on 911 calls for service or police incident data for user-selected crime types. Users choose the time period (for example, changes over the past month) as well as the areal unit by which they would like to aggregate the data. The areal units can either be pre-defined, such as by Census tracts or patrol sectors, or user-defined cells derived by overlaying a grid on the City of Pittsburgh. Finally, the user chooses the class intervals for shading the map. These are either calculated automatically according to standard deviations or frequencies, or defined by the user. The output of the early warning system is a citywide map that shades areas according to changes in criminal activity relative to other areas in the city. Those areas that experienced negative changes are shaded from light blue to deep blue depending on the relative magnitude of change ("cold areas"), whereas those with positive changes, or increases, are shaded from light red to deep red ("hot areas"). Users can also zoom in to hot areas to look at specific addresses or intersections responsible for the increase in criminal activity.

The early warning system described above was a significant step ahead in terms of providing police administrators with an automated tool to analyze changes in spatial crime patterns on a citywide basis. However, the system does not provide for any predictive capabilities. As mentioned earlier, police administrators also have a need for tools allowing them to anticipate changes in criminal activity. Thus, the following pages outline how the early warning system was modified to provide space-time forecasts of changes in 911 calls for service for drugs.

SPATIAL FORECASTING MODELS AND METHODS

Somewhat surprisingly, it was not until the early 1950s that the first models were developed that took spatial context into consideration, even though temporal context, or time series modeling, was introduced as early as the 1920s (Cliff et al., 1975). Since then geographers and regional scientists have devised a variety of techniques for space-time forecasting, many of which are spatial extensions of time-series models. Anselin (1988) notes that the regional science and geography literature provides much evidence that the effects of space are heterogeneous rather than homogeneous. As a result, he argues, modeling strategies have to account for regional, or local, features.

A univariate example of space-time models is the Space-Time Autoregressive model, or STAR (Tobler, 1969). STAR, an extension of the purely temporal autoregressive model originating with Box and Jenkins (1970), assumes that the influence of neighboring observations declines with distance from the current observation according to a set of pre-defined spatial weights. A related model is the Space-Time Autoregressive Integrated Moving Average model, which incorporates repeated differencing for trend elimination and the exponential smoothing model (Cliff et al., 1975).

One of the most basic multivariate models that takes into account local context is the spatially varying parameter model, defined as follows:

$$Y_i = \sum_{k=0}^{p} \beta_{ki} x_{ki} + \varepsilon_i, i \in C \qquad (1)$$

where C is an index for the space-time context of parameter variation, i is an index in C, Y_i is the independent variable at observation i, β_{ik} is the parameter for the k_{th} independent variable for observation I (k = 0,1,2...p), and ε_i is the error term for observation i. Implementing this model in unconstrained form is impossible because the number of parameters increases with the number of observations (Anselin, 1988). Consequently, researchers have devised a number of strategies to counter this problem.

Two such methods are locally weighted regression (see, for example, Cassetti, 1982, and Cleveland and Devlin, 1988) and Kriging (David, 1977; Haining, 1990). Locally weighted regression techniques require that the weights are specified a priori. This often occurs via trial and error as an attempt is made to see which set of weights produces the best fit of the dependent variable. Kriging — or, in the multivariate case, cokriging — uses an empirically estimated function, called a variogram, to determine the spatial weighting of data observations. Both methods assume that the influence of other observations declines with distance from the current observation.

Model (1) is also often used for exploratory data analysis (Gorr and Olligschlaeger, 1994): maps of residuals can show undetected spatial heterogeneity suggesting additional theory or model structure, and maps of estimated spatially varying parameters are useful in determining the functional form of parameter variation. This type of exploratory data analysis is also used in expansion modeling. One example is a stepwise regression model using polynomial or other functions of time and space coordinates that interact with an initial model's variables (see, for example, Cassetti, 1982 and Cassetti and Jones, 1992).

Two final examples of estimating spatially varying parameter models are spatial adaptive filtering (SAF) and weighted spatial adaptive filtering (WSAF), both of which are based on adaptive filtering originating with Widrow and Hoff (1960). Foster and Gorr (1986) introduced SAF as an extension of multivariate damped negative feedback estimation by using a heuristic approach to optimizing individual damping factors for each β_k in model (1). WSAF was introduced by Gorr and Olligschlaeger (1994) as an extension of SAF. It incorporates a pattern recognizer into SAF that reduces an inherent bias created by applying equal weights to feedback signals from neighboring observations. Based on the magnitude of forecast errors using the β_k of neighboring observations, WSAF automatically assigns appropriate weights to feedback signals: those observations with small forecast errors receive relatively large weights, whereas those with larger errors receive smaller weights. The resulting weighting scheme is similar to those used in time-series combination forecasting (see, for example, Bates and Granger, 1969 and Clemen, 1989).

At this point it is important to note that both SAF and WSAF use a feedback scheme very similar to the Widrow-Hoff (1960) rule and the perceptron convergence procedure originating with Minsky and Papert (1969). In addition, the scheme resembles the generalized Delta Rule employed in estimating feed-forward artificial neural networks with backpropagation (Rumelhart and McClelland, 1988). The significance of this will become apparent in a later section.

All of the examples discussed above assume that the distribution of data fits a certain functional form. As practitioners know, this is only very rarely if ever the case, especially when it comes to crime data. Second, with the exception of WSAF and Kriging, the functional form of the spatial variation of parameters as well as the weights defining the influence of neighboring observations must be specified a priori. From a practical viewpoint, this requires much exploratory analysis and experimentation with different model specifications in order to arrive at a model with good predictive capabilities. WSAF, while generally more efficient at automatically detecting spatial patterns, is very sensitive to the heuristics used in determining optimal damping factors and sometimes tends to overfit the model. In addition, it is more of an exploratory technique rather than a predictive one.

Law enforcement practitioners rarely have the time or the expertise to arrive at predictions of criminal activity using the above models. Rather, they require techniques that provide reasonably accurate forecasts of crime patterns with a minimum of user intervention, with results being displayed in such a way that they are easy to understand and intuitive. In addition, the forecasting models used to make predictions must be adaptive, i.e., they must be able to automatically recognize and adapt to changes in the functional form underlying spatio-temporal crime patterns. For example, drug dealers are constantly changing their method of operation in response to various law enforcement efforts as well as changes in the nature of their business. This, in turn, leads to changes in behavior as evidenced, for example, by the geographic displacement of drug markets. One technique that could accomplish the above-mentioned goals are artificial neural networks.

A BRIEF OVERVIEW OF ARTIFICIAL NEURAL NETWORKS

As with many newer technologies, there is still much confusion and skepticism among applied researchers over what artificial neural networks are and how useful they can be. There is confusion because there are so many different types of artificial neural networks (also known as "connectionist" or "parallel distributed processing" models) and because little, if anything is known about their statistical properties. On the one hand, artificial neural networks seem to be able to do things that no other statistical method can do, but on the other no one quite understands how and why they can do it. Skeptics argue that, like expert systems, neural networks are just another much-ballyhooed technology that may have some usefulness for a small set of well-defined applications but that they are not quite the greatest thing since sliced bread that their proponents make them out to be.

Exactly how widespread the use of neural networks will be remains to be seen. However, some very important developments have recently occurred in the field that show great promise for a wide range of potential applications. All indications are that research into neural networks is not going to be as short-lived as some people believe. The current interest in neural networks actually represents the second wave of research into the area. The first wave occurred after McCulloch and Pitts (1943) introduced a simple form of neurons as an attempt to emulate biological neurons. The authors envisioned using these mathematical neurons as components that could perform computational tasks in electronic circuits (Kroese and Van der Smagt, 1993). After two decades or so of research by a variety of authors, Minsky and Papert (1969) showed that perceptrons (their term for neural networks) had a number of deficiencies that prevented their use for general purposes. One of the most important deficiencies was the fact that they were unable to perform non-linear calculations. Consequently, many researchers left the field, although some key authors continued their work (Rumelhart and McClelland, 1988).

A resurgence of interest in the field occurred when Rumelhart and McClelland (1988) published their two volume set *Parallel Distributed Processing*. It consisted of a series of articles written by the PDP Research Group, a group of researchers who had continued to work on neural networks during the 1970s and 1980s. One of the chapters that is of particular interest to this paper outlined an approach incorporating multiple layers of neurons and nonlinear signal processing that allowed perceptron-like neural networks to estimate nonlinear functions. Since then there has been a remarkable amount of research in the field, including efforts at using neural networks for prediction (see, for example, Poli and Jones, 1994, and White, 1988).

Due to the large variety of artificial neural networks, it is beyond the scope of this paper to discuss even a representative sample (for an excellent introduction to the topic, see Rumelhart and McClelland, 1988 or Carpenter and Grossberg, 1991). However, one neural network architecture — feed-forward networks with backpropagation — will be outlined because it forms the basis of the neural net architecture of the early warning system described in the next section. Multi-layer feed-forward networks with backpropagation are probably the most studied type of artificial neural network, and are essentially a non-linear extension of Minsky and Papert's (1969) perceptrons.

Regardless of type, all artificial neural networks consist of a number of processing units that send signals to one another via a large number of weighted connections (Kroese and Van der Smagt, 1993). The main difference between network architectures is how signals are processed by each unit and the way in which the weights on each connection are updated. The internal representation of a processing unit in a backpropagation network is shown in Figure 1.

Figure 1: A Neural Processing Unit

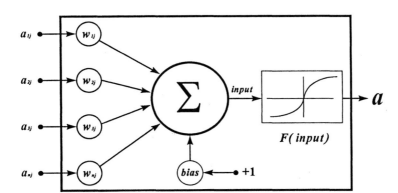

Each processing unit, via weighted connections, receives input in the form of the outputs (activations) from the processing units in the previous layer. These outputs are multiplied by the weight on each connection, and, together with a bias, are summed to form the net input for the processing unit. More formally:

$$net_{pi} = \sum_j w_{ij} a_{pj} + \theta_{pi} \qquad (2)$$

where net_i is the net input for processing unit i for input pattern p, w_{ij} is the weight of the connection between processing unit i and processing unit j in the previous layer, a_{pj} is the activation of unit j in the previous layer, and θ_{pi} is the bias associated with unit i. The function used to process the net input varies, but generally takes on a sigmoid functional form. The most commonly used function is the logistic function. It yields values in the range [0,1] and determines the activation of the processing unit at the next step as follows:

$$a_{ip} = \frac{1}{1 + e^{-net_{ip}}} \qquad (3)$$

where a_{ip} is the activation of unit i for input pattern p.

Figure 2: A Multilayer Feed-forward Network

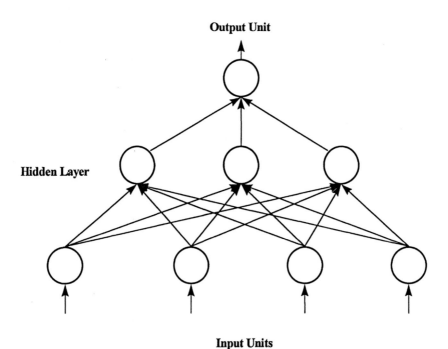

Figure 2 shows an example of a simple multi-layer neural network architecture. The network consists of three layers: input, output and hidden. Each layer consists of a number of units (neurons) that process information passed to them by units in the layer below, as described in (2) and (3). The input layer has four nodes and the hidden layer has three. In this example there is only one output node, although it possible to have more than one. In feed-forward networks information is input into each node, processed, and then passed on to each node in the layer above. In the case of an output node, information is simply passed out of the network.

The goal is to map the input units to a desired output similar to the way in which the dependent variable is a function of the independent variables in regression analysis. The difference is that regression analysis uses linear direct mapping whereas multi-layer feed-forward networks use non-linear indirect mapping. The hidden layer creates an internal representation of the patterns to be mapped. The internal representation is then mapped to the output unit. It is the hidden layer, along with the use of a non-linear activation function, that allows multi-layer networks to map far more complex functions than simple direct input-to-output unit mappings.

Feed-forward networks with backpropagation "learn" to map the input units to the output units by adjusting the weights on the connections in response to error signals transmitted back through the network. During training, the network is presented with each input pattern and computes the activation of the output unit(s) using the current network weight structure (the weights are initialized randomly prior to training). The difference between the output of the network and the target mapping constitutes the error signal. This signal is then propagated back through the network via the processing units, and their connections and the weights are updated. The goal is to continually update the weights until the sum of all error signals is minimized.

In backpropagation networks, weight updates are performed using the generalized delta rule derived by Rumelhart et al. (1988) from the perceptron convergence procedure originating with Minsky and Papert (1969). The latter, in turn, is a variation of the delta rule proposed by Widrow and Hoff (1960). The generalized delta rule can be summarized in three equations (for a formal derivation of the generalized delta rule, see Kroese and Van der Smagt, 1993 or Rumelhart et al., 1988). The first specifies that the weight change should be proportional to the product of the error signal sent to a receiving unit along a connection, and the activation of the sending unit. More formally,

$$\Delta_p w_{ij} = \eta \delta_{pj} a_{pi} \quad (4)$$

where $\Delta_p w_{ij}$ is weight change for training pattern p and the connection between processing units i and j, δ_{pj} is the error signal sent to unit j, a_{pi} is the activation of unit i for input pattern p, and η is the "learning rate." The learning rate is usually some small number less than 1. The definition of the error signal differs between output units and hidden units. For output units using a logistic activation function, it is defined as:

$$\delta_{pj} = (t_{pj} - a_{pj})a_{pj}(1 - a_{pj}) \quad (5)$$

where t_{pj} is the target activation for the output unit. For hidden units the error signal is given by

$$\delta_{pj} = a_{pj}(1 - a_{pj})\sum_i \delta_{pi} w_{ij} \quad (6)$$

The generalized delta rule implements a gradient descent in the error term. Training of the network proceeds by repeatedly presenting all input patterns and adjusting the weights until the sum of all errors is minimized, i.e., the network converges to a solution. In this respect, it is crucial to select a learning rate that during training will allow the network to iterate toward a true global minimum rather than getting stuck in local minima. Too-large learning rates can lead to oscillations between local minima, whereas small learning rates can require hundreds of thousands of iterations to converge. While it is theoretically possible that even with small learning rates the network will converge to a local minimum, empirical evidence suggests that this is rarely the case (Weiss and Kulikowski, 1991). One way to avoid this is to train the network several times with different random initializations of the weights, and to compare the results.

When implementing a backpropagation network, there are a number of factors to take into account. For example, the derivation of the generalized delta rule assumes that the network weights are updated each epoch, i.e., the error signal used in equation (4) is taken to be the sum of all error signals computed for each input pattern in the training data set. It has been shown that in some cases, updating the weights after each input pattern is presented can yield better results, i.e., the total mean squared error is smaller (Weiss and Kulikowski, 1991).

A further consideration is to determine how many processing units to include in the hidden layer. It appears that the number is directly related to the complexity of the function to be estimated (Hecht-Nielsen, 1990). Since in empirical applications the functional form of the input-to-output unit mapping is rarely known, the number of processing units has to be determined by trial and error. Too few hidden units may produce sub-optimal results, whereas too many may result in overfitting, i.e., the network simply "memorizes" all of the input and output patterns and yields zero error. While in some cases this may be desirable it is inappropriate for forecasting. One commonly used approach to determine the correct number of hidden units is to use about two thirds or three-quarters of the sample data for network training, and to keep adding hidden units until the network no longer generalizes well. Network generalization refers to how well the network performs with "unseen" data, i.e., data that was not used in training. If the performance is significantly worse, then the network has overfitted the data.

Depending on the number of weights present in the network and the type of architecture, feed-forward networks with backpropagation can require a large number of data points to train. If the sample size is not large enough, the network once again will simply "memorize" the input-to-output mappings and overfit the data. This can pose a problem for spatial data. Often only annual data are available at the Census tract level, so that even with a relatively large study area (say, on the order of 150 Census tracts) and 10 years worth of data the total number of observations would only be 1,500. For social science data this is typically not enough to train a neural network without overfitting the data. Depending on the complexity of the function to be estimated, neural networks can require tens of thousands of observations. As will be demonstrated in a later section, GISs allow for the production of very large data sets due to the nature in which data is stored and the manner in which it can be queried.

Depending on the sample size and the size of the network, the task of determining the ideal network structure for a specific application can prove to be very time-consuming. However, artificial intelligence algorithms do exist that can automatically design and optimize application-specific network structures. The genetic algorithm due to Holland (1975), which "evolves" the network architecture based on a "survival of the fittest" scheme, has been used quite successfully (see, for example, Harp et al., 1990 and Rogers, 1990). Regardless of how the network architecture is optimized, once this has been accomplished the network can readily adapt to changes in the functional form of the input-to-output unit mapping. In a time series, for example, the network is simply retrained as new data are collected using the previous network weight structure as initial weights.

Neural networks have one drawback in their potential as a spatial modeling tool, however. The algorithm described above requires that the number of input units is the same for all input-to-output mappings, i.e., there can be no missing variables in the sample data. Many spatial models (such as the Spatial Adaptive Filter discussed in the previous section) use a contiguity matrix to determine the neighborhood of the current observation. A contiguity matrix is an n by n dimensional matrix of ones and zeroes, where n is the total number of geographic regions in the study area. If a region is a neighbor of the current observation, then the matrix entry for those two regions has a value of one. If the two regions are not neighbors, the matrix entry has a value of zero. One of the most common geographic units used to estimate spatial models are Census tracts. The problem with using Census tracts as a geographic basis for spatial modeling using neural networks is that each Census tract has an inconsistent number of neighbors. Including neighboring observations as input units, as is most often the case in spatial modeling methods violates the rule that the number of input units must be the same for all observations. This problem will be addressed and a solution to it provided in the next section.

Feed-forward networks with backpropagation have some very important properties that make them suitable for the kind of modeling discussed in the previous section. First, they do not require that the functional form of the input-to-output unit mapping is specified a priori. The theoretical underpinnings of many statistical models, on the other hand, require that the data sample and the input-to-output mapping have a certain functional form. For example, in Kriging or Cokriging the functional form of parameter variation must be specified a priori. While there are certainly many types of statistical models with different assumptions as to the distribution of data or parameters, they often require much exploratory analysis and experimentation with different functional dependencies before satisfactory results are achieved.

A second important discovery with regard to the nature of backpropagation networks was made by Hornik et al. (1989), who proved mathematically that, provided sufficiently many hidden units are available, multi-layer feed-forward networks with backpropagation form a class of universal approximators capable of estimating any functional form to any desired degree of accuracy.

A NEURAL NETWORK ARCHITECTURE FOR SPACE-TIME FORECASTS

In summarizing the previous sections it is possible to define the following requirements for a neural network architecture for space-time forecasting:

(1) The number of input units must be constant across all input-output mappings, i.e., each observation must have an equal number of observations in its neighborhood.

(2) The size of the data set must be sufficiently large to train the network without overfitting, or "memorizing," the input-to-output mappings.

(3) The number of hidden processing units must be large enough to facilitate an internal representation of the input-to-output mappings, but not too large to cause overfitting of the data.

(4) The network must be able to generalize, i.e., the weight structure arrived at during training should perform reasonably well on data that were not used during training.

(5) The network should not get stuck in a local minimum, i.e., should perform equally well with different random initializations of the connection weights.

The idea for a neural network architecture for space-time forecasting that satisfies the above criteria was originally conceived when the author was conducting research on cellular automata and chaos theory. Chaos theory, like artificial neural networks, has been the focus of much attention in recent years. It basically involves the study of phenomena or systems that are very sensitive to initial conditions. In chaotic systems or equations minute changes in parameters can result in very different outcomes — ranging from long-term stability to apparently random and unpredictable chaotic behavior (for an excellent introduction to chaos theory, see Schroeder, 1991). Some real-world examples of chaotic systems include weather patterns, neurological and cardiac activity, and the stock market. Chaos theory postulates that although chaotic systems seem to display totally random and unpredictable behavior, they are actually following strict mathematical rules that can be derived and studied (Pickover, 1990). These rules can range in sophistication from simple decision trees to complex non-linear functions.

Cellular automata are a specific type of chaotic system. They differ from other chaotic systems in that they act on discrete space or grids rather than a continuous medium such as a surface. In a cellular automata machine, each frame (representing all cells in a population) is replaced by a new one according to a specific "recipe," or rule, in the next epoch (Toffoli and Margolus, 1987). A key determinant of cellular automata rules is how each cell is influenced by neighboring cells. Consider the example given below.

Figure 3: A Game of Life

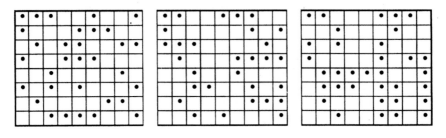

Epoch 0   Epoch 1   Epoch 2

Figure 3 shows three epochs in the life of a population of cells occupying a 9 x 9 grid. An empty square represents a dead cell, whereas a dotted square represents a live cell. Upon initial examination of the three epochs it appears that cells are born and die randomly. As it turns out, however, this is not the case. The behavior of the cell population from one epoch to the other actually follows a very simple set of rules introduced by mathematician John Conway in his game of "life" (Gardner, 1970). Assuming that the "neighborhood" of a cell consists of all immediately adjacent cells, the rules are as follows:

(1) A live cell will only stay alive if it has two or three living neighbors. Otherwise it will die of either "overcrowding" or "loneliness."

(2) A dead cell will come to life if it has exactly three living neighbors. Otherwise it remains dead.

The above example can easily be expressed in terms of a neural network. Designate the target output of the network as the state of a cell in the next epoch (where the target output is one if the cell is alive and zero otherwise). The next step is to determine the input units. Since the rules of the game consider the state of all adjacent cells, as well of the current observation, we will need a total of nine input units representing a nine-cell square with the current observation being in the middle. If the current observation is located at the edge of the grid then all neighbors not on the grid — i.e., "missing" neighbors — are assumed to have a value of zero. Incidentally, this definition of a neighborhood is identical to that used in spatial adaptive filtering and weighted spatial adaptive filtering outlined earlier (see Gorr and Olligschlaeger, 1994). However, in the original Game of Life, cells are assumed to "wrap around" to the other edge of the grid (see Toffoli and Margolus, 1987). The mapping of the input-to-output units is a simple binary-to-binary mapping, i.e., a combination of nine zeros and ones map to either a single zero or a single one. If we assign three hidden units to the network the architecture would look like that in Figure 4.

Figure 4: Game of Life Neural Network

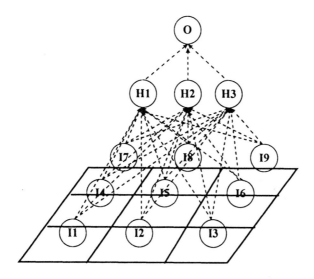

The neural net architecture in Figure 4 was in fact trained to "learn" the rules of the Game of Life when the author was first exploring the idea of using neural networks for space-time modeling. The algorithm used in training centered the network on each observation, and used the input mappings of the nine cells in the neighborhood to arrive at the output of the network for the current observation in the next epoch. The difference between the target output and the actual output of the network constituted the error signal. Thus, for each epoch (or time period) the number of patterns presented to the network is equal to the number of cells in the grid. The total number of training patterns is equal to the number of cells in the grid, multiplied by the number of epochs in the game presented to the network.

Presenting the results of the network outlined above would be beyond the scope of this paper. Suffice it to say, however, that the network was able to learn the rules of the Game of Life perfectly, i.e., without error. Moreover, the network performed flawlessly even when shown patterns that were not used during training: different random initializations of the grid cells had no effect on the performance of the network. In addition, it was able to predict successive generations of cells ad infinitum, requiring only the first epoch of randomly initialized cells to do so. This indicates that the network is very robust and able to generalize well, at least for this particular problem.

The rules of the Game of Life are certainly very simple. In the real world, rules governing space-time phenomena are far more complex. However, as demonstrated earlier, feed-forward networks with back-propagation are capable of "learning" extremely complex input-to-output mappings. In addition, the inputs or outputs need not be binary; they can take on any functional form (continuous or discontinuous) and do not have to fall into the [0,1] range. Finally, there is no reason why each cell in the neighborhood need only have one input unit. The rules can depend on more than one input that is unique to each cell.

It should therefore be possible to extend the neural network architecture outlined in Figure 4 in order to accommodate a variation of model (1). If for the moment we assume that we can obtain grid-based data for a geographical area, then using the same definition of a neighborhood as that for the Game of Life we can rewrite (1) as follows:

$$Y_i(t+1) = \sum_{k=0}^{p} \beta_k x_{ik}(t) + \sum_{j=0}^{8}\sum_{l=0}^{p} \beta_{jl} x_{jl}(t) + \varepsilon \quad (7)$$

where p is the number of independent variables and j represents each observation (1,2...8) in the neighborhood. Model (7) assumes that the parameters are spatially constant. For the spatially varying parameter case we can write:

$$Y_i(t+1) = \sum_{k=0}^{p} \beta_{ik} x_{ik}(t) + \sum_{j=0}^{8} \sum_{l=0}^{p} \beta_{jlm} x_{jl}(t) + \varepsilon; i, m \in C$$

(8)

where i and m are indexes in C, the context of spatial parameter variation. Therefore, the only difference between (7) and (8) is that in model (8) each cell has its own set of parameters. Note that models (7) and (8) also assume that the dependent variable is a linear function of the independent variables. Feed-forward networks with back-propagation do not require this assumption since functional dependencies do not need to be specified a priori.

A neural network architecture to estimate models (7) and (8) would look very similar to that presented in Figure 4. The only difference is that the number of input units for each cell is equal to p, and the number of hidden processing units will presumably be greater. For the spatially varying case, each cell would have its own unique set of input-to-hidden unit connections along with a unique set of weights. The hidden-to-output unit weight structure would be the same for all observations.

The neighborhood defined above satisfies requirement 1 outlined earlier, that the number of input units must be constant for all input-to-output mappings. Requirement 3 is usually determined via trial and error, i.e., the number of hidden units is increased over repeated training sessions until the network performance does not significantly improve. The fourth requirement can be determined by comparing the performance of the network to patterns previously unseen, i.e., not used during training. Finally, requirement 5 can be satisfied by repeatedly training the network using the same number of hidden units but different random initializations of the weight structure, and comparing the results. Thus requirements 3, 4 and 5 are satisfied during the optimization of the network, i.e., by repeated training and comparing of results.

What remains to be determined, however, is how to obtain not only grid-based data but also a large enough number of observations to train the network (requirements 1 and 2). This is where GIS and geocoding, discussed in section 2, come into the picture. Recall that one of the main advantages of GIS-based data is that it can be queried according to any geographic area, including user-defined ones. If we create a grid-based polygon coverage and overlay it on a study area such as a city, then we can easily determine the number of data points that fall within each grid cell. In addition, we can break down the data further according to other characteristics. For example, with 911 or police data we can count the frequencies of drug calls for service, robbery arrests or burglaries. In addition, if property ownership data is geocoded by address, then for each grid cell we can also determine variables such as the average assessed value of homes, the proportion of commercial properties, etc. Thus requirement 1 is also satisfied.

The final requirement that still needs to be satisfied is the number of data points. If we have four years' worth of annual data and 400 grid cells, we would have 1,600 observations distributed over four epochs. This is not enough to train a neural network. However, if the geocoded data points also have a date associated with them, then we can break down the data even further into time slices such as months or weeks and thus increase the total number of data points considerably. For example, four years' worth of monthly data and 400 grid cells would yield 19,200 observations distributed over 48 epochs. This would conceivably be enough. Thus requirement 2 would also be satisfied.

The next section describes how the neural network architecture discussed in this section was used and trained to create an early warning system for 911 drug calls for service. The data for the early warning system was created using the DMAP GIS outlined in the second section.

A NEURAL NETWORK-BASED EARLY WARNING SYSTEM FOR 911 DRUG CALLS FOR SERVICE

Like many other cities of its size, Pittsburgh experienced a marked increase in street-level drug trafficking during the late 1980s and early 1990s as a result of the crack epidemic. Although crack cocaine use was already prevalent in larger cities such as Los Angeles, Detroit and New York before that time, historical evidence shows that it generally takes a few years for new illicit drugs to disperse to smaller cities that are not ports of entry for drug smugglers. Prior to the appearance of crack cocaine, street-level drug dealing in Pittsburgh was largely confined to two areas that specialized primarily in heroin and marijuana. Other sporadic areas of open-air drug dealing did exist, but were mainly limited to the sale of prescription drugs such as painkillers and the "Yuppie" drug powder cocaine.

In the summer of 1991, Pittsburgh also experienced a surge in gang-related violence. While initially most gangs were merely loosely organized groups of adolescents, experienced gang members from larger cities quickly attempted to gain a foothold in what they perceived as "virgin territory" for crack cocaine sales. Street-level drug markets in other major cities were already saturated by dealers, and there was little opportunity for entry into a market tightly controlled by gangs. Pittsburgh, on the other hand, was still a "free-for-all": demand was greater than supply. Thus, at least a part of the increase in violence can be attributed to street gangs setting up and defending "turfs" within which they conducted their illicit drug trade.

In reacting to the increase in street-level drug dealing, the Pittsburgh Bureau of Police used disruptive enforcement strategies that were proven highly successful in other cities: reverse stings, undercover buys, on-sight arrests of drug dealers after having observed illicit transactions and placing community-oriented police officers in plain view of established drug hot spots. These strategies were used because street-level drug dealing is widely regarded as a weak link in the chain: once a street market has been disrupted it is very difficult for dealers to relocate (Cohen et al., 1993). They are unable to advertise their new location, and are severely restricted in establishing new ones because they might infringe upon turfs already claimed by other drug dealers. However, there were a few instances where new hot spots did eventually surface.

While DMAP performed quite well at tracking the geographic displacement of drug dealers via its ability to plot the locations and frequencies of the number of drug calls for service and drug arrests, it did not perform as well at identifying emerging drug markets. The reason for this is twofold: first, police officers rarely make arrests in areas in which they are unaware that street-level drug dealing is going on unless they happen to stumble upon a transaction. Street sweeps tend to concentrate on known drug markets. Second, residents of areas in which street-level drug dealing is a new phenomenon frequently are unaware of what is going on. They initially do not perceive the activity as drug dealing. Rather, they tend to notice an increase in the level of crimes associated with street-level drug dealing such as robberies, burglaries and assaults. Thus there is a lag between the time a drug market has established itself and when residents begin to make drug-related calls for service.

An early warning system for emerging street-level drug markets must therefore be able to predict drug calls for service based on factors other than the level of drug calls for service in previous time periods. Based on the results of previous work and the availability of data from DMAP, it was decided to use three types of calls for service as indicators of emerging drug activity: weapon-related calls (shots fired, person shot, person with a gun, etc.), robbery calls and assaults-related calls. Cohen et al. (1993) showed that ecological factors such as the proportion of commercial properties in an area are important contributors to the level of drug calls for service. Commercial areas, especially older ones, lend themselves more to open-air drug dealing because of factors such as the relative lack of population outside of business hours (there are fewer residents to observe drug dealing). Thus the proportion of residential and commercial properties were included as indicator variables. Open-air drug dealing is a seasonal phenomenon: in the winter months drug dealers tend to stay inside not only because it is cold, but also because fewer people are on the streets and they become more visible. A seasonality index was therefore also included.

The data for the early warning system were obtained by superimposing a grid on the area of the city of Pittsburgh (see Figure 5), and aggregating data for each grid cell. The cells are 2,150 feet square, resulting in a total number of 445 cells. It was important not to make the cells too small. Otherwise, only few cells would have more than one or two calls for service, while cells that were too large would have resulted in too few data points for neural net modeling.

Call-for-service data were obtained by counting the number of calls per month within each cell using the xy coordinates of the geocoded locations. The data spanned the years 1990 to 1992, resulting in 35 months' worth of data (December 1992 could not be used since there was no value for the number of drug-related calls for service in January 1993). With 445 cells, the total number of data points was therefore 15,575. The relative proportions of commercial and residential properties were arrived at by relating property ownership information to parcel polygons via the lot and block number. The xy coordinates of the geographic center of a parcel were then used to determine which grid cell a particular property falls into. The zoning classification for each property provided the basis for the relative frequencies. Finally, the seasonal index was arrived at by assigning values between 0.1 and 0.9 in equal increments to each month, where a value of 0.9 was assigned to June and July and 0.1 to December and January.

Figure 5: EWS Tile Structure vs. 1990 Census Tracts

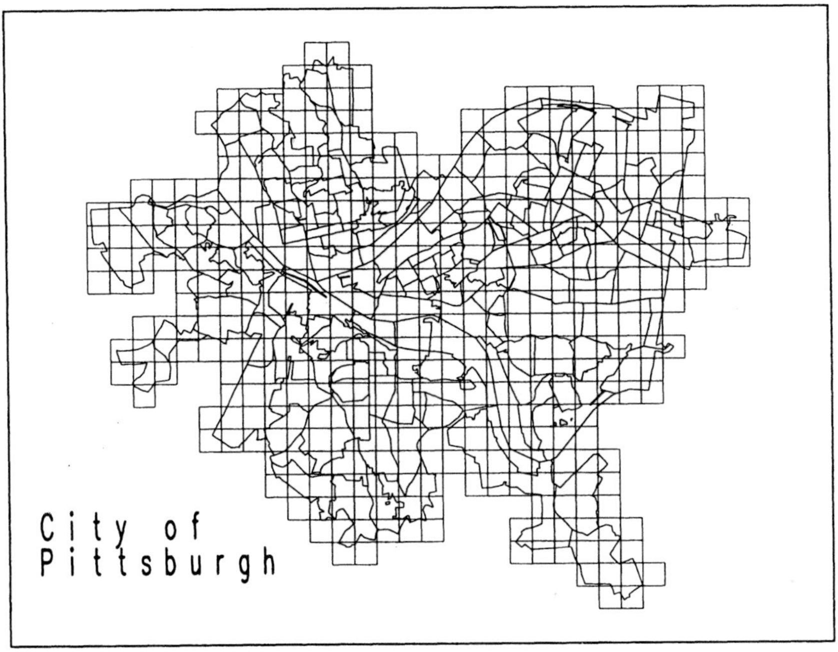

City of
Pittsburgh

Table 1: Annual Total Number of Calls for Service

	Drugs	Weapons	Robberies	Assaults
1990	5053	3580	1922	8618
1991	6397	4523	2309	7154
1992	6223	6622	2699	6147

Table 1 shows the total number of calls for service, by year, for each of the four nature codes used in this study. Notice the remarkable increase in the number of weapon-related calls for service of almost 100% over three years. The number of drug- and robbery-related calls for service also increased; only assaults showed a decline. Figure 6 shows the number of calls for each nature code broken down by month. The seasonal variation is quite noticeable, especially for drugs, weapons and assaults. The figure also shows how, with the exception of assaults, most of the increase in the number of calls for service is accounted for in the summer months.

Using the data described above, three methods were employed to estimate the one-step-ahead forecasting model specified in equations (7) and (8). Ordinary least squares regression with six independent variables for each cell in the neighborhood and a neural network with an architecture similar to that shown in Figure 4 were used to estimate model (7). The only difference between the network shown in Figure 4 and that used to estimate (7) was that each cell in the neighborhood had six input units instead of just one, and the number of hidden units was nine instead of three. Model (8) was estimated using a neural network with spatially varying input-to-hidden unit weights. In other words, each cell had its own unique set of weights between the input and hidden layers. The neural network with spatially varying weights also had six input units per cell and nine hidden units.

Both neural networks were estimated using a value of 0.001 for the learning rate. In order to determine whether the neural networks were overfitting the data and to compare the robustness of each methodology, only two years' worth of data (1990 and 1991) were used to estimate the regression parameters and to train the networks (the training data set). The 1992 data were used to test how well each method performed on data not used during training or for estimation (the unseen data set). The program utilized to estimate the neural networks was custom written using the C programming language, and was run on a Sun Microsystems Sparc 20 workstation with 128 Megabytes of RAM. In order to limit the amount of computer time used, the number of iterations was limited to 15,000. In spite of the relatively powerful hardware and code optimization techniques, it took between three and six days for each network to either converge or reach the limit of 15,000 iterations.

Each network architecture was estimated four times with different random initializations of the weights in order to determine whether the results were consistent and the networks were not stuck in a local minimum. This was indeed the case. For each network architecture and in all four replications the residual sum of squared errors differed by no more than 0.5%.

Table 2 shows a comparison of the results of the three methodologies. For reasons of brevity, the estimated regression parameters (of

Figure 6: Monthly Calls for Service

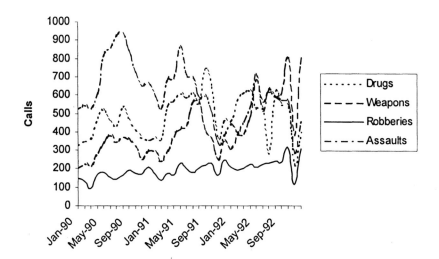

Table 2: Performance Comparison of Forecasting Methods

	Regression		Constant Weights		Varying Weights	
	Residual Sum of Squares	R^2	Residual Sum of Squares	R^2	Residual Sum of Squares	R^2
Training	120,481	.4185	120,589	.4117	95,032	.5343
Unseen	61,345	.3457	51,719	.3983	41,257	.5326

which there were 47) are not presented and only one replication of each of the network architectures is shown. The constant weight version of the neural network took 9,447 iterations to converge to a minimum, whereas the varying weight version was stopped at 15,000 iterations. On the training data set, the regression model and the constant weight network architecture performed about the same while the varying weight architecture did significantly better.

The differences in performance were more pronounced when the estimated parameters and weights were used on the unseen data set.

The fit of the regression model dropped sharply, from an r square of .4185 to .3457, while that of both network architectures only did so very slightly. This is a strong indicator, although by no means statistical proof, that neural networks are a robust and consistent spatial forecasting methodology. The constant weight architecture performed 15.2% better than regression on the unseen data set, whereas the varying weight network outperformed regression by 54.1%. This is a highly significant difference.

Figures 7 through 10 are choropleth maps of actual and predicted drug calls for service, by grid cell, for the month of August 1992. This month is part of the unseen data set. Unfortunately, some of the detail on the maps is lost due to the lack of color (black-and-white choropleth maps allow for fewer class intervals; color maps show the differences to be more pronounced). It is nevertheless clear that the neural network architecture with spatially varying weights more accurately predicts hot spots of drug activity than the other two methods.

In looking at the map of actual calls for service it is apparent that most cells are zero, i.e., had no drug calls for service during the month of August 1992. Notice how both the regression and the constant weight models tend to perform relatively poorly on those cells with no calls. Table 3 shows the mean absolute percent forecast error for all cells and for those with at least one drug call for service. All methods tend to perform better on non-zero cells. However, the difference in performance is much less pronounced for the neural network with spatially varying weights. Finally, both neural network models perform better than regression for both zero and non-zero cells. Again, this is highly significant: the mean absolute percent error is often viewed by forecasters to be more indicative of a model's forecasting capability than the r squared.

Table 3: Mean Absolute Percent Forecast Error on Unseen Data Set

	Regression	Constant Weights	Varying Weights
All Data Points	678.68	549.20	253.86
Non-Zero Cells	137.49	127.34	110.98

Figure 7: Drug Calls for Service, by Tile, August 1992

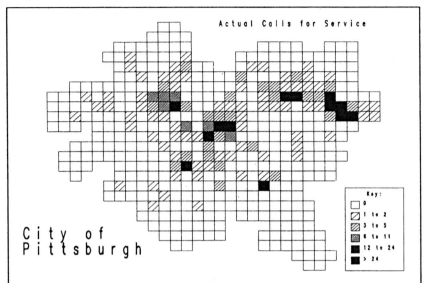

Figure 8: Drug Calls for Service, by Tile, August 1992

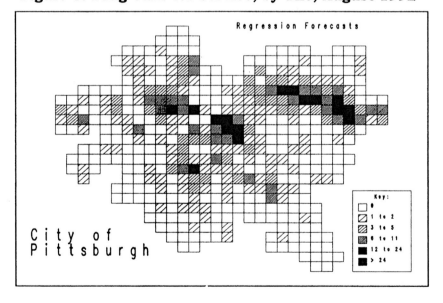

Figure 9: Drug Calls for Service, by Tile, August, 1992

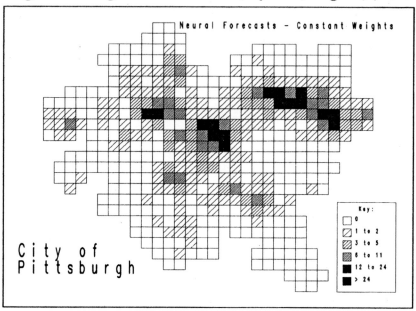

Figure 10: Drug Calls for Service, by Tile, August 1992

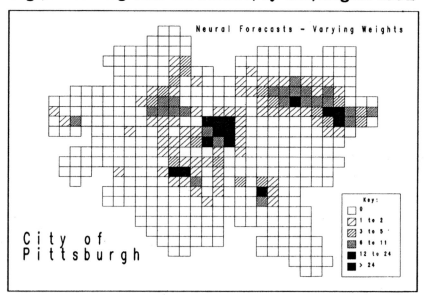

CONCLUSION

The results described in the previous section are very encouraging. Both neural network architectures performed at least as well in terms of model fit as a fairly complex ordinary least squares regression model, and, in one case, significantly better. In both cases artificial neural networks appear to be more robust at estimating forecasts than regression. One disadvantage of neural networks is that there currently are no tests of statistical significance for the estimated weight structures. However, if the main goal of a model is to provide good forecasts rather than to analyze relationships between dependent and independent variables, then this should not be an issue.

Producing the data set, estimating the neural networks and mapping the results took a lot of computing power. The reader should not be discouraged by this fact. While the average desktop computer in use today does not have the computing capabilities of the hardware employed in this study, recent advances in computer technology indicate that this will change in the very near future. For example, the code used for the neural networks was developed on a now five-year-old Sun Microsystems Sparc 2 workstation with only 32 megabytes of RAM. At the time it was purchased the Sparc 2 was one of the fastest workstations commercially available, at a cost of around $25,000. In contrast, a high-end Pentium PC available for about $4,000 today is two or three times faster than the Sparc 2.

The early warning system described in this study represents only a first attempt at using artificial neural networks for GIS-based space-time forecasting. As far as neural networks are concerned the algorithm used is a fairly simple one. In developing the algorithm, the primary focus was on adapting existing neural network technology to work with spatial data and to simply see if it would work. However, the fact that even two fairly simple artificial neural network algorithms are able to outperform a fairly complex statistical model is highly significant. Certainly more work remains to be done in order to determine whether this is also true for other data sets. Rigorous testing with Monte Carlo data would also provide more insight.

A further next step is to employ some of the recent advances made by researchers in other areas of neural network applications. For example, there are many ways in which feed-forward networks with backpropagation can be modified to converge more quickly to a solution. An additional improvement would be to employ genetic algorithms to develop self-optimizing network architectures.

Finally, there are a variety of types of neural networks, many of which can potentially be adapted for spatial modeling and integration into GIS. In addition, forecasting is only one of countless ways in which GIS can be used for modeling. Exploring and improving the ways in which neural networks can be applied to GIS promises to be an exciting field in the years to come.

Acknowledgments: Funded in part by the U.S. National Institute of Justice, Drug Market Analysis Program, Grant 90-IJ-CX-007. Special thanks to Darrell Packer and Glenn Bigler for the extra CPU time.

REFERENCES

Anselin, L. (1988). *Spatial Econometrics: Methods and Models*. Dordrecht, NETH: Kluwer.

Bates, J.M. and C.W.J. Granger (1969). "The Combination of Forecasts." *Operations Research Quarterly* 20:451-68.

Bookser, M.C. (1991). "The Future of Information Management in Pennsylvania Law Enforcement." Paper presented at the International Symposium on the Future of Law Enforcement, Quantico, VA, April.

Box, G.E.P. and G.M. Jenkins (1970). *Time Series Analysis, Forecasting and Control*. San Francisco, CA: Holden-Day.

Canter, P. (1993). "State of the Statistical Art: Point Pattern Analysis." In: C.R. Block and M. Dabdoub (eds.), *Workshop on Crime Analysis Through Computer Mapping Proceedings*. Chicago, IL: Illinois Criminal Justice Information Authority.

Carpenter, G.A. and S. Grossberg (1991). *Pattern Recognition by Self-Organizing Neural Networks*. Cambridge, MA: MIT Press.

Cassetti, E. (1982). "Drift Analysis of Regression Parameters: An Application to the Investigation of Fertility Development Relations." *Modeling and Simulation* 13:961-66.

—— and J.P. Jones (1992). *Applications of the Expansion Method*. London, UK: Routledge.

Clemen, R. T. (1989). "Combining Forecasts: An Annotated Bibliography." *International Journal of Forecasting* 5:559-83.

Cleveland, W.S. and S.J. Devlin. (1988). "Locally Weighted Regression: An Approach to Regression Analysis by Local Fitting." *Journal of the American Statistical Association* 83:596-610.

Cliff, A.D., P. Haggett, J.K. Ord, K. Bassett, and R. Davies (1975). *Elements of Spatial Structure*. Cambridge, UK: Cambridge University Press.

Cohen, J., W.L. Gorr, and A.M. Olligschlaeger (1993). *Modeling Street-Level Illicit Drug Markets*, Working Paper #93-64. Pittsburgh, PA: H. John Heinz III School of Public Policy and Management, Carnegie Mellon University.

David, M. (1977). *Geostatistical Ore Reserve Estimation*. Amsterdam, NETH: Elsevier.

Foster, S.A. and W.L. Gorr (1986). "An Adaptive Filter for Estimating Spatially Varying Parameters: Application to Modeling Police Hours Spent in Response to Calls for Service." *Management Science* 32: 878-89.

Gardner, M. (1970). "The Fantastic Combinations of John Conway's New Solitaire Game 'Life.'" *Scientific American* 223(4):120-123.

Gorr, W.L. and A.M. Olligschlaeger (1994). "Weighted Spatial Adaptive Filtering: Monte Carlo Studies and Application to Illicit Drug Market Modeling." *Geographical Analysis* 26:67-87.

Green, L.A. (1993). "Drug Nuisance Abatement, Offender Movement Patterns, and Implications for Spatial Displacement Analysis." In: C.R. Block and M. Dabdoub (eds.), *Workshop on Crime Analysis Through Computer Mapping Proceedings*. Chicago, IL: Illinois Criminal Justice Information Authority.

Haining, T. (1990). *Spatial Data Analysis in the Social and Environmental Sciences*. Cambridge, UK: Cambridge University Press.

Harp, S.A., T. Samad, and A. Guha (1990). "Designing Application-Specific Neural Networks Using the Genetic Algorithm." In: D.S. Touretzky (ed.), *Advances in Neural Information Processing Systems* vol. 2. San Mateo, CA: Morgan Kaufmann.

Hecht-Nielsen, R. (1990). *Neurocomputing*, Reading, MA: Addison-Wesley.

Holland, J. (1975). *Adaptation in Natural and Artificial Systems*. Ann Arbor, MI: University of Michigan Press.

Hornik, K., M. Stinchcombe, and H. White (1989). "Multilayer Feedforward Networks are Universal Approximators." In: *Neural Networks*, vol. 2. Elmsford, NY: Pergamon Press.

Kroese, B. J. and P.P. Van der Smagt, (1993). *An Introduction to Neural Networks*. Lecture Notes. Amsterdam, NETH: University of Amsterdam.

Maltz, M.D. (1993). "Crime Mapping and the Drug Market Analysis Program (DMAP)." In: C.R. Block and M. Dabdoub (eds.), *Workshop on Crime Analysis Through Computer Mapping Proceedings*. Chicago, IL: Illinois Criminal Justice Information Authority.

McCulloch, W.S. and W. Pitts (1943). "A Logical Calculus of the Ideas Imminent in Nervous Activity." *Bulletin of Mathematical Biophysics* 5:115-33.

McEwen, J.T., and F.S. Taxman, (1994). "Applications of Computerized Mapping to Police Operations." In: J. Eck and D. Weisburd (eds.), *Crime and Place*. Crime Prevention Studies, vol. 4. Monsey, NY: Criminal Justice Press.

Minsky, M. and S. Papert (1969). *Perceptrons*. Cambridge, MA: MIT Press.

Pickover, C.A. (1990). *Computers, Pattern, Chaos and Beauty*. New York, NY: St. Martin's Press.

Poli, I. and R.D. Jones (1994). "A Neural Net Model for Prediction." *Journal of the American Statistical Association* 89:117-121.

Rogers, D. (1990). "Predicting Weather Using a Genetic Memory: A Combination of Kanerva's Sparse Distributed Memory with Holland's Genetic Algorithms." In: D.S. Touretzky (ed.), *Advances in Neural Information Processing Systems*, vol. 2. San Mateo, CA: Morgan Kaufmann.

Rumelhart, D.E. and J.L. McClelland (1988). *Parallel Distributed Processing*, vols. 1 and 2. Cambridge, MA: MIT Press.

—— G.E. Hinton, and R.J. Williams (1988). "Learning Internal Representations by Error Propagation." In: D.E. Rumelhart and J.L. McClelland (eds.), *Parallel Distributed Processing*, vol. 1. Cambridge, MA: MIT Press.

Schroeder, M. (1991). *Fractals, Chaos and Power Laws*. New York, NY: W.H. Freeman.

Tobler, W.R. (1969). "Geographical Filters and their Inverses." *Geographical Analysis* 1:234-253.

Toffoli, T. and N. Margolus (1987). *Cellular Automata Machines: A New Environment for Modeling*, MIT Press Series in Scientific Computation. Cambridge, MA: MIT Press.

Trojanowicz, Robert (1986). *Community Policing Programs: A Twenty-Year View*, Community Policing Series No. 10. East Lansing, MI: National Neighborhood Foot Patrol Center.

Weiss, S.M. and C.A. Kulikowski (1991). *Computer Systems That Learn*. San Mateo, CA: Morgan Kaufmann.

White, H. (1988). "Economic Prediction Using Neural Networks: The Case of IBM Daily Stock Returns." *Proceedings of the IEEE International Conference on Neural Networks.* San Diego, CA.

Widrow, G. and M.E. Hoff (1960). *Adaptive Switching Circuits,* Western Electronic Show and Convention Record, Part 4, pp.96-104. New York, NY: Institute of Radio Engineers.

SMART MAPPING FOR LAW ENFORCEMENT SETTINGS: INTEGRATING GIS AND GPS FOR DYNAMIC, NEAR-REAL TIME APPLICATIONS AND ANALYSES

by

Severin L. Sorensen
SPARTA Consulting Corporation

Abstract: Crime analysis has long relied on maps for plotting crimes. Plotting crimes after they occur is a static process of historical data collection and reporting wherein data might not be plotted for many days, weeks, or months after the criminal event. SMART (Spatial Management, Analysis and Resource Tracking) mapping in law enforcement settings means integrating geographic information systems with dynamic location acquisition technology where near-real time data collection and analysis are possible. This article explores several possibilities for dynamic near-real time mapping applications for law enforcement. Examined are potential uses for small hand-held field equipment to plot "hot spots," boundaries, and other geographic characteristics, and for large automated vehicle location and artificial intelligence-guided emergency services dispatch.

INTRODUCTION

Historically, mapping out crime has been an important component of crime analysis. Today, whether by traditional pushpin or modern electronic plotting methods, crime mapping has become even more important as an analytical component of crime analysis. A review of

Address correspondence to: Severin L. Sorensen, President, SPARTA Consulting Corporation, Social Political Analysis, Research & Technical Assistance, 4720 Montgomery Lane, Suite 310, Bethesda, MD 20814.

**Figure 1: Picture Of Trimble Navigation's Scoutmaster GPS
Receiver Capable Of Capturing Field Readings For Later
Downloading On Computer For Precise Mapping Of
Boundaries, Hot Spots, And Recordable Attributes**

earlier chapters within this volume demonstrates many advances of
crime analysis made through electronic mapping. However, with few
exceptions, the uses of crime analysis and electronic mapping described in earlier chapters of this volume have been largely limited to
examining static (non-real-time) data through temporal snapshots or
maps of crime in time. Analysis of crime is routinely conducted days,
weeks, or months after data are collected. This kind of electronic
crime mapping can be a valuable intelligence tool to aid police in
problem solving, but most of these analyses can be characterized as
reactive and not proactive examples of crime analysis.

Mapping out crime in "real time" (i.e., as it occurs and is reported)
can: reduce police response time; increase officer safety through real-
time location identification; and increase the predictive capability of
crime analysis, which in turn can lead to increased offender's risks of
crime — a primary objective of situational crime prevention.[1] Mapping out crime in real time can enable law enforcement to conduct
real-time monitoring, incident tracking, risk identification, and resource allocation. This chapter examines the integration of off-the-
shelf technologies to conduct SMART (Spatial Management, Analysis
and Resource Tracking) mapping for law enforcement. These tools
have the potential to alter the mode of crime analysis currently conducted, enabling greater predictive functionality and operability. For
example, dynamic or near-real time data collection and analysis can

expedite the delivery of appropriate emergency responses through use of artificial intelligence algorithms that can rapidly identify crime incident location, closest emergency response personnel, and other characteristics to help the emergency response dispatcher to work smarter.

Real-time mapping operations require the integration of geographic information systems (GIS), global positioning systems (GPS), automated vehicle location (AVL) monitoring, and management information systems (MIS) integration. Together this alphabet soup of technologies constitute the SMART technologies.

This paper provides a primer on SMART mapping technologies and explores how they may be applied in law enforcement settings. SMART mapping technologies will be examined with respect to how spatial mapping, real-time analysis, and resource tracking can improve law enforcement data analysis and performance. Suggestions for crime data collection, spatial analysis, and the visualization of geographic data are provided. The chapter concludes with a discussion of potential advantages and drawbacks of using SMART technologies in law enforcement settings.

PRIMER ON SMART MAPPING TECHNOLOGIES

The backbone of the SMART mapping technologies are GIS, GPS, Management Information Systems (MIS), and AVL systems. On its own, none of these systems is sufficient for an effective SMART mapping system, yet together they create many opportunities for improving law enforcement.

Geographic Information Systems

GIS is a system of computer spatial analysis that links tabular (rows and columns) data to geographic boundaries and reference points. GIS computer programs may combine two types of data types: vector and raster. Vector data include typical row- and column-type data commonly used in spreadsheets. Raster data comprise other visual data that are mappable such as satellite images, photographs, and grid-system data, and that do not rely on vector-based row and column structures. Pioneered by the defense, energy, environment, and space research communities, GIS is one of the fastest growing technology areas worldwide.

The application of GIS to law enforcement is a relatively new phenomenon compared to the robust application of GIS within the engineering sciences.[2]

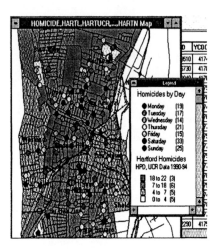

Figure 2: Example of a GIS Desktop Mapping System, MapInfo Being Used to Analyze Homicides in Hartford for Years 1990 to 1994

Figure 2 depicts a typical crime analysis using a desktop GIS system. Using incident-based data from the Hartford CT Police Department, Sorensen (1995) found that clusterings of homicides were geographically linked to ethnicity in public housing settings. This MapInfo for Windows chart uses shaded circles to show incidences of homicide by location, proximity, day of week, and neighborhood in Hartford from 1990 to 1994. The irregularly shaped polygons represent recognized neighborhoods and reporting areas. These neighborhoods are shaded according to density of homicides by area. Behind the map and legend appears a table in spreadsheet form that is the source of the crime data for the map.

Many law enforcement departments already conduct some form of crime analysis through mapping. The U.S. Department of Justice's Drug Market Analysis Program sponsored crime mapping projects in Hartford; Jersey City; Kansas City; Pittsburgh and San Diego, California. Subsequently, the U.S. Department of Justice sponsored two other pilot studies of mapping with the Montgomery County (MD) Police Department and the Warrenton (VA) Police Department. U.S. government-sponsored crime mapping projects represent limited coverage of what is happening in law enforcement departments nationwide. Many innovations are occurring worldwide as crime analysts are integrating mapping into their routine reporting and analysis.

The International Association of Crime Analysts reports that member analysts are mapping crime and related statistics in law enforcement departments throughout North America. A recent survey of members found that the most frequently used mapping program for crime analysis in law enforcement departments was MapInfo, followed by Arc/Info, Arc/View, Atlas, and other packages (Sanford, 1996).[3]

Global Positioning Systems

GPS is a satellite array that provides a precise method of measuring latitude, longitude, altitude, direction, time, velocity, and other data at any location on Earth. While other methods are available to determine these measures, GPS performs these methods with great ease, accuracy and timeliness. A person only needs to push a few buttons on a mobile GPS receiver to record the information instantly. Depending upon the application, locational bearing information can be updated on a second-by-second basis.

A constellation of 24 semi-synchronous satellites (21 satellites and three active spares), located in orbit approximately 11,000 miles from Earth, makes GPS possible. Each satellite broadcasts specific atomic clock readings that are received and interpreted by GPS receivers. A GPS receiver must receive signals from three satellites to establish a two-dimensional fix (e.g., latitude and longitude or map grid coordinates, etc.), and four satellites to get a three-dimensional fix (e.g., latitude, longitude, and altitude). An unobstructed GPS receiver will see between six and to 8 GPS satellites at any one time.

The GPS system is funded and controlled by the U.S. Department of Defense. Initially, two accuracy levels for GPS receiver readings were created. Precise Position Service (PPS), is officially reported to pinpoint a receiver's location within ten meters and Standard Positioning Service (SPS), with an accuracy designed to be within 30 to 100 meters, was provided for state and local government and civilian usage. SPS-GPS readings, with error correction known as differential GPS (DGPS), are the signal readings most likely to be useful in law enforcement use settings. Although SPS-GPS signal readings are deliberately biased by the U.S. Defense Department to decrease pinpoint accuracy, commercial vendors have developed error-correction software that can increase accuracy to within 1 to 3 meters. This increased accuracy is achieved by using a fixed-point location with a known reference position, and introducing differential GPS algorithms to enable location positioning to filter out bias and other errors. The end result is that the DGPS is sufficiently accurate for law enforcement use, and much more cost-effective, than PPS-GPS.

GPS receivers range in price from several hundred dollars to many thousands of dollars. Hand-held units range from $100 to $4,000, depending on the accuracy level and features desired. Shown below are examples of two types of GPS receivers. The first is a hand-held unit that can be taken to the field to collect precise location readings that can subsequently be downloaded into a computer and mapped.

Figure 3: Hand-Held GPS Receiver

The second image is of a personal computer (PC) card-based GPS receiver that allows real-time data collection and monitoring. This system is used in vehicles with dynamic GIS maps that provide a second-by-second map with refreshed positioning. When this system is combined with a portable radio transmitter, such as a cellular phone or a two-way radio, it can receive GPS signals from a receiver at a distance from the data interpretation point (limited only by the signal strength of the transmitter and radio receivers).

Figure 4: PC Card-Based GPS Receiver

Alternately, the GPS receivers can be mounted on the automobile dashboard, window, or exterior of the vehicle. Miniature GPS receivers can be hand carried, uniform holstered, or wrist mounted. The application purpose determines the equipment, size, accuracy, and features required.

Management Information Systems

MIS computer databases are used extensively by GIS and GPS applications. MIS databases include accessible data with reference points that are mappable. Such spatial data include boundaries such as Census blocks, block groups and tracts, street addresses, zip codes, police zones and districts, patrol areas, political boundaries and jurisdictions. These systems are essential to providing storage for access and application of GIS and GPS data. Examples of law enforcement GIS applications include emergency response systems, drug market analysis programs, offender tracking programs, gang identification programs, and historical databases.

The following image illustrates an example of using *On Target Mapping's* "Drive" time analysis software, a MapInfo add-on module, to determine the best paths by time and distance measurements. Notice that the dispersion of shaded paths is uneven, and that rivers and unnavigatable areas are not eligible for consideration. Through this module, the operator can control up to 36 variables to create realistic representations of time-distance relationships. This type of drive time analysis is an excellent illustration of the integration of MIS and GIS systems. When combined with a GPS receiver, the map could be used to track distances by car, foot, train, or other distance-time measures.

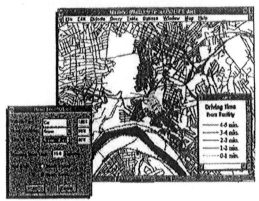

Figure 5: Example Of A Screen From On Target Mapping's "Drive" Time Analysis Software

Use of integrated tools allows analysts to make distance calculations in terms of the following distances:

- Euclidean (i.e., "as the crow flies")
- Manhattan (i.e., "as the taxi drives")
- Drive time under non-optimal conditions, walk time, etc.
- Network
- Ground
- Spherical, and
- Map projection

Use of the appropriate distance measure increases data reliability for analysts and law enforcement officers. For example, using Manhattan distance following only allowable street patterns can help determine the optimal emergency response personnel based on drive-time distance.

CURRENT AND FUTURE RESEARCH APPLICATIONS FOR INCIDENT-BASED CRIME DATA

In 1991, the U.S. Department of Justice's *Incident-Based Reporting Project Advisory Board* conducted a survey of current and potential uses for incident-based data.[4] Applications included identifying largely static mapping outcome such as:

(1) Victim-offender relationships
(2) Costs of crime
(3) Drug/alcohol involvement in crime
(4) Crime rates by population characteristics
(5) Spatial analysis of offenses
(6) Residency of victim and offender
(7) Use/involvement of weapons
(8) Hate/bias-related crimes
(9) Secondary crimes in events
(10) Crime rates by offense type
(11) Tracking arrested offenders
(12) Development of new indices
(13) Characteristics of cleared offenses

All of these are reported as static measures of measurable data, and are most often collected and analyzed some time after the events occur. Some of the measures, such as tracking arrested offenders (or probationers), lend themselves to dynamic tracking. The accuracy and real-time use of the above crime measures and indices (excluding 2 and 13) may be improved or made more valuable or predictive through dynamic, real-time, SMART mapping.

Situational Crime Prevention and Applied Technology

The emergence of new mobile technologies such as cellular phones and portable radios has challenged the supposition that rapid response is not efficacious. Near-real-time and mobile responses made possible with new technologies have enabled emergency response personnel to respond more quickly and with increased intelligence to time-sensitive events. In the past, the time lag between the time when crimes occurred and when law enforcement responded was significantly long so as to discredit the notion of rapid response as a crime deterrent. Rapid response was discredited as a crime prevention tool as the distance decay from criminal event to reporting made even efficient events time-lagged responses. Community policing reemerged as the crime prevention approach of choice. However, recent advances in technology will enable real-time and near real-time response.

Linking GPS tracking capability with GIS mapping programming can significantly lessen the distance decay from point of infraction to intervention. Several possibilities for crime prevention are availed through these technologies. Computer-aided dispatch can be made smarter through the ability of GPS to inform GIS emergency response systems with accuracy and timeliness. Linkages to MIS can provide best-route information, reference traffic congestion, and predict close approximations of response times to assure callers. GPS receivers linked to mobile computers can be used to map out the locations of crime, drug markets and gang activity, or to map out the boundaries of roads, fence lines, reporting areas, etc., or other characteristics impacting crime reporting. Standard-mounted GPS receivers located on emergency response vehicles can provide real-time position monitoring, and can potentially reduce emergency response times by providing vehicle location, drive time analysis, and database referencing to provide the most appropriate and timely response for each situation. Miniature and disguised GPS receivers with radio or cellular transmitters can be used to provide discreet real-time position monitoring of personnel, vehicles, shipments, and other targets to increase operational safety in sensitive law enforcement operations by allowing for non-human technical surveillance at a distance. Wrist-worn GPS units could become part of standard uniform for patrol and operations officers, allowing for real-time technical support and officer-down alerts and tracking. The additional option of remotely turning off the GPS units could make them inoperable if compromised or stolen. Crime analysts can gain data integrity improvement through the use of GPS- and GIS-linked real-time position monitoring. GPS asset tracking (personnel and vehicles) can increase analytical power of law enforcement by providing better data useful in modeling crime events by time, location, and proximity to other geographic characteristics.

In the future, dynamic real-time crime maps will be available for law enforcement officers on patrol. GPS-assisted law enforcement asset position monitoring and radio feedback can allow for active data exchange of historical data to create dynamic crime contour maps (e.g., three-dimensional topographical maps) that can be useful to officers on patrol. Moving maps displayed on mobile computer notebook screens could provide predictive and historical crime pattern information of offenders and victims, as well as use of space information. Other potential uses of dynamic mapping in criminal justice settings are described in the following section.

SMART MAPPING LAW ENFORCEMENT APPLICATIONS

This section describes how specific objectives can be achieved through SMART mapping to reduce response times, and to increase appropriate response likelihood, officer safety, and offender risks associated with crime.

Real-Time Response and Opportunity Reduction

When GPS and GIS are linked with emergency response systems, they can systematically reduce dispatch time and error, which in turn can lead to more rapid response and crime opportunity reduction. One such system, AVL, is an enhancement to computer-aided dispatch. A combination of AVL and GPS provides a public safety agency with the ability to identify the location of every emergency response vehicle, and to dispatch the closest, most appropriate units to the scene. AVL requires the capability to determine emergency vehicle location, communicate with the response vehicle, and track the vehicle's location into an interpretable format for the dispatcher. With GPS, AVL can operate within seconds. AVL can use several methods of locational proximation, of which GPS is the most dynamic and accurate. The best AVL systems use GPS to increase their accuracy and timeliness of response. Many older AVL systems require the dispatcher to manually consult a map and locate the nearest assets to respond to an emergency. When GPS is linked with AVL, human interaction is guided and time between need and dispatch is minimized. Consider the following situation.

A call for assistance is received. While the operator speaks with the caller, the emergency response computer quickly identifies the location of the call through GIS tracking enabled by enhanced 911. The computer swiftly "pings" its visual "radar screen" to determine which emergency vehicles are available to respond swiftly. The system then selects the most appropriate vehicle and alerts it. The GPS system is able to update the computer system each second with new information on the location, availability, and status of each law enforcement officer and asset within the system, and thus can consistently provide the most accurate information. While the system is locating a vehicle, an automated search request is forwarded to the MIS system database that aids the process by identifying technical resources, equipment, and the training level of officers within each vehicle. Accordingly, a set of predetermined algorithms guides the law enforcement response selection process, as the SMART mapping system identifies and ranks law enforcement personnel by proximity to the location. At the same time, a GIS drive time analysis is identifying natural barriers of rivers, obstructions, street types, traffic congestion, and road closures, and estimating drive time. The GPS system updates the process on a second-by-second basis. An estimated time of arrival is communicated to the caller, and real-time monitoring is available to the dispatcher.

The components of this scenario could be conducted in a matter of seconds, almost seamlessly, enabling the computers to increase operational response through appropriate law enforcement asset selection and resource allocation. Such situations are not merely hypothetical. Several early integrators of AVL applications in law enforcement include: the Michigan State Police, the California Highway Patrol, the Montgomery County (MD) Police Department, and the Schaumburg (IL) Police Department.

Real-Time Tracking and Risk Reduction

A second use of this technology for law enforcement is to improve operational safety. Consider the following situations.

In the first example, narcotics detectives wish to follow a known suspect. A discreet GPS device has been mounted on the suspect's vehicle. GPS signals are transmitted from the suspect's vehicle, via miniature radio receiver, and are captured by the tracking vehicle. The signals provide latitude and longitude coordinates or map grid coordinates, as well as altitude (height) bearings (e.g., geographic topography, building floor elevation, etc.). Officers tail at a safe distance, observing the signal of the target vehicle as it appears on their portable notebook computer screen is equipped with GIS-GPS tracking software.

The second example concerns organized crime detectives who are working on foot and who become separated. Miniature wristband GPS devices signal, on a near-real-time basis, each agent's whereabouts to other field agents who are supervising the undercover operation. A man-down switch on one of the detectives' GPS receivers is toggled. The supervisor observes that the signal from the officer's GPS unit is rapidly leaving the target area. Monitoring software enables the supervisor to swiftly identify the direction and bearings of the signal. The GPS tracking beacon enables support officers to locate and rescue the detective, who had been taken hostage and was being held in a previously unknown warehouse operated by a criminal organization.

Clearly, in both these situations officer safety and operation integrity are improved through the use of SMART mapping technologies.

Forecasting and Crime Opportunity Avoidance

Use of SMART mapping need not be limited to responding to current events. Consider the following proactive situation. A metropolitan city has invested in a SMART mapping systems that integrates GPS, GIS, MIS, and AVL systems technologies. Patrol officers' automobiles are equipped with notebook computers linked to GPS devices. As each vehicle moves throughout the city, a dynamic three-dimensional map showing latitude, longitude, and crime incident probability (or history) would provide a real-time cityscape of crime probability in visual topographical form. Peaks and valleys, representing crime hot spots and cold spots, are visible. Data is updated from departmental computers via radio signals that are fed into the notebook computers. Day of week, time of day, weather patterns, and historical data guide the visualization of data projected on the screen. The forecasting model visually represented may also include actuarial data informed by known probabilities of crime in and around different types of buildings. Officers observe their assigned communities with new eyes. As an infrared camera brings new vision to the night blind, a GPS-GIS law enforcement visualization model can bring new vision to officers' perception of the crime around them. This new vision could greatly assist officers in being proactive in crime situations. Officers trained to use this information to seek out the high-crime areas in their communities could proactively reduce crime opportunity by patrolling and suppressing locations that were identified as having a high likelihood of crime incidents.

Other Research-Based Applications for Mapping and Crime Analysis

Cutting-edge work in crime mapping is being conducted by several influential criminologists, geostatisticians, and practitioners. Recent innovations include:

- Rossmo's (1995a, 1995b, 1994) Isocrime Mapping and Criminal Geographic Targeting.
- C.R. Block and R. Block's (1994) STAC Hot Spot Ellipse Identification tool.
- P.L. Brantingham and P.J. Brantingham's (1994) offender location and place pattern analysis, which incorporates actuarial data such as building site, zoning, use profiling, and risk assessments.

- LeBeau's (1994) incorporation of three-dimensional crime interpolations into spectral analysis.
- Canter's (1994) integration of health and police data into drug market analysis.
- Weisburd (1995, 1992) and Green's (1994) identification and definition of drug markets in geographic settings.
- Additional mapping contributions on various topics by Rengert (1994), by Maltz (1995, 1994), and by Eck (1995, 1994).

These research applications and many others have been incorporated into practical-use crime mapping in U.S. law enforcement settings.

Similarly, crime offender and victimization profiling can be integrated into mapping for specific purposes. For example, the San Bernadino Sheriff's Office uses mapping to recognize and detect serial burglary patterns using factors of:

- Time
- Date
- Weapons involved
- Victim statistics
- Offender statistics
- City map data

Environmental factors influencing theft of cars (Poyner and Webb, 1991) also could be integrated into algorithms suitable for identification of markets and potential victim locations. Auto theft's mappable traits include:

- Crime rates
- Owner-occupied housing
- Presence of driveways
- Presence of garage
- On- and off-street parking
- Communal parking
- Facing direction of house
- Through pathways on the property

Drug investigations can be enhanced through the integration of mapping of factors that include:

- Computer searches
- Offender investigations
- Vehicular investigations
- Historical conspiracy investigations
- Laboratory forensics investigations

- Habitual offender tracking
- Financial document tracking
- Offender asset tracking

Police performance and understanding of crimes can be improved through mapping of such physical evidence as:

- Laboratory analysis of drug samples
- Fingerprint analysis
- Field testing of drug samples
- Weapons seizures
- Bullet analysis

Electronic surveillance data can be integrated with mapping to produce near-real-time and real-time applications that would improve officer safety, enhance law enforcement performance, and reduce response time. Such applications and technologies include:

- Mobile communications-assisted vehicle, personnel, and target tracking
- Hand-held GPS data collection and monitoring tools
- Wireless microphones used at peripheral locations creating audio tripwires that report back location of incoming or outgoing targets
- Counter-surveillance equipment

Undercover operations, collateral intelligence-gathering activities, and performance records can be mapped with information on the location, offenders (buyers and sellers), setting, and time. Among these covert efforts are:

- Buy/Bust
- Buy/Walk
- Reverse-Sting
- Sting
- Precursor chemical enforcement

Precursor chemical enforcement can be dramatically enhanced through the integration of the following data sources.

- Precursor chemical control
- Audits of suppliers
- Audits of manufacturers
- Audits of pharmacies
- Audits of medical doctors
- Seizure data

Although the legal and moral implications of using this electronic equipment must be considered carefully before implementation, the following additional electronic technical measures can be highly valuable when integrated into mapping:

- Still camera systems
- Video/closed-circuit television systems
- Mobile video systems
- Night vision equipment
- Thermal sensing equipment
- Aerial photography
- Remote sensing
- Offender photos
- Suspect trails

A comprehensive listing of mapping possibilities for crime analysis appears in the Appendix.

SMART MAPPING ANALYTICAL AND VISUALIZATION POSSIBILITIES

The value of mapping in relaying complex information cannot be overstated. Simply expressed, if it is true that a picture is worth a thousand words, then it is also true that a map is worth a thousand numbers (paraphrased from Berry [1993]). Visualizing data communications helps transfer information through the lowest common denominators of expression. The French proverb, "that which is understood, can be expressed simply" applies to mapping. Visualization of data is useful in presenting concrete facts, directions, processes, bits of data, comparative data, data recorded over time, organizational structures, places, chronologies, generalizations, and theories (Wileman, 1993).

Why Analytical Visualization?

Mapping is statistics made simple. The eye can easily understand visual depictions of the results of complex mathematical computations. Peaks and valleys in maps inform the viewer of high spots and low spots without requiring that he or she understand how such information was mathematically created. Consider the following illustration of a two-dimensional Interpolation.

Data that lie on a two-dimensional grid can be interpolated by using splines that run in two directions. These data may be characterized by the following function.[5]

Consider the relation:

$$i := 0..10 \qquad j := 0..10 \qquad A_{i,j} := \sin(i) \cdot \cos(j)$$

where the following equations create a smooth csplined surface map.

$$m := 0..40$$

$$n := 0..40$$

$$Y_m := \frac{1}{4} \cdot m$$

$$D^{\langle j \rangle} := \text{cspline}\left(R, A^{\langle j \rangle}\right)$$

$$K_{j,m} := \text{interp}\left(D^{\langle j \rangle}, R, A^{\langle j \rangle}, Y_m\right)$$

$$V^{\langle m \rangle} := \text{cspline}\left(R, K^{\langle m \rangle}\right)$$

$$S_{n,m} := \text{interp}\left(V^{\langle n \rangle}, R, K^{\langle n \rangle}, Y_m\right)$$

The result of these calculations can be shown in a contour map. Completing such calculations will yield numerical data that are not easily interpretable. These numerical data pale in comparison to the observational intuitiveness of visual mapping and cognitive identification. The results of the calculations are depicted in the contour map below. Hot spots and cold spots are readily observed as peaks and valleys. Color differentiation shows gradations of effects along a continuous surface map.

Other spatial data reference coordinates such as streets, places, boundaries, operations, zoning, occupancy, and rates of crime can be represented in a similar map. The opportunities for crime analysis and law enforcement operations are enormous. Maps such as these would enable law enforcement officers on the street to visually associate these peaks and valleys with surface coordinates at the neighborhood level. Such visualization would greatly enhance the translation of crime data analysis to on-the-street policing.

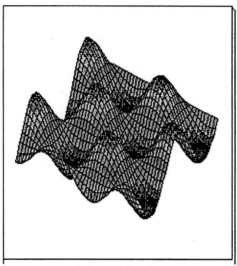

Figure 6: This Contour Map Displays The Results Of The Above Equations

SMART Rooms or "Situation Rooms" with Large Screen Monitoring

Visualization of data may be eventually be extended to SMART rooms or "situation rooms." Real-time monitoring of emergency response system assets can improve situation management. Such situation rooms could serve as dispatch and emergency response headquarters, or, in a portable form, be used for tactical law enforcement operations and planning.

Mobile Crime Topography and Dynamic Contouring

Eventually, advances in communications and crime modeling will enable officers to view historical crime pattern data on mobile computer screens, perhaps projected on the front windshields of their patrol cars. As officers passed through neighborhoods, the GPS receiver would update their position coordinates and their maps would be refreshed, with crime data appearing as peaks and valleys in a topographical layout.

The display could include streets, crime modalities, and crime hot spots. As a dynamic map, it could serve as a predictive play book for crime prevention. Officers could direct their efforts to suppress criminal activity to the peak areas, as indicated by the map. Fast rates of data exchange and monitor refreshing, combined with mobile data terminals, could enable officers to confirm identification of vehicles and persons contacted.

SMART MAPPING CAVEATS AND VULNERABILITIES

While SMART mapping has many obvious potential benefits, there are also some caveats which should be considered before pursuing widespread acceptance of the technology within law enforcement settings.

Does Real-Time (or Near-Real-Time) Response Prevent Crime?

One must address the issue of real-time or near-real time response. One of SMART mapping's greatest strengths is its ability to relay data in near real-time and thus increase officer response speed. It is important to determine whether this access to near real-time data in this form will help law enforcement officers to be more effective in fighting crime. The question that must be answered is, "Does real-time (or near-real time) response prevent crime?" In the 1990s, the cycle of law enforcement practices has come full circle so that community-oriented policing is again in vogue. Once-popular rapid response methods have gradually been overtaken by community policing methods.

While SMART mapping can clearly support community-oriented policing, most mapping applications to date have been problem-oriented. A potential outcome of law enforcement use of crime mapping is that enforcement agencies with short-term performance goals may stray away from community policing models in favor of specific situational intervention models, in the hope that SMART responses (being both rapid and appropriately efficient) might bring early success. It is important that community policing not be abandoned. Law enforcement agencies that plan to introduce SMART mapping need to be aware of its impact on alternate models and programs.

Privacy Concerns

For some purposes, SMART technologies may be too smart. To individuals concerned with conspiracy, the specter of "big brother" watching is reinforced by the onset of smart technologies that include integrated GIS, GPS, MIS, and AVL technologies.

Anecdotal reports collected while preparing this article included repeated concerns from police union members that law enforcement officers risk losing their privacy through real-time surveillance of officers. The fear that the power of GPS tracking technology might be turned inward and used for internal police manpower analysis purposes is not unreasonable.

Reports of intra-department GIS system sabotage by police officers and damage to GPS tracking systems on patrol units is not uncommon. The purpose of GPS systems in law enforcement settings needs to be clearly defined. Limited goals of smart response (being both rapid and appropriate), officer safety, and operational integrity may be required to encourage acceptance of the technology within law enforcement settings.

Potential Misuse of SMART Technologies

Beyond privacy concerns, there are other — more sinister — possibilities for SMART technologies. Rarely have tools made for positive purposes not been turned to negative purposes by someone seeking gain or reward. Criminals and terrorists could potentially access such technologies for tracking or targeting individuals. An organized crime operation would have a considerable advantage if it knew the exact location of all law enforcement assets at any given time. Governments (or individuals with government access) could also abuse this power. The courts have kept a tight hold on the use of eavesdropping technologies. The use of GPS technologies for tracking has many uncharted and unlitigated boundaries that must be established. It is likely that abuses of this tracking technology will provide the impetus for instituting these regulations. However, the potential for misuse is inherent in the technology.

Technical Limitations

Beyond concerns of harmful human misappropriation, there are technical limitations that will be encountered in implementing an aggressive technology policy. The best crime modeling approximations are still not entirely free from error. In law enforcement settings predictive capability is valuable, yet cannot replace the need for conventional law enforcement coverage. For example, a crime predictive model could predict with some certainty that crimes were likely to occur during certain periods or days at particular locations. However, while increased patrols could be assigned to the identified areas, one could not reasonably abandon enforcement of other areas without increasing crime opportunity risks in those areas.

GIS data are limited by the accuracy of several inputs that directly influence outcomes. Incomplete incident reports, wrong addresses, improperly entered dispatch reports, geocoding errors, street-file imperfections, and human error all complicate the analysis of data and can introduce bias that limits its usefulness. GPS receiver signals are imperfect. GPS error sources are a combination of noise, intended bias, and blunders. Noise and clock bias occur within the GPS receiver itself, which distorts readings. GPS receivers use crystal oscillators that are much more inaccurate than atomic clocks used in GPS satellites.

Beyond mechanical bias, some errors are deliberately instituted by the U.S. government when it seeks to degrade the signal quality through a time-varying bias. Recent GPS and GIS field testing (Sorensen et al., 1996) conducted in August 1996 in and around the San Francisco Bay area found that deliberate GPS signal bias was greater during nighttime hours, rendering simple GPS receivers worthless without Precise Positioning Capability to adjust for error. Further, each satellite's bias is different, which complicates correcting the bias and thus adds to the overall inaccuracy. The combined biases of all the satellites reduce the basic accuracy of signal readings for around 30 to 100 meters, or, in the case of San Francisco, several blocks during nighttime use. Consequently, bias-correcting differential algorithms are necessary to increase accuracy for law enforcement purposes. Other bias errors occur through satellite clock errors; topospheric delays (due to changes in humidity, pressure, and temperature); ephemeris data errors; and unmodeled ionosphere delays, etc. (Dana, 1997).

Beyond bias and system errors, GPS is also vulnerable to human interventions such as jamming of signals and spoofing or false signals. Dithering of signal accuracy at variable levels beyond the designated 100-meter error level can be expected during increased national security uncertainty. Presently, such dithering or distorting signals are largely limited to national security situations, but it is not entirely unwarranted to consider the possibility of interventions by organized crime groups if they were aware of law enforcement's use of the system.

Another problem encountered in using GPS systems is that GIS maps are conceived on a national level and so do not always reflect local settings. For example, addresses in many public housing settings are listed in terms of individual building names. A GIS map, however, might group the entire development by its street address, and not make the distinction between particular buildings or apartments. GPS can overcome this by precisely locating positions within formerly non-mappable locations. For example, a hand-held or portable GPS receiver could be carried or driven on new streets, fence lines, building exteriors, etc. to create a digital file of points representing the previously non-mapped characteristic. This data can be amended to one's existing GIS data files to incorporate the new geographic characteristics found in the field. However, in this instance, prior to use a human-resource cost of labor, time, and equipment must be used to characterize the new street or geographic feature. Beyond static map files, dynamic mapping places additional memory resource requirements on GIS computer systems to respond to multiple requests in dynamic environments. The capital costs can be enormous.

Certainly, it would not be cost-efficient to fund implementation of a GPS system if reliable backup technologies were not already included in the emergency response plan. Too great a reliance on GPS systems could prove to be disastrous if something were to interfere with law enforcement's ability to use the system. For instance, the same GPS system that guides police vehicles can guide missiles. It is unrealistic to think that the standard-positioning GPS guidance systems would remain operational during wartime. Other tracking systems such as dead-point reckoning, LORAN (long-range radio positioning system), cellular phone, or other radio-based tracking system can be used as backups and should be factored into the design phase.

Incompleteness

To accurately map crime, one must ascertain that crimes have been committed, and that the crimes have been recorded accurately down the data chain. James Q. Wilson's (1975) caution concerning data validity is doubly true with respect to crime mapping. For data to reflect real-world conditions, crime must be perceived, defined, and reported. Mapping requires additional measures to ensure accuracy, including: testing and routinely upgrading street files for integrity and accuracy; filtering data for imperfections; and ensuring that data is accurately recorded, processed and analyzed by all persons who handle them, from the officer responding who files the report, to the booking clerk at the jailhouse, to the data entry clerk preparing data for computer analysis, to the crime analyst examining the data.

Cost and Training

Financial barriers to implementing mapping systems have decreased dramatically over the past five years, but are still not insignificant. Mainframe systems can be replaced by smaller yet still powerful RISC workstations, and desktop mapping systems have increased in power and sophistication. Desktop GIS systems with the highest numbers of licensed users include high-end GIS packages such as ESRI's ArcInfo (ESRI) and desktop packages such as MapInfo Professional, V.4, ESRI's ArcView 2.0, and Strategic Mappings (Atlas GIS). Numerous other packages are available and documented on the Internet and can be found using search tools querying "GIS," mapping, etc.

Digital files required for mapping streets in the U.S. once cost many thousands of dollars, but can now be purchased on a series of CD-ROMs for less than $400. Recent U.S. Geological Survey Map files (Tiger 94) have improved in accuracy since the Tiger 92 version. Still, in order to fully work within a seamless GIS system, these files need messaging as new streets may be created, numbering systems may change, etc.

Basic hand-held GPS receiver units now cost between $100 and $350, while more sophisticated hand-held units now cost upward of $500 dollars each. This price does not include additional accessories that are necessary for an interface "box," such as the GPS system, modems, radios, sensors, monitors, and other peripheral devices. It also does not include the price for radio frequency transmitting devices with repeaters or digipeaters; an interface "box" (device to pass data from the radio to the computer), charges for local GPS error correction, or a local running AVL-inclusive SMART mapping package. These things together will result in a GPS system capable of managing law enforcement assets using real-time information. Fortunately, today's trend toward off-the-shelf (as opposed to design-built) technologies will probably continue to lower prices while keeping compatibility (and interchangeability) high. This can only benefit law enforcement.

The time needed to learn SMART mapping applications can be great. Training costs are high in terms of dollar costs per hour. However, as more GIS-GPS applications become available in the form of off-the-shelf commodity packaging, their user-friendliness should increase, thus minimizing training times and costs. Currently, the learning curve for all software packages mentioned above is steep. Desktop packages require several days of training, and the more complex workstation packages can require six months or more.

CONCLUSION

Crime mapping plays an increasingly important role in crime analysis. Spatial analysis tools and techniques, accompanied by the improved data accuracy afforded by GPS systems, can improve law enforcement response time, officer safety, asset allocation, and crime analysis. If an offender's perceived risks of crime increase, so much the better.

Crime Analysis Implications of Mapping

As a technology tool, GIS will continue to evolve and improve our sensitivity, understanding, identification, and forecasting of reported mappable events (Worrall, 1991). Where crime analysis and law enforcement are concerned, GIS mapping technologies will evolve to equip crime analysts with improved analytical tools and dynamic, near-real-time SMART technology capabilities that include:

(1) *More sensitive monitoring* of demographic, social, economic, ecological and environmental factors and their effect on crime offender and victimization conditions.

(2) *Better understanding of patterns* of criminal offenders and of the complex interactions among place, time, offender, victim, and opportunity.

(3) *More accurate forecasting* of changing needs of law enforcement through more precise situation assessments.

(4) *More precise identification* of spatial variations in crime conditions as a basis of targeting resources for intervention.

(5) *More rigorous identification* of crime targets and magnets, which will promote local services in needed areas and reduce the expense of programming in unneeded areas.

(6) *More effective and responsive crime service planning*, vehicle tracking, and automated vehicle dispatch through more accurate identification of the determining factors of crime and expert forecasting of the changing patterns of crime, enabling operations to reflect changing needs.

(7) *Improving the quality of law enforcement service* management by developing more economical approaches for undertaking routine activities through more efficient scheduling.

(8) *Improving the cost-effectiveness of asset management* by developing more accurate asset disbursement, tracking, monitoring, and mapping in near-real time or real-time conditions.

(9) *Improving law enforcement planning processes* by developing means for modeling and simulating alternative scenarios, and by developing techniques to assess the suitability of new proposals.

(10) *Improving law enforcement policy-making processes* by developing more sensitive methods for evaluation and analysis of policies and programs.

SMART mapping technologies are evolving quickly, rapidly becoming even smarter. The integration of SMART technologies in law enforcement settings will set a new benchmark for policing and crime analysis. While caveats and other considerations should be reviewed on a departmental basis, the potential improvements to crime analysis, police response time, officer safety, and specific deterrence provided by SMART technologies are worth considering for nearly all mid-to-large size law enforcement agencies.

NOTES

1. Clarke (1992), in *Situational Crime Prevention*, defines primary situational crime prevention objectives as: (1) increasing offender effort needed to commit crimes; (2) increasing offender risks associated with crime; (3) reducing rewards of crime. Subsequently, a fourth objective has been added, namely, (4) removing excuses for non-performance.

2. As this entire volume is dedicated to GIS, the reader is referred to the introductory chapter and internet sources (http://www.gisworld.com) for more information on GIS systems.

3. Ray Sanford, "GIS User Agencies," survey of International Association of Crime Analysts" members, Winter, 1996. Contact, rsanford@community.net for more information.

4. The Incident-Based Reporting Project Advisory Board conducted a survey of current and potential uses for incident based data and identified fourteen applications (Coyle, Schaff, and Coldren, 1991).

5. Visualization of 2-D illustration is a modified example of an interpolation illustration provided in *MathCad's Mathsoft* Handbook, 1991.

REFERENCES

Berry, J.K. (1993). "Maps as Data: An Emerging Map-ermatics." In: *Beyond Mapping: Concepts, Algorithms, and Issues in GIS*. Colorado: GIS World Books.

Block, C. R. (1994). "STAC Hot Spot Areas: A Statistical Tool for Law Enforcement Decisions." In: C.R. Block and M. Dabdoub (eds.), *Workshop on Crime Analysis Through Computer Mapping: Proceedings: 1993*. Chicago, IL: Illinois Criminal Justice Information Authority and Sociology Department, Loyola University Chicago.

Brantingham, P.L. and P.J. Brantingham (1994). "Location Quotients and Crime Hot Spots in the City." In: C.R. Block and M. Dabdoub (eds.), *Workshop on Crime Analysis Through Computer Mapping: Proceedings: 1993*. Chicago, IL: Illinois Criminal Justice Information Authority and Sociology Department, Loyola University Chicago.

Canter, P. (1994). "State of the Statistical Art: Point Pattern Analysis." In: C.R. Block and M. Dabdoub (eds.), *Workshop on Crime Analysis Through Computer Mapping: Proceedings: 1993*. Chicago, IL: Illinois Criminal Justice Information Authority and Loyola University Chicago.

Clarke, R.V. (ed.) (1992). "Introduction." *Situational Crime Prevention: Successful Case Studies*. New York, NY: Harrow and Heston.

Coyle, K.R., J.C. Schaaf, and J.R. Coldren (1994). "The Incident Based Reporting." In: *National Incident Based Reporting Project: Final Report*. U.S. Department of Justice.

Dana, P.H. (1997). "The Geographer's Craft Project.." Department of Geography, University of Texas at Austin. Also available on the Internet at: http://wwwhost.cc.utexas.edu/ftp/pub/grg/gcraft/notes/gps/gps.html

Eck, J.E. (1995). "A General Model of Geography of Illicit Retail Marketplaces." In: J. Eck and D. Weisburd (eds.),*Crime and Place*. Crime Prevention Studies, vol. 4. Monsey, NY: Criminal Justice Press.

—— (1994). "The Usefulness of Maps for Area and Place Research: An Example from a Study of Retail Drug Dealing." In: C.R. Block and M. Dabdoub (eds.), *Workshop on Crime Analysis Through Computer*

Mapping: Proceedings: 1993. Chicago, IL: Illinois Criminal Justice Information Authority and Sociology Department, Loyola University Chicago.

GIS World, http://www.gpsworld.com

Greene, L. (1994). "Drug Nuisance Abatement, Offender Movement Patterns, and Implications for Spatial Displacement." In: C.R. Block and M. Dabdoub (eds.), *Workshop on Crime Analysis Through Computer Mapping: Proceedings: 1993.* Chicago, IL: Illinois Criminal Justice Information Authority and Sociology Department, Loyola University Chicago.

LeBeau, J. (1994). "The Temporal Ecology of Calls for Police Service." In: C.R. Block and M. Dabdoub (eds.), *Workshop on Crime Analysis Through Computer Mapping: Proceedings: 1993.* Chicago, IL: Illinois Criminal Justice Information Authority and Sociology Department, Loyola University Chicago.

Maltz, M.D. (1995). "Criminality in Space and Time: Life Course Analysis and the Micro Ecology of Crime." In: J. Eck and D. Weisburd (eds.), *Crime and Place.* Crime Prevention Studies, vol. 4. Monsey, NY: Criminal Justice Press.

—— (1994). "Crime Mapping and the Drug Market Analysis Program (DMAP)." In: C.R. Block and M. Dabdoub (eds.), *Workshop on Crime Analysis Through Computer Mapping: Proceedings: 1993.* Chicago, IL: Illinois Criminal Justice Information Authority and Sociology Department, Loyola University Chicago.

MathSoft (1991). "Contour Plots." *MathSoft MathCad for Windows 5.0: Users Guide.* Cambridge, MA: MathSoft, Inc.

Poyner, B. and B. Webb (1991). *Crime-Free Housing.* London, UK: Butterworth-Heinemann Architectural Books.

Rengert, G.F. (1994). "Comparing Cognitive Hot Spots to Crime Hot Spots." In: C.R. Block and M. Dabdoub (eds.), *Workshop on Crime Analysis Through Computer Mapping: Proceedings: 1993.* Chicago, IL: Illinois Criminal Justice Information Authority and Sociology Department, Loyola University Chicago.

Rossmo, D.K. (1995a). "Profiling Raptors: An Examination of Mapping Predictive Behavior Patterns of Violent Sex Offenders." Working Paper, Fourth Annual Seminar on Environmental Criminology and Crime Analysis, Cambridge, UK, July, 1995.

—— (1995b). "Place, Space, and Police Investigations: Hunting Serial Violent Criminals." In: J. Eck and D. Weisburd (eds.), *Crime and Place.* Crime Prevention Studies, vol. 4. Monsey, NY: Criminal Justice Press.

—— (1994). "Strategic Crime Patterning: Problem-Oriented Policing and Displacement." In: C.R. Block and M. Dabdoub (eds.), *Workshop on Crime Analysis Through Computer Mapping: Proceedings: 1993*. Chicago, IL: Illinois Criminal Justice Information Authority and Sociology Department, Loyola University Chicago.

Sanford, R. (1996). "GIS User Agency Profile: Survey Results." Newsletter of the International Association of Crime Analysts, Winter 1996. http://rsanford@dcommunity.net

Sorensen, S.L. (1995). "Homicides in Hartford, 1990-94." *Mapping out Drugs, Crime and Violence in Hartford Public and Assisted Housing: Technical Report*. Hartford, CT: Hartford Housing Authority.

—— (1995b). "Crime Map-e-matics: Visualization Tools for Crime Analysis." Paper presented at the 4th International Seminar on Environmental Criminology and Crime Analysis, Cambridge, UK, July 1995 (unpublished.)

—— J.G. Hayes, and N.D. Bellamy (1996). *Safety and Security Improvement Assessment: San Francisco Housing Recovery Team — Technical Report*. Research notes on observations from field testing GPS and GIS locational capabilities using standard GPS in day and nighttime situations. Bethesda, MD: SPARTA Consulting Corporation.

Weisburd, D. (1994). "Drug Market Analysis Program (DMAP)." Technical Report(s), U.S. Department of Justice, multiple documents (1992-95).

—— and L. Greene (1995). "Measuring Immediate Spatial Displacement: Methodological Issues and Problems." In: J. Eck and D. Weisburd (eds.), *Crime and Place*. Crime Prevention Studies, vol. 4. Monsey, NY: Criminal Justice Press.

Wieman, R.E. (1993). "Visual Data as Language." *Visual Communicating*. Educational Technology Publications.

Wilson, J.Q. (1975). *Thinking About Crime*. New York, NY: Basic Books.

Worrall, L. (1991). "GIS for Spatial Analysis and Spatial Policy: Developments and Directions." In: L. Worrall (ed.), *Spatial Analysis and Spatial Policy Using Geographic Information Systems*. London, UK: Bellhaven Press.

Appendix: Comprehensive Listing of Potential Uses of Mapping in Crime Analysis

The following list was prepared after culling through volumes of articles on mapping, geography, criminology, and crime analysis.

Each of the items listed represent potential mappable features or analysis presently or potentially predictable using mapping. The integration of GPS and GIS technologies will expedite the onset of use of these technologies in law enforcement generally and in crime analysis particularly.

Beats and redistricting

Before-and-after intervention analysis

Building structure, zoning, occupancy, vacancy

Calls for police assistance

CAP indexing of crime risk reduction

Catchment areas analysis

Community policing resources tracking

Change in contacts

Crime magnets identification

Crime pattern analysis

Crime prevention through environmental design

Diffusion

Dispatch

Dispersion

Displacement

Domestic dispute calls

Drug enforcement outpost location mapping

Drug market analysis

Emergency response planning

Extremes and outliers identification

Feature identification (abandoned autos, buildings, and drug incidents)

First abuse or offense analysis

Functional displacement

Gang territory and disputed space

Geographic displacement

Geographic profiling

Health sites and health risk hot spots

Homeomorphic vs. geometric space analysis

Hot clusters

Hot-spot areas

Hot-spot ellipses

Intertemporal comparisons

Journey to crime analysis

Lighting surveys

Location of lattice points

Location of new nodes

Magnet identification

Major landmarks

Mobility pattern analysis

Offender flexibility, mobility, and opportunity

Offender movement patterns

Patrol method optimization

Proximity

Public housing and public parks

Radial (buffering) searches

Safehouse location mapping

Scale and perception of clusters

Serial pattern recognition

Spatial autocorrelation

Spatial behavior of offenders by type

Special event planning (e.g., concerts, parades, holidays)

STAC hot-spot analysis

Street-gang-related incidents

Structure type and purpose

Tactical displacement

Tactical early warning system

Target displacement

Temporal displacement

Terminal and transportation crime risk

Testing the accuracy of cognitive maps

Use of space analysis

Topological transformations

Zoning and redistricting

WHAT DO THOSE DOTS MEAN?
MAPPING THEORIES WITH DATA

by

John E. Eck

University of Maryland
Washington/Baltimore High Intensity Drug
Trafficking Area, Greenbelt MD

Abstract: Criminologists have expanded their use of maps as the costs of mapping have plummeted. Using two cases of drug dealing, this paper examines the way in which theory influences how we interpret maps. The first study is a hypothetical case using fictitious data; the second, an actual case using real data. We show that when the explicit theoretical content of maps is low, it is difficult to interpret the data. As the theoretical content of maps increases, their utility increases. We show that theory also enhances the utility of computer algorithms designed to find point clusters on maps. The implications for crime control and prevention practitioners and researchers are discussed.

INTRODUCTION

We are experiencing a revolution in the use of mapping in criminology and criminal justice research. The proliferation of easy-to-use, high-speed mapping software that runs on inexpensive personal computers has contributed to this revolution, just as easy to use statistical software contributed to the use of increasingly advanced statistical tools for the study of crime. Much attention has been focused

---

Address correspondence to: John E. Eck, Washington/Baltimore High Intensity Drug Trafficking Area, Suite 900, 7500 Greenway Center Drive, Greenbelt, MD 20770.

on the variety of data that can be placed on maps and the methods of mapping that can be used (for useful summaries, see Block et al., 1995, or McEwen and Taxman, 1995).

Though mapping a variety of data using advanced software can help criminologists understand crime patterns, our ability to use maps effectively depends as much on how we incorporate theories in the maps of data. This paper describes why it is critical that we pay more attention to theory when using maps. The thesis is that adding explicit conjectural information to maps provides insights that are not available if one maintains a strict empiricist perspective. Though this papers emphasizes research applications of mapping, there are important parallel implications for the application of mapping to crime control and prevention operations.

THEORY, DATA AND METHOD IN MAPPING

Science advances through a complex interplay among speculation, observation, and method. This is no less true for criminology than it is for economics or physics. The simple paradigm we were taught in our first undergraduate research course stated that we entertain a hypothesis, derive some expected observable consequences from the hypothesis, compare the actual observations to these expectations, and then assess the meaning of the differences between our expectations and our observations. We might abandon the hypothesis if our expectations are dashed, amend it if our expectations are merely bruised, or celebrate it if our observations meet our expectations.

Though this process is overly simple, it does highlight the interplay among method, data, and theory. Theory is deeply imbedded in the data we apply to criminological questions. Indeed, to have a question about crime suggests that something is not as one expects. An expectation implies a theory. That we collect data — an expensive, time-consuming, and often difficult undertaking — suggests a theory about crime and a desire to find support for it, or a reason to choose an alternative theory. In the absence of an explicit theory, an implied theory guides the research. A researcher cannot know what data to collect, how to collect it, and how to analyze it without a theory (explicit or implied). A researcher without any theoretical guidance will find it impossible to determine the meaning of any data collected and will not be able to describe what was learned.

The decision to select a particular research method is also laden with theory. If the theory implies a linear relationship between two variables, then ordinary least squares regression might be useful.

But if the theory rules out a linear relationship in favor of a non-linear function, then an analysis method in accord with the theory needs to be selected. If a researcher is interested in the evolution of a crime pattern, he or she would use time-series analysis. Maps are only of use if we are interested in a phenomena that produces spatial patterns of crime.

Mapping crime data is a scientific enterprise, but it is often done without an explicit theory. The researcher plots crime points on a map or shades areas of the map in accordance with the presence or frequency of some attribute. In the absence of an explicit theory, the researcher must be acting on the implicit theory that space is related to crime. If the researcher maps political boundaries (police beats, council wards, city boundaries, or state lines), he or she implies that these boundaries matter in some way. If the researcher plots crime data on a street grid, he or she is stating that the pattern of the streets has some relationship to the crimes plotted.

It might be argued that there is no implied theory; that the streets, for example, are drawn as a reference for the reader and not because the researcher assumed there was a relationship between streets and crime patterns. This may be a valid explanation for the work of a police crime analyst who needs to direct patrol attention to a small area with a big crime problem. But it is not a valid explanation for the researcher communicating to an audience who will never visit the area. Few readers of the researcher's map are likely to visit the areas mapped; these readers want to know what the map tells them about areas in other cities and neighborhoods. If the researcher does not expect the street layout to help explain the crime pattern, or is not interested in testing the hypothesized relationship, then plotting the crimes on a blank page would be as meaningful as plotting them on the street grid. In other words, everything displayed on a map should be of theoretical importance.

The absence of explicit theories in crime mapping makes it difficult to interpret the data. This is particularly true when individual events are plotted. These are the simplest maps because the researcher has not aggregated the data. But they are also the most confusing. If data are aggregated by area and the frequencies of events in areas are compared, it is obvious what the maps are trying to show — some areas have more crime events than others (either absolutely or relative to some other factor, such as population). But when points are plotted it is not certain what is being examined. Should we be looking for clusters of dots? If so, how many dots and how close should they be to one other to make a cluster? Or should we be looking at the association of crime dots with other features drawn on the map? If so, which features should be shown and how close do the dots have to be to the feature to demonstrate an association? Whether we are looking for clusters or associations with features, how do we separate systematic patterns from chance or random patterns?

There are no methodological answers to these and similar questions; the answers depend on the theory being examined. And if the researcher has not been precise in describing his or her theory, readers can draw differing interpretations from the same map displays, regardless of the methodological tools used. As we will see later, methodological aids for interpreting spatial patterns plotted on maps are far more useful when an explicit and powerful theory is applied than when implicit and weak theories are used. Methodological tools, such as the example used later in this paper, are like carpentry tools; there are appropriate and inappropriate situations for their use, and there are different tools for different purposes. But ultimately, the quality of the finished product built will depend less on the tools than on the plans for the thing being built (as well as the skill of the user). This is not an evaluation of any general-purpose analytical tool but of the plans.

MAPS OF A HYPOTHETICAL AREA

To illustrate the role of theory in mapping, we will look at a series of maps of a fictitious area in a hypothetical city. In this example we will look at plots of drug locations. We will assume that these data came from narcotics investigation arrest reports, citizen calls over a drug tip phone line, and patrol officers reports, and that the data shown represent known sites of persistent drug dealing. In other words, we are going to assume that the data are reasonably valid indicators of drug dealing locations and that we can safely ignore data validity issues. We will examine the same hypothetical data pattern on a series of maps where the theory has been made increasingly explicit. Thus, we will hold the data set constant, vary the theory and examine how this influences our interpretation of the maps.

Figure 1 is a theory-free map (ignore the ellipse, we will come back to it later). It shows the dots on a featureless terrain. We see that there is a cluster of drug sites toward the upper right. What this means is unclear. The only context shown in this map is the distance scale, which tells us that the dots are relatively close together. But by itself, the scale does not provide sufficient context to interpret the map. That Figure 1 makes little sense is not surprising, but it reminds us that without a context data is meaningless.

Figure 1: A Theory-Free Map

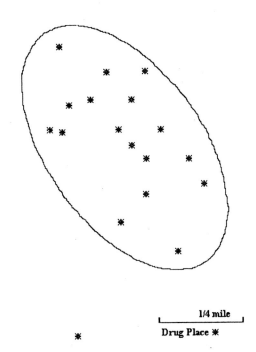

How can this context be shown? We cannot map everything. Many interesting attributes cannot be mapped because they are not part of an easy-to-use database. But even if they were and we tried to map all these features, the map would be hopelessly cluttered and would be as uninterpretable as Figure 1. Some contextual features are irrelevant and could be left off of the map. But which features are irrelevant? The choice of the features that describe the relevant context depends on the theory being examined. To interpret the dots we need a theory so we can display the relevant context and leave out the irrelevant context.

Under what circumstances is it preferable to display data on a virtually blank map? Consider a researcher studying the covariance of two crime types in a large area. A map with just the outline of a city would show the borders of the data collection area. The researcher would plot the data for the two crime types on this featureless terrain. Since the researcher is interested only in whether the two crimes are found at the same locations, features like streets and police precinct boundaries would be irrelevant to the question being examined, would clutter the graphical display, and would make the map more difficult to interpret. There are many examples of featureless maps in criminological research. Canter (1995) and LeBeau (1995) use featureless maps to examine drug markets and police calls for service, respectively. Reboussin et al. (1995) discuss the use of "mapless mapping" to examine spatial relationships between the locations of rapists' homes and crime scenes. Since they are using data from several different cities, there are no features common to the areas used by the rapist. These examples show that when the theory being examined does not include spatial features and the data provides its own context, only the data needs to be shown on the map and little else needs to be displayed.

Even when spatial features are central to the theory, featureless maps may be useful. Brantingham and Brantingham (1995) display isopleths for crime in Burnaby, British Columbia. The authors label the places "under" the peaks of the isopleth surfaces to illustrate how crime concentrates at these locations. They do not show the streets of this city or other features. Clearly, many of the features we commonly associate with maps are not needed for some applications.

However, for most criminologists an important function of maps is to show how crime is related to spatial features. Which features should one select to show on the map? And which features should one leave off? To answer this question, we will continue with the hypothetical case we began with in Figure 1. Figure 2 shows the same dots we saw earlier on Figure 1, but superimposed on a street grid. The fact that a street grid is used (instead of elevation contours, soil type, or land use patterns, for example) suggests that the researcher feels that street layouts matter (and elevation, soil, and land use do not) for understanding the pattern of drug dealing places. If the researcher did not think that the street pattern was somehow important for understanding the pattern of drug locations, then any street configuration would be equally meaningful. Three types of streets are shown (side streets, arterials, and highways) with three line sizes because this is theoretically important. If street size was unimportant then the streets could be shown using only one line width. We can further explore the relationship between theory and map features by examining another set of features on Figure 2.

Figure 2: Map with Street Grid

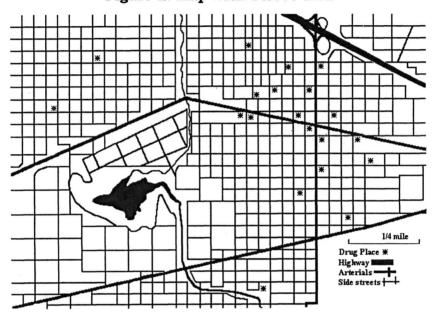

Figure 2 also shows a lake and two rivers. How are they related to the spatial organization of drug dealing? The water features are related to the street configuration. Many streets end at the rivers, and other streets bend around the lake. So the possible relationship between water features and drug dealing is mediated by the street pattern. If this is the hypothesis that the researcher is interested in, then it makes sense to include the water features on the map. However, many other topographical and land use features also influence street configurations, and these are not shown. But if the researcher is only interested in showing the relationship between street patterns and drug dealing, then there is no useful purpose of showing the features that influence street patterns. These features just clutter the map and distract the reader from the hypothesis being examined. For this reason, the water features have been deleted from subsequent maps of this area. As we will see, deleting these theoretically irrelevant features does not reduce our ability to interpret the map. If anything, removing the water features makes it easier to see the patterns we are interested in because there are fewer distractions.

We can see at least two patterns on Figure 2. First, the map shows the cluster of dots we noted originally, along with the three outliers (one toward the bottom and two toward the left of the map). This cluster is centered roughly around the intersection of two arterial streets. Another pattern visible is the relationship between the large streets and the dots. All of the drug locations are within three blocks of an arterial street, with two exceptions (a dot to the left and top, and another toward the center and top). Two of the outliers to the original cluster (Figure 1) fit this pattern, and one dot that was part of the original pattern is an outlier to the second pattern. Clearly, the pattern of dots observed depends on the expectations of the observer. Similarly, which dots are part of patterns and which are outliers depend on the expectations observers brings to the map. When the theory is explicit (e.g., all drug dealing should be close to arterial streets), the researcher and the reader can examine the same pattern. But when the theory is not clearly stated (e.g., street patterns provide structure to drug dealing), the reader and the researcher may be examining different patterns.

There are a variety of analytic tools that researchers can use to study spatial data. These procedures are useful for addressing a variety of questions, for example: Are these dots part of a single cluster? Are the events found in one area related to events found in nearby areas? Do spatial patterns change over time? Regardless of the question, the utility of the procedure will depend on the explicitness and power of the theory being examined.

To illustrate this point we will focus on one type of question: Does this set of points represent a meaningful cluster? Let us focus attention on the original cluster of dots noted in Figure 1. Is this observed cluster centered on the intersection of the two arterial routes in Figure 2, or is this just our imagination? Recently, there have been attempts to develop decision rules for defining clusters of crime events. Buerger et al. (1995) describe a manual procedure that employed computer maps and direct observations of potential clusters to draw "hot-spot" boundaries for use in a randomized experiment (Sherman and Weisburd, 1995). A similar set of decision rules has been used by Weisburd and Green (1995a, 1995b) to study drug markets. This manual approach has the advantage of using a great deal of information, much of it not available on computer files or easily mapped, to create precise boundaries. Additionally, the borders of these clusters can enclose odd and complex shapes. The drawback is that the approach is time-consuming and requires many subjective decisions (Buerger et al., 1995).

Another approach is to fully automate the cluster-finding process by using a computer algorithm. The Illinois Criminal Justice Information Authority (ICJIA) has developed an easy-to-use software program (STAC) that allows us to detect point clusters (Block, 1995). This tool can help us interpret the dots on maps by offering a non-substantive standard for what a cluster means. By non-substantive we mean that the interpretation is not based on crime theory but is instead drawn from a mathematical algorithm that will identify clusters of points (representing anything) on a map. Though the ICJIA developed this software to assist police agencies detect crime patterns, it can be useful for research (see, for example, Rengert, 1995 and Block and Block, 1995). Because it is well-known and widely used, we will use STAC as an example from which make general statements about the relationship between spatial theory and analytical tools for examining spatial data.

Returning to Figure 1, if the ellipse were the result of an algorithm like STAC (it was in fact drawn by hand to mimic what such an algorithm would produce), then how much more information was added to what we can learn from Figure 1? The answer is, very little. We can see that some dots are inside the ellipse and some are outside. But absent map features the ellipse is not much more helpful than the dots by themselves. The problem is not with the analytic tool, but with the lack of contextual information for interpreting the analysis results.

Figure 3 displays the dots, streets and ellipse. Now the ellipse provides some guidance. With the streets added, the ellipse suggests that the cluster is centered on the intersection. If the researcher had begun with a theory that drug locations cluster around intersections, then this ellipse would be evidence in support of that hypothesis. The ellipse also draws attention to another intersection of arterial streets that does not have a cluster of dots. This might suggest a deficiency in the original theory (e.g., intersections may be important for understanding drug markets, but why are some intersections involved and not others?). Thus, the value of such algorithms is tied to the use of theories. In the absence of a theory, such algorithms will add less to understanding the data being mapped than would be the case if a theory had been used. Clearly, the problem is not with the analytical tools being applied or the data being examined, but with the amount of theory being used.

Figure 3: Map with Street Grid and Ellipse

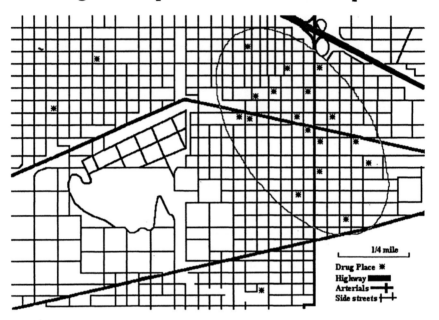

If we had another theory, however, the ellipse might not be as useful. Consider Figure 4. Here the researcher shaded an area of the city that is economically depressed. The theory being examined here is that economic investment in an area is associated with drug sites (no streets are shown because they are unimportant to this particular theory). We see at once that most of the dots fall within the economically depressed area. Four dots are outside the economically depressed area (the three outliers noted above and another dot on the extreme right). The ellipse is less useful here because it captures one of the outliers and suggests that the cluster is larger than it really is. The utility of the algorithm could be enhanced if the theory was more precise (e.g., explaining which parts of the economically depressed area are particularly vulnerable to drug dealing locations). But the theory is weak in that it does not explain how the dots are clustered or scattered within the shaded areas. Though the ellipse draws attention to large parts of the economically depressed area that are outside its boundaries, there are some areas within the ellipse that are without drug dealing places. This is an example of a theory being too weak for the statistical tool being used. The value of these types of algorithms depends on the precision, or power, of the theory. A more powerful theory would make the cluster-finding algorithm more useful.

Figure 4: Map with Poverty Area and Ellipse

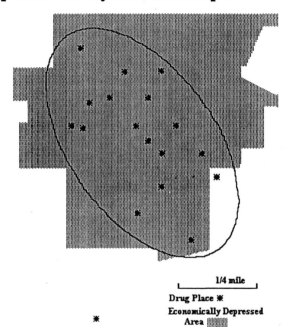

1/4 mile

Drug Place ✳
Economically Depressed
Area

The power of a theory is directly related to the patterns that are ruled out by the theory (Popper, 1992). Theories that permit fewer patterns are more powerful than theories that permit many. What we would like to do with maps is to specify where the dots should not fall and where they should. Let us see how this might work with a more detailed theory of drug market places, a theory that considerably restricts the allowable dot patterns. In other words, there are few dot patterns that are consistent with the theory compared to the many possible dot patterns that are inconsistent with the theory.

The theory we will use is based on a general model of illicit retail marketplaces (Eck, 1995). Though the theory covers a variety of consensual crimes, we will only describe it in reference to retail drug dealing. The theory asserts that there are only two ways to sell drugs. The first method, to sell to acquaintances or people vetted by acquaintances, reduces the dealers' and buyers' risk of theft and arrest. But it also reduces the number of sales that can be made by sellers and the shopping opportunities for buyers. This is called a "network market."

The second way of marketing drugs is for dealers to sell to strangers and for customers to buy from strangers. This style of drug market is called a "routine activity market." This strategy increases drug market participants' risk of theft and arrest, but allows sellers to make more sales and buyers to have more sources of drugs. To reduce their risks, buyers and sellers will meet where they both feel safe. This will occur in areas with which they are both familiar. Buyers and sellers will be familiar with these areas because they transact many of their legitimate routine activities in them. Routine activities such as shopping, playing, learning, working, and commuting are usually located along busy arterial routes. So are large multi-family apartment complexes. Many people, some of whom participate in drug transactions, will be familiar with these areas. Since both buyers and sellers will be familiar with these areas, drug dealing will take place along these routes. Locations near arterial routes let sellers "advertise" to passing customers that they are open for business.

Network dealing will take place over a much larger area and will not necessarily be concentrated along arterial routes. This is because the participants know one other, which reduces their risks and thus the need to seek familiar areas. It also reduces sellers' need to advertise: buyers can call dealers and arrange to meet, or buyers can contact the sellers through intermediaries or by other means.

Routine activity market dealing is not just limited by arterial routes. Because routine activity sales operations will draw many customers, dealers must be at locations where property owners and managers will not bother them. Thus, they will be concentrated where place management is the weakest. And place management will be weakest, according to this theory, in economically depressed areas.

Network marketplaces will not necessarily be located in economically depressed areas because the risks of detection by place managers is lower. There are fewer people coming and going as a result of the network drug trade, and there is less need to sell from a single location. Any location will serve as long as buyers and sellers can make contact through their network to arrange exchanges at mutually satisfactory locations.

This implies that the two types of drug markets will have two different spatial patterns. Network places will be widely scattered and will display little clustering. Routine activity market places will be concentrated along arterial routes through economical depressed areas.

Figure 5: Map with Explicit Theory of Drug Dealing Places

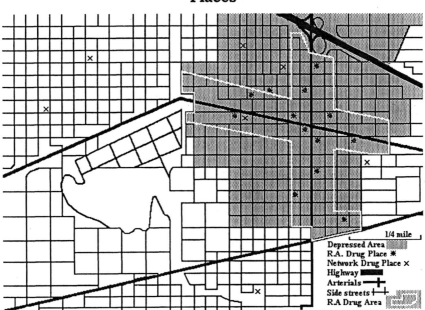

If this theory is mapped along with the drug sites we might get a display like that shown in Figure 5. Here the researcher has noted the two differing drug sales types as specified by the theory. The Xs represent network dealing sites, and the dots represent routine activity marketplaces. Street sizes are theoretically important and are displayed on the map. Similarly, the economically depressed area is shown. Finally, the map shows the boundaries for the routine activity market area. The boundaries in Figure 5 are draw roughly a block and a half from the arterials. The theory does not say how close these boundaries should be to the arterials, so the boundaries drawn are somewhat arbitrary. A more powerful theory might specify the boundaries or a gradient around the arterials, perhaps based upon knowledge of drug users' search behaviors.

Interpreting the meaning of the dots is relatively simple because the theory tells us what we should expect. In this hypothetical example the theory is supported. The network Xs are widely scattered, in and out of the economically depressed area, near and far from arterial routes. The routine activity dots are within the market boundaries, with one exception.

The theory also tells us what dot patterns we should not expect. It rules out routine activity sites outside the economically depressed areas. Thus we can answer a question raised when we examine Figure 2: Why isn't there a cluster of dots around the lower intersection of two arterials? The answer is that much of the area around this second intersection is outside the economically depressed area. The theory also rules out routine activity market dealing far from arterials. There are no clusters of drug dealing in large parts of the economically depressed area (see Figure 4) because much of this area is far from arterial routes. Finding routine activity dealing sites outside the predicted boundaries would be grounds for seriously questioning the theory.

How useful would an algorithm for drawing ellipses around clusters be for examining this theory? First, we would want to analyze the two types of markets separately. For the network marketplaces, we would expect to see either a single very large ellipse encompassing most of the map, a set of many small ellipses each containing few points, or no ellipse at all. Any of these outcomes would suggest that it is difficult for the algorithm to identify a meaningful cluster.

Second, for the routine activity marketplaces, we would want to compare the orientation of the ellipse drawn around the dots to the orientation of the two arterial routes. This theory suggests a cross-shaped pattern (in the area shown in this example). Ideally, we would see two intersecting ellipses — one with its main axis going up and down, and the second with its main axis going left to right. The axes for the ellipses should be close to and roughly parallel to the two arterials. Unfortunately, a single ellipse cannot describe this shape (Block, 1995). This suggests that alternative mapping tools should be used. In this example, plotting iso-crimes may be more useful (Zepp, 1989).

MAPS OF AN ACTUAL CASE

In the preceding case we looked at maps of a hypothetical area. Invented examples are useful because they allow one to examine just the factors one is interesting in without complicating the discussion with extraneous factors that create unexplainable loose ends. In short, these examples make the world pure and simple. But things are seldom this simple. Therefore, it is useful to examine a real-world case.

The actual case comes from an area in Baltimore County, MD. The maps were produced by the Baltimore County Police Department's Planning Division using MapInfo.[1] The dots (stars on these maps) represent the locations of arrests for the sales and distribution of cocaine. We must note, therefore, that though the first hypothetical case mapped persistent drug locations with multiple indicators, in this actual case we are using a single indicator so that any specific dot may or may not represent a persistent dealing location. Nevertheless, patterns of arrest sites many indicate zones where drug dealing may be found, even if the precise location of each dot cannot be interpreted as evidence of persistent dealing at that place.

Let's begin by assuming we know nothing about this area but we are interested in the relationship between street patterns and drug dealing. Under these circumstances we might produce Figure 6, which displays a wide scatter of dots. Several patterns are evident. There are several tight clusters in the upper center of the map. These have been labeled A, B, C, and D. Cluster C is particularly large. Two other smaller clusters at the center of the map, E and F, are also notable. Though we may be interested in clusters, we can also see that most of the dots (including those in the six clusters just mentioned) are: (1) on arterial routes; (2) within two blocks of an arterial; or (3) on streets that loop off and back onto arterials. All four of the arterials have cocaine dealing arrest sites along them. Finally, there are a few widely scattered deviant cocaine arrest sites that do not fit this larger pattern. They can be seen at the bottom and left edge of the map.

Figure 6: Drug Arrests and Streets

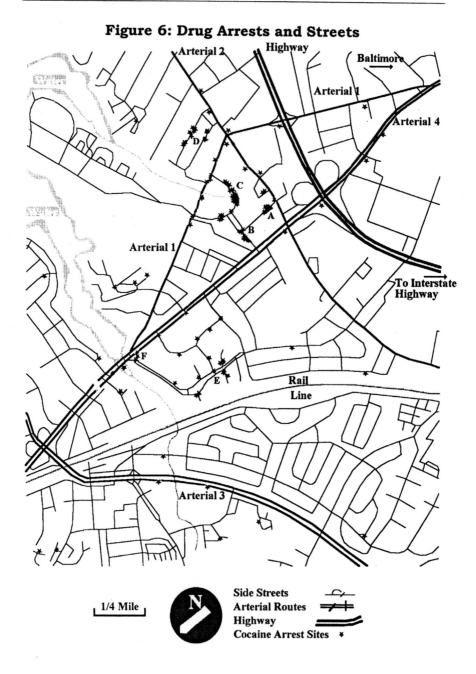

Arterial 2　　Highway

Baltimore

Arterial 1

Arterial 4

D

C

A

B

Arterial 1

To Interstate
Highway

F

E

Rail
Line

Arterial 3

1/4 Mile　　**N**

Side Streets
Arterial Routes
Highway
Cocaine Arrest Sites ✶

This map supports the theory that drug dealing is associated with street patterns. Nevertheless, the map reveals several deficiencies with this simple theory. Though most cocaine sites are associated with arterials (either on them or within easy access), there are many stretches of arterial routes without cocaine arrests. In addition, there are many street segments within two blocks of an arterial without cocaine arrests. Further, there are many short loops off and on to arterial routes with no cocaine arrests. The clusters at A, B, C, D and F can be explained using this simple theory, but it is more difficult to explain cluster E. In short, there are many theoretically high-risk locations for drug dealing that do not have obvious clusters.

More context is needed to better understand what the drug arrest pattern on this map shows, and this requires showing more features. Of the many possible features we could show on a map, which should we choose? Notice that the two ellipses are located near two inlets to the Chesapeake Bay. In the absence of a theory, we could create an ad hoc hypothesis that drug dealing concentrates around water courses. Perhaps drug dealing in Baltimore County is associated with water courses or branches of the Chesapeake Bay, but this would not help us understand drug dealing in San Diego, or New York, or Tulsa, or Kalamazoo, or most other areas. Though ad hoc speculation can be useful, we require something more — a generalizable theory. The water course hypothesis seems too arbitrary, an accident of what the MapInfo program used by the Baltimore County Police Department happens to print and the peculiar topography of this part of the county. What widely applicable theory could we use to find information we could add to these maps?

If we apply the theory of illicit retail marketplaces to Figure 7, we find that the pattern of cocaine dealing sites (both where they are found and where they are not found) becomes more interpretable and the ellipses become more helpful. Much of the cocaine dealing in this part of Baltimore County is sold in routine activity markets, some of which are open-air street markets. The area is only four miles from the eastern border of Baltimore via arterials 1 and 4 that cut across the top and bottom of the upper ellipse and the top of the lower ellipse. The highway on the top right of maps 6 and 7 connects into the interstate highway circling the city. The area has a mixture of middle- and working-class residences, along with a variety of businesses. The economy of this area used to be primarily industrial, but the number of manufacturing jobs has declined. There is a substantial recreational industry in the area, concentrated around the Chesapeake

Figure 7: Drug Arrests, Streets and Ellipses

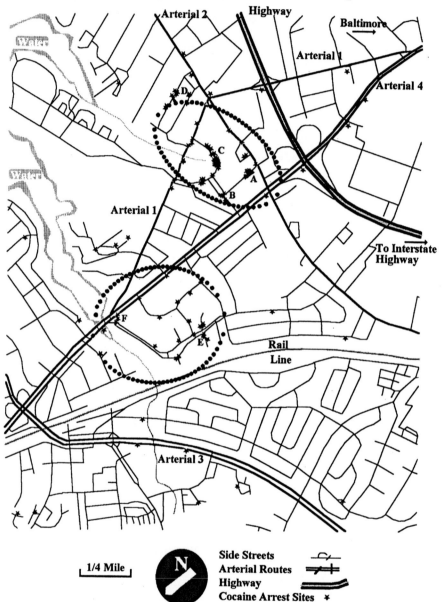

Bay. Though the entire area is not economically depressed, neither is it thriving and there are pockets of poverty.

Three of these pockets of poverty are found in three low-rent, large, multi-family apartment complexes. Two of these complexes are well-known for being poorly managed, and the third has undergone some changes in 1988 to improve property management (Carson, 1995a). According to the theory of illicit retail marketplaces, routine activity marketplaces should be located in areas where place management is weak and near arterial routes or major activity nodes. These complexes are shown in Figure 8.

Clusters A, B, and C are in the Village of Tall Trees. This complex has 828 residential units, in 105 buildings divided among 38 separate owners. Some owners have a single building, and some own many buildings. Buildings owned by a single person are often not adjacent to each other but are scattered throughout the complex. So if one place manager is diligent, poor place management by adjacent owners can undercut their efforts. Rents are low throughout the complex, but rentals are handled by each owner individually. If a person is evicted from one building they can move to a nearby building (Carson, 1995a, 1995b).

The street layout of Tall Trees contributes to its suitability as a site for drug dealing as can be seen in the sketch shown in Figure 9. This map is not to scale, but illustrates the location of clusters A, B, and C in relation to the streets within the complex, the parking lots, and external arterial routes. Dot cluster A is on an arterial route and includes a parking lot. Cluster B is at an intersection within the complex that gives ready access to three arterial routes (one to the north of the complex, one to the south, and another to the east). Cluster C is on a horseshoe street that provides easy exit off and onto a major arterial route to the south of the complex. Probably as important is the concentration of parking lots near cluster C. The ability of cocaine buyers to drive in, meet a dealer, and then leave seems to contribute to the drug problems of this area. In fact, from January through November 1994, 76% of the drug arrests in Tall Trees were of people who were not residents of the complex. In one eight-hour survey of vehicles in the complex, less than 6% belonged to residents of Tall Trees (Carson, 1995b).

Figure 8: Drug Arrests, Streets, Ellipses and Apartment Complexes

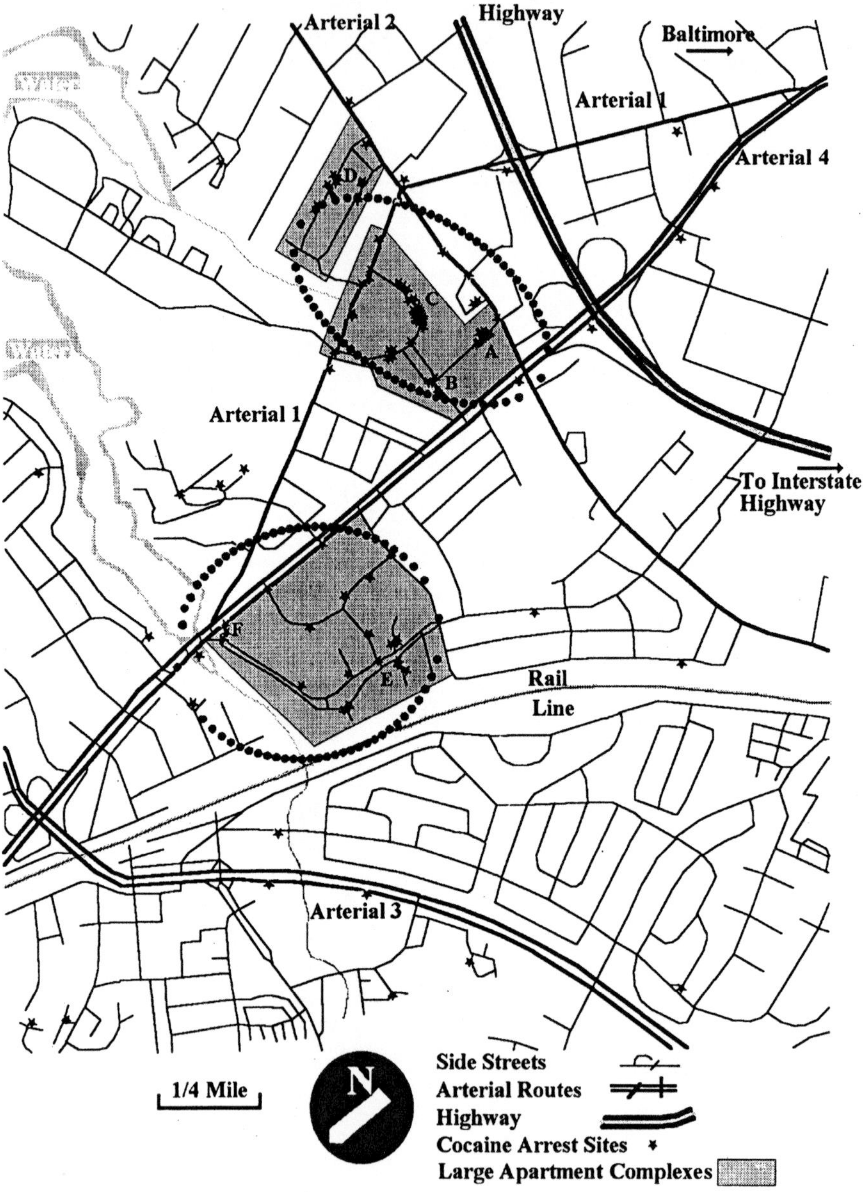

Arterial 2 Highway Baltimore

Arterial 1

Arterial 4

D

C

A

B

Arterial 1

To Interstate Highway

F

E

Rail Line

Arterial 3

1/4 Mile

N

Side Streets
Arterial Routes
Highway
Cocaine Arrest Sites
Large Apartment Complexes

Figure 9: Detailed Street Layout of One Apartment Complex

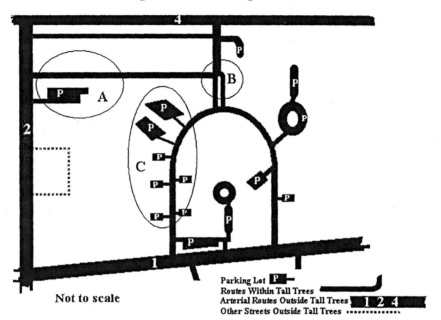

Not to scale

Parking Lot
Routes Within Tall Trees
Arterial Routes Outside Tall Trees
Other Streets Outside Tall Trees

Clusters E and F (on Figure 8) are in the Riverdale Village Apartments. This complex is in an advanced stage of decay. It has 1,100 units, but half are vacant and a third are closed. The complex had the highest percentage of code violations of any other multi-family apartment complex in the county. Unlike Tall Trees, Riverdale has a single owner, who lives in New York (Carson, 1995a). Drug buyers can easily drive through Riverdale, though not as conveniently as through Tall Trees. Cluster E is located at the back entrance to Riverdale. Cluster F is located at the front entrance, and on a major arterial route. The road connecting F and E is the major route through the complex, and directly connects arterials 1 and 4 to the north with arterial 2 (on the map) and arterial 4 (off of the map) to the south.

There is another low-income apartment complex in the area, Kingsley Apartments. These apartments are located at cluster D. This complex is not as badly managed as Tall Trees or Riverdale (Carson, 1995a), but its 312 units serve a low-income clientele. All tenants at Kingsley receive some form of federal rent subsidy (compared to 10 and 7%, respectively, of the renters in Tall Trees and Riverdale (Carson, 1995a). Though 55% of the cocaine arrests in the precinct came from these three apartments, only 9% came from Kingsley (36% came from Tall Trees and 10% from Riverdale) (Carson, 1995a, 1995b). Like the other two apartment complexes, it is convenient for drug buyers to come by entering from one arterial route and to go by leaving another.

If one set out to test the theory of illicit retail marketplaces, then STAC is particularly useful. The ellipses shown in Figure 8 provide evidence supporting this theory. The ellipses highlight at least two of the three areas that are predicted to have drug dealing. The one apartment complex partially missed by an ellipse is the best managed of the three. Without detailed information of the management practices of other properties in the area, but not shown on the map, we cannot be certain that there are no other properties that are theoretical candidates for drug dealing sites but that have no evidence of drug dealing. Figure 8 does not provide a complete test of the theory. Still, when we examine this actual case, we see the same relationship we explored with the hypothetical case; the more theory we bring to the data, the more interpretable the map and the more useful the analytic procedures.

IMPLICATIONS

In this paper, we have shown that theory changes how we interpret the data displayed on maps by changing what features we display on them. The map conveys the theory we are examining. This implies that we should display all of the relevant theoretical concepts, along with the data and any annotations that help us interpret the data and the theory. It also implies that anything that is not a theoretical concept or data, or does not help us interpret the theory or data (e.g., labels), should be left out.

We have seen that as the theoretical content of maps is increased, the easier it is to make sense of the data. Spatially organized data plotted on a blank page provide little information. But the same data, when plotted on maps annotated with increasingly powerful theories, become increasingly interesting and useful. This implies that the more precisely the researcher can specify his or her expectations of where the dots should and should not be found, before the dots are placed on the map, the more useful the map will be once the researcher plots the observations. If the researcher can say that the dots will only be found in a very few specific areas, or clustered around specific features, then the actual dot displays will be more useful than if the researcher only expects to find some clustering in unspecified areas. In the first instance, the researcher will know if the data are confirming or disconfirming his or her expectations. In the second case, the researcher will only learn that some clustering occurred or did not occur.

These findings also apply to procedures designed to find dot clusters using non-substantive computer algorithms. In the absence of a powerful theory, these procedures can find clusters but what these clusters mean is unclear. When the same procedure is applied to the same data but in light of a more powerful theory, the utility of such algorithms increases. These algorithms may be more useful for theory testing than for their original purpose — finding dot clusters in the absence of any expectation of where the clusters should be found (Block, 1995). In fact, Block and Block (1995) use the STAC cluster-finding algorithm to test hypotheses about the relationship between clusters of liquor-related crimes and of taverns and liquor stores in Chicago. Analytical techniques are not substitutes for powerful theories. Instead, they are complements (also see Block, in this volume).

We have restricted our attention to research applications of maps. Do the lessons of this discussion apply to operational uses of maps, by police departments, for example? The answer is yes. Maps 6, 7 and 8 illustrate this point under two different conditions. In the first condition, the police department is unaware of the pattern of cocaine sales arrests in this part of the county.[2] If the head of the narcotics section wanted to find out where the biggest drug problems are located, then Figure 6 would show several small clusters where a great deal of enforcement activity had taken place. Figure 6 suggests that there are at least six separate problems. In this scenario, where the police are in relative ignorance of what is taking place, the map suggests that further investigation is required to determine what could be done to address the problem. If STAC ellipses were drawn around these clusters, the resulting map (Figure 7) would suggest that there are two large clusters of seemingly related dots. Note that a police agency that has such limited information about the areas it serves could hardly be called community-oriented or problem-oriented. Thus, the type of mapping described in this scenario is probably typical of a traditional police agency that simply uses maps to augment its crime analysis function.

In the second scenario, the police are very aware of the cocaine problems in this part of the county, and they know about the involvement of the apartment complexes shown in Figure 8. The ellipses provide a different, and potentially more valuable, type of information under these conditions. Because the algorithm that drew the ellipses uses a procedure independent of the problem being investigated, the police could use Figure 8 as evidence that the Village of Tall Trees and the Riverdale Apartments have peculiarly high levels of drug selling activity. This evidence may be useful in presentations to community groups, and regulatory agencies, or in civil court proceedings. Note that the same map does not present good evidence that the Kingsley Apartments are a particular problem.

Police agencies taking a problem-oriented approach (Goldstein, 1990) would probably find this method useful. It is not uncommon for police officers to identify a troublesome location (e.g., a bar, convenience store, bus stop, movie theater, entertainment arcade, or liquor store), and to become convinced that many of the crimes near (but not necessarily on) the location arise because of the way the place is used. Is this claim justified? How can the officers test this hypothesis in a manner that would be convincing to an independent observer (senior commanders, community groups, the owner of the location, or a court, for example)? Plotting ellipses for the crimes in question is one method. If the ellipse showing a crime hot spot encloses the target location, this is evidence that the location may be a cause of the problem. If the ellipse does not enclose the target site, this is evidence that the location may not be responsible for the problem. Additional evidence may be required to make a strong case, depending on the circumstances, who the police officers are trying to convince, and the rules of evidence (if any) used by the independent observer. A rough analogue of the use of cluster-finding algorithms is the use of physical evidence in investigations. Most physical evidence is more valuable for verifying (or ruling out) an already-identified suspect than for identifying an unknown offender (Eck, 1983).

If the police do not know much about the area then they cannot form a testable hypothesis. This is the case in most situations when the police look for fast-breaking crime patterns so they can focus enforcement activity on a troubled area — by means of saturation patrolling, decoy operations, surveillance, or other tactics. Though the crime maps and even cluster-detection algorithms may be useful for these operations, these mapping techniques are probably more useful when officers already have a good understanding of the area in question.

This suggests that the police, like researchers, should pay as much attention to criminological theories as they do to the data they examine (dots) and the methods they apply (maps). Several eminently useful theories have direct application to research and operational mapping. These theories try to explain why crimes occur under specific circumstances (event theories) rather than try to explain why some individuals become criminal offenders and others do not (offender theories) (Eck and Weisburd, 1995). Routine activity theory (Felson, 1994) describes how criminal events are linked to everyday routines in society. Offender search theory (Brantingham and Brantingham, 1981) attempts to explain how offenders select crime targets. Both theories try to explain how crime is distributed in space and time. Rossmo (1995a) has used offender search theory to help police investigators solve serial homicides and rapes. The theory of the geography of illicit retail markets (described earlier) is based in large part on these two perspectives (Eck, 1994, 1995). Two applied theories used by the police and others interested in reducing crime events draw on routine activity theory and offender search theory. Problem-oriented policing (Goldstein, 1990) demands greater analysis of problems, and maps are particularly helpful in this regard (Rossmo, 1995b). Situational crime prevention (Clarke, 1992) seeks to find methods to block opportunities for crime. Often maps are useful for understanding the opportunities for crime and the development of methods for blocking these opportunities (see Matthews, 1992 and 1993, for example).

In summary, the investment in mapping technology and databases can be greatly enhanced if combined with an interest in theories of criminal events. The more explicit and precise analysts (researchers and practitioners) can state their expectations of the dot patterns, the greater their ability to interpret the observed dots and the more useful the maps will become.

Acknowledgments: I want to thank David Weisburd for encouraging me to write this paper and Becky Block, who gave me very helpful comments on an earlier draft. I must give special thanks to Phil Cantor for producing the original Baltimore County maps used in this paper. Finally, Major Kim Ward of the Baltimore County Police Department deserve thanks for informing me of the history of the Village of Tall Trees and Riverdale Village Apartments, and for giving me a tour of these apartment complexes and the surrounding area. Despite this assistance, I alone am responsible for any errors in this paper.

NOTES

1. The maps from MapInfo were scanned and the digital images edited to make the original map more legible. The arterial routes and highways were widened. When the arterial and highway enhancements obscured a cocaine arrest dot, the dot was moved slightly to the side of the street so it would still be visible. Two water features (a river and a creek flowing into the Chesapeake Bay) were deemphasized and annotations and labels were added. Finally, the areas of the apartment complexes were shaded.

2. In reality, the police department and other county agencies are working together to address a host of problems in the three complexes described in this paper.

REFERENCES

Block, C.R. (1995). "STAC Hot-Spot Areas: A Statistical Tool for Law Enforcement Decisions." In: C.R. Block, M. Dabdoub and S. Fregley (eds.), *Crime Analysis Through Computer Mapping.* Washington, DC: Police Executive Research Forum.

—— M. Dabdoub and S. Fregly (1995). *Crime Analysis Through Computer Mapping.* Washington, DC: Police Executive Research Forum.

Block, R.L. and C.R. Block (1995). "Space, Place and Crime: Hot Spot Areas and Hot Places of Liquor Related Crime." In: J. E. Eck and D. Weisburd (eds.), *Crime and Place.* Crime Prevention Studies, vol. 4. Monsey, NY: Criminal Justice Press.

Brantingham, P.L. and P.J. Brantingham (1981). "Notes on the Geometry of Crime." In: P.J. Brantingham and P.L. Brantingham (eds.), *Environmental Criminology.* Beverly Hills, CA: Sage.

—— (1995). "Criminality of Place: Crime Generators and Crime Attractors." *European Journal of Criminal Justice Policy and Research* 3:5-26.

Buerger, M., E.G. Cohen, and A.J. Petrosino (1995). "Defining the 'Hot Spots of Crime': Operationalizing Theoretical Concepts for Field Research." In: J.E. Eck and D. Weisburd (eds.), *Crime and Place.* Crime Prevention Studies, vol. 4. Monsey, NY: Criminal Justice Press.

Canter, P. (1995). "State of the Statistical Art: Point Pattern Analysis." In: C. R. Block, M. Dabdoub and S. Fregley (eds.), *Crime Analysis Through Computer Mapping.* Washington, DC: Police Executive Research Forum.

Carson, L. (1995a). "Essex Housing Complexes are Targeted for Cleanup." *Baltimore Sun,* March 30, p.1b.

—— (1995b). "In Essex, Halting Crime at Ground Zero." *Baltimore Sun,* February 25, p.1b.

Clarke, R. V. (1992). *Situational Crime Prevention: Successful Case Studies.* New York, NY: Harrow and Heston.

Eck, J.E. (1983). *Solving Crimes: The Investigation of Burglary and Robbery.* Washington, DC: Police Executive Research Forum.

—— (1994). Drug Markets and Drug Places: A Case-Control Study of the Spatial Structure of Illicit Drug Dealing. Doctoral dissertation, University of Maryland, College Park.

—— (1995). "A General Model of the Geography of Illicit Retail Marketplaces." In: J.E. Eck and D. Weisburd (eds.), *Crime and Place.* Crime Prevention Studies, vol. 4. Monsey, NY: Criminal Justice Press.

—— and D. Weisburd (1995). "Crime Places in Crime Theory." In: J. E. Eck and D. Weisburd (eds.), *Crime and Place.* Crime Prevention Studies, vol. 4. Monsey, NY: Criminal Justice Press.

Felson, M. (1994). *Crime and Everyday Life: Insight and Implications for Society.* Thousand Oaks, CA: Pine Forge Press.

Goldstein, H. (1990). *Problem-Oriented Policing.* New York, NY: McGraw Hill.

LeBeau, J.L. (1995). "The Temporal Ecology of Calls for Police Service." In: C.R. Block, M. Dabdoub and S. Fregley (eds.), *Crime Analysis Through Computer Mapping.* Washington, DC: Police Executive Research Forum.

Matthews, R. (1992). "Developing More Effective Strategies for Curbing Prostitution." In: R.V. Clarke (eds.), *Situational Crime Prevention: Successful Case Studies.* New York, NY: Harrow and Heston.

—— (1993). *Kerb-Crawling, Prostitution and Multi-Agency Policing.* Crime Prevention Unit Series Paper 43. London, UK: Police Research Group, Home Office.

McEwen, J.T. and F.S. Taxman (1995). "Application of Computerized Mapping to Police Operations." In: J.E. Eck and D. Weisburd (eds.), *Crime and Place.* Crime Prevention Studies, vol. 4. Monsey, NY: Criminal Justice Press.

Popper, K.P. (1992). *The Logic of Scientific Discovery*. London, UK: Routledge.

Reboussin, R., J. Warren, and R.R. Hazelwood (1995). "Mapless Mapping in Analyzing the Spatial Distribution of Serial Rapes." In: C.R. Block, M. Dabdoub and S. Fregley (eds.), *Crime Analysis Through Computer Mapping*. Washington, DC: Police Executive Research Forum.

Rengert, G. F. (1995). "Comparing Cognitive Hot Spots to Crime Hot Spots." In: C.R. Block, M. Dabdoub and S. Fregley (eds.), *Crime Analysis Through Computer Mapping*. Washington, DC: Police Executive Research Forum.

Rossmo, D. K. (1995a). "Place, Space, and Police Investigations: Hunting Serial Violent Criminals." In: J.E. Eck and D. Weisburd (eds.), *Crime and Place*. Crime Prevention Studies, vol. 4. Monsey, NY: Criminal Justice Press.

—— (1995b). "Strategic Crime Patterning: Problem-Oriented Policing and Displacement." In: C. R. Block, M. Dabdoub, and S. Fregley (eds.), *Crime Analysis Through Computer Mapping*. Washington, DC: Police Executive Research Forum.

Sherman, L.W. and D. Weisburd (1995). "General Deterrent Effects of Police Patrol in Crime 'Hot Spots': A Randomized, Controlled Trial." *Justice Quarterly* 12:625-648.

Weisburd, D. and L. Green (1995a). "Measuring Immediate Spatial Displacement: Methodological Issues and Problems." In: J. E. Eck and D. Weisburd (eds.), *Crime and Place*. Crime Prevention Studies, vol. 4. Monsey, NY: Criminal Justice Press.

—— (1995b). "Policing Drug Hot Spots: The Jersey City Drug Market Analysis Experiment." *Justice Quarterly* 12:711-736.

Zepp, J. (1989). "Illinois Criminal Justice Authority Develops Crime Analysis Software." *CJSA Forum* 7:10-11.

SUBJECT INDEX

Page numbers that appear in *italics* refer to figures or tables.

Printed in the United States
202826BV00003B/163-180/A